# HORSE SCHOOLS

## The International Guide to Universities, Colleges, Preparatory and Secondary Schools, and Specialty Equine Programs

**SECOND EDITION**

ANGELIA ALMOS

Trafalgar Square Publishing

North Pomfret, Vermont

First published in 2005 by
**Trafalgar Square Publishing**
North Pomfret, Vermont 05053

*Disclaimer of Liability*
The author and publisher shall have neither liability nor responsibility to any person or entity with respect to any loss or damage caused or alleged to be caused directly or indirectly by the information contained in this book. While the book is as accurate as the author can make it, there may be errors, omissions, and inaccuracies.

Library of Congress Cataloging-in-Publication Data

Almos, Angelia.
Horse schools : the international guide to universities, colleges, preparatory and secondary schools, and specialty equine programs / Angelia Almos.—2nd ed.
        p. cm.
Includes bibliographical references.
ISBN 1-57076-297-X (pbk.)
1. Horses—Study and teaching (Higher) 2. Horses—Study and teaching (Secondary)
I. Title.
SF285.27.A46 2004
636.1'0071—dc22

                                        2004019340

Book design by Heather Mansfield
Typeface: Minion, Meta

Printed in the United States of America

9 8 7 6 5 4 3 2 1

Front cover photos

Left: **Wilson College** students Rachel Douglas (left), Veterinary Medical Technology major—Class of 2005; April Claar (right), Veterinary Medical Technology major—Class of 2005, see page 138. Photo by Kristin Garrett courtesy of Wilson College.
Middle: **Texas A&M University** student Quincy Cahill on Boomon N Seven, Class of 2002, see page 147. Photo by Waltenberry, Inc.
Right: **Mount Holyoke College** student Kenzie Snyder on Milltown, Class of 2008, see page 100. Photo by Mustphoto, Inc.

# Table of Contents

# Acknowledgments

I would like to thank the many people who made the creation and production of this book possible. My first thanks go to all of you who are searching for a horse school. This guide would never have been created and updated for this second edition without you.

Thank you to the schools, equestrian federations, and associations that provided information and pointed me in the right direction; without their help, some countries would not have been represented in this guide.

A huge thanks to my wonderful editor, Martha Cook, and to all the staff at Trafalgar for their work on this edition.

To my parents, Scott and Jan Derrick, for always standing behind my projects. And of course last, but not least, my husband Greg and our daughter Jessica Lynne for their many hours of patience as I plugged along on this book.

# How to Use This Book

This book has been created as a resource to aid you in the search for a horse school. In the pages to come, you will find the following:

**Introduction:** A discussion of different kinds of horse schools and tips on how to choose one that's right for you.

**Horse School Questionnaire:** A list of questions to ask school representatives, both on the phone and during visits. Add to the questionnaire as you think of things you may want to know about a school.

**Possible Careers:** An extensive list of over 250 careers involving horses.

**Fields of Study:** An index of fields of horse-related study, as well as the schools that offer majors in those fields. If you already know what you want to study, this is a good place to start. Be sure to skim the entire list, though, as some majors fall under more than one category.

**Descriptions of Schools:** Basic information on each school, including the type of school, the kind of majors and degrees offered, and a summary of costs (tuition, room, and board). Also included is a short description of the school or program, a description of the equestrian facilities, the ratio of classroom courses to hands-on equine courses, opportunities for competition, and contact and website information. The description notes whether the school is approved or accredited by any association or organization.

Please note that whenever possible, school information has been provided by the school itself and was correct at the time that it was provided. All websites were up-to-date at the time of publication. All tuition costs listed are correct for the 2004-2005 school year. However, be aware that, because of fluctuating exchange rates, any international tuition entries listed in American dollars are approximate and were correct only at the time of publication. Most international costs were provided in foreign currencies.

Readers should also consider the issue of language when researching study abroad. When the information was provided, I have listed whether classes are taught in English or in another language. If international schooling appeals to you, I urge you to include on your "Horse School Questionnaire" queries regarding language requirements and what opportunities might be available to learn the native language, should it be necessary.

Be sure to verify the information provided in this manual when you contact your list of possible schools. Contact persons, tuition costs, facilities, requirements, etcetera, often change from year-to-year.

School listings have been organized as follows:

**Name of School or Program**
School's mailing address. Contact person. Phone and fax number. Email address.
**Accreditation:** Associations and organizations that the school is accredited or approved by.
**Degrees Offered:** The level of degree that is offered in an equine subject. Example: Bachelor of Science.
**Majors Offered:** The subject area that the degree is offered in. Example: Equine Science.

**Tuition Costs:** Form of currency if not U.S. dollars. Cost for attending school. Housing and additional fees will be included if available.

**Description of Program:** A short description of the equine program.

**Facilities:** A description of the equestrian facility.

**Classroom/Hands-On Equine Classes:** The ratio of equine classroom time to equine hands-on time.

**Showing:** Indicates competition opportunities for students while attending the school.

Each school is accompanied by a quick reference sidebar. Website information and "type of school" (for example, community college or specialty school) is included here, as well as descriptive icons to help you determine with one glance whether a school offers the kind of opportunities you are looking for.

## Icon Key

 School offers English and/or Western riding.

 School teaches and/or competes in rodeo and Western show events.

 School teaches and/or competes in dressage.

 School teaches driving.

 School teaches horseshoeing or natural trimming techniques.

 School teaches and/or competes in jumping and/or eventing.

 School teaches breeding management and/or hands-on techniques.

 School teaches performance skills: jousting, reenactments, vaulting, tricks, circus, etc.

 School teaches horse racing (flat/harness): jockey, management, groom, driver, trainer, etc.

**Scholarships:** A list of equine-oriented scholarships.

**Intercollegiate Associations:** Descriptions and contact information for intercollegiate associations that offer students a chance to compete, as well as a list of schools that participate (if applicable).

**Equestrian Federations:** If you are seeking horse sports and/or schools in a particular country, contacting the country's equestrian federation can be a good place to begin your search.

**Bibliography:** A list of the books and websites used to create this book.

**Index of Schools:** The easy way to find any school in this book.

**Other Resources**

Visit www.horseschools.net for a list of equine-program textbooks, other horse career-oriented books, links to equine employment sites, a bulletin board to communicate with other searchers, and much more.

# Introduction

## What is a "horse school"?

The term "horse school" covers a wide range of educational opportunities, from secondary schools and accredited universities, to the clinics and camps of well-known trainers and specialty riding programs. As long as the focus of what you are learning involves horses, the place in which you are learning can be termed a horse school. The two main classifications of horse schools are (1) universities and colleges, which offer an accredited degree (A.A., A.S., B.A., B.S., etc.), and (2) specialty schools, which typically offer a certificate or diploma upon completion of the program.

If you choose to pursue a degree, you will learn about a lot more than just horses. Every college or university has general education requirements that are mandatory for all degree candidates. Classes typically include math, English, history, and a foreign language. However, if you choose to pursue a certificate or diploma from a specialty school, typically you will only take classes in the equine skill you are learning.

## Questions to Ask Yourself

When choosing a horse school, first decide what you're looking for. Be specific! Here is a list of questions that may prove helpful in deciding which school is right for you.

- Do you want a career in the equine industry, or do you just want to keep horses in your everyday life?
- What do you want to learn from this experience? Do you want to improve your riding skills, learn about breeding, learn how to manage a stable, become a certified instructor, or learn how to retrain problem horses? (Be specific in stating your goals.)
- How much time can you devote to your education? (For example, a bachelor's degree will take four years or more; a certificate or diploma program usually requires a year or less.)
- Do you have your heart set on attending a prestigious or highly ranked university? (Unfortunately, none of the Ivy League universities offer equine degrees, though several of them have very active equestrian teams.)
- Is it important to receive a certain type of degree? How would this degree impact your career goals?
- Do you want or need to stay close to home, in the state, or in the same geographical area? Do you have a specific area in mind?
- Do you want to travel to other countries? (If so, you may want to consider schools located in other countries, or schools that provide internships or apprenticeships in other countries.)
- Will you be more comfortable in a small school or a large school?
- Do you have a specific career path in mind? Or are you still undecided? If you are undecided, take a look at the list of possible careers. Do any of them appeal to you? (If you still aren't sure, a generalized degree, such as Equine Science or Animal Science with an equine concentration, may be a good place to start.)
- Do you want to have your own business or work for others?
- Do you want mostly hands-on experience (riding and training) or more class room work (business management classes, lectures, labs, etc.)?
- Do you want to pursue a graduate degree (master's, Ph.D.) eventually? Will that degree also be horse-related?

- Do you want exposure to lots of different types of horses?
- Do you want to take your horse with you to school? (Some schools don't allow students to bring their horses. If this is the case, you will need to find and pay for an outside boarding facility, and make time to see your horse.)
- How much can you afford? (If your parents are providing financing, you need to discuss this with them. Remember to factor in living expenses for yourself, and possibly, your horse.)
- Will you need to have a part-time job while attending school?
- Do you want job placement after you graduate?

## Why choose a college or university?

Many students choose a university because "that's what their parents want." But there are other advantages. When you complete a college or university, you will have an associate or bachelor degree in hand. That can be a big advantage in any career.

Your parents may also be concerned about your choice of majors. Attending a college or university can be a good compromise for horsey teenagers and their parents. The student satisfies the parents by attending a university, and the equine major allows the student to pursue something that he or she loves and is interested in.

Some college students are adults who generally fall into two categories: horse professionals seeking a degree, or individuals who have decided to change careers and enter the horse world.

## Why choose a "specialty school"?

Most people choose a specialty school to learn a certain technical skill or to study with a specific person. Many specialty schools, such as farrier schools and equine massage schools, are designed to provide you with a skill that will enable you to find employment immediately after graduation. Many schools offer apprenticeships or working-student arrangements that provide hands-on experience for successful graduates.

You may also decide to supplement a university education with a specialty school. Some specialty schools are linked with universities or community colleges, so be sure to ask them about the possibility of college credit and its transferability.

## Combining a College/University Education with Specialized Schooling

If you want a traditional degree, but are very interested in a specialty school, you may be able to combine the two. Many universities offer internship credit, which allows you to earn college units for attending a specialty school, or for working in an apprenticeship or specialized job. Once you are enrolled in the university, you may be able to attend a specialty school during your summer break (typically, three months).

To obtain internship credit, be sure to talk to your college advisor first. Often, you will have to fill out forms just to get the process started. At the end of your internship, the college may want to see your contract (for an apprenticeship or a job) or certificate (for a specialty school) with the dates of attendance (start date to finish date). You may also be required to write a paper on the experience.

If you have already attended the specialty school, or your college doesn't offer internship credit, ask about "life credit." If such credit is available, you will often be required to submit a portfolio or take a written/verbal test to prove what you know about the topic. Then, credit is granted for what you have already learned.

## Taking Your Education International

Don't limit yourself to the borders of your own country. Check out the international programs in this book. Many people who have studied abroad consider it one of their best experiences. Take advantage of this opportunity if there are several strong international schools in the area of your interest. For instance, the British Horse Society has one of the most organized and well-respected certification processes for riding instructors. In fact, most of the riding instructor certification programs in the world are based in the United Kingdom. In contrast, while there are trainers throughout the world in Natural Horsemanship, some of the best-known trainers are based in the United States. If you want to become a professional dressage, combined training, or jumper rider, several large and well-respected schools are located in Europe. Studying abroad can also be a great opportunity to learn to speak a second language.

## Financial Concerns

Are you worried about getting your money's worth from a program? If you choose a college or university education, you will earn a degree that will be recognized nationally, but it may or may not help you get a job in your chosen field. And, a certificate or diploma from a specialty school or program may not be recognized in other areas of the equine world or in a different state or country.

To check out a college, university, or specialty school, contact your local Better Business Bureau or the one closest to the school. (A complete list of offices is available at www.bbb.org.) Find out from the BBB if any complaints have been issued. If so, were the complaints settled, with both sides satisfied? Also, talk to current students and previous graduates of the program. Contact the associations and organizations that accredit or approve the school.

You might also be worried about tuition costs. Most university and college equine programs have "equine fees," which are not included in the normal tuition costs. And, many colleges offering equine programs are private schools—therefore, the tuition will be higher than the in-state tuition of state universities.

Don't worry! There are plenty of books available to help you finance your education with loans, grants, and scholarships. You should be able to qualify for financial aid at any college or university, and many specialty schools are starting to offer financial aid and scholarships. Ask potential schools about financial aid, and request a list of scholarships and grants that they offer. Be sure to check the *Scholarships* section of this book for an extensive list of equine-oriented scholarships.

## Making Your Own Education

Perhaps what you are looking for isn't in the pages of this book. You want to learn a particular skill or go into a certain field that has few (if any) schools representing it. Don't despair! With a little legwork, you can design your own education. Start by identifying the field that interests you. Are there any associations or organizations that represent that field? Include sport and breed associations on your list. Contact these associations and ask them how you could find out more information about your particular field of interest. Can they direct you to a particular person or to another association? Is there any organized form of certification or licensing for that field? How would you go about obtaining the education necessary to receive a certificate or license? This experience may include jobs, working student positions, apprenticeships, etc. If there is not a form of certification or licensing available, then what is the average background of someone with a career in that field?

## Choosing a Horse School

First, answer the questions at the beginning of this chapter. This will help you figure out what you are looking for in a school. Second, look through this book and make a list of the schools that you are interested in. Once you have created your initial list of candidate schools, contact each school (via e-mail, postal mail, or phone) and request an information packet on both the school and its equine or equestrian program. Take time to review the information they send, and jot down notes to yourself on your list. You may want to rank schools from your most favorite to your least favorite.

Once you have familiarized yourself with the schools you are interested in, utilize the questionnaire on pp. 00. Read over the questionnaire first, adding any questions of your own. Then, sit down with the telephone, revised questionnaire, and some sheets of paper. Allow at least one sheet of paper for each school that you would like to know more about. (It helps to write the name of each school at the top of a sheet of paper.) Now you can begin calling the schools.

If most of the questions you want to ask about a school are related to the equine program, it is best to talk to someone in the program. However, if most of your questions are about the school in general, then you will want to talk to someone in the admissions office. Either way, introduce yourself and explain a little bit about your interest (indicate whether you have questions about the school, or about the equine program). If the individual you are talking to seems knowledgeable, begin asking the questions on your list. If the person you are speaking with is not helpful, ask him or her to connect you with someone who can answer your questions. Be sure to get a name and contact number for the appropriate person.

After you have the answers to all of your questions, feel free to "chitchat" about any additional concerns you may have—ask for an overview of the program or details regarding campus life, if applicable. Finally, ask if you can contact current students or graduates who can tell you more about the program, and be sure to thank the person for taking the time to answer your questions.

After the phone interviews, reevaluate the schools on your list and reassign ratings (most favorite to least favorite) based on any new information you acquired. On each individual school's sheet of notepaper, highlight any areas of concern or excitement. This will make it easy for you to find this information again. Unless you have chosen a very unusual area of study, you should still have several candidates on your list. Call or e-mail any additional contact people (current students, equestrian team coaches, etc.) provided by the schools that most interest you. It is helpful to write out your questions before beginning your calls or e-mails, but again, don't be afraid to relax and informally chat. Even a general conversation about the school's program can give you a "feel" for another person's experience. (It is often useful to ask current students about their own backgrounds. Those with backgrounds and interests similar to yours may be better able to provide an accurate perspective.)

This process should allow you to narrow your list to a fairly reasonable number. Now, decide how many of the schools you can visit in person. Do your best to visit while classes are in session. Many schools have open houses that allow you to tour the campus, visit the equestrian facilities, meet current students, and talk with instructors or professors. If your parents are not thrilled with the idea of pursuing a career in horses, this can be a great opportunity to ease their fears. Ask your parents to visit colleges with you. Once you are on campus, school staff can help explain various careers and how their program provides the experience necessary to secure jobs in those careers.

If the schools you are interested in are close by, visiting them with your parents shouldn't be a problem. If you are interested in schools several-hundred-miles away, however, you may need to make other arrangements. For example, if you live on the West Coast, but you're interested in schools on the East Coast, consider arranging visits to several schools within a one- or two-week period, and suggest that one parent accompanies you. Be sure to allow a full day's visit for each school, plus travel time.

If the schools are in session during your visits, try to talk to as many current students as possible. Listen for both praise and complaints. Bring a notebook with you and jot down anything that seems important. Over time, the schools you visit may run together in your mind, and your notes will help you remember important details. Otherwise, a month after your visit, you may not remember whether the school in West Virginia had mirrors in its indoor arena—or even if it *had* an indoor arena!

If all the schools you are considering are in the same country, purchase a map of that country. (If they are all in one region of a country, you'll only need a map of that region.) Post the map on a wall and hang a name tag for each school to a map pin. Use pins of various colors and establish a coding system—for example, yellow for schools contacted, red for schools visited, blue for your favorites, etc. This will provide a visual record of your progress.

Finally, you will have to narrow your list down to one school. Only you (and your parents) can make this decision. Take every detail into consideration, including finances, geography, and your educational and career goals. Remember that in the end, this is supposed to be fun! This decision should make you happy. If for some reason it doesn't, keep in mind that no decision is permanent. If one school doesn't work out, you can always go back to your final list and try again.

# Horse School Questionnaire

This list of questions will help you evaluate potential schools. Every question will not apply to every school. Some questions are geared towards universities, while others are more applicable for specialty schools. Skip questions that don't apply to a particular school, or rework them so they do. Add your own questions to the list as they come to mind.

When you call or visit a school, keep this list in front of you. Scribble answers to the questions on sheets of paper, clearly labeled with the names of the schools that you are interested in. Otherwise, you may not remember which answers belong to which schools.

- What type of degree or certificate does the school offer?

- Is the program accredited?

- What association or organization is responsible for accrediting the program?

- What is the length of the program?

- What is the cost of the entire program?

- What does the tuition cover?

- Is housing provided?

- What is the cost of housing?

- Is financial aid available?

- Are there scholarships I can apply for?

- What are the additional costs for the equestrian program?

- Is there a clearly stated goal for the program?

- Is the program carrying out that goal?

- How long has the program been in existence?

- What is the admission policy for the program?

- What kind of educational goals does the typical student possess?

- Are graduates leaving the program with the skills and knowledge they hoped to acquire?

- What is a typical day like for an equestrian student?

- What is the ratio of general education to equine classes per semester or quarter?

- How many hours of hands-on experience do students get per semester or quarter?

- Can you describe the curriculum for the major I'm interested in?

- How often is the curriculum updated and reevaluated?

- Are the goals for each class clearly stated?

- Are the goals achievable for the students?

- Does each course build on the last as students progress?

- How are students graded in the hands-on (non-classroom) courses?

- How often are students evaluated?

- What is the average class size for hands-on courses?

- For hands-on courses, are the classes organized by skill level?

- How often do students ride, in hours, per semester or quarter?

- Does the school own the equestrian center, or is the program run at a nearby stable?

- How often has the school changed the location of the equestrian center?

- Is the equestrian center within walking distance of the campus?

- Is transportation provided to the equestrian center?

- How often is transportation provided, and at what times?

- How many horses are available for the program?

- Are students assigned their own horses or do they share with other students?

- Are horses of various ages and levels of ability available?

- May I bring my own horse?

- Will my horse be used in the program?

- What is the cost of boarding?

- Are barn safety rules and regulations clearly posted and upheld?

- Can you provide a detailed description of the equestrian facilities?

- What kind of training and degrees do members of the faculty have?

- Is the faculty currently involved in the equine industry outside of the school?

- Do assistants or other students (such as seniors) teach any classes?

- How easily accessible are the teachers outside of class?

- Do program directors teach classes?

- Are internships and apprenticeships available for students?

- Does the program help students find employment after graduation?

- How many students find jobs in the equine industry within a year of graduation?

- What types of jobs do graduates now hold?

- Are records kept of graduates that have found jobs and, if so, may I view them?

- Are students allowed to use the school's career services after graduation?

# Possible Careers

If you want a job in the equine industry, your choices are not limited to being a rider or a trainer. There are more than 250 careers listed on the next few pages, and every one of them can be considered a "horsey job." Some of them are office jobs that do not require a four-year degree; however, you will typically earn a higher salary if you have a degree. The same is true of many "hands-on" positions—you will find that many employers are willing to accept a degree in place of a certain number of years of experience.

To learn more about various horse careers and how to prepare for them, I recommend consulting *The Complete Guide to Horse Careers* by Sue Reynolds and *Careers with Horses: The Comprehensive Guide to Finding Your Dream Job* by Vicki Hogue.

**Accountant:** Keeps accounts for a farm or a horse-related business or has a private practice.

**Acupuncturist:** Practices alternative healing for horses.

**Administrator of Equestrian Program:** Manages the equine program for a school.

**Advertising Copywriter:** Writes the text for advertisements.

**Advertising Director:** Manages the advertising office and approves all ads.

**Advertising Sales Manager:** Manages the sales force in the advertising office.

**Advertising Salesperson:** Sells ad space to clients.

**Agricultural Engineer:** Designs and builds stables, water systems, feed systems, etc.

**Alternative/Eastern Medicine Provider:** Provides holistic care for horses, such as acupuncture, acupressure, herbal remedies, etc.

**Animal Behaviorist:** Studies and researches equine behavior.

**Animal Nutritionist:** Works for a food distributor; ensures products are nutritionally sound and teaches nutrition classes.

**Announcer:** Announces at shows, races, and events.

**Architect:** Designs buildings.

**Artificial Inseminator:** Performs artificial insemination under supervision of vet or breeding manager.

**AI Technician:** Assists artificial inseminator.

**Artist, Commercial/Creative:** Draws, paints, sculpts, etc.

**Attorney:** Specializes in equine law and/or works for a horse-related business.

**Auction Clerk:** Handles paperwork at an auction house.

**Auctioneer:** Announces at auctions.

**Auction Ring Assistant:** Handles horses in auction ring.

**Auditor, Equine Organization:** Attends to organization's financial records.

**Author:** Writes fiction and/or nonfiction books on horses.

**Award Manufacturer/Salesperson:** Makes and sells trophies, ribbons, etc. for competitions.

**Backstretch Worker:** Works on the backstretch of a racetrack.

**Barn Manager/Assistant:** Manages the day-to-day operations at a barn and hires staff.

**Bedding Supplier:** Supplies bedding to stores and large ranches.

**Blacksmith:** Makes horseshoes and other items, usually from iron.

**Blanket Cleaning & Repair Serviceperson:** Cleans and repairs horse blankets.

**Bloodstock Agent:** Buys and sells horses for clients.

**Blood Typing Specialist:** Types blood to aid in horse identification.

**Boarding Barn Manager/Assistant:** Manages the day-to-day operations at a boarding barn and hires staff.

**Bookkeeper:** Keeps the financial books for a barn, business, or company.

**Boot Manufacturer:** Makes riding boots.

**Braider:** Braids the manes and tails of horses for competitions, sales, and races.

**Brand Inspector:** Inspects brands on horses for identification purposes and to settle legal issues.

**Breed Association Official:** Handles leadership duties in a breed association.

**Breeding Farm Staff:** Cares for stallions, mares, and foals.

**Breeding Manager/Assistant:** Manages the stallions, mares, and foals, and hires staff.

**Broodmare Manager/Assistant:** Manages the mares and foals.

**Business Manager, Magazine:** Manages the business side of the magazine.

**Camp Equestrian Director:** Designs and runs the equestrian program at a camp.

**Caretaker:** Lives on-site to take care of property and animals at stables, farms, and estates.

**Carpenter:** Makes items from wood and/or handles construction/repair of buildings.

**Carriage Driver:** Drives a carriage for weddings, shows, and other special events.

**Chemist:** Analyzes blood, urine, and saliva for illegal substances.

**Chiropractor:** Adjusts horses to relieve pain or correct problems.

**Circulation Manager, Magazine:** Manages the circulation department in a magazine.

**Clerk of Course:** Maintains all paperwork and certificates for racehorses.

**Clerk of Scales:** Weighs-in jockeys at a race.

**Clinician:** Teaches clinics in a particular field of expertise.

**Clocker:** Clocks workouts at racetracks and provides information to "scratch sheet" editor.

**Clothing Designer/Tailor:** Designs and tailors equestrian clothing.

**Clothing Salesperson:** Sells equestrian clothing to resellers or directly to consumers.

**Collections Manager of a Museum or Library:** Manages and maintains an equine-oriented collection.

**College Instructor/University Professor of Equestrian Science:** Teaches courses in equine subjects.

**Computer Programmer:** Designs and writes horse-related computer programs.

**Computer Screensaver Designer:** Designs horse-related screensavers.

**Concession Operator:** Operates concession stands at shows, fairs, and events.

**Condition-Book Technician:** Records data into a horse condition book.

**Conditioning Rider:** Rides horses and maintains their level of conditioning.

**Country Club Manager:** Manages the day-to-day operations at a country club.

**Course Designer:** Designs cross-country, hunter/jumper, or trail courses for competition.

**Crewman/Props:** Sets up courses for competitions.

**Dentist:** Maintains dental health of the horse.

**Director of Public Relations:** Handles public relations duties at a company or association.

**Driver, Harness:** Races harness horses or drives carriages and buggies.

**Drugging Inspector:** Inspects horses that may have been drugged.

**Drug/Pharmaceutical Salesperson:** Sells drugs/pharmaceuticals for horses.

**Dude or Guest Ranch Host/Hostess:** Greets and entertains guests at dude or guest ranch.

**Dude or Guest Ranch Manager:** Manages the day-to-day operations.

**Dude Ranch Wrangler:** Manages the horses and equestrian staff at a dude ranch.

**Editor:** Edits books and magazines.

**Equine Appraiser:** Appraises horse's worth for insurance companies and purchases.

**Equine Consultant:** Provides consultant services in a particular area of expertise.

**Estate Manager:** Manages the day-to-day operations of an estate.

**Executive Secretary or Director of Equine Organization:** Manages the organization.

**Exercise Rider:** Exercises and conditions racehorses.

**Exhibitor:** Exhibits horses or horse products at shows, events, and fairs.

**Expert Witness:** Testifies in court or in depositions.

**Extension Horse Specialist:** Oversees horse activities for extension department of a university.

**Farm Maintenance:** Maintains and repairs equipment and facilities of a farm.

**Farm Office Staff:** Works in a farm's office, handling filing, answering phones, etc.

**Farm Sitter:** Stays on farm to take care of property and animals while owners are away.

**Farm Vet:** Works for farm as on-site vet.

**Farrier:** Trims and shoes horses.

**Feed Company Representative:** Represents the feed company to farms and to resellers.

**Feed Manufacturer:** Manufactures feed to be distributed to farms and resellers.

**Feed Salesperson:** Sells feed to farms and to resellers.

**Field Secretary for Equine Organization:** Represents the organization's interests at events.

**Film Editor/Distribution Specialist:** Edits and distributes horse-oriented commercials, programs, and movies.

**Financial Advisor:** Provides financial advice to companies or individuals.

**First Aid Personnel:** Provides first aid at events for horses or equestrians.

**Foaling Crew Personnel:** Takes care of mares in labor and their foals.

**4-H Instructor/Director:** Instructs and directs 4-H groups.

**Gardener:** Maintains landscaping at horse facilities.

**Geneticist:** Studies equine genetics.

**Gift Shop Manager:** Manages the day-to-day operations and employees at an equine gift shop.

**Groom, General:** Grooms, tacks-up, and takes care of horses on a day-to-day basis at a stable.

**Groom, Race:** Takes care of, grooms, and tacks-up racehorses.

**Groom, Show:** Takes care of, grooms, and tacks-up show horses.

**Grounds Maintenance:** Maintains and repairs show, race, and stable grounds.

**Handicapper:** Handicaps (determines how much weight the horse will carry) race horses for races.

**Harness Driver:** Drives harness-racing horses.

**Harness Maker:** Designs and makes harness gear.

**Hay Salesperson/Distributor:** Sells and distributes hay to farms or to resellers.

**Horse-Drawn Tour Guide:** Leads tours in a carriage.

**Horse-and-Buggy Driver:** Drives buggies for weddings, tours, etc.

**Horse Feed Development Specialist:** Develops various feeds.

**Horse Feed Wholesale Distributor:** Sells feed to resellers.

**Horsehair Products Producer:** Uses horsehair to create items for sale (blankets, ropes, etc.).

**Horse Identifier:** Identifies horses before classes at horse shows.

**Horse Show Secretary:** Manages the paperwork in the office and in the announcer's booth at horse shows.

**Horse Show Steward:** Monitors activities at horse shows to prevent illegal practices.

**Horse Show Vet:** Provides on-site vet services at a show.

**Horse Trader:** Buys and sells horses.

**Hot Walker:** Walks and cools down racehorses after workouts and races.

**Humane Society Official:** Investigates animal cruelty complaints.

**Identification File Clerk:** Maintains files on horses for shows and races.

**Identifier:** Checks the lip tattoos of racehorses against registration papers.

**Illustrator for Equine Publications:** Creates illustrations for horse publications.

**Insurance Actuary:** Calculates insurance rates and premiums.

**Insurance Agent:** Maintains the insurance policy and handles all questions from clients.

**Insurance Investigator:** Investigates insurance claims.

**Insurance Salesperson:** Sells insurance for horses.

**Instructor:** Teaches people how to ride or drive.

**Jewelry Designer/Salesperson:** Designs, makes, and sells equine-oriented jewelry.

**Jockey:** Rides horses in races.

**Jockey Room Custodian:** Maintains the jockey's locker room.

**Jockey's Agent:** Solicits horses for a particular jockey to ride.

**Jockey Valet:** Assists jockeys in preparing for a race.

**Judge:** Evaluates participants in horse shows and events.

**Jump Crew:** Puts up and takes down jumps at shows and events.

**Jump Equipment Manufacturer:** Makes and distributes the equipment to make jumps.

**Landscape Architect:** Designs the landscaping for horse facilities.

**Landscaper:** Handles landscaping tasks at horse facilities.

**Leather Dealer:** Distributes leather directly to saddlers.

**Lobbyist:** Talks to key politicians about issues on behalf of an organization.

**Loper:** Warms up Western horses and maintains their conditioning.

**Maintenance Rider:** Maintains level of fitness in assigned horses.

**Marketing Director of Equestrian Program:** Handles marketing (advertising) for an equine program.

**Massage Therapist:** Provides massage therapy for horses.

**Merchandise Retailer:** Sells equine items to consumers.

**Model Horse Designer:** Designs and paints model horses.

**Motion Pictures Worker:** Works in the motion picture business with equines.

**Mounted Police Officer:** Works as a police officer or deputy sheriff in the mounted unit.

**Mutuels Manager:** Manages the betting in horse racing.

**Nanny/Housekeeper:** Oversees the children and/or the house at an equestrian estate.

**Night Watch/Foaling Manager:** Patrols farms at night and monitors the barns during foaling season.

**Official Race Timer:** Maintains and manages the automatic timer at horse races.

**Outrider:** Leads and follows the post parade before races and assists jockeys that are in trouble.

**Packer/Guide:** Takes clients on wilderness camping trips on mules or on horseback.

**Paddock Judge:** Supervises the paddock area before a race.

**Paddock Master:** Manages and calls classes to the entry gate at horse shows and events.

**Painter:** Paints portraits for customers.

**Parade Organizer:** Organizes the order and manner in which a parade proceeds.

**Paymaster of Purses:** Handles all purses, entry fees, claiming money, and jockey fees at a racetrack.

**Pedigree Analyst:** Analyzes pedigrees for purposes of breeding and competition.

**Pedigree Researcher:** Researches the pedigrees of horses for breeding purposes.

**Photo Finish Operator:** Photographs the finish line at a racetrack.

**Photographer:** Takes pictures of horses for clients, shows, magazines, etc.

**Polo Clinician:** Gives clinics on the sport of polo.

**Polo Coach:** Coaches (instructs and trains) polo teams.

**Polo Field Caretaker:** Takes care of the polo grounds.

**Polo Instructor:** Teaches people the sport of polo.

**Polo Trainer:** Trains horses for polo.

**Pony Rider:** Leads racehorses in the post parade.

**Professional Huntsman:** Organizes and leads foxhunts.

**Producer, Film/Video:** Handles the financial responsibility for equine films.

**Publications Distributor:** Researches markets and distributes equine publications to suitable markets.

**Publicity Agent/Assistant:** Designs publicity campaigns.

**Publisher:** Publishes books and magazines.

**Racing Chemist:** Checks blood, urine, and saliva for illegal substances.

**Racing Commissioner:** Oversees horse racing in a particular state.

**Racing Forms & Programs Distributor:** Oversees the printing of racing programs.

**Racing Manager:** Manages the overall operation at the track.

**Racing Secretary:** Oversees the day-to-day operation at the track.

**Racing Steward:** Monitors racing practices to prevent illegal activities.

**Ranch Hand:** Takes care of horses and other livestock on ranches and farms.

**Ranch Manager/Assistant:** Manages the day-to-day operations on a ranch or farm.

**Real Estate Agent:** Specializes in equine-oriented real estate.

**Rehabilitation Therapist:** Works with horses to help them recover after injuries.

**Reporter/Journalist:** Reports on equine-related stories.

**Rescue Worker/Agency Representative:** Rescues horses from auctions and other harmful situations.

**Ribbon/Trophy Designer:** Designs and creates ribbons and trophies.

**Rider, Circus:** Rides horses under saddle, performs vaulting maneuvers, and works horses at liberty in a circus.

**Rider, Dressage:** Rides dressage horses in competitions.

**Rider, Endurance:** Competes in endurance events.

**Rider, English:** Rides in general equitation and hunter competitions.

**Rider, Hunter:** Rides in hunter competitions.

**Rider, Jumper:** Rides in jumper competitions.

**Rider, Stunt/Trick:** Rides trick horses and performs stunts for movies, shows, and fairs.

**Rider, Western:** Rides in Western competitions.

**Rodeo Producer:** Oversees the rodeo and handles the hiring of all staff.

**Rodeo Staff:** Works a rodeo event.

**Rodeo Secretary:** Handles the paperwork at a rodeo.

**Rodeo Stock Contractor:** Supplies the stock (cows and horses) for a rodeo.

**Saddler:** Designs, makes, and repairs horse tack.

**Schooling Rider:** Rides horses and maintains their level of training for lessons and/or competition.

**Secretary of Racing Commissioner:** Represents and carries out the policies of the racing commissioner.

**Security:** Handles the security and safety of horses and patrons.

**Show Manager/Assistant:** Manages the overall operation of a show.

**Sign Maker:** Designs and makes equine-oriented banners and signs.

**Software Developer:** Designs and develops computer programs.

**Soring Inspector:** Inspects horses at shows for illegal soring.

**Stable Manager/Assistant:** Manages the day-to-day operations at a stable and hires staff.

**Stable Owner:** Owns a stable, farm, or ranch.

**Stallion Handler:** Handles everyday care of stallions.

**Starter:** Leads racehorses into the starting gate and ensures that the start of the race is fair.

**State Vet:** Enforces animal protection laws and helps prevent animal disease from spreading.

**Summer Camp Staff Member:** Works with children and horses.

**Tack & Equipment Designer:** Designs tack and equine-oriented equipment.

**Tack Company Representative:** Represents a tack company to the public and to resellers.

**Tack Salesperson:** Sells tack to customers and to resellers.

**Tack Shop Owner:** Owns and operates a tack store.

**Tax Specialist:** Specializes in tax laws for horses.

**Teacher/Professor:** Teaches equine courses in schools.

**Television Announcer:** Announces equestrian events for sports networks.

**Theme Park Horse Manager:** Oversees the equine-related operations at a theme park.

**Therapeutic Riding Instructor:** Teaches handicapped children how to ride.

**Therapeutic Riding Program Manager:** Directs and manages the program.

**Ticket Seller:** Sells tickets for horse events.

**Timing Equipment Salesperson:** Sells timing equipment for horse events.

**Track Security Staff:** Maintains security and control on race day and patrols track areas.

**Track Vet:** Provides on-site vet services at a racetrack.

**Trail Engineer:** Designs and maintains trails to keep erosion and damage at a minimum.

**Trail Guide:** Leads trail rides.

**Trailer Design, Manufacture, and Salesperson:** Designs, manufactures, and sells horse trailers.

**Trainer, Race:** Trains racehorses.

**Trainer, Show:** Trains show horses.

**Transportation Specialist:** Transports horses.

**Travel Agent:** Specializes in finding and booking reservations for equine-oriented vacations.

**Turf Club Director:** Manages and oversees the operations of a race club.

**Veterinarian:** Takes care of equine medical needs.

**Veterinarian Assistant:** Assists vets in the field and at the office.

**Veterinarian Lab Tech:** Assists vets in the laboratory.

**Videographer:** Creates videos of horses for companies or as a freelancer.

**Video Race Patrol:** Videotapes horse races.

**Web Page Designer:** Designs equine-oriented web sites.

**Whipper-In:** Handles control and direction of dogs during foxhunts.

**Wild Horse Preservationist:** Works with Bureau of Land Management (BLM) or wild horse organizations to protect and preserve wild horses.

**Writer:** Writes articles on equine-related subjects and events.

**Youth Director for Horse-Oriented Organization:** Oversees the youth programs in the organization.

# Fields of Study

## Alternative Therapies

Academy of Equine Dentistry (Idaho, U.S.A.)
American School of Equine Dentistry (Virginia, U.S.A.)
Aspen Equine Studies, Inc. (Colorado, U.S.A.)
The Association of Chartered Physiotherapists in Animal Therapy Education
(Hampshire, England)
Australian College of Natural Animal Medicine (Australia)
BC College of Equine Therapy (British Columbia, Canada)
D'Arcy Lane Institute (Ontario, Canada)
Don Doran's Equine Sports Massage Program (Florida, U.S.A.)
Equi-Myo Training Program (Connecticut, U.S.A.)
Equinology, Inc. ® (California, U.S.A.)
Equissage (Virginia, U.S.A.)
Equitouch Systems® (Colorado, U.S.A.)
Geary Whiting's Equine Massage School (California, U.S.A.)
Hartpury College (Gloucestershire, England)
A Healthy Horse the Natural Way (Australia)
HJW Equine Therapy (British Columbia, Canada)
Hocking College (Ohio, U.S.A.)
Institute of Equine Podiatry (Massachusetts, U.S.A.)
Integrated Touch Therapy, Inc. (Ohio, U.S.A.)
International Academy of Equine Sports Therapy (Germany)
McTimoney College of Chiropractic (Oxfordshire, England)
Meredith Manor International Learning Center (West Virginia, U.S.A.)
New England Academy of Therapeutic Sciences (New Hampshire, U.S.A.)
Prairie Winds Equine Massage Therapy College (Colorado, U.S.A.)
Teikyo Post University (Connecticut, U.S.A.)
Tellington Method Training (New Mexico, U.S.A.)
University of Melbourne (Australia)

## Animal Science (Agriculture) with an Equine Emphasis

ACS Distance Education (Wallingford, England)
Auburn University (Alabama, U.S.A.)
Australian Correspondence School (Australia)
Berry College (Georgia, U.S.A.)
Brooksby Melton College (Leicestershire, England)
California Polytechnic State University, San Luis Obispo (California, U.S.A)
California State Polytechnic University, Pomona (California, U.S.A.)
California State University–Fresno (California, U.S.A.)
Casper College (Wyoming, U.S.A.)
Clemson University (South Carolina, U.S.A.)
CNEAP (France)
Coleg Sir Gâr (Wales)
The College of West Anglia (Cambridgeshire, England)
Conners State College (Oklahoma, U.S.A.)
Cook College, Rutgers University (New Jersey, U.S.A.)

- Cornell University (New York, U.S.A.)
- Delaware Valley College (Pennsylvania, U.S.A.)
- Feather River College (California, U.S.A.)
- Imperial College London (Kent, England)
- Iowa State University of Science and Technology (Iowa, U.S.A.)
- Kansas State University (Kansas, U.S.A.)
- Kemptville College/University of Guelph (Ontario, Canada)
- Landbúnaðarháskólinn á Hvanneyri—Hvanneyri Agricultural University (Iceland)
- Lassen Community College (California, U.S.A.)
- Los Angeles Pierce College (California, U.S.A.)
- Louisiana State University (Louisiana, U.S.A.)
- Louisiana Tech University (Louisiana, U.S.A.)
- Mesalands Community College (New Mexico, U.S.A.)
- Michigan State University (Michigan, U.S.A.)
- Middle Tennessee State University (Tennessee, U.S.A.)
- Mississippi State University (Mississippi, U.S.A.)
- Montana State University (Montana, U.S.A.)
- Morehead State University (Kentucky, U.S.A.)
- Murray State University (Kentucky, U.S.A.)
- New Mexico State University (New Mexico, U.S.A.)
- North Carolina State University (North Carolina, U.S.A.)
- Ohio State University (Ohio, U.S.A.)
- Oregon State University (Oregon, U.S.A.)
- Pennsylvania State University (Pennsylvania, U.S.A.)
- Plumpton College (Sussex, England)
- Purdue University (Indiana, U.S.A.)
- Redland's Community College (Oklahoma, U.S.A.)
- South Dakota State University (South Dakota, U.S.A.)
- Southern Illinois University–Carbondale (Illinois, U.S.A.)
- Southwest Missouri State University (Missouri, U.S.A.)
- State University of New York–Cobleskill (New York, U.S.A.)
- Sul Ross State University (Texas, U.S.A.)
- Tarleton State University (Texas, U.S.A.)
- Texas Tech University (Texas, U.S.A.)
- Thompson School of Applied Science (New Hampshire, U.S.A.)
- Truman State University (Missouri, U.S.A.)
- University of Arizona (Arizona, U.S.A.)
- University of California–Davis (California, U.S.A.)
- University of Connecticut (Connecticut, U.S.A.)
- University of Delaware (Delaware, U.S.A.)
- University of Georgia (Georgia, U.S.A.)
- University of Idaho (Idaho, U.S.A.)
- University of Illinois at Urbana–Champagne (Illinois, U.S.A.)
- University of Kentucky (Kentucky, U.S.A.)
- University of Louisiana–Monroe (Louisiana, U.S.A.)
- University of Maine–Orono (Maine, U.S.A.)
- University of Maryland (Maryland, U.S.A.)
- University of Massachusetts–Amherst (Massachusetts, U.S.A.)
- University of Minnesota–Crookston (Minnesota, U.S.A.)
- University of Nebraska–Lincoln (Nebraska, U.S.A.)
- University of Nevada–Reno (Nevada, U.S.A.)
- University of New Hampshire (New Hampshire, U.S.A.)

University of Tennessee–Knoxville (Tennessee, U.S.A.)
University of Tennessee–Martin (Tennessee, U.S.A.)
University of Vermont (Vermont, U.S.A.)
University of Wisconsin–River Falls (Wisconsin, U.S.A.)
Utah State University (Utah, U.S.A.)
Virginia Tech (Virginia, U.S.A.)
Walters State Community College (Tennessee, U.S.A.)
Welsh College of Horticulture (Wales)
West Texas A & M Univerity (Texas, U.S.A.)
Western Kentucky University (Kentucky, U.S.A.)
Wilmington College (Ohio, U.S.A.)

## Announcing

Sam Howry's Rodeo Academy (Oklahoma, U.S.A.)

## Apprenticeships/Internships/Working Student Opportunities

American Horse Publications Internship Program (Florida, U.S.A.)
Bishop Burton College (Yorkshire, England)
C. W. Training (California, U.S.A.)
Donna Snyder-Smith Apprenticeship (California, U.S.A.)
Equestrian International (California, U.S.A.)
Equine Research Foundation (California, U.S.A.)
Experience International (Washington, U.S.A.)
Jim Graham & Meadow Run Ranch (Alabama, U.S.A.)
Kent Equine Industry and Training Services Ltd. (Hertfordshire, England)
Kentucky Equine Management Internship Program (Kentucky, U.S.A.)
Monty Roberts International Learning Center (California, U.S.A.)
Oatridge Agricultural College (Scotland)
Robert O. Mayer Riding Academy (Pennsylvania, U.S.A.)
Warwickshire College (Warwickshire, England)
Wellington Equestrian Education Ltd. (Hampshire, England)
Wesleyan College (Georgia, U.S.A.)

## Art

American Academy of Equine Art Workshops (Kentucky, U.S.A.)
Taos School of Equine Art (New Mexico, U.S.A.)

## Breeding

Australian Correspondence School (Australia)
British Stud Staff Training Scheme (Suffolk, England)
California Polytechnic State University, San Luis Obispo (California, U.S.A.)
Cazenovia College (New York, U.S.A.)
Central Florida Community College (Florida, U.S.A.)
Centre de Formation d'Armor (France)
CNEAP (France)
Dannevirke High School (New Zealand)
Doubletree Horse Farm Breeding Management School (Colorado, U.S.A.)
Ecole d'Agriculture St. Joseph (France)

Equine-Reproduction.com (California, U.S.A.)
Hartpury College (Gloucestershire, England)
Hocking College (Ohio, U.S.A.)
Kansas State University (Kansas, U.S.A.)
Kentucky Equine Management Internship Program (Kentucky, U.S.A.)
Kwantlen University College (British Columbia, Canada)
Kyrewood Equestrian Centre Ltd. (New Zealand)
Lake Erie College (Ohio, U.S.A.)
Lakeland Equestrian Centre (Cumbria, England)
L.A.P. du Tricastin-Baronnies (France)
L.A.P. Le Cluzeau (France)
L'Ecole des Courses Hippiques AFASEC (France)
Lycée d'Enseignement Professionnel Agricole St Hilaire du Harcouet (France)
Lycée General et Technologique Agricole Paysager Equestre (France)
New Mexico State University (New Mexico, U.S.A.)
North Carolina State University (North Carolina, U.S.A.)
North Central Texas College (Texas, U.S.A.)
Ohio State University Agriculture Technical Institute (Ohio, U.S.A.)
Olds Colleges (Alberta, Canada)
Sierra College (California, U.S.A.)
South Dakota State University (South Dakota, U.S.A.)
Southern Illinois University–Carbondale (Illinois, U.S.A.)
Southwest Missouri State University (Missouri, U.S.A.)
State University of New York–Cobleskill (New York, U.S.A.)
State University of New York–Morrisville (New York, U.S.A.)
Swedish University of Agricultural Sciences (Sweden)
Torrens Valley Institute of TAFE (Australia)
University of Idaho (Idaho, U.S.A.)
Utah State University (Utah, U.S.A.)
Waikato Institute of Technology (New Zealand)
William H. Miner Agricultural Research Institute (New York, U.S.A.)
Writtle College (Essex, England)
Yrkesinstitut Sydväst (Finland)

## Carriage Driving

British Driving Society (Warwickshire, England)
La Ferme du Sonvaux (France)
Lakeland Equestrian Centre (Cumbria, England)
Norwegian Equine College (Norway)
Queensland Race Training (Australia)
State University of New York–Morrisville (New York, U.S.A.)
University of Melbourne (Australia)
Ypäjän Hevosopisto/Equine College Ypäjä (Finland)

## Course Designer

Equitation School of the Armored Calvary School–Army of Chile (Chile)

## Dressage

Brookfields Riding & Livery Centre (Warwickshire, England)
Equitation School of the Armored Calvary School–Army of Chile (Chile)

Escola de Equitacao do Exercito—Brazillian Army Riding School (Brazil)
Robert O. Mayer Riding Academy (Pennsylvania, U.S.A.)

## Equine Business Management

Averett University (Virginia, U.S.A.)
Berkshire College of Agriculture (Berkshire, England)
Bicton College (Devon, England)
Cannington College (Somerset, England)
Cazenovia College (New York, U.S.A.)
Centenary College (New Jersey, U.S.A.)
Clemson University (South Carolina, U.S.A.)
Dawson Community College (Montana, U.S.A.)
Duchy College (Cornwall, England)
Global Equine Academy (Wyoming, U.S.A.)
Hartpury College (Gloucestershire, England)
Imperial College London (Kent, England)
Institute of Rural Studies, University of Wales, Aberystwyth (Wales)
Johnson and Wales University (Rhode Island, U.S.A.)
Lake Erie College (Ohio, U.S.A.)
Laramie County Community College (Wyoming, U.S.A.)
Marcus Oldham College (Australia)
Midway College (Kentucky, U.S.A.)
Mount Ida College (Massachusetts, U.S.A.)
Mt. San Antonio College (California, U.S.A.)
Northwest College (Wyoming, U.S.A.)
Olds Colleges (Alberta, Canada)
Otterbein College (Ohio, U.S.A.)
Pencoed College (Wales)
Reaseheath College (Cheshire, England)
Rocky Mountain College (Montana, U.S.A.)
Royal Agricultural College (Gloucestershire, England)
St. Andrews Presbyterian College (North Carolina, U.S.A.)
Saint Mary-of-the-Woods College (Indiana, U.S.A.)
State University of New York–Cobleskill (New York, U.S.A.)
Stephens College (Missouri, U.S.A.)
University of Arizona (Arizona, U.S.A.)
University of Findlay (Ohio, U.S.A.)
University of Limerick (Republic of Ireland)
University of Louisville (Kentucky, U.S.A.)
University of Maryland (Maryland, U.S.A.)
University of Sydney–Orange (Australia)
University of West England–Bristol (Avon, England)
Walford and North Shropshire College (Shropshire, England)
Warwickshire College (Warwickshire, England)
Western Kentucky University (Kentucky, U.S.A.)
William Woods University (Missouri, U.S.A.)
Writtle College (Essex, England)

## Equine Science (Studies)

Agricultural School of Lambach (Austria)
Alfred University (New York, U.S.A.)

Averett University (Virginia, U.S.A.)
Berkshire College of Agriculture (Berkshire, England)
Bethany Hills College (West Virginia, U.S.A.)
Bicton College (Devon, England)
Bishop Burton College (Yorkshire, England)
Black Hawk College (Illinois, U.S.A.)
Brinsbury College (Sussex, England)
Centenary College (New Jersey, U.S.A.)
Central Wyoming College (Wyoming, U.S.A.)
Charles Sturt University (Australia)
Colby Community College (Kansas, U.S.A.)
Coleg Gwent (Wales)
Coleg Sir Gâr (Wales)
Colorado State University (Colorado, U.S.A.)
Delaware Valley College (Pennsylvania, U.S.A.)
Dodge City Community College (Kansas, U.S.A.)
Duchy College (Cornwall, England)
Eastern Institute of Technology–Hawke's Bay (New Zealand)
Easton College (Norfolk, England)
Enniskillen College and Greenmount College (Northern Ireland)
Equi Study (Warwickshire, England)
Fairview College (Alberta, Canada)
Feather River College (California, U.S.A.)
Hadlow College (Kent, England)
Hartpury College (Gloucestershire, England)
Herdword (New Zealand)
Hólar í Hjaltadal (Iceland)
Horses and Courses Ltd. (Buckinghamshire, England)
Houghton College (New York, U.S.A.)
Institut de Technologie Agroalimentaire (Quebec, Canada)
Institute of Rural Studies, University of Wales, Aberystwyth (Wales)
Johnson and Wales University (Rhode Island, U.S.A.)
Judson College (Alabama, U.S.A.)
Kanadiana International Equestrian Centre Inc. (Saskatchewan, Canada)
Kingston Maurward College (Dorset, England)
Kirkwood Community College (Iowa, U.S.A.)
Kishwaukee College (Illinois, U.S.A.)
Kwantlen University College (British Columbia, Canada)
Laramie County Community College (Wyoming, U.S.A.)
Lord Fairfax Community College (Virginia, U.S.A.)
Los Angeles Pierce College (California, U.S.A.)
Lycée Agro-environnemental privé St Joseph (France)
Martin Community College (North Carolina, U.S.A.)
Massey University (New Zealand)
Middle Tennessee State University (Tennessee, U.S.A.)
Midway College (Kentucky, U.S.A.)
Morehead State University (Kentucky, U.S.A.)
Moulton College (Northamptonshire, England)
Murray State University (Kentucky, U.S.A.)
Myerscough College (Lancashire, England)
New Horizons Equine Education Center, Inc. (Colorado, U.S.A.)
Northeastern Jr. College (Colorado, U.S.A.)

Nottingham Trent University/Brackenhurst (Nottinghamshire, England)
Oaklands College (Hertfordshire, England)
Ohio State University Agriculture Technical Institute (Ohio, U.S.A.)
Olds Colleges (Alberta, Canada)
Open College of Equine Studies (Suffolk, England)
Oregon State University (Oregon, U.S.A.)
Oxford Brookes University (Oxfordshire, England)
Parkland College (Illinois, U.S.A.)
Pembrokeshire College (Wales)
Pencoed College (Wales)
Reaseheath College (Cheshire, England)
Redland's Community College (Oklahoma, U.S.A.)
Rocky Mountain College (Montana, U.S.A.)
Rodbaston College (Staffordshire, England)
Royal Agricultural College (Gloucestershire, England)
The Royal (Dick) School of Veterinary Studies (Scotland)
St. Andrews Presbyterian College (North Carolina, U.S.A.)
Saint Mary-of-the-Woods College (Indiana, U.S.A.)
Salem International University (West Virginia, U.S.A.)
Santa Rosa Junior College (California, U.S.A.)
Schoolcraft College (Michigan, U.S.A.)
Scottsdale Community College (Arizona, U.S.A.)
Shasta College (California, U.S.A.)
Sierra College (California, U.S.A.)
Southern Illinois University–Carbondale (Illinois, U.S.A.)
Southwest Missouri State University (Missouri, U.S.A.)
Sparsholt College Hampshire (Hampshire, England)
State University of New York–Morrisville (New York, U.S.A.)
Stephens College (Missouri, U.S.A.)
Stockbridge School of Agriculture (Massachusetts, U.S.A.)
Swedish University of Agricultural Sciences (Sweden)
Sweet Briar College (Virginia, U.S.A.)
Teikyo Post University (Connecticut, U.S.A.)
Telford Rural Polytechnic (New Zealand)
Texas A & M University (Texas, U.S.A.)
University College Northampton (Northamptonshire, England)
University of Aberdeen (Scotland)
University of Bristol (Avon, England)
University of Findlay (Ohio, U.S.A.)
University of Limerick (Republic of Ireland)
University of Lincoln (Lincolnshire, England)
University of Maine–Orono (Maine, U.S.A.)
University of Massachusetts–Amherst (Massachusetts, U.S.A.)
University of New Hampshire (New Hampshire, U.S.A.)
University of Veterinary Sciences and the College of Agriculture (Austria)
The University of Wales–Aberystwyth (Wales)
University of West England–Bristol (Avon, England)
University of Wolverhampton (Warwickshire, England)
University Putra Malaysia (Malaysia)
Virginia Intermont College (Virginia, U.S.A.)
Walford and North Shropshire College (Shropshire, England)
Warwickshire College (Warwickshire, England)

William Woods University (Missouri, U.S.A.)
Wilmington College (Ohio, U.S.A.)
Windhurst Riding & Training Centre (Ontario, Canada)
Writtle College (Essex, England)

## Eventing

Equitation School of the Armored Calvary School–Army of Chile (Chile)
Escola de Equitacao do Exercito—Brazillian Army Riding School (Brazil)
Gillian Watson International Equestrian Training (Buckinghamshire, England)
Jim Graham & Meadow Run Ranch (Alabama, U.S.A.)

## Farrier Training or Natural Trimming

Butler Graduate Farrier Trimming (Colorado, U.S.A.)
Casey & Son Horseshoeing School (Georgia, U.S.A.)
Central Wyoming College (Wyoming, U.S.A.)
Colorado School of Trades (Colorado, U.S.A.)
Colorado State University (Colorado, U.S.A.)
Cornell University (New York, U.S.A.)
Cowtown Horseshoeing School (Montana, U.S.A.)
East Texas Horseshoeing School (Texas, U.S.A.)
Education Center of Japan Farriers Association (Japan)
Eques Coop (Italy)
Equine Education Institute (Illinois, U.S.A.)
Escola de Equitacao do Exercito - Brazillian Army Riding School (Brazil)
Far Hills Forge (New Jersey, U.S.A.)
The Farriery Training Service (Petersborough, England)
Heartland Horseshoeing School (Missouri, U.S.A.)
Hocking College (Ohio, U.S.A.)
Institute of Equine Podiatry (Massachusetts, U.S.A.)
Kentucky Horseshoeing School (Kentucky, U.S.A.)
Kwantlen University College (British Columbia, Canada)
Lassen Community College (California, U.S.A.)
Lookout Mountain School of Horseshoeing (Alabama, U.S.A.)
Malaysian Equestrian Council (Malaysia)
Maritime Farrier School (Nova Scotia, Canada)
Maryland Horseshoeing School (Maryland, U.S.A.)
Merced College (California, U.S.A.)
Meredith Manor International Learning Centre (West Virginia, U.S.A.)
Mesalands Community College (New Mexico, U.S.A.)
Midwest Horseshoeing School (Illinois, U.S.A.)
Minnesota School of Horseshoeing (Minnesota, U.S.A.)
Mission Farrier School (Washington, U.S.A.)
Montana State University (Montana, U.S.A.)
NC School of Horseshoeing and Equine Lameness (North Carolina, U.S.A.)
Northwest College (Wyoming, U.S.A.)
Oklahoma Horseshoeing School (Oklahoma, U.S.A.)
Oklahoma State Horseshoeing School (Oklahoma, U.S.A.)
Olds Colleges (Alberta, Canada)
Pacific Coast Horseshoeing School (California, U.S.A.)
Pikes Peak Community College (Colorado, U.S.A.)

Queensland Race Training (Australia)
Shur Shod Horseshoeing School (Missouri, U.S.A.)
Sierra Horseshoeing School (California, U.S.A.)
Sul Ross State University (Texas, U.S.A.)
Tucson School of Horseshoeing (Arizona, U.S.A.)
Village Farrier School (Alberta, Canada)
Walla Walla Community College (Washington, U.S.A.)
Warwickshire College (Warwickshire, England)
Western School of Horseshoeing (Arizona, U.S.A.)
Wolverine Farrier School (Michigan, U.S.A.)
Ypäjän Hevosopisto/Equine College Ypäjä (Finland)

## Graduate Programs (Not Including Veterinary Programs)

Auburn University (Alabama, U.S.A.)
California State Polytechnic University, Pomona (California, U.S.A.)
California State University–Fresno (California, U.S.A.)
Charles Sturt University (Australia)
Colorado State University (Colorado, U.S.A.)
Cook College, Rutgers University (New Jersey, U.S.A.)
Institute of Rural Studies, University of Wales, Aberystwyth (Wales)
Iowa State University of Science and Technology (Iowa, U.S.A.)
Kansas State University (Kansas, U.S.A.)
Louisiana State University (Louisiana, U.S.A.)
Michigan State University (Michigan, U.S.A.)
Montana State University (Montana, U.S.A.)
Murray State University (Kentucky, U.S.A.)
New Mexico State University (New Mexico, U.S.A.)
Prescott College (Arizona, U.S.A.)
Royal Agricultural College (Gloucestershire, England)
The Royal (Dick) School of Veterinary Studies (Scotland)
Salem International University (West Virginia, U.S.A.)
Southern Illinois University–Carbondale (Illinois, U.S.A.)
Southwest Missouri State University (Missouri, U.S.A.)
Sul Ross State University (Texas, U.S.A.)
Tarleton State University (Texas, U.S.A.)
Tufts University (Massachusetts, U.S.A.)
University College Dublin (Republic of Ireland)
University of California–Davis (California, U.S.A.)
University of Connecticut (Connecticut, U.S.A.)
University of Delaware (Delaware, U.S.A.)
University of Florida (Florida, U.S.A.)
University of Georgia (Georgia, U.S.A.)
University of Idaho (Idaho, U.S.A.)
University of Illinois at Urbana–Champagne (Illinois, U.S.A.)
University of Kentucky (Kentucky, U.S.A.)
University of Maine–Orono (Maine, U.S.A.)
University of Maryland (Maryland, U.S.A.)
University of Missouri–Columbia (Missouri, U.S.A.)
University of Nebraska–Lincoln (Nebraska, U.S.A.)
University of Nevada–Reno (Nevada, U.S.A.)
University of Tennessee–Knoxville (Tennessee, U.S.A.)

University of Vermont (Vermont, U.S.A.)
University of Veterinary Sciences and the College of Agriculture (Austria)
Virginia Tech (Virginia, U.S.A.)
Western Kentucky University (Kentucky, U.S.A.)

## Grooming

Association of British Riding Schools (Cornwall, England)
British Driving Society (Warwickshire, England)
Central Florida Community College (Florida, U.S.A.)
Centre de Formation d'Armor (France)
Eques Coop (Italy)
Hayfield Equestrian Centre (Scotland)
La Chabraque (France)
Lakeland Equestrian Centre (Cumbria, England)
Lucky Braids™ Top Turnout™ Clinics (Massachusetts, U.S.A.)
New Zealand Equine Academy (New Zealand)
Norwegian Equine College (Norway)
Raviopisto Kaustinen (Finland)
Päijänne Instituutti (Finland)
TM International School of Horsemanship (Cornwall, England)
Urchinwood Manor Equitation Centre (Avon, England)
Ypäjän Hevosopisto/Equine College Ypäjä (Finland)

## Horse Care

Abbots Bromley Equestrian Centre (Staffordshire, England)
Abingdon and Witney College (Oxfordshire, England)
Acre Cliff Riding School & Equestrian Centre (Yorkshire, England)
Askham Bryan College (Yorkshire, England)
Association of British Riding Schools (Cornwall, England)
Associazione Sportiva I Due Laghi (Italy)
Ayrshire Equitation Centre (Scotland)
Ballingale Farm Riding School (Republic of Ireland)
Barleyfields Equestrian Centre (Derbyshire, England)
Beaus River Riding School (Hong Kong)
Berkshire College of Agriculture (Berkshire, England)
Berriewood Farm (Shropshire, England)
Bicton College (Devon, England)
Bishop Burton College (Yorkshire, England)
Blackborough End Equestrian Centre (Norfolk, England)
Blacknest Gate Riding Centre (Berkshire, England)
Bold Heath Equestrian Centre (Cheshire, England)
Brampton Stables (Northamptonshire, England)
Brennanstown Riding School Ltd. (Republic of Ireland)
Brinsbury College (Sussex, England)
British Horse Society (Warwickshire, England)
Brookfields Riding & Livery Centre (Warwickshire, England)
Brooksby Melton College (Leicestershire, England)
Bryanston Riding Centre (Dorset, England)
Calliaghstown Riding Centre (Republic of Ireland)
Callum Park Riding Centre (Kent, England)

Cannington College (Somerset, England)
Capel Manor College (Middlesex, England)
Central Florida Community College (Florida, U.S.A.)
Centro Equestre Epona (Spain)
Checkendon Equestrian Centre (Berkshire, England)
Cherry Tree Livery Stables (Yorkshire, England)
Clevedon Riding Centre (Avon, England)
Cobham Manor Riding Centre (Kent, England)
Coleg Gwent (Wales)
Coleg Meirion-Dwyfor (Wales)
College Farm Equestrian Centre (Nottinghamshire, England)
The College of West Anglia (Cambridgeshire, England)
Contessa Riding Centre (Hertfordshire, England)
Courses for Horses (Staffordshire, England)
Croft End Equestrian Centre (Lancashire, England)
Curragh Equestrian Center (Texas, U.S.A.)
Dannevirke High School (New Zealand)
Diamond Centre for Handicapped Riders (Surrey, England)
Ditchling Common Stud (Sussex, England)
Dubai Equestrian Centre (United Arab Emirates)
Easterton Stables (Scotland)
Eastminster School of Riding (Essex, England)
Easton College (Norfolk, England)
Eccleston Equestrian Centre (Lancashire, England)
Endon Riding School (Staffordshire, English)
Enniskillen College and Greenmount College (Northern Ireland)
Equi Study (Warwickshire, England)
Escuela de Arte Ecuestre (Spain)
The Fortune Centre of Riding Therapy (Dorset, England)
Foxes Riding School (Cheshire, England)
GGH Equitation Centre Ltd. (Isle of Man, England)
Gleneagles Equestrian Centre (Scotland)
Goodnestone Court Equestrian (Kent, England)
Grand Cypress Equestrian Center (Florida, U.S.A.)
Grennan College Equestrian Centre (Republic of Ireland)
Grove House Stables (Yorkshire, England)
Hadlow College (Kent, England)
Hargate Equestrian (Derbyshire, England)
Hargate Hill Riding School (Derbyshire, England)
Hartpury College (Gloucestershire, England)
Hayfield Equestrian Centre (Scotland)
Hill House Equestrian Centre (Lincolnshire, England)
Hinckley Equestrian Centre (Leicestershire, England)
Hocking College (Ohio, U.S.A.)
Holme Lacy College (Herefordshire, England)
Honeysuckle Farm Equestrian Centre (Devon, England)
Huntley School of Equitation (Gloucestershire, England)
Ingestre Stables (Staffordshire, England)
Insight Learning Academy (New Zealand)
Isle of Anglesey Stud Farm & Riding Centre (Wales)
Kent Equine Industry and Training Services Ltd. (Hertfordshire, England)
Kingston Maurward College (Dorset, England)

The Kingston Riding Centre (Surrey, England)
Kirkley Hall College (Northhumberland, England)
Kyrewood Equestrian Centre Ltd. (New Zealand)
Lakeland Equestrian Centre (Cumbria, England)
L.A.P. du Tricastin-Baronnies (France)
Lavant House Stables (Sussex, England)
Lessans Riding Stables (Northern Ireland)
Liege Manor Farm Equestrian Centre (Wales)
Lincoln College (Lincolnshire, England)
Limes Farm Equestrian Centre (Kent, England)
Lingfield Correspondence (Somerset, England)
Littledean Riding Centre (Gloucestershire, England)
Logie Farm Riding Centre (Scotland)
Longacres Riding School (Merseyside, England)
Longfield Equestrian Centre (Yorkshire, England)
Lords House Farm Education Centre (Lancashire, England)
Low Fold Riding Centre (Durham, England)
Manas de la Hoz (Spain)
Merrist Wood College (Surrey, England)
Middleton Park Equestrian Centre (Yorkshire, England)
Moulton College (Northamptonshire, England)
Myerscough College (Lancashire, England)
Naburn Grange Riding Centre (Yorkshire, England)
National Equestrian Academy (New Zealand)
The Naval Riding Centre (Hampshire, England)
Necarne Stable (Northern Ireland)
Newton Hall Equitation Centre (Suffolk, England)
New Zealand Equine Training Ltd. (New Zealand)
North Devon Equestrian Centre (Devon, England)
Northern Racing College (Yorkshire, England)
Northern Riding Centre (Yorkshire, England)
The North Highland College (Scotland)
North Humberside Riding Centre (Yorkshire, England)
Oakfield Riding School (Oxfordshire, England)
Oatridge Agricultural College (Scotland)
Open College of Equine Studies (Suffolk, England)
Orchard Cottage Riding Stables (Surrey, England)
Otterbein College (Ohio, U.S.A.)
Pakefield Riding School (Suffolk, England)
Palmerston North Girls High School (New Zealand)
Pembrokeshire College (Wales)
Pencoed College (Wales)
Penshaw Hill Equestrian Centre (Northhumberland, England)
Plumpton College (Sussex, England)
Poplar Park Equestrian Training Centre (Suffolk, England)
Portlaoise Equestrian Centre (Republic of Ireland)
Portree Riding and Trekking Stables (Scotland)
Pound Cottage Riding Centre (Dorset, England)
Prescott Equestrian Centre (Shropshire, England)
Queen Ethelburga's College/Chapter House Preparatory School (Yorkshire, England)
Queen's High School (New Zealand)
Queensland Race Training (Australia)

Quob Stables (Hampshire, England)
Rayne Riding Centre (Essex, England)
Reaseheath College (Cheshire, England)
Rheidol Riding & Holiday Centre (Wales)
Ringer Villa Equestrian Centre (Derbyshire, England)
Rodbaston College (Staffordshire, England)
Runningwell Equestrian Club (Essex, England)
Rycroft School of Equitation (Hampshire, England)
Ryder Farm Equestrian Centre (Cheshire, England)
St. Peter's School (New Zealand)
Selston Equestrian Centre (Nottinghamshire, England)
Snowdon Farm Riding School (Yorkshire, England)
Snowdonia Riding Stables (Wales)
South Medburn Farm Ltd. (Hertfordshire, England)
Stonar School (Wiltshire, England)
Sue Adams Riding School (Herefordshire, England)
Summerhouse Education and Equitation Centre (Gloucestershire, England)
Suzannes Riding School (Middlesex, England)
Swan Lodge Equestrian Centre (Leicestershire, England)
The Talland School of Equitation (Gloucestershire, England)
Thorpe Grange Equestrian Centre (Lincolnshire, England)
TM International School of Horsemanship (Cornwall, England)
Torrens Valley Institute of TAFE (Australia)
Traditional Equitation School (California, U.S.A.)
Trent Park Equestrian Centre (London, England)
Tuen Mun Public Riding School (Hong Kong)
University of Lincoln (Lincolnshire, England)
Urchinwood Manor Equitation Centre (Avon, England)
Valley Farm Riding & Driving Centre (Suffolk, England)
Veterinary Field Station (Scotland)
Wadlands Hall Equestrian Centre (Yorkshire, England)
Waikato Institute of Technology (New Zealand)
Wellington Equestrian Education Ltd. (Hampshire, England)
Wellow Park Stables & Saddlery (Nottinghamshire, England)
Welsh College of Horticulture (Wales)
Wheal Buller Riding School (Cornwall, England)
Wickstead Farm Equestrian Centre (Wiltshire, England)
Wildwoods Riding Centre (Surrey, England)
Willington Hall Riding Centre (Cheshire, England)
Wiltshire College, Lackham (Wiltshire, England)
Wimbledon Village Stables (London, England)
Witham Villa Ltd. (Leicestershire, England)
Wrea Green Equitation Centre (Lancashire, England)
Writtle College (Essex, England)
The Yorkshire Riding Centre Ltd. (Yorkshire, England)

## Horse Management

Abingdon and Witney College (Oxfordshire, England)
Asbury College (Kentucky, U.S.A.)
Agricultural School of Lambach (Austria)
Askham Bryan College (Yorkshire, England)

Bedgebury School (Kent, England)
Berkshire College of Agriculture (Berkshire, England)
Bethany Hills College (West Virginia, U.S.A.)
Bicton College (Devon, England)
Bishop Burton College (Yorkshire, England)
Brinsbury College (Sussex, England)
Brooksby Melton College (Leicestershire, England)
Cannington College (Somerset, England)
Capel Manor College (Middlesex, England)
Central Texas College (Texas, U.S.A.)
Central Wyoming College (Wyoming, U.S.A.)
Coleg Gwent (Wales)
College of Southern Idaho (Idaho, U.S.A.)
The College of West Anglia (Cambridgeshire, England)
Delaware Valley College (Pennsylvania, U.S.A.)
Duchy College (Cornwall, England)
Easton College (Norfolk, England)
Ellsworth Community College (Iowa, U.S.A.)
Enniskillen College and Greenmount College (Northern Ireland)
Global Equine Academy (Wyoming, U.S.A.)
Hadlow College (Kent, England)
Hartpury College (Gloucestershire, England)
J. Sargeant Reynolds Community College (Virginia, U.S.A.)
Kemptville College/University of Guelph (Ontario, Canada)
Kent Equine Industry and Training Services Ltd. (Hertfordshire, England)
Kentucky Equine Management Internship Program (Kentucky, U.S.A.)
Kentucky Horse Park Education Program (Kentucky, U.S.A.)
L.A.P. Le Cluzeau (France)
Lake Erie College (Ohio, U.S.A.)
Lamar Community College (Colorado, U.S.A.)
Linn-Benton Community College (Oregon, U.S.A.)
Merced College (California, U.S.A.)
Michigan State University (Michigan, U.S.A.)
Midway College (Kentucky, U.S.A.)
Moulton College (Northamptonshire, England)
Myerscough College (Lancashire, England)
National American University (South Dakota, U.S.A.)
New Mexico State University (New Mexico, U.S.A.)
North Central Texas College (Texas, U.S.A.)
Northeastern Jr. College (Colorado, U.S.A.)
Nottingham Trent University/Brackenhurst (Nottinghamshire, England)
Oaklands College (Hertfordshire, England)
Oatridge Agricultural College (Scotland)
Ohio State University Agriculture Technical Institute (Ohio, U.S.A.)
Parkland College (Illinois, U.S.A.)
Pencoed College (Wales)
Plumpton College (Sussex, England)
Reaseheath College (Cheshire, England)
Rodbaston College (Staffordshire, England)
Sparsholt College Hampshire (Hampshire, England)
State University of New York–Cobleskill (New York, U.S.A.)
State University of New York–Morrisville (New York, U.S.A.)

Teikyo Post University (Connecticut, U.S.A.)
Thompson School of Applied Science (New Hampshire, U.S.A.)
Türi School of Technology & Rural Economy (Estonia)
University of Lincoln (Lincolnshire, England)
University of Melbourne (Australia)
Walford and North Shropshire College (Shropshire, England)
Welsh College of Horticulture (Wales)
William H. Miner Agricultural Research Institute (New York, U.S.A.)
Wilson College (Pennsylvania, U.S.A.)
Wiltshire College, Lackham (Wiltshire, England)
Yrkesinstitut Sydväst (Finland)

## Horsemanship

Escola de Equitacao do Exercito–Brazillian Army Riding School (Brazil)
Fairview College (Alberta, Canada)
Intelligent Horsemanship from Kelly Marks (Berkshire, England)
Kanadiana International Equestrian Centre Inc. (Saskatchewan, Canada)
Kemptville College/University of Guelph (Ontario, Canada)
Lassen Community College (California, U.S.A.)
Midway College (Kentucky, U.S.A.)
Morehead State University (Kentucky, U.S.A.)
Olds Colleges (Alberta, Canada)

## Independent Study (Distance Education)

ACS Distance Education (Wallingford, England)
Aspen Equine Studies, Inc. (Colorado, U.S.A.)
Austin Education Center (Florida, U.S.A.)
Australian Correspondence School (Australia)
Australian College of Natural Animal Medicine (Australia)
Charles Sturt University (Australia)
East Texas Horseshoeing School (Texas, U.S.A.)
Enniskillen College and Greenmount College (Northern Ireland)
Equine Education Institute (Illinois, U.S.A.)
Equissage (Virginia, U.S.A.)
Equi Study (Warwickshire, England)
Equitouch® Systems® (Colorado, U.S.A.)
A Healthy Horse the Natural Way (Australia)
Horses and Courses Ltd. (Buckinghamshire, England)
Lingfield Correspondence (Somerset, England)
New Horizons Equine Education Center, Inc. (Colorado, U.S.A.)
Open College of Equine Studies (Suffolk, England)
Prescott College (Arizona, U.S.A.)
Saint Mary-of-the-Woods College (Indiana, U.S.A.)
Scottsdale Community College (Arizona, U.S.A.)
Telford Rural Polytechnic (New Zealand)
University of Limerick (Republic of Ireland)
Waikato Institute of Technology (New Zealand)

## Instructing or Coaching

Abbots Bromley Equestrian Centre (Staffordshire, England)
Acre Cliff Riding School & Equestrian Centre (Yorkshire, England)
American Association of Horsemanship Safety (Texas, U.S.A.)
American Riding Instructor Certification Program (Florida, U.S.A.)
The Arabian Riding School (Kansas, U.S.A.)
Association of British Riding Schools (Cornwall, England)
Ayrshire Equitation Centre (Scotland)
Beaus River Riding School (Hong Kong)
Bedgebury School (Kent, England)
Berriewood Farm (Shropshire, England)
Bold Heath Equestrian Centre (Cheshire, England)
Brampton Stables (Northamptonshire, England)
Brennanstown Riding School Ltd. (Republic of Ireland)
Brinsbury College (Sussex, England)
British Driving Society (Warwickshire, England)
British Horse Society (Warwickshire, England)
Bryanston Riding Centre (Dorset, England)
Calliaghstown Riding Centre (Republic of Ireland)
Callum Park Riding Centre (Kent, England)
Centenary College (New Jersey, U.S.A.)
Centered Riding® Inc. (Pennsylvania, U.S.A.)
Centre Equestre de la Houssaye (France)
Centro Equestre Epona (Spain)
Certified Horsemanship Association (Texas, U.S.A.)
Cherry Tree Livery Stables (Yorkshire, England)
Cobham Manor Riding Centre (Kent, England)
Coleg Gwent (Wales)
Coleg Meirion-Dwyfor (Wales)
Collège Equestre de Conches/Equestrian Village of Conches (France)
College Farm Equestrian Centre (Nottinghamshire, England)
The College of West Anglia (Cambridgeshire, England)
Contessa Riding Centre (Hertfordshire, England)
Courses for Horses (Staffordshire, England)
Curragh Equestrian Center (Texas, U.S.A.)
Diamond Centre for Handicapped Riders (Surrey, England)
Ditchling Common Stud (Sussex, England)
Donna Snyder-Smith Apprenticeship (California, U.S.A.)
Dubai Equestrian Centre (United Arab Emirates)
Dutch Equestrian School (The Netherlands)
Eccleston Equestrian Centre (Lancashire, England)
The Equestrian Centre (Wales, U.K.)
Equestrian Education Systems (Montana, U.S.A.)
Equi Study (Warwickshire, England)
Equitation School of the Armored Calvary School–Army of Chile (Chile)
GGH Equitation Centre Ltd. (Isle of Man, England)
Gleneagles Equestrian Centre (Scotland)
Goodnestone Court Equestrian (Kent, England)
Grand Cypress Equestrian Center (Florida, U.S.A.)
Grennan College Equestrian Centre (Republic of Ireland)
Hadlow College (Kent, England)

Hayfield Equestrian Centre (Scotland)
Hólar í Hjaltadal (Iceland)
Honeysuckle Farm Equestrian Centre (Devon, England)
Horsemanship Safety Association, Inc. (Florida, U.S.A.)
Huntley School of Equitation (Gloucestershire, England)
Ingestre Stables (Staffordshire, England)
Institut de Technologie Agroalimentaire (Quebec, Canada)
International Group for Qualifications in Training Horse & Rider (Bermuda)
Kanadiana International Equestrian Centre Inc. (Saskatchewan, Canada)
Kemptville College/University of Guelph (Ontario, Canada)
Kingston Maurward College (Dorset, England)
The Kingston Riding Centre (Surrey, England)
Kirkley Hall College (Northhumberland, England)
Kwantlen University College (British Columbia, Canada)
Kyrewood Equestrian Centre Ltd. (New Zealand)
Lake Erie College (Ohio, U.S.A.)
Lakeland Equestrian Centre (Cumbria, England)
Lavant House Stables (Sussex, England)
Lessans Riding Stables (Northern Ireland)
Liege Manor Farm Equestrian Centre (Wales)
Limes Farm Equestrian Centre (Kent, England)
Lincoln College (Lincolnshire, England)
Littledean Riding Centre (Gloucestershire, England)
Longacres Riding School (Merseyside, England)
Longfield Equestrian Centre (Yorkshire, England)
The Lord Newcastle Stables (Belgium)
Low Fold Riding Centre (Durham, England)
Malaysian Equine Council (Malaysia)
Merrist Wood College (Surrey, England)
Midway College (Kentucky, U.S.A.)
Monte Roberts International Learning Center (California, U.S.A.)
Myerscough College (Lancashire, England)
Naburn Grange Riding Centre (Yorkshire, England)
The Naval Riding Centre (Hampshire, England)
Necarne Stable (Northern Ireland)
New Zealand Equestrian Federation (New Zealand)
North American Riding for the Handicapped Association Inc. (Colorado, U.S.A.)
The North Highland College (Scotland)
North Humberside Riding Centre (Yorkshire, England)
Norwegian Equine College (Norway)
Otterbein College (Ohio, U.S.A.)
Päijänne Instituutti (Finland)
Pakefield Riding School (Suffolk, England)
Pat Parelli International Study Center (Colorado, U.S.A.)
Penshaw Hill Equestrian Centre (Northhumberland, England)
Plumpton College (Sussex, England)
Portree Riding and Trekking Stables (Scotland)
Prescott Equestrian Centre (Shropshire, England)
Queen Ethelburga's College/Chapter House Preparatory School (Yorkshire, England)
Queen Margaret's School (British Columbia, Canada)
Rayne Riding Centre (Essex, England)
Rheidol Riding & Holiday Centre (Wales)

Robert O. Mayer Riding Academy (Pennsylvania, U.S.A.)
Rocky Mountain College (Montana, U.S.A.)
Runningwell Equestrian Club (Essex, England)
Ryder Farm Equestrian Centre (Cheshire, England)
Saint Mary-of-the-Woods College (Indiana, U.S.A.)
Selston Equestrian Centre (Nottinghamshire, England)
Snowdon Farm Riding School (Yorkshire, England)
Snowdonia Riding Stables (Wales)
South Medburn Farm Ltd. (Hertfordshire, England)
Stonar School (Wiltshire, England)
Sue Adams Riding School (Herefordshire, England)
Summerhouse Education and Equitation Centre (Gloucestershire, England)
Suzannes Riding School (Middlesex, England)
The Talland School of Equitation (Gloucestershire, England)
Thorpe Grange Equestrian Centre (Lincolnshire, England)
TM International School of Horsemanship (Cornwall, England)
Traditional Equitation School (California, U.S.A.)
Trent Park Equestrian Centre (London, England)
Tuen Mun Public Riding School (Hong Kong)
United States Dressage Federation, Inc. (Kentucky, U.S.A.)
University of Lincoln (Lincolnshire, England)
Urchinwood Manor Equitation Centre (Avon, England)
Veterinary Field Station (Scotland)
Waikato Institute of Technology (New Zealand)
Warwickshire College (Warwickshire, England)
Wellington Equestrian Education Ltd. (Hampshire, England)
Wheal Buller Riding School (Cornwall, England)
Wildwoods Riding Centre (Surrey, England)
Willington Hall Riding Centre (Cheshire, England)
Wiltshire College, Lackham (Wiltshire, England)
Windhurst Riding & Training Centre (Ontario, Canada)
Witham Villa Ltd. (Leicestershire, England)
Woodcock Hill Riding Academy Inc. (Connecticut, U.S.A.)
Workshops for Riding Instructors (Alabama, U.S.A.)
Wrea Green Equitation Centre (Lancashire, England)
The Yorkshire Riding Centre Ltd. (Yorkshire, England)
Ypäjän Hevosopisto/Equine College Ypäjä (Finland)
Yrkesinstitut Sydväst (Finland)

## Judge

Equitation School of the Armored Calvary School–Army of Chile (Chile)
United States Dressage Federation, Inc. (Kentucky, U.S.A.)

## Logging

La Ferme du Sonvaux (France)

## Massage Therapy

Aspen Equine Studies, Inc. (Colorado, U.S.A.)
Australian College of Natural Animal Medicine (Australia)

BC College of Equine Therapy (British Columbia, Canada)
D'Arcy Lane Institute (Ontario, Canada)
Don Doran's Equine Sports Massage Program (Florida, U.S.A.)
Equinology, Inc. ® (California, U.S.A.)
Equissage (Virginia, U.S.A.)
Equitouch Systems® (Colorado, U.S.A.)
Geary Whiting's Equine Massage School (California, U.S.A.)
HJW Equine Therapy (British Columbia, Canada)
Hocking College (Ohio, U.S.A.)
Integrated Touch Therapy, Inc. (Ohio, U.S.A.)
New England Academy of Therapeutic Sciences (New Hampshire, U.S.A.)
Prairie Winds Equine Massage Therapy College (Colorado, U.S.A.)
Tellington Method Training (New Mexico, U.S.A.)

## Natural Horsemanship

C. W. Training (California, U.S.A.)
Intelligent Horsemanship from Kelly Marks (Berkshire, England)
John Lyons Certification Program (Colorado, U.S.A.)
Lassen Community College (California, U.S.A.)
Monty Roberts International Learning Center (California, U.S.A.)
Pat Parelli International Study Center (Colorado, U.S.A.)
Waikato Institute of Technology (New Zealand)

## Performance (Circus, Jousting, Exotic Animals, Vaulting, etc.)

Cheval Art Action (France)
L'Ecole des Courses Hippiques AFASEC (France)
Minnesota Horse Training Academy (Minnesota, U.S.A.)
Moorpark College (California, U.S.A.)
Seattle Knights (Washington, U.S.A.)
U.S. Calvary School (Washington, U.S.A.)

## Polo

Ascot Park Polo Club (Surrey, England)
El Trebol Polo School (Argentina)
Mark Harris Polo School (New Zealand)
Potomac Polo School (Maryland, U.S.A.)
Rege Ludwig Polo School (California, U.S.A.)

## Professional Riding

Centre de Formation d'Armor (France)
Ecole Nationale d'Equitation [ENE] (France) ]
Escola de Equitacao do Exercito - Brazillian Army Riding School (Brazil)
Gillian Watson International Equestrian Training (Buckinghamshire, England)
Fairview College (Alberta, Canada)
Kemptville College/University of Guelph (Ontario, Canada)
Meredith Manor International Learning Centre (West Virginia, U.S.A.)
Norwegian Top Athelethichs Gymnasium for Elite riders (Norway)

## Racing (Flat and Harness)

Armidale Racing Academy (Australia)
Beaus River Riding School (Hong Kong)
British Horseracing Training Board (Suffolk, England)
British Racing School (Suffolk, England)
Curragh House Education Institute (Republic of Ireland)
Enniskillen College and Greenmount College (Northern Ireland)
Eques Coop (Italy)
Institut de Technologie Agroalimentaire (Quebec, Canada)
Kemptville College/University of Guelph (Ontario, Canada)
Kentucky Equine Management Internship Program (Kentucky, U.S.A.)
Kyrewood Equestrian Centre Ltd. (New Zealand)
L'Ecole des Courses Hippiques AFASEC (France)
New Zealand Equine Academy (New Zealand)
Northern Racing College (Yorkshire, England)
Norwegian Equine College (Norway)
Queensland Race Training (Australia)
Racing Academy and Centre of Education (Republic of Ireland)
Rancho Del Castillo (Florida, U.S.A.)
State University of New York–Cobleskill (New York, U.S.A.)
State University of New York–Morrisville (New York, U.S.A.)
Swedish University of Agricultural Sciences (Sweden)
Torrens Valley Institute of TAFE (Australia)
University of Arizona (Arizona, U.S.A.)
University of Louisville (Kentucky, U.S.A.)
University of Melbourne (Australia)
Ypäjän Hevosopisto/Equine College Ypäjä (Finland)

## Ranch, Pack, Trail Guide, Wrangler

American Association of Horsemanship Safety (Texas, U.S.A.)
Argyll Trail Riding (Scotland)
British Horse Society (Warwickshire, England)
Certified Horsemanship Association (Texas, U.S.A.)
College Farm Equestrian Centre (Nottinghamshire, England)
Hayfield Equestrian Centre (Scotland)
Hocking College (Ohio, U.S.A.)
Horsemanship Safety Association, Inc. (Florida, U.S.A.)
La Ferme du Sonvaux (France)
Lakeland College (Alberta, Canada)
Lycée General et Technologique Agricole Paysager Equestre (France)
Portree Riding and Trekking Stables (Scotland)
University of Central Lancashire (Cumbria, England)
Ypäjän Hevosopisto/Equine College Ypäjä (Finland)

## Rodeo and Western Sports

Josey Ranch Barrel Racing and Roping Clinics (Texas, U.S.A.)
Olds Colleges (Alberta, Canada)
R.T.S. Professional Team Roping Schools (Texas, U.S.A.)
Sankey Rodeo Schools (Missouri, U.S.A.)

## Saddle Making (Saddlery)

Cumbria School of Saddlery (Cumbria, England)
Oklahoma State University–Okmulgee Technical Branch (Oklahoma, U.S.A.)
The Saddlery Training Centre (Wiltshire, England)
The Walsall College of Arts & Technology (Warwickshire, England)

## Secondary, Preparatory, Middle, and Elementary Schools

Academy of the Sacred Heart (Louisiana, U.S.A.)
The Andrews School (Ohio, U.S.A.)
Bethany Hills School (Ontario, Canada)
The Brewster Academy (New Hampshire, U.S.A.)
Chatham Hall (Virginia, U.S.A.)
Cheltenham Ladies College (Gloucestershire, England)
The Culver Academies (Indiana, U.S.A.)
Cushing Academy (Massachusetts, U.S.A.)
Dana Hall School (Massachusetts, U.S.A.)
Dannevirke High School (New Zealand)
Ecole d'Agriculture St. Joseph (France)
Ecole privée Charles Péguy (France)
Ethel Walker School (Connecticut, U.S.A.)
Fountain Valley School (Colorado, U.S.A.)
Foxcroft School (Virginia, U.S.A.)
Garrison Forest School (Maryland, U.S.A.)
George School (Pennsylvania, U.S.A.)
Gould Academy (Maine, U.S.A.)
Grier School (Pennsylvania, U.S.A.)
Hawaii Preparatory Academy (Hawaii, U.S.A.)
Kent School (Connecticut, U.S.A.)
Kents Hill School (Maine, U.S.A.)
The Kildonan School (New York, U.S.A.)
The Knox School (New York, U.S.A.)
Leysin American School (Switzerland)
Linden Hall (Pennsylvania, U.S.A.)
Lowell Whitman School (Colorado, U.S.A.)
Lycée d'Enseignement Professionnel Agricole St Hilaire du Harcourt (France)
The Madeira School (Virginia, U.S.A.)
Midland School (California, U.S.A.)
The Millbrook School (New York, U.S.A.)
Millfield School (Somerset, England)
Monte Vista Christian School (California, U.S.A.)
North Country School (New York, U.S.A.)
Oak Creek Ranch School (Arizona, U.S.A.)
Ojai Valley School (California, U.S.A.)
Oldfields Schools (Maryland, U.S.A.)
The Orme School (Arizona, U.S.A.)
Palmerston North Girls High School (New Zealand)
The Phelps School (Pennsylvania, U.S.A.)
Proctor Academy (New Hampshire, U.S.A.)
Purnell School (New Jersey, U.S.A.)
The Putney School (Vermont, U.S.A.)

Queen Ethelburga's College/Chapter House Preparatory School (Yorkshire, England)
Queen Margaret's School (British Columbia, Canada)
Queen's High School (New Zealand)
St. Peter's School (New Zealand)
St. Timothy's School (Maryland, U.S.A.)
San Domenico School (California, U.S.A.)
Sorenson's Ranch School (Utah, U.S.A.)
Stevenson School (California, U.S.A.)
Stonar School (Wiltshire, England)
Stoneleigh-Burnham School (Massachusetts, U.S.A.)
The Taft School (Connecticut, U.S.A.)
Tauranga Girls College (New Zealand)
The Thacher School (California, U.S.A.)
Verde Valley School (Arizona, U.S.A.)
Virginia Episcopal School (Virginia, U.S.A.)

## Side-Saddle Riding

Pittern Hill Stables (Warwickshire, England)

## Stable Management

British Horse Society (Warwickshire, England)
Bukit Kiara Resort Berhad (Malaysia)
College Farm Equestrian Centre (Nottinghamshire, England)
Dutch Equestrian School (The Netherlands)
Kyrewood Equestrian Centre Ltd. (New Zealand)
Norwegian Equine College (Norway)
Open College of Equine Studies (Suffolk, England)
Portree Riding and Trekking Stables (Scotland)
Traditional Equitation School (California, U.S.A.)
Treasure Valley Community College (Oregon, U.S.A.)
University of California—Santa Barbara (California, U.S.A.)
Wheal Buller Riding School (Cornwall, England)
Ypäjän Hevosopisto/Equine College Ypäjä (Finland)

## Therapeutic Riding

British Driving Society (Warwickshire, England)
Centenary College (New Jersey, U.S.A.)
Certified Horsemanship Association (Texas, U.S.A.)
Diamond Centre for Handicapped Riders (Surrey, England)
New Zealand Riding for the Disabled Association Inc. (New Zealand)
North American Riding for the Handicapped Association Inc. (Colorado, U.S.A.)
Rocky Mountain College (Montana, U.S.A.)
St. Andrews Presbyterian College (North Carolina, U.S.A.)
Saint Mary-of-the-Woods College (Indiana, U.S.A.)
Teikyo Post University (Connecticut, U.S.A.)
Wilson College (Pennsylvania, U.S.A.)
Ypäjän Hevosopisto/Equine College Ypäjä (Finland)

# Training

Austin Education Program (Florida, U.S.A.)
Centenary College (New Jersey, U.S.A.)
Central Wyoming College (Wyoming, U.S.A.)
C. W. Training (California, U.S.A.)
Donna Snyder-Smith Apprenticeship (California, U.S.A.)
Duchy College (Cornwall, England)
Escola de Equitacao do Exercito - Brazillian Army Riding School (Brazil)
Fairview College (Alberta, Canada)
Global Equine Academy (Wyoming, U.S.A.)
Hólar í Hjaltadal
John Lyons Certification Program (Colorado, U.S.A.)
Lake Erie College (Ohio, U.S.A.)
Lamar Community College (Colorado, U.S.A.)
Laramie County Community College (Wyoming, U.S.A.)
L'Ecole des Courses Hippiques AFASEC (France)
Lycée d'Enseignement Professionnel Agricole St Hilaire du Harcourt (France)
Meredith Manor International Learning Centre (West Virginia, U.S.A.)
Minnesota Horse Training Academy (Minnesota, U.S.A.)
North Central Texas College (Texas, U.S.A.)
Northwest College (Wyoming, U.S.A.)
Norwegian Equine College (Norway)
Pat Parelli International Study Center (Colorado, U.S.A.)
Queensland Race Training (Australia)
Raviopisto Kaustinen (Finland)
Rocky Mountain College (Montana, U.S.A.)
Saint Mary-of-the-Woods College (Indiana, U.S.A.)
Utah State University (Utah, U.S.A.)
Ypäjän Hevosopisto/Equine College Ypäjä (Finland)

# Veterinary and Pre-Vet Programs

Atlantic Veterinary College (Prince Edward Island, Canada)
Auburn University (Alabama, U.S.A.)
Australian College of Natural Animal Medicine (Australia)
Bel-Rea Institute of Animal Technology (Colorado, U.S.A.)
Bethany Hills College (West Virginia, U.S.A.)
Chulalongkorn University (Thailand)
Clemson University (South Carolina, U.S.A.)
Colorado State University (Colorado, U.S.A.)
Cook College, Rutgers University (New Jersey, U.S.A.)
Cornell University (New York, U.S.A.)
Delaware Valley College (Pennsylvania, U.S.A.)
Ecole Nationale Vétérinaire d'Alfort (France)
Escola de Equitacao do Exercito - Brazillian Army Riding School (Brazil)
Freie Universität Berlin (Germany)
Helsingon Yliopisto (Finland)
Houghton College (New York, U.S.A.)
Instituto Superior Técnico (Portugal)
Iowa State University of Science and Technology (Iowa, U.S.A.)
Judson College (Alabama, U.S.A.)

Kansas State University (Kansas, U.S.A.)
Koret School of Veterinary Medicine (Israel)
Los Angeles Pierce College (California, U.S.A.)
Louisiana State University (Louisiana, U.S.A.)
Louisiana Tech University (Louisiana, U.S.A.)
Massey University (New Zealand)
Michigan State University (Michigan, U.S.A.)
Middle Tennessee State University (Tennessee, U.S.A.)
Mississippi State University (Mississippi, U.S.A.)
Montana State University (Montana, U.S.A.)
Mount Holyoke College (Massachusetts, U.S.A.)
Mount Ida College (Massachusetts, U.S.A.)
Murdoch University (Australia)
Murray State University (Kentucky, U.S.A.)
Myerscough College (Lancashire, England)
National Chung Hsing University (Taiwan)
New Mexico State University (New Mexico, U.S.A.)
Nihon University College of Bioresource Sciences (Japan)
Norges veterinærhøgskole (Norway)
North Carolina State University (North Carolina, U.S.A.)
Ohio State University (Ohio, U.S.A.)
Oklahoma State University College of Veterinary Medicine (Oklahoma, U.S.A.)
Oregon State University (Oregon, U.S.A.)
Otterbein College (Ohio, U.S.A.)
Purdue University (Indiana, U.S.A.)
The Royal Veterinary College (London, England)
The Royal (Dick) School of Veterinary Studies (Scotland)
Salem International University (West Virginia, U.S.A.)
South Dakota State University (South Dakota, U.S.A.)
State University of New York–Cobleskill (New York, U.S.A.)
Swedish University of Agricultural Sciences (Sweden)
Tarleton State University (Texas, U.S.A.)
Texas A & M University (Texas, U.S.A.)
Truman State University (Missouri, U.S.A.)
Tufts University (Massachusetts, U.S.A.)
Tuskeegee University (Alabama, U.S.A.)
Universidad de León (Spain)
Università degla Studi di Milano (Italy)
Università di Bologna (Italy)
Universität Leipzig  (Germany)
Université de Montreal (Quebec, Canada)
Universiteit Utrecht (The Netherlands)
University College Dublin (Republic of Ireland)
University of Bern (Switzerland)
University of Bristol (Avon, England)
University of California–Davis (California, U.S.A.)
University of Cambridge (Cambridgeshire, England)
University of Florida (Florida, U.S.A.)
University of Georgia (Georgia, U.S.A.)
University of Glasgow (Scotland)
University of Idaho (Idaho, U.S.A.)
University of Illinois at Urbana–Champagne (Illinois, U.S.A.)

University of Kentucky (Kentucky, U.S.A.)
University of Liverpool (Liverpool, England)
University of Louisiana–Monroe (Louisiana, U.S.A.)
University of Maryland (Maryland, U.S.A.)
University of Massachusetts–Amherst (Massachusetts, U.S.A.)
University of Minnesota College of Veterinary Medicine (Minnesota, U.S.A.)
University of Minnesota–Crookston (Minnesota, U.S.A.)
University of Missouri–Columbia (Missouri, U.S.A.)
University of Nebraska–Lincoln (Nebraska, U.S.A.)
University of Pennsylvania (Pennsylvania, U.S.A.)
University of Tennessee–Knoxville (Tennessee, U.S.A.)
University of the Philippines Los Baños (The Philippines)
University of Vermont (Vermont, U.S.A.)
University of Veterinary Medicine in Kosice (Slovakia)
University of Veterinary Sciences and the College of Agriculture (Austria)
University of Wisconsin–Madison (Wisconsin, U.S.A.)
University of Zurich (Switzerland)
Universté de Liège (Belgium)
Univerzitet u Beograd (Yugoslavia)
Utah State University (Utah, U.S.A.)
Virginia-Maryland Regional College of Veterinary Medicine (Virginia, U.S.A.)
Virginia Tech (Virginia, U.S.A.)
Washington State University (Washington, U.S.A.)
Western College of Veterinary Medicine (Saskatchewan, Canada)
Western Kentucky University (Kentucky, U.S.A.)
Wilson College (Pennsylvania, U.S.A.)

# United States of America

## *ALABAMA*

## Auburn University

Animal & Dairy Sciences, 210 Upchurch Hall, Auburn University, AL 36849-5415.
Contact: Drs. Dale Coleman, Undergraduate Teaching Coordinator or Cindy McCall.
Email: dcoleman@acesag.auburn.edu or cmccall@acesag.auburn.edu.
**Accreditation:** Southern Association of Colleges and Schools
**Degrees Offered:** Bachelor of Science, Master of Science, Doctor of Philosophy, Doctor of Veterinary Medicine
**Majors Offered:** Animal Science (B.S.), Animal & Dairy Science with equine research (M.S., Ph.D.), Veterinary Medicine (D.V.M.)
**Tuition Costs:** $1,825 in-state, $5,575 out-of-state, plus $1,110 room and board per year
**Program Description:** Two instructors. Hunt and stock seat styles taught. The undergraduate program has two curriculum options. The pre-vet/pre-professional option gives students a foundation in biological and physical sciences for careers in emerging areas of biotechnology while satisfying requirements for application to Auburn's College of Veterinary Medicine, other professional schools, or graduate school. The production option prepares students for animal production management and agribusiness while electives allow the students to develop an expertise in fields such as animal genetics, nutrition, reproduction, biology of growth, meat science, animal behavior, equine science, and companion animals. Internships are encouraged for credit, conducted away from the university under outstanding mentors in various fields of endeavor. The graduate programs provide advanced education and technical training in preparation for careers in public and private sectors related to animal science and technology, food science and technology, animal biotechnology, agribusiness, and university-level research and education. Areas of specialization include animal nutrition, animal behavior, biochemistry and molecular biology, quantitative/population genetics, and reproductive biology.
**Facilities:** Horse Unit is two miles from campus and has 50 school-owned horses, two lighted arenas (100ft x 250ft), a reproduction lab, and round pens.
**Classroom/Hands-On Equine Classes:** 1:1
**Showing:** Local, open, breed, varsity show team

**Website:**
www.auburn.edu

**Type of School:**
Public University

## Jim Graham & Meadow Run Farm

7901 County Road 61, Florence, AL 35634. Phone: (256) 766-2914 (Stable) or (256) 767-6077 (Home). Fax: (256) 767-7810.
**Degrees Offered:** Working Student/Apprentice
**Majors Offered:** Eventing
**Description of Program:** Jim is always looking for quality people who want to be "on the inside" of the equestrian business. Jim interviews through out the year for apprentices for the next year. Working pupils must be willing to work long hours for at least a year in exchange for "learning the ropes." Students must have their own horses and be at least 16 years old. Housing is on the property. This program shows the apprentices the inner workings of the horse business and helps many decide whether they

**Website:**
www.jimgraham.net

**Type of School:**
Specialty Ranch

want this as a career or not. The University of North Alabama is nearby.

**Facilities:** The 200-acre facility includes a 200ft x 400ft show jumping arena, a lighted dressage arena, various cross-country jumps, four turnout paddocks, several individual pastures, and great hacking.

**Showing:** As Jim's competition schedule allows, the students travel and compete at all levels.

## Judson College

**Website:**
www.judson.edu

**Type of School:**
Private University

Equine Science Department, Judson College, PO Box 120, Marion, AL 36756. Contact: Jennifer Johnston Hoggle, Director of Equine Science.
Phone: (334) 683-5456. Fax: (334) 683-6399. Email: jjohnst@future.judson.edu.
**Accreditation:** Southern Association of Colleges and Schools
**Degrees Offered:** Minor, Bachelor, Pre-Professional
**Majors Offered:** Equine Science (M), Pre-Vet, Independent Major (B)
**Tuition Costs:** $4,275 per semester, $2,815 room and board, $130 riding fee per class, $275 horse board per month
**Program Description:** Two instructed rides per week, with class size averaging five students. Judson College welcomes all students who want to participate in the equestrian program. You may choose this program so that you can use the knowledge to gain an edge professionally, or you may simply want to learn how to ride. Either way, you will be comfortable in the riding program at Judson College. The Equine Science minor helps prepare students for veterinary medicine, veterinary medical technology, show riding, breeding, training, jumping, working with various aspects of the equine, and the etiquette of the show world. As a Judson Equestrian, you will learn all that you can about the equine and equine industry. The program includes exhibition shows, presentations, field trips, IHSA (Intercollegiate Horse Show Association), and many more opportunities. Students have an opportunity to gain experience showing horses in hunter, jumping, western horsemanship, and reining classes. Students may tryout to become a member of the Judson College Equestrian Team. The Judson College Equestrian Team competes in the IHSA.
**Facilities:** Equestrian center is located on campus. Sixteen school horses, one covered arena (175ft x 200ft), and one jumping field. Eighteen-stall barn. Approximately, twenty-five acres of rolling woods for trail riding and turnout.
**Classroom/Hands-On Equine Classes:** 15/6 credits
**Showing:** IHSA, exhibition shows, presentations, shows and performances on campus

## Lookout Mountain School of Horseshoeing

**Website:**
www.horseshoeingschool.com

**Type of School:**
Private Trade School

400 Lewis Road, Gadsden, AL 35904. Phone: (256) 546-2036. Contact: Tom McNew. Email: tmcnew@microxl.com.
**Accreditation:** Alabama Department of Education, Veteran's Association and Disabled Veteran's Association approved.
**Degrees Offered:** Diploma
**Majors Offered:** Farrier
**Tuition Costs:** $3,000/eight-week class, $1,000/two-week class
**Description of Program:** Founded in 1987. Two instructors. The program is Monday through Friday from 8 a.m. to 4 p.m. for eight weeks. The first week, students do half a day in forge work and half a day in anatomy. After that, students shoe and trim everyday. The courses are presented in understandable terms, and each student, upon graduation, is a qualified, well-informed farrier. The students learn in great

detail about the horse and his conformation, how to form and use handmade shoes, welding, and brazing.

**Facilities:** The forge room is 25ft x 40ft with eleven forges. Each student is provided an individual forge, work bench, vice, coal bin, anvil, and tools. Dormitory is a modern home with 1500 square feet of space; will house sixteen male students and four female students.

**Classroom/Hands-On Equine Classes:** Daily hands-on experience

## Tuskegee University

College of Veterinary Medicine, Nursing & Allied Health, Tuskegee University, Tuskegee, AL 36088. Phone: (334) 727-8174. Fax: (334) 727-8177. Email: cvmnah@tuskegee.edu.

**Degrees Offered:** Master of Science, Doctor of Veterinary Medicine

**Majors Offered:** Veterinary Medicine (D.V.M.), Veterinary Science (M.S.)

**Website:**
www.tuskegee.edu

**Type of School:**
Private University

## Workshops for Riding Instructors

5940 Robinson Springs Rd., Millbrook, AL 36054. Contact: Jo Struby, MA Eq. Ed. Phone: (334) 285-5185.

**Degrees Offered:** Certificate of Completion

**Majors Offered:** Riding Instructor

**Tuition Costs:** Elementary Workshop less than $100, Standard and Advanced Workshops about $200

**Description of Program:** One- and two-day riding instructor clinics to improve your teaching skills. Jo Struby's teaching workshops for Horseback Riding Instructors are offered at three levels: Elementary One-Day Workshop for the aspiring instructor; Standard Two-Day Workshop for the instructor with experience; Advanced Two-Day Workshop for the tenured instructor. In all three workshop formats, classroom activities are combined with actual teaching. Struby encourages peer evaluation to develop productive interaction and dialogue; healthy and informative exchanges result. Meanwhile, Struby shares her expertise, plus empirical research findings on how physical and sport skills are more easily learned. Horseback Riding Instructors leave with new ways to approach their teaching, along with useful tools for evaluating their lessons as well as student learning. Instructors completing Struby's Standard and Advanced Workshops receive a Certificate of Completion and are added to Struby's database of instructors who have completed her programs. This database is made available to all national programs involved with certifying/licensing horseback riding instructors. The workshops are recognized by most certification programs as a valuable experience. Information booklet available upon request.

**Facilities:** Classroom and riding areas

**Classroom/Hands-On Equine Classes:** 50:50

**Type of School:**
Specialty School

## Oak Creek Ranch School

Website:
www.ocrs.com

Type of School:
Secondary Boarding School

P.O. Box 4329, West Sedona, AZ 86340-4329. Contact: Jay K. Wick, Headmaster. Phone: (928) 634-5571. Fax: (928) 634-4915. Email: admissions@ocrs.com.
**Accreditation:** North Central Association of Colleges and Schools
**Degrees Offered:** High School Diploma
**Tuition Costs:** $26,000
**Description of Program:** The Oak Creek Ranch School Horseback Riding Program is experiential in nature. The skills that are learned there, stay with the students for a lifetime and are reflected in the personal growth demonstrated both on campus and in any future endeavors that the student may find themselves in. In keeping with this philosophy, besides learning about horses and riding, our students learn such skills as leadership, teamwork, decision making, wilderness expertise and compassion.

## The Orme School

Website:
www.ormeschool.org

Type of School:
Secondary Private Day/Boarding School

HC 63, Box 3040, Mayer, AZ 86333. Phone: (928) 632-7601. Fax: (928) 632-7605. Email: admissions@ormeschool.org.
**Accreditation:** North Central Association of Colleges and Schools
**Degrees Offered:** High School Diploma
**Tuition Costs:** Boarding school: $27,800; Day school: $14,200
**Description of Program:** Qualified and experienced instructors teach skills from beginning to advanced levels. Horsemanship (Western & English) and 4-H are two of the major programs offered by Orme. For more than 70 years, the Orme School has offered students the opportunity to experience first-hand the workings of a cattle ranch. Though the program has changed with the times, students are provided the chance to work with the ranch. In addition to the ranching experience, Orme offers 4-H projects for those students interested in learning more about ranch/farm animals. The 4-H'ers compete against other students from around the state, region, and nation. All of these wonderful opportunities for Orme students complement the outstanding college preparatory academic course work offered by the school.
**Facilities:** Lighted rodeo arena, an English riding arena, two barns, covered stalls, and riding trails across the 40,000-acre Orme Ranch.
**Showing:** Students participate year-round in rodeo events, compete in English and Western pleasure events, and are perennial winners at livestock shows.

## Prescott College

Website:
www.prescott.edu

Type of School:
Liberal Arts College, Independent Study

220 Grove Ave., Prescott, AZ 86301. Contact: Lisa Mauldin, Admissions Counselor. Phone: (800) 628-6364. Phone/Fax: (928) 776-5242.
Email: admissions@prescott.edu.
**Accreditation:** Higher Education Commission of the North Central Association of Colleges and Schools
**Degrees Offered:** Bachelor of Arts, Bachelor of Science, Master of Arts
**Majors Offered:** Equine Assisted Mental Health (M.A.), Self-Designed Degree Program (B.A., B.S.)
**Tuition Costs:** $5,490 full-time per enrollment period

**Description of Program:** The Master of Arts program allows students seeking licenser or certification as a psychotherapist or in counseling psychology to develop competence in the rapidly evolving area of EAMH. In addition to the established core requirements designed for professional licenser, this course work explores the theoretical understanding, ethical issues, facilitation skills, and relational horsemanship skills crucial for mastery in this area of counseling. Both undergraduate programs allow for student-designed degree programs. There are not horse facilities on campus, so students must have access to their own horses and equipment elsewhere.

**Facilities:** None on campus

**Classroom/Hands-On Equine Classes:** Dictated by student

## Scottsdale Community College

Equine Science, Scottsdale Community College, 9000 E. Chaparral Road, Scottsdale, AZ 85256. Contact: Diane Blazer, Program Director. Phone:(480) 423-6231.
Fax: (480) 423-6421. Email: diane.blazer@sccmail.maricopa.edu.
Distance Education Course: Contact: Zhara Dean, Director of Continuing Education. Phone: (480) 423-6305. Email: zhara.dean@sccmail.maricopa.edu.
Website: www.horsecoursesonline.com.

**Accreditation:** North Central Association of Colleges and Schools Commission on Institutions of Higher Education

**Degrees Offered:** Certificate of Completion, Associate of Applied Science

**Majors Offered:** Equine Science

**Tuition Costs:** In-county: $51/credit hour; Out-of-state: $216/credit hour; plus assorted lab and horse usage fees, $75 to $200 per online noncredit course

**Description of Program:** Eight instructors. Program includes: anatomy and physiology, business practices, behavior, equine management, equine massage, nutrition, health and disease management, conformation evaluation, reproduction and internship opportunities. English and western horsemanship classes available as electives. The online Horse Sense Success Series certificate program is noncredit. Students earn a certificate of recognition for each online course taken and a Horse Sense Success Series certificate for completing 6 required courses and 2 of 8 elective courses. Students are in e-mail contact with nationally recognized "celebrity" instructors. Students get one on one assistance with any specific questions or problems at any time. Start a course anytime; take one course or several at a time. Work at your own pace and complete courses at your convenience.

**Facilities:** On and off campus teaching units

**Website:**
www.sc.maricopa.edu
www.horsecoursesonline.com

**Type of School:**
Community College, Independent Study

## Tucson School of Horseshoeing

2230 North Kimberlee Road, Tucson, AZ 85749. Phone: (520) 749-5212 or (800) 657-2779. Fax: (520) 760-0886. Email: director@tucsonhorseshoeing.com.

**Degrees Offered:** Certificate

**Majors Offered:** Horseshoeing Course, Primary Horseshoeing Course, Farrier Course, Two-Month Farrier Course, Three-Month Farrier Course

**Website:**
www.tucsonhorseshoeing.com

**Type of School:**
Specialty School

## University of Arizona

University of Arizona, Race Track Industry Program, Education Building #69 Rm. 104, P.O. Box 210069, Tucson, AZ 85721-0069. Phone: (520) 621-5660.

**Website:**
ag.arizona.edu

**Type of School:**
Public University

Fax: (520) 621-8239. Contact: Betty Prewitt. Email: bprewitt@ag.arizona.edu, or Department of Animal Sciences, University of Arizona, Tucson, AZ 85721. Contact: Mark Arns. Phone: (520) 621-7623. Email: marns@ag.arizona.edu.

**Accreditation:** North Central Association of Colleges and Schools

**Degrees Offered:** Bachelor of Science

**Majors Offered:** Race Track Industry Program (RTIP) with an emphasis in Business or Animal Management (B.S.), Animal Science with Equine Option (B.S.)

**Tuition Costs:** $3,604 in state, $12,374 out of state, $6,810 room and board

**Description of Program:** Five instructors. RTIP: The Business path is structured for those students planning careers in management, marketing, or regulation. The Animal paths are offered for those students interested in pursuing careers in the industry or in pursuing post-graduate training. The Industry path prepares students for entering the job market in areas such as training, sales, the breeding industry, or farm management. The Science path prepares students for entering post-graduate programs such veterinary medicine, equine research, etc. An exchange program is offered for qualified students with the University of Limerick's International Equine Institute, located in Limerick City, Ireland. Students participate in the world's largest racing conference each year (the Symposium on Racing), which UA hosts. Internships are provided throughout the country and sometimes overseas, and about ten "guest lecturers" are brought in each semester from various professions in the industry to teach classes.

**Facilities:** The University of Arizona Horse Center has been used as a teaching aid for classes such as Horsemanship, Yearling Sales Preparation, Equine Reproduction, and Introduction to Horse Science. Field trips are taken to racetracks and breeding farms.

**Classroom/Hands-On Equine Classes:** Several hands-on courses are available for students. In addition, part-time employment is available for qualified students.

**Showing:** Students enrolled in the Yearling Sales Preparation class travel each year to the Thoroughbred Breeder's sale and present the UA yearlings to buyers from around the country. In addition, an Intercollegiate Equestrian team is currently being developed.

## Verde Valley School

**Website:**
www.verdevalleyschool.org

**Type of School:**
Secondary School

3511 Verde Valley School Road, Sedona, AZ 86351. Contact: Don Smith, Director of Admissions. Phone: (928) 284-2272 ext. 128. Fax: (928) 284-0432. Email: info@verdevalleyschool.org.

**Accreditation:** Member of National Association of Independent Schools, A Better Chance, the College Board, the Secondary School Admission Test Board, the Western Boarding Schools Association, and the American Schools for International Students and Teachers

**Degrees Offered:** High School Diploma

**Tuition Costs:** $29,500 boarding, $15,600 day

**Description of Program:** Verde Valley School's Riding Program offers a broad range of horseback riding experiences. English riding instruction is available, including jumping and dressage, with the possibility of competing in local shows. Some students may choose to train for endurance competition. If a casual trail ride is to your liking, the school is surrounded by thousands of acres of national forest and extensive trails. Riding is one of the most popular attractions at Verde Valley School. Students are welcome to bring their own horses to campus and stable them in our facilities.

## Western School of Horseshoeing

**Website:**
www.westernschool.com

**Type of School:**
Specialty School

2801 W. Maryland Avenue, Phoenix, AZ 85017. Phone: (602) 242-2560.

Fax: 602-242-6670. Email: westerns_school@hotmail.com.
**Accreditation:** Post-secondary school system of Arizona
**Degrees Offered:** Diploma
**Majors Offered:** Farrier
**Tuition Costs:** $3,500 for course, approximately $525 for tools
**Description of Program:** Eight week course, six days week. Students go off-site to shoe customers' horses.
**Facilities:** School is on five acres and consists of a blacksmithing shop, classroom, and two rental units for out-of-state students.

# CALIFORNIA

## California Polytechnic State University, San Luis Obispo

Animal Science Department, Cal Poly State University, San Luis Obispo, CA 93407. Contact: Mike Lund, Equine Specialist. Phone: (805) 756-2558. Fax: (805) 756-5069. E-mail: mlund@calpoly.edu.
**Accreditation:** Western Association of Schools and Colleges
**Degrees Offered:** Bachelor of Science
**Majors Offered:** Animal Science with equine option
**Tuition Costs:** Residents: $11,877/year; non-residents: $17,781/year; costs include tuition, room and board, and other expenses
**Description of Program:** The horse program revolves around the breeding and training of Thoroughbreds and Quarter Horses. The classes are designed to give students a foundation in the principles of horsemanship. Students will receive valuable experience in artificial insemination, veterinary work, and the training of horses through the various classes offered. Experience is also gained through enterprises such as the Breeding Enterprise, Ranch Horse Enterprise, Thoroughbred Yearling Enterprise, and the Quarter Horse Enterprise. The unit has Foundation-owned horses, which include Quarter Horse broodmares, Thoroughbred broodmares, two-year-olds, yearlings, and weanlings. Also, privately-owned horses are brought in each quarter for enterprises and classes such as equitation and colt breaking.
**Facilities:** Equine facilities are located on campus. Outdoor arena.
**Classroom/Hands-On Equine Classes:** All classes have a hands-on component
**Showing:** IHSA, Polo, NIRA

**Website:**
www.calpoly.edu

**Type of School:**
Public University

## California State Polytechnic University, Pomona

Animal Science Department, California State Polytechnic University, 3801 W. Temple Ave., Pomona, CA 91768. Contact: Rhonda Ostrowski, Recruitment Coordinator. Phone: (909) 869-3718 or (888) 2DAYS AG. Fax: (909) 869-4454. Email: rlostrowski@csupomona.edu.
**Accreditation:** Western Association of Schools and Colleges
**Degrees Offered:** Bachelor of Science, Master of Science
**Majors Offered:** Animal Science with emphasis in Equine Sciences (B.S.), Agriculture with emphasis in Animal Science (M.S.)
**Tuition Costs:** $2,505 per year; out-of-state students pay additional $188 per unit; $6,900 room and board
**Description of Program:** The Equine Science option is designed to prepare students

**Website:**
www.csupomona.edu

**Type of School:**
Public University

for employment as managers and for related agribusiness opportunities in the equine industry. The option combines course work in equine production, nutrition, breeding, genetics, and diseases with studies in the management aspects of an equine enterprise. At the W.K. Kellogg Arabian Horse Center, one of the world's outstanding Arabian horse breeding farms, the Arabians are utilized in the animal science courses related to light horse production, research, and training. The Equine Research Center (ERC) offers both undergraduate and graduate students an opportunity to study horse health and function, reproductive physiology, exercise physiology, energetics and kinematics of locomotion, animal behavior, parasitology, and immunology. Students may also study exercise physiology using a modern high-speed treadmill shared by the two centers. Students perfect their knowledge and technical skills by collecting and processing semen and embryos, growing tissue cultures, assaying hormones, and analyzing scientific data. They are also instructed in the use of sophisticated computer programs (e.g., the Peak motion analysis system) that assist in the analysis of scientific data. Quality research is emphasized, and student researchers are encouraged to present the results of their work at local, national, and international scientific forums.

**Facilities:** The W.K. Kellogg Arabian Horse Center is located on the edge of campus; it includes a main barn, show arena, grooming stalls, wash racks, farrier workshop, snack bar, museum, classrooms, boarding barns, pasture, veterinary clinic, equine treadmill, equine force plate, rodeo arena, hot walker, and breeding facilities. The Kellogg herd consists of approximately 135 Arabians. The Equine Research Center includes a research laboratory, mini equine library, graduate student work room, and offices. Arabian Horse Collection (world renowned Arabian horse library) is also available.

**Classroom/Hands-On Equine Classes:** Classroom: 7 required/5 optional; Hands-on: 2 required/4 optional

**Showing:** IHSA, WIHSA, Arabian Mounted Drill Team, Horse Judging Team, Rodeo Team, Sunday Arabian Horse shows

**Website:**
www.csufresno.edu

**Type of School:**
Public University

# California State University–Fresno

Animal Sciences & Agriculture Education, CSU Fresno, 2415 E. San Ramon · MS AS75, Fresno, CA 93740-8033. Contact: Dr. Anne Rodiek. Phone: (559) 278-2971 or (559) 278-5623. Fax: (559) 278-4101. Email: anner@csufresno.edu.

**Accreditation:** California Board of Education and the Western Association of Schools and Colleges

**Degrees Offered:** Bachelor of Science, Master of Science

**Majors Offered:** Animal Science with emphasis in Equine Science (B.S.), Animal Science (M.S.)

**Tuition Costs:** Residents: $1,207/semester for undergraduates, $1,312/semester for graduate students; non-residents: $282/per unit; room and board: average of $7,000/year

**Description of Program:** The Bachelor of Science degree in Animal Science is a broad-based, scientific program with a large component of hands-on learning. An emphasis in Equine Science allows students to specialize in horses within the broader Animal Science curriculum. The Master of Science degree in animal science offers in depth study in animal nutrition, reproduction, and management. The M.S. program has considerable flexibility, and students interested in horses may, with the direction of an adviser and a thesis committee, conduct a research project in an area of equine interest. Hunt seat and Western styles taught. Horse Production, Advanced Horse Management, Equine Nutrition, Stable Management courses are offered. All courses except

Equine Nutrition have a laboratory component. Experiential learning at our two campus horse units is strongly emphasized.

**Facilities:** The program has two on-campus horse units: A Quarter Horse Unit that houses approximately 90 head of horses for educational and research purposes, and a Student Horse Center to house 40 student-owned horses and to support the campus NCAA Division I Equestrian Team.

**Classroom/Hands-On Equine Classes:** 50:50

**Showing:** IHSA (NCAA Equestrian Team), various Western events (Quarter Horse Unit), rodeo (Rodeo Club)

## C.W. Training

6496 Crow Canyon Rd., Castro Valley, CA 94552. Phone: (510) 886-9000. Email: cwtraining@attbi.com.

**Degrees Offered:** Horsemanship Program, Apprenticeship

**Majors Offered:** Foundation Program: Colt Starting & Re-schooling (A)

**Tuition Costs:** Apprenticeship program: $12,000; housing: $35/day. One-week horsemanship program: $700/week for tuition, $275 for lodging, $200 for horse board. Two-week horsemanship program: $1,300 for tuition, $500 for lodging, $300 for horse board. Three-week horsemanship: $1,800 for tuition, $700 for lodging, $400 for horse board.

**Description of Program:** The C.W. Training program is overseen by Charles Wilhelm, owner/trainer. The Horsemanship Program is a one- to three-week working program for trainers and owners. Participants are introduced to the conditioned response method used as a foundation for starting colts, re-schooling, and as a remedy to a variety of behavioral and gymnastics problems. These methods apply to all horses and all disciplines. By working and learning at the central training facility, you will experience the full range of tools used to enhance the equine-human partnership and to allow the horse to work at its full potential. A maximum of two people will be trained at the same time. The Apprenticeship Program is a twelve-week program where trainers and owners can develop the expertise to create a solid foundation with any horse, for any riding discipline. The program is divided into four units given over a 12-month period, which offers you time between units to practice and apply the material learned. Each participant must have his/her own horses, two for each segment. One well broke and one green-broke is okay. Stabling and feed is provided.

**Facilities:** Show barn with covered arena, two outdoor arenas, round pens, and miles of beautiful trails.

**Website:**
www.cwtraining.com

**Type of School:**
Specialty School

## Donna Snyder-Smith Apprenticeship

Donna Snyder-Smith, 32628 Endeavour Way, Union City, CA 94587.
Phone: (510) 487-9001. Email: Rightrider@cs.com.

**Accreditation:** American Riding Instructor's Association, Centered Riding®

**Degrees Offered:** Apprenticeship

**Majors Offered:** Instructor of Riding Apprenticeship, Trainer Apprenticeship

**Tuition Costs:** Work exchange (average responsibility is for four to eight horses–no mucking)

**Description of Program:** The apprenticeships are two years long, and only one student/apprentice is taken at a time. The training apprenticeship is designed to provide the apprentice with the basic skills necessary to start and school horses into well-balanced, responsive athletes and/or pleasure mounts on the flat. Dealing with horses

**Type of School:**
Balanced Seat/English/Pleasure Riding

with extreme behavioral problems is not a part of the course. The instructor apprenticeship is focused on a universal "balanced seat" and requires that the apprentice take the American Riding Instructor Association (ARIA) teaching exams by the end of the 24 months. The course is designed to help you achieve certification by the ARIA. Some competition exposure is often a part of the course; however, the course is not "competition" focused. Applicants must be fit and healthy with a good attitude and work ethic. They must be intermediate or better riders. In the second year, some small income is usually generated from either teaching revenue or training revenue, as students keep a portion of the fees when they become competent enough to function without constant supervision in either a teaching or training capacity.

**Facilities:** The stable is located in Northern California. Can be hot in summer months (no snow). Simple boarding barn with all-weather arena, two sand round pens, hot walker, tack room, wash rack (clean, neat and functional, not fancy). No housing provided.

**Classroom/Hands-On Equine Classes:** The apprenticeships involve hands-on training, but also require a fair amount of textbook and video study and there are periodic written exams.

**Showing:** Some competition exposure is often a part of the course; however, the course is not "competition" focused.

# Equestrian International

1840 N. San Marcos Rd, Santa Barbara, CA 93111.
Email: info@equestrian-international.com.
**Degrees Offered:** Apprenticeship/Job/Working Student
**Majors Offered:** Bronze Medal Program (3-12 month working student), Silver Medal Program (2 weeks to 3 months regular student), Gold Medal Program (2 weeks to 6 months ultimate student)
**Tuition Costs:** $60 application fee. Bronze Medal: $500 fee split between student and host. Silver Medal: $1,500-$3,500 per month. Gold Medal: $3,500+ per month.
**Description of Program:** Equestrian International is an organization that creates training, educational, and competition opportunities for riders in foreign countries. By using a large network of contacts and a unique application and interview process, riders are screened and individually placed in appropriate barns throughout the world. This provides an invaluable service for participating riders and the professionals they are placed with. A select group of professionals is presented with serious students, which, in addition, serves riders well because they are sent only to qualified, talented professionals who match them in terms of goals and ability. Stays can run from two to four weeks, to three months or more. It is possible for college students to get credit from this program through their own schools, typically as overseas study credits or language credits.
**Facilities:** Barns in United States, Europe, Southeast Asia, Mexico
**Showing:** Showing opportunities are available for those who choose to take advantage of them.

# Equine-Reproduction.com

P.O. Box 2876, McKinleyville, CA 95519. Phone: (720) 272-5998.
**Majors Offered:** Equine Reproduction
**Tuition Costs:** $250 per person, per seminar, housing not included

**Description of Program:** Equine-Reproduction.com offers one- and two-day seminars that are designed to educate horse breeders to more fully understand the intricacies of equine reproduction. Because it is understood that most horse breeders have full-time jobs outside their horse interests, seminars are scheduled on weekends. Furthermore, the seminars are brought to you, because travel costs and time away from home to attend a seminar can make attendance difficult. These courses are excellent for the new breeder, as well as the reproductive veterinarian looking for an update on the latest technologies and methods of breeding. Although the courses are easily understandable, they are intensive and cover all aspects of equine reproduction and breeding. They include study of the anatomy and physiology of both the mare and the stallion reproductive systems; management of mare and stallion for optimal breeding; the mare's reproductive cycle and hormonal relationships; fertility evaluation; manipulation of the estrous cycle in the mare; techniques for live cover and artificial insemination of the mare; and the use of fresh, cooled, or frozen semen.

**Facilities:** Various locations across the U.S. and Canada

**Classroom/Hands-On Equine Classes:** 90 percent classroom/10 percent hands-on/wet lab

## Equine Research Foundation

Equine Research Foundation, Learning and Riding Vacations and Internships, P.O. Box 1900, Aptos, CA 95001. Phone: (831) 662-9577. Fax: (831) 662-9575. Email: EquiResF@aol.com.

**Accreditation:** The ERF is a nonprofit organization with tax-exempt status. We are supported by grants and tax-deductible public and corporate donations.

**Degrees Offered:** Internship, College Credit

**Majors Offered:** Research in Equine Cognition and Perception

**Tuition Costs:** One week: $1,095. Two weeks: $1,795. Internships are $1,500 per month, with one- to three-month options. Costs include food, lodging, instruction, riding. A portion of the cost is tax-deductible.

**Description of Program:** Research Facility with Public Programs covering equine learning abilities, perception, behavior, training, riding, care and welfare. The program is multifaceted and includes a focus on a unique scientific research project geared toward gaining a deeper understanding of the horse's mind. During your stay as a volunteer, you will participate in all phases of the research, including operation of testing apparatus, handling the animals during the tests, videotaping sessions, collecting data, computer data entry, journal record keeping, and more. Through seminars, observation, and hands-on experience, you will learn how the findings of the Equine Research Foundation relate to human dealings with horses, and how cognition and behavior principles apply to handling and training. You will also receive instruction and hands-on experience working and playing with horses using the Equine Research Foundation alternative methods of ground schooling and bond formation. Based on equine social dynamics, herd behavior, psychology, and positive reinforcement, these techniques will help you develop a better relationship with any horse. All methodology emphasizes positive interaction, creates strong human/horse bonds, and develops willing partnerships between humans and horses.

**Facilities:** Forty-acre ranch. Part of the ranch includes a vineyard with horse trails; part of it is pasture. Much of the ranch contains riding trails through the hills, among redwoods and oaks. Excursions to the coastal beaches and mountain trails are also part of the program. Horses are kept together in large pastures with access to shelter and to the stable in bad weather. A three-bedroom, two and a half-bath ranch house with a

**Website:**
www.equineresearch.org

**Type of School:**
Research Facility

pool is situated in the middle of the vineyard; typically, two persons share a bedroom. Arrangements can be made to allow couples to have private rooms.

<table>
<tr><td>

**Website:**
www.equinology.com

**Type of School:**
Specialty School

</td><td>

## Equinology, Inc.®

P.O. Box 1248, Grover Beach, CA 93483. Phone: (866) 829-2086.
Email: office@equinology.com.
**Accreditation:** The International Massage Association, USDF University, and McTimineony Animal Chiropractic School (United Kingdom)
**Degrees Offered:** Certificate
**Majors Offered:** Equine Body Worker, Equine Body Worker Level II, Advanced Equine Body Worker, Specialized Equine Body Worker
**Tuition Costs:** $95-$1,395 per course
**Description of Program:** Courses offered in a modular format. Courses included massage, acupressure, MFR, craniosacral, biomechanics, anatomy, saddle fitting, neuromuscular reeducation, nutrition, exercise physiology and more. All courses are taught by veterinarians and specialists. Equine sports massage is the therapeutic application of hands-on techniques that have been long recognized for their ability to increase circulation and range of motion, as well as to improve the horse's stamina and overall performance. It also relieves muscle spasms and tension and enhances muscle tone. Overuse, overstretching, and overloading muscles can cause tissue lesions, which can restrict motion and create pain. The goal of this program is to teach the pupil how to locate these points and break them up using various therapeutic methods and techniques. This course differs from others in that the student's ability to locate points and issues is developed by instilling a strong groundwork of anatomy. The student will learn to identify muscles and their functions, evaluate and observe the horse's movement and development, administer an entire sports massage, and perform correct range-of-motion stretching and warm-up exercises. Some courses are accredited or counted as continuing education by the McTimoney Animal Chiropractic School, the USDF University, and other colleges.
**Facilities:** Housing is not provided for students. The northern California venue, Flying Cloud Farm located in Petaluma, has a large covered arena, indoor stalls, pole barn, pipe paddock, pasture, one outdoor jumping arena, one outdoor regulation dressage court, a large classroom, and three round pens. The central and southern California venues are equally suitable for courses. A Florida location has been added for 2004. In addition, all or some of the program courses are offered in Australia, England, Canada, Brazil and South Africa.
**Classroom/Hands-On Equine Classes:** 50 to 90 percent hands-on

</td></tr>
<tr><td>

**Website:**
www.frc.edu

**Type of School:**
Community College

</td><td>

## Feather River College

570 Golden Eagle Ave., Quincy, CA 95971. Phone: (800) 442-9799 or
(530) 283-0202. Email: equinestudies@frc.edu.
**Accreditation:** California Community College Chancellor
**Degrees Offered:** Associate in Science, Certificate
**Majors Offered:** Equine Studies (A.S.), Animal Science (C)
**Tuition Costs:** In-state: $18/unit; housing costs as stated by Feather River Apartments
**Description of Program:** Two instructors. This unique program offers college-level course work to students who wish to become professionals in horse-related enterprises. In this program, you will gain the skills needed for various jobs in the horse indus-

</td></tr>
</table>

try choose; stable managers, wrangler for guest ranches and resorts, packer, horse training apprentice, farrier apprentice, or just go on to a four year college.

**Facilities:** The equestrian center is located on campus, and includes two arenas (150ft x 300ft outdoor and 80ft x 100ft heated indoor arena) 3 round pens (outdoors), 23 stalls, and five pastures, including a breeding pasture. Also included are a shoeing barn, two tack rooms, one grain room, one classroom, and living quarters for four student interns. Housing is provided through the Feather River Apartments (530-283-9713).

**Classroom/Hands-On Equine Classes:** All hands-on, except one course

**Showing:** May form a show club if enough interest is shown.

## Geary Whiting's Equine Massage School

P.O. Box 435, Douglas City, CA 96024. Phone: (888) 794-5555 (Pin#9446) or (530) 623-6485. Email: ftnsdr@shasta.com.

**Degrees Offered:** Certificate

**Majors Offered:** Equine Sports Massage Therapist

**Tuition Costs:** $1,300 includes lodging, meals, and outings, as well as a $1,000,000 liability insurance policy upon graduation, and membership in the Ancient Healing Arts Association.

**Description of Program:** This school is unique because it addresses both horse and human performance problems. Geary Whiting has been in the fitness business for over 43 years and feels that a fitness program for students is very important to their futures as equine massage therapists. To do a thorough job on a horse, it requires strength and stamina. Whiting also knows that if school is fun, people learn better. In order to enhance the students' educations, each student lives at the school in their own cozy cabin nestled under the trees. Meals are served at the main house in a family environment, and often the evenings include fireside storytelling. Thursday evenings are movie nights, and the marketing part of school is incorporated when inspirational films based on true stories are shown. Students learn very quickly and achieve remarkable results. This is much more than a school...it is an experience.

**Facilities:** Individual cabins for students to stay in. Four-stall barn, work in and out of the barn. Nature trails for those moments you wish to be alone and do some thinking.

**Classroom/Hands-On Equine Classes:** 60:40

**Website:**
www.gearywhiting.com

**Type of School:**
Private Specialty School

## Lassen Community College

P.O. Box 3000, Susanville, CA 96130. Contact: Brian Wolf, Agriculture Instructor. Phone: (530) 251-8803. Email: bwolf@lassen.cc.ca.us.

**Accreditation:** Accrediting Commission for Community and Junior Colleges Western Association of Schools and Colleges

**Degree Offered:** Certificate of Completion, Certificate of Achievement, Associate of Science

**Majors Offered:** Agriculture (A.S., C.A.), Horsemanship (C.A.), Horseshoeing (C.C.L.)

**Tuition Cost:** In-state: $18/credit hour; out-of-state: $171/credit hour; room and board: $1,700 per nine-meal plan, $2,050 per fourteen-meal plan; horse board: $600/semester

**Description of Program:** Five instructors. Three to four instructed rides per week with an average class size of twelve. An excellent training program that offers everything from beginning riding to advanced colt training. Classes such as Cutting, Reining, Working Cow Horse, Natural Horsemanship, and English are available. There is a

**Website:**
www.lassen.cc.ca.us

**Type of School:**
Community College

livestock judging team that also does some horse judging. Lassen offers a horse husbandry course that is academic, but the rest of the courses are hands-on training courses.

**Facilities:** On campus. Two arenas (200ft x 300ft & 100ft x 200ft), and two 45ft round pens. Every semester, eight horses are available for lease to beginning and intermediate horse students who do not have their own horse.

**Classroom/Hands-On for Equine Courses:** 1/3 classroom : 2/3 hands-on

**Showing:** Some students show independently; instructors are happy to assist them as needed.

## Los Angeles Pierce College

**Website:**
www.piercecollege.com

**Type of School:**
Community College

6201 Winnetka Ave., Woodland Hills, CA 91371

**Accreditation:** Western Association of Schools and Colleges, Accrediting Commission for Community and Junior Colleges (ACCJC)

**Degrees Offered:** Certificate, Associate of Science

**Majors Offered:** Agriculture, Horse Science, RVT, Pre-Veterinary Sciences, Horticulture

**Tuition Costs:** In-State: $18/credit hour; out-of-state: $130/credit hour; horse board: starting at $125/month

**Facilities:** Equestrian Center is on campus. Sixty stalls, plus outside pens. The covered arena is 80' x 140'. Plus six other show arenas.

## Merced College

**Website:**
www.mccd.edu

**Type of School:**
Community College

Agriculture Division, Merced College, 3600 M Street, Merced, CA 95348.
Contact: Karen Wallace. Phone: (209) 384-6250. Fax: (209) 381-6444.
Email: wallace.k@mccd.edu.

**Accreditation:** Western Association of Schools and Colleges

**Degrees Offered:** Certificate of Completion, Associate of Science

**Majors Offered:** Horseshoeing (C), Horse Management (A.S.)

**Tuition Costs:** In-state: $18/credit; out-of-state: $141/credit

**Description of Program:** The eighteen-week Horseshoeing Program meets 20 hours per week for ten units of college credit. The course consists of five hours of lecture and fifteen hours of laboratory experience. This includes the actual trimming and shoeing of horses, as well as iron and forge work. It also introduces the student to the construction of man-made horseshoes, the anatomy and physiology of the equine foot and leg, horse psychology, proper hoof balances in relation to conformation, and safety for the horse and horseshoer. The Horse Management Program is designed to meet the need for trained personnel in a broad range of occupational opportunities involved with or related to the horse industry. Students enrolled in the program study theory and apply practical experiences in a variety of classes that are related to the horse, and receive a platform of experiences that help to prepare them for a very competitive business.

**Facilities:** Equestrian center is located on campus. Outdoor arena, covered stalls, animal science agriplex with demonstration pavilion for indoor live animal instruction. No housing available; there are reasonably priced apartments near campus.

**Classroom/Hands-On Equine Classes:** 1:2

**Showing:** Club-sponsored horse shows

## Midland School

P.O. Box 8, Los Olivos, CA 93441. Contact: David S. Lourie, Interim Head of School. Phone: (805) 688-5114 Ext. 12. Fax: (805) 686-2470.
Email: dlourie@midland-school.org.
**Degrees Offered:** High School Diploma

**Website:**
www.midland-school.org

**Type of School:**
Secondary Boarding School

## Monte Vista Christian School

2 School Way, Watsonville, CA 95076. Phone: (831) 722-8178 x167. Fax: (831) 722-0864. Email: equestrian@mvcs.org or info@mvcs.org.
**Accreditation:** Western Association of Schools and Colleges, Association of Christian Schools International
**Degrees Offered:** High School Diploma
**Tuition Costs:** $25,000 Residential Domestic Students; $27,600 Residential International Students; $7,100 High School Day Students; $6,880 Middle School Day Students. Tuition costs include room and board, books, P.E. clothing, athletic and class fees, and some transportation.
**Description of Program:** Grades 6-12. Resident program grades 9-12. With both English and Western riding arenas and numerous trails around the campus, the equestrian program is a visible part of the curricular and extracurricular offerings. Many students enjoy the opportunity to learn horsemanship. A stable of mounts and experienced instructors provide the opportunity for any level of equitation a student may possess.
**Facilities:** The campus occupies almost 100 acres of rolling lawns, ponds, playing fields, equestrian facilities, and more than 25 buildings.

**Website:**
www.mvcs.org

**Type of School:**
Private Day and Boarding School

## Monty Roberts International Learning Center

Flag Is Up Farms, 901 E. Hwy. 246, P.O. Box 246, Solvang, CA 93464. Phone: (805) 688-3483. Fax: (805) 693-8223. Email: learningcenter@montyroberts.com.
**Accreditation:** Currently seeking accreditation
**Degrees Offered:** Certificate
**Majors Offered:** Introductory Course, Advanced Course, Instructor's Internship
**Tuition Costs:** $4,000 Introductory Course; $3,000 Advanced Course. Housing and meals are not included, but local facilities give student discounts
**Description of Program:** Both the Introductory and Advanced Courses are 12-month programs and are presented in three segments. Section A: Takes place at the Flag Is Up Farms and is a four-week course. Section B: Is a ten-month fieldwork (student's place of origin) that allows the students to enhance their work from the four-week section. Section C: Two-week summary and examination program. The first week of this segment will be spent evaluating and refining each student's ten-month fieldwork. During the second week, the student will be asked to complete a written, oral, and practical exam. The Introductory course commences (Section A) as a four week intense study period covering feeding & nutrition, breeding & foaling, horse performance, stable management and a large emphasis on horse psychology and Monty's methods. The Advanced Course commences (Section A) as a three week intense study of dealing with horses that present remedial behavioral problems. This course aids the student in a deeper understanding of horse psychology and problem-solving. The Instructor's Internship is an internship in which the student has been specially selected and approved to complete. This is for those students who wish to become an instructor in

**Website:**
www.montyroberts.com

**Type of School:**
Specialty School

Monty Roberts' concepts. The internship is completed at Flag Is Up in California, where the student aids in assisting the MRILC for a minimum one year training period.

**Facilities:** The 110-acre farm includes lush, green, manicured lawns and pastures, beautiful stables and barns, and a 24,000-square-foot covered arena, one-half-mile training track, starting gate, round pens and chute.

**Classroom/Hands-On Equine Classes:** 40:60

## Moorpark College

**Website:**
www.moorparkcollege.edu

**Type of School:**
Community College

7075 Campus Road, Moorpark, CA 93021. Phone: (805) 378-1441. Email: eatm@vcccd.net.

**Accreditation:** Western Association of Schools and Colleges

**Degrees Offered:** Certificate of Achievement, Associate of Science

**Majors Offered:** Exotic Animal Training and Management

**Tuition Costs:** In-state: $18/unit; out-of-state: $150/unit (additional); $1,000 books and supplies

**Description of Program:** This program is geared toward all exotic animals (not just equines). The increasing importance of zoos and wildlife education to the efforts of conservation, and the use of animals in various entertainment fields present many career options to graduates of this curriculum. The EATM program prepares the student for positions in the animal care industry that often involve working with dangerous animals. The students work with some dangerous animals at the college's facility and at other animal facilities during their course of study. Students are required to work at America's Teaching Zoo, located on the Moorpark College campus, many nights and weekends. This requirement is in addition to the long hours and days spent working with and caring for the animals and attending classes. The zoo currently has a miniature horse in the collection, and in the past, an Arabian horse and a zebra have also been in residence. Several camels, goats, pigs, water buffalo, and other types of "hoofstock" animals such as llamas, alpacas, and deer are always included in the program.

**Facilities:** America's Teaching Zoo has more than 150 different animals, and is maintained and run entirely by the students. Hoofstock area has pipe corrals for the animals, and a shelter area for them. Housing for students is not supplied by the school.

**Classroom/Hands-On Equine Classes:** 50:50

## Mt. San Antonio College

**Website:**
www.mtsac.edu

**Type of School:**
Community College

Animal Health Technology Program, Mt. San Antonio College, 1100 N. Grand Ave., Walnut, CA 91789. Contact: Lee Pettey. Phone: (909) 594-5611 or 594-4540. Fax: (909) 468-3917. Email: admissions@mtsac.edu.

**Accreditation:** Western Association of Schools and Colleges

**Degrees Offered:** Certificate, Associate of Science

**Majors Offered:** Horse Ranch Management

**Tuition Costs:** In-state: $18/unit

**Showing:** Judging

## Ojai Valley School

**Website:**
www.ovs.org

**Type of School:**
Private PreK-12 School

723 El Paseo Road, Ojai, CA 93023. Lower School Phone: (805) 646-1423. Upper School Phone: (805) 646-5593. Lower Fax: (805) 646-0362. Upper Fax: (805) 933-1096. Email: admission@ovs.org.

**Accreditation:** Western Association of Schools and Colleges, Interscholastic Equestrian League

**Degrees Offered:** High School Diploma

**Tuition Costs:** $32,600 boarding for grades 6-12. $26,100 boarding for grades 3-5. Day tuition varies depending on grade level.

**Description of Program:** Preparatory boarding school for grades 3-12. The Lower School: The English and Western equestrian program is included in the PreK-3rd grade curriculum. Students may choose riding for their physical education class in grades 4 through 8 for an additional fee. The Lower School also has a competitive riding team and a drill team. These teams meet after school for practice and attend competitions. Students go "horse camping." The Upper School: Students may choose riding for their physical education requirement. In addition, the equestrian program offers both competitive English and Western riding. OVS Upper students compete in eventing, and quadrille, hunter-jumper, and dressage shows. They attend Western "play days," ride on trails, and camp out. A favorite location is Montana de Oro State Park, a camp on the beach where the students can ride their horses into the ocean one day and through the mountains the next.

**Facilities:** Full stable facility, barn, tack rooms, and riding arena. The facilities are located directly on the grounds of both the Upper and Lower School campus. Each campus has its own equestrian facility.

**Showing:** Competitive riding team, drill team, eventing, hunter/jumper, dressage

## Pacific Coast Horseshoeing School

9625 Florin Road, Sacramento, CA 95829-1009. Phone: (916) 336-6064. Fax: (916) 366-6618. Email: pchs@farrierschool.com.

**Degrees Offered:** Certificate

**Majors Offered:** Horseshoeing

**Tuition Costs:** $4,500; $50/week for housing

**Description of Program:** An eight week program. Twelve to fourteen students per class, with two instructors. The program is broken into three categories: classroom training, forge work and shoeing/trimming. Classroom training consists of studying the equine anatomy, conformation and movement, lameness and therapeutic shoeing, gait analysis, shoeing for disciplines, and business skills (bookkeeping, marketing strategies). Forge work consists of creating fourteen handmade shoes that have use either in therapeutic shoeing or a specific discipline. In shoeing/trimming, all feet are shod and trimmed to the American Farriers Association's certification standards.

**Facilities:** 7,500 square feet of forge and shoeing area, 200-square-foot tool room with private lockers for each student, 1000-square-foot metal shop, 600-square-feet of modern classroom space, complete with central heat and air.

**Classroom/Hands-On Equine Classes:** 6 hours/34 hours per week

**Website:**
www.farrierschool.com

**Type of School:**
Specialty School

## Rege Ludwig Polo School

The Ludwig Polo Company, 74-350 Primrose Dr., Palm Desert, CA 92260. Contact: Janet. Phone: (760) 773-3558. Fax: (760) 773-3658. Email: info@regeludwigpolo.com.

**Accreditation:** United States Polo Association, Polo Training Foundation

**Degrees Offered:** Certificate of Completion

**Majors Offered:** Polo

**Tuition Costs:** $1,200 includes horses

**Website:**
www.regeludwigpolo.com

**Type of School:**
Specialty Polo School

**Description of Program:** Three- and six-day polo clinics, held on grass polo fields. There are six to seven hours of instruction per day, beginning at 7 a.m.; however, the hours will be flexible enough to allow students to watch the high-goal games. Enrollment is limited to eight students. Clinics are available for beginning and experienced polo players. The intermediate-level clinics are for experienced polo players up to the two-goal level. To enter the beginning-level clinics, participants need to be adequate riders—able to stop, turn and hand gallop on an outdoor polo field with confidence. Daily schedule: Riding (balanced seat) from 8-10 a.m. Foot polo, hitting cage and wooden horse from 10-11 a.m. Sandwiches and class in rules/umpiring, positions/tactics, or team plays from 11 a.m.-12:30 p.m. Play polo from 12:30-2 p.m.

**Facilities:** El Dorado Polo Club near Palm Springs, California features twelve grass polo fields and a club house, stick-and-ball field, exercise track, and stabling for 1,000 horses. The Virginia Polo Center is nestled in the Blue Ridge Mountains in Charlottesville, Virginia. It features a grass polo field, a freestanding indoor arena, and an indoor arena in a covered facility for play during bad weather. The University of Virginia Polo Team is based at these facilities. Housing is not included (though the school has a list of hotels).

**Showing:** Chukkers

**Website:**
www.sandomenico.org

**Type of School:**
Secondary School

## San Domenico School

Director of Admission, San Domenico School, 1500 Butterfield Road, San Anselmo, CA 94960-1099. Phone: (415) 258-1905. Fax: (415) 258-1906. Email: admissions@sandomenico.org.
**Degrees Offered:** High School Diploma

**Website:**
www.santarosa.edu

**Type of School:**
Junior College

## Santa Rosa Junior College

1501 Mendocino Avenue, Santa Rosa, CA 95401. Contact: Jim Porter.
Phone: (707) 527-4646. Fax: (707) 527-4651. Email: jporter@santarosa.edu.
**Degrees Offered:** Associate of Science
**Majors Offered:** Equine Science
**Tuition Costs:** $18.00/unit
**Facilities:** Indoor arena (125ft x 200ft), outdoor arena (100ft x 200ft), and a new 16-stall barn with a completion date of 2005.
**Classroom/Hands-On Equine Classes:** 75 percent : 25 percent, not including internships

**Website:**
www.shastacollege.edu

**Type of School:**
Community College

## Shasta College

Ctr. For Science, Industry & Natural Resources, 11555 Old Oregon Trail, PO Box 496006, Redding, CA 96049. Contact: Dr. Ross Tomlin. Phone: (530)225-4660. Fax: (530)225-4823. Email: info@shastacollege.edu.
**Accreditation:** Western Association of Schools and Colleges
**Degrees Offered:** Certificate, Associate of Science
**Majors Offered:** Equine Science
**Tuition Costs:** Tuition: $18 per unit; Student Health Fee: $12; Campus Center Fee: $20.50; Non-Resident Tuition: $163 per unit. Parking fee is $25 per vehicle per semester or $1 per day.
**Description of Program:** Veterinary practices, feeds & feeding, training. Western and English riding styles taught.

**Facilities:** 90-acre farm, training pen, arena
**Showing:** Schooling shows

## Sierra College

Agriculture Department, Sierra College, 5000 Rocklin Rd., Rocklin, CA 95667-3397. Contact: Jerry Van Rein, Ag. Dept. Chair. Phone: (916) 624-3333. Fax: (916) 789-2918. Email: jvanrein@scmail.sierra.cc.ca.us.
**Degrees Offered:** Certificate, Associate of Arts, Associate of Science
**Majors Offered:** Animal Husbandry, Equine Studies

## Sierra Horseshoeing School

Rt. 2 Box 22B, Bishop, CA 93514. Phone: (760) 872-1279 or (760) 788-8115. Email: info@sierrahorseshoeing.com.
**Accreditation:** California Sate Department of Education, courses are approved for selected VA Job Retraining and BIA Rehabilitation Programs
**Degrees Offered:** Certificate
**Majors Offered:** Horse Shoeing
**Tuition Costs:** $4,000 (textbook and shoeing tools included in tuition); $500 housing
**Description of Program:** Classes meet for eight hours a day, five days a week for eight weeks, and include a combination of lecture, shop, and practical shoeing. Students handle horses and tools from the first week of school and continue with as much hands-on experience as time allows throughout the course. Hand-forged shoes are fabricated for corrective and therapeutic shoeing as students study anatomy, physiology, and the conformation of the horse. The motivated student has virtually unlimited opportunities to shoe a wide variety of horses under the supervision of an experienced instructor. The student-to-teacher ratio is low, allowing for individualized feedback and instruction that includes customer relations, business practice, and other skills necessary for students to successfully begin their own businesses. Instruction includes but is not limited to the following subjects: equine anatomy and physiology, equine conformation, correctional shoeing, equine congenital and environmental problems and causes, practical and physiological shoeing, blacksmithing and forging, and business practices.
**Facilities:** Comfortable classroom in addition to a spacious and fully-equipped workshop. The school maintains rental accommodations for male and female students that include satellite TV, full kitchen facilities, pool, and spa.
**Classroom/Hands-On Equine Classes:** 20:80

## Stevenson School

Director of Admission, Stevenson School, 3152 Forest Lake Road, Pebble Beach, CA 93953. Phone: (831) 625-8309. Fax: (831) 625-5208. Email: info@rlstevenson.org.
**Accreditation:** Western Association of Schools and Colleges, National Association of Independent Schools member, California Association of Independent Schools, Council for Advancement and Support of Education, Secondary School Admission Test Board, National Association for College Admission Counseling
**Tuition Costs:** $31,550 Boarding; $18,850 Day
**Description of Program:** Lower/Middle School day students only; Upper School day and boarding students

## The Thacher School

5025 Thacher Road, Ojai, CA 93023. Contact: Monique DeVane, Director of Admission and Financial Aid. Phone: (805) 640-3210. Fax: (805) 640-9377.
Email: admission@thacher.org.
**Degrees Offered:** High School Diploma

## Traditional Equitation School

c/o The Los Angeles Equestrian Center, 480 Riverside Drive, Burbank, CA 91506.
Phone: (818) 569-3666. Fax: (818) 549-1128. Email: info@tes-laec.com.
**Degrees Offered:** BHS Certificate, Working Student
**Majors Offered:** Stages 1-4, Assistant Instructor, Intermediate Stable Manager, Intermediate Instructor, Stable Manager, Instructor, Fellowship of the British Horse Society

## University of California–Davis

Animal Science, University of California–Davis, One Shields Ave., Davis, CA 95616-8521. Contact: Dr. Janet Roser. Phone: (530) 752-2918. Fax: (530) 752-0175.
Email: jfroser@ucdavis.edu.
UCD Equestrian Center, University of California-Davis, Equestrian Lane, Davis, CA 95616. Contact: Holly Fox, Program Manager. Phone: (530) 752-2372. Fax: (530)752-3192. Email: wcpayne@ucdavis.edu Website: campus recreation.ucdavis.edu.
**Accreditation:** Western Association of Schools and Colleges
**Degrees Offered:** Bachelor of Science, Master of Science, Doctor of Philosophy, Doctor of Veterinary Medicine
**Majors Offered:** Animal Science with Equine concentration (B.S., M.S.), Animal Science and Management with Equine concentration (B.S., M.S.), Physiology (Ph.D.), Veterinary Medicine (D.V.M.)
**Tuition Cost:** In-state: $6,437 per year; out-of-state: $20,647 per year; room and board $8,202 per year; horse board: $195-295/month; eight group lessons: $135/quarter
**Description of Program:** Candidates accepted in the M.S. or Ph.D. programs in Animal Science, Physiology, or Endocrinology are eligible to specialize in equine reproductive endocrinology research conducted by Dr. Roser, whose research focus is endocrine regulation of fertility in the mare and stallion. Students in the B.S. degree program can specialize in equine sciences in both the AS and ASM. Equine courses that satisfy the specialization are Horse Husbandry, Advance Horse Production and Management, Equine Exercise Physiology, Equine Nutrition, Farrier Science, Equine Enterprise Management, and Advanced Equine Reproduction. Advanced Horse Production and Management and Farrier Science include lecture and laboratories. There are also a number of internship programs that students can take. Two of these internships courses take six months to complete and prepare students for a career as a stud or broodmare manager. Students learn how to handle stallions for breeding, and learn to breed and foal out mares. The UC Davis Equestrian Center offers recreational and competitive horseback riding lessons in English and western disciplines. Horse shows, trail rides, summer youth camps, lease horses, clinics, work exchange program, Guardian Angel program, and special activities are offered. Employment for student staff includes instructors, barn supervisors, feeders, maintenance and stall cleaners.
**Facilities:** Located on main campus and on central bike trail. Facility includes 25 acres, 200ft x 250ft main jumping arena, small jumping arena, western arena, large dressage court, round pen, and large irrigated grass riding field with limited cross country

jumps, and track. Several turn out paddocks are available. Arena footing consists of sand/rubber mixture. Facility houses approximately 120 horses, 60 which are lesson horses and 60 are privately owned and boarded horses. Stalls, pipe pens and dry lot pastures available.

**Classroom/Hands-On For Equine Courses:** 18/2 courses

**Showing:** IHSA (Intercollegiate Horse Show Association) Hunter / Jumper and Western Team, IDA (Intercollegiate Dressage Association) Team, and Eventing Teams form Competitive Sports Club.

## University of California—Santa Barbara

West Campus Stables, P.O. Box 14082, Santa Barbara, CA 93107.
Contact: Karinna Hurley. Phone: (805) 893-4208. Email: fizzdorado@yahoo.com.
**Accreditation:** Western Association of Schools and Colleges
**Degrees Offered:** Bachelors, Masters, Doctorate
**Majors Offered:** No equine majors
**Tuition Costs:** $3,300/year; $5,000/year room and board; $165/month horse board
**Description of Program:** Student-run boarding stable on UCSB's campus. The stable is managed by a student group, the Horse Boarders Association (HBA). Heading the group is the Executive Board, consisting of a Chairperson, Treasurer, and Secretary. These officers are elected by the HBA membership each October. Board includes alfalfa hay, forage hay, grass hay, and two bags of pellets per month, if needed. The club is run on a co-op basis. The university does not provide funding and members are responsible as a group for all operating and maintenance costs, including damage and repairs as needed. Each member is responsible for feeding and cleaning on a daily basis (small-group feed schedules are formed and work study students can be hired for stall cleaning during the school year). In addition, members must do four chores a month, four work hours a quarter, and hay barn duty on a rotation roster. Membership meetings are held monthly, and all members are encouraged to attend. There are two mandatory vet clinics per year and worming takes place every three months—all horses must participate in this schedule.
**Facilities:** Large jumping arena, two smaller arenas, round pen, beach and trail access, turnouts, 24 stalls with paddocks.
**Showing:** Some individual students go to shows.

**Website:**
www.ucsb.edu

**Type of School:**
Public University

# *COLORADO*

## Aspen Equine Studies, Inc.

5821 County Road 331 Silt, CO. Phone: (970) 876-5839.
Email: aspenequine@yahoo.com.
**Accreditation:** International Massage and Movement Schools Association, Kathy Duncan is approved by the National Certification Board for Therapeutic Massage and Bodywork (NCBTMB) as a continuing education Approved Provider
**Degrees Offered:** Certificate
**Majors Offered:** Equine Massage Therapy, Equine Sports Trainer, Hydrotherapy
**Tuition Costs:** $995 EMT (on site), $199 (home study), $95 EST (home study), $35 Hydrotherapy course (home study)
**Description of Program:** Courses are written by Kathy Duncan NCTMB, who has

**Website:**
www.equinemassageschool.com

**Type of School:**
Specialty School, Independent Study

been a health and fitness educator since 1976, and a lifetime horsewoman. Her thorough programs include many facets of horsemanship, including conformation, behavior, injury rehabilitation, and proper athletic training. Students are instructed in the methods of training and rehabilitation used by Kathy Duncan in her 19 year practice in Aspen, Colorado. Kathy Duncan is a member of the International Massage Association, International Fitness Association, Colorado Horse Council, the American Society of Equine Appraisers, and the International Massage & Movement Schools Association. ◆ Massage Therapy: Courses include conformation, study of muscles and joints and their movements, strokes and technique, and stretching. Sports Trainer: Course includes musculoskeletal function, specificity training, strength and endurance training, interval and cross training, stretching / flexibility, and optimum physical fitness. **Facilities:** Home Study, or small ranch in Silt, Colorado

## Bel-Rea Institute of Animal Technology

**Website:**
www.bel-rea.com

**Type of School:**
Technical School

1681 S. Dayton, Denver, CO 80231. Phone: (303) 751-8700 or (800) 950-8001. Email: admissions@bel-rea.com.
**Degrees Offered:** Associate of Applied Science
**Majors Offered:** Veterinary Technology

## Butler Graduate Farrier Training

**Website:**
www.farrierfocus.com

**Type of School:**
Specialty School

Doug Butler Enterprises, Inc., P.O. Box 1390, La Porte, CO 80535. Phone: (800) 728-3826. Fax: (970) 482-8621. Email: products@farrierfocus.com.
**Majors Offered:** Farrier
**Tuition Costs:** Varies
**Description of Program:** Customized program for individualized needs. Advanced skills training programs have been designed to fit your busy schedule by providing you several learning options. You may apply for One-On-One Training, where you receive undivided attention, hands-on instruction, and mentoring. You may want to attend or host a Small Group Workshop or Large Group Seminar held at your location. Or, choose a self-study collection, where you work at your own pace to achieve the mastery level you desire. Dr. Butler has dedicated more than 35 years of his life to studying, teaching, writing, and learning from expert farriers around the world. Farriers who have received advanced training with Dr. Butler have found that his educational style transcends the traditional classroom learning experience. His practical, hands-on approach to training has helped farriers build successful careers and solid incomes. Invest in your future by taking the next step with one of Dr. Butler's Advanced Skills Training programs. You'll gain confidence, expand your skills, and increase your income as you advance through the mastery skills levels.

## Colorado School of Trades

**Website:**
www.schooloftrades.com

**Type of School:**
Specialty School

1575 Hoyt Street, Lakewood, CO 80215. Phone: (303) 233-4697 or (800) 234-4594. Fax: (303) 233-4723.
**Accreditation:** Approved for Veteran's Training
**Degrees Offered:** Certificate
**Majors Offered:** Farrier Science
**Tuition Costs:** Ask school; financial aid available
**Description of Program:** Four months. The program uses hands-on techniques to

teach you all aspects of the farrier business, from anatomy to keg shoes, from corrective shoeing to handmade shoes, including the necessary forge work and everything in between. This program is designed for the serious student. Much of the lab work is performed on live animals located either in the fully equipped farrier shop, or on location–the school has many customers in the Denver/Boulder/Golden area. If the animals can't come to the school, the mobile farrier shop will go to them! This program teaches the craft through hands-on techniques, not just classroom work.

**Facilities:** Housing not provided (school will assist in locating housing)

**Classroom/Hands-On Equine Classes:** 65/550 hours

## Colorado State University

Equine Sciences Program, Colorado State University, Fort Collins, CO 80523. Email: equinesc@colostate.edu.

**Degrees Offered:** Certificate, Bachelor of Science, Master of Science, Doctor of Philosophy, Doctor of Veterinary Medicine

**Majors Offered:** Farrier (C), Equine Science (B.S.), Animal Science–Physiology (M.S., Ph.D.), Veterinary Medicine (D.V.M.)

> **Website:**
> www.csuequine.com
>
> **Type of School:**
> Public University
>
>

## Doubletree Horse Farm Breeding Management School

800-1400 Lane, Delta, CO 81416. Contact: Carl Wood, Director. Phone: (970) 874-7456. Fax: (970) 874-8391. Email: doubletree@tds.net.

**Degrees Offered:** Certificate of Completion

**Majors Offered:** Equine Breeding Management

**Tuition Costs:** $550; housing, meals, and transportation extra

**Description of Program:** A one-week, short course covering all aspects of a breeding facility. Maximum class size is twelve. Stallion and Mare Management. Collecting, evaluating, and shipping semen. Mare management including use of hormonal drugs, understanding anatomy, ultrasound technology, Artificial Insemination, the foaling mare and newborn, and use of equipment needed. The course also covers business management, advertising, taxes, hiring, and much more. Courses offered in February, April, May, and November each year. After the course has been completed, students are encouraged to contact the school anytime about problems they encounter, or about new technology.

**Facilities:** Doubletree Horse Farm is a working facility standing ten or more stallions.

**Classroom/Hands-On Equine Classes:** Over 36 hours of instruction, about half in the classroom

> **Website:**
> www.dbthorses.com
>
> **Type of School:**
> Specialty School

## Equitouch® Systems

PO Box 7701, Loveland, CO 80537. Phone: (800) 483-0577. Email: equitouch1@aol.com.

**Degrees Offered:** 150-Hour Certificate

**Majors Offered:** Equine Sports Massage Therapist

**Tuition Costs:** Equitouch Equine Anatomy Studies Primer (home study): $37.95; Equitouch ten-day onsite course: $1,595

**Description of Program:** Class size is normally four to six students with a four-to-one student/instructor ratio to ensure individualized instruction. Upon completion of this course, you will be trained to begin a business in equine massage therapy. You will be

> **Website:**
> www.equitouch.net
>
> **Type of School:**
> Specialty School, Independent Study

able to identify and discuss major muscles and muscle groups. You'll also understand how muscles work and what can cause problems in the equine musculature. You'll spend an extensive amount of time learning hands-on massage, various strokes, application techniques, and theory. The unique, hands-on lecture series allows you to learn and comprehend more than you would believe possible. The 150-hour program has been accepted by several fully accredited universities for full semester credit, and students from those institutions can apply that credit toward their bachelor or master degrees.

**Facilities:** Lazy J Bar S Ranch : a working training & boarding facility with more than 80 horses, barns with a heated indoor arena, 100ft x 250ft outdoor arena, regulation dressage arena, driving arena, jumping arena, limited cross country, regulation 5/8-mile race track, and approximately eight miles of riding trails. Housing for students is not provided.

**Classroom/Hands-On Equine Classes:** 30 percent / 70 percent

**Website:**
www.fvs.edu

**Type of School:**
Secondary School

## Fountain Valley School

Colorado Springs, CO 80911. Contact: Kilian Forgus, Director of Admissions.
Phone: (719) 390-7035. Fax: (719) 390-7762. Email: admis@fvs.edu.
**Degrees Offered:** High School Diploma

**Website:**
www.johnlyons.com

**Type of School:**
Specialty School

## John Lyons Certification Program

John Lyons Symposiums, Inc., 8714 County Road 300, Parachute, CO 81635.
Contact: Linda Wingstrom, Certification and Select Trainer Director.
Phone: (970) 285-9797. Fax: (970) 285-7530. Email: select@johnlyons.com.
**Accreditation:** Recognized by the Veterans Administration
**Majors Offered:** John and Josh Lyons Certified Trainer
**Tuition Costs:** $18,000 for the full program ($1,500 a week). Traveling expenses, lodging, food, etc., are your responsibility. Portable box stalls will be provided. Stall fees are $10 per day per stall. Feed and bedding for your horses during your stay will be your responsibility.
**Description of Program:** The program is twelve weeks. Participants will bring two horses for the entire program: two broke horses or one broke horse and one unbroke horse. The broke horses must be able to be ridden on a trail ride safely. Horses must be able to walk, trot, and canter; it is not necessary for them to be able to pick up both leads, but that would be ideal. Age is not important, but they both need to be in good health and sound. Stallions are not suggested for these programs. No student under nineteen years of age accepted. Group size is limited to fifteen students per program. It is strongly suggested that all students be familiar with all of the printed materials and videos that this program offers. While not mandatory, it will help you to understand the material, give you the best opportunity to make the program of optimal value, you will move forward faster, and more information will then be covered. This is a very exclusive, educational equine program. Since there are many people who would like to participate in this program and only a limited number of students are accepted, your total commitment to the program is essential.

## Lamar Community College

Horse Training and Management, Lamar Community College, 2401 South Main,

Lamar, CO 81052.   Contact: J.J. Rydberg.. Phone: (719) 336-1590 or (800) 968-6920.
Fax: (719) 336-2448. Email: JJ.Rydberg@lamarcc.edu.
**Accreditation:** North Central Association of Colleges and Secondary Schools
**Degrees offered:** Certificate, Associate of Applied Science, Associate of General Studies
**Majors Offered:** Horse Training and Management, concentration in Trainer or Horsemanship/Management
**Tuition Costs:** In-state: $66.05/credit; out-of-state: $276.10/credit; room and board: $4,470
**Description of Program:** Western style taught. The HTM program offers two options; both are designed to provide the knowledge and experience needed to be successful in the equine industry. Students may pursue either a Horse Trainer or Horsemanship/Management program of study. Classroom and practical laboratory experiences are provided through the program courses in both option areas. Classroom courses in the horse trainer option provide the student the opportunity to learn the physiology of the horse, horse evaluation and selection, stable management, nutrition, diseases, and breeding practices. Lab experiences progress from an "un-broke" horse to green broke to more advanced and specialized stages of training. Students are also provided with a foal to halter break. Classroom courses in the horsemanship/management option provide the student the opportunity to learn the physiology, basic care and training of gentle broke horses, horse evaluation and selection, fundamentals of riding instruction, business, business management, and equine management courses. An internship, required in the spring semester of the sophomore year, gives the student the opportunity to participate in a supervised work experience in the horse industry prior to graduation. Students help to acquire the internships in the areas of their special training interests.
**Facilities:** The equestrian center is a quarter-mile from campus. Seventy-four stalls, one indoor arena (95ft x 175ft), two outdoor arenas (300ft x 150ft), seven round pens, and trails. Prominent breeders from Colorado, Oklahoma, Kansas, Nebraska, Texas, and New Mexico furnish high-quality horses for students to train.
**Classroom/Hands-On Equine Courses:** 26/35 (A.S.), 7/1 (C)
**Showing:** Judging team, rodeo

**Website:**
www.lamarcc.edu

**Type of School:**
Community College

# Lowell Whiteman School

42605 RCR 36, Steamboat Springs, CO 80487. Phone: (970) 879-1350 Ext. 15.
Fax: (970) 879-0506. Email: admissions@whiteman.edu.
**Accreditation:** Association of Colorado Independent Schools, National Association of Independent Schools member
**Degrees Offered:** High School Diploma
**Tuition Costs:** $28,120 boarding; $14,935 day
**Description of Program:** Lowell Whiteman is a high school for 9-12 graders. Each fall, Lowell Whiteman students have the option of participating in a program that has been in place for more than 45 years and is part of the school's enduring romantic western heritage. Founder Lowell Whiteman once said, "One of the best experiences you can give students is to put them in the saddle and show them the Rocky Mountains on horseback. They'll never forget it.....They will soon have a wonderful appreciation of their own abilities, horses, and the American West." Back in the early days of the Lowell Whiteman School, Whiteman required each and every student to learn to ride. "There is nothing like a horse to teach kids all about themselves." Today, the horse program is one of many activities offered, but its magical tradition remains. All riding abilities are welcome and beginners are given instruction in all the basics. Both West-

**Website:**
www.whiteman.edu

**Type of School:**
College-Preparatory
Secondary School

ern and English (if there are enough students interested) styles of riding are offered. Though the program concentrates on trail riding four days a week, the program also involves some arena work, a gymkhana, and a fall pack trip.

**Showing:** Gymkhana

## New Horizons Equine Education Center, Inc.

**Website:**
www.newhorizonsequine.com

**Type of School:**
Specialty School,
Independent Study

New Horizons Equine Education Center, Inc., 425 Red Mountain Rd., Livermore, CO 80536. Phone: (970) 484-9207. Email: nheec@frii.com.

**Accreditation:** Approved by American Paint Horse Association, American Quarter Horse Association, Appaloosa Horse Club, International Arabian Horse Association

**Degrees Offered:** Certificate of Achievement

**Majors Offered:** General Equine Science, American Paint Horse General Equine Science, American Quarter Horse General Equine Science, Appaloosa Horse General Equine Science, Arabian Horse General Equine Science

**Tuition Costs:** New Student Enrollment Fee: $35; individual courses: $48-75; entire series: $450; Equine Science Youth Series: $45

**Description of Program:** The most comprehensive equine education available through the mail today. Whether you are new to the horse world or have years of experience, you will find just the right courses to help you achieve your equestrian goals. A successful series of courses to guide you, step-by-step, from the basics in horsemanship through the more advanced principles of equine management has been designed. Whether you are preparing for a career with horses or simply want to improve your equestrian skills, education will be the key to your success. Offered curriculums: Equine Science Series, Young Equestrian Series, Careers in the Horse Industry, Understanding Equine Behavior, Establishing Training Goals, Showing Courses, Tailoring Courses, Stable Management, Breeding Courses, First Aid Courses, Quarter Horse Series, Appaloosa Series, Arabian Series, Paint Series, and more!

**Facilities:** Your own backyard.

## North American Riding for the Handicapped Association, Inc.

**Website:**
www.narha.org

**Type of School:**
Specialty School

P.O. Box 33150, Denver, CO 80233. Phone: (800) 369-7433. Fax: (303) 252-4610. Email: narha@narha.org. The following locations offer a therapeutic riding instructor training course that has been approved by NARHA: *Equest Center for Therapeutic Horsemanship*, Lili Kellogg, 2902 Swiss Avenue, Dallas, TX 75204, (972) 412-1099. *High Hopes Therapeutic Riding Inc.*, Kitty Stalsburg, P.O. Box 254, 36 Town Woods Rd., Old Lyme, CT 06371, (860) 434-1974. *St. Andrews College*, Lorrie Renker, 1700 Dogwood Mile, Laurinburg, NC 28352, (910) 277-5243. *Fran Joswick Therapeutic Riding Center*, Anthony Busacca, 26284 Oso Rd., San Juan Capistrano, CA 92675, (949) 240-8441. *Centenary College*, Octavia Brown, 400 Jefferson Street, Hackettstown, NJ 07840, (908) 852-1400 x2174.

**Accreditation:** North American Riding for the Handicapped Association, Inc.

**Degrees Offered:** Certification

**Majors Offered:** Registered Instructor, Advanced Instructor, Master Instructor

**Tuition Costs:** NARHA membership: $45 per year; Instructor Certification application: $40; NARHA Approved Training Courses: $800-$1,000; NARHA Registered On-Site Workshop and Certification: $300 and up

**Description of Program:** The following are the options for becoming a NARHA Certified Instructor at the Registered Level. Option A: Attend and successfully complete a

NARHA Approved Training Course which satisfies all certification process requirements. Option B: A new multi-step certification process that culminates in successfully completing an On-Site Workshop and Certification. One of the advantages of the new process is that applicants can proceed at their own pace and that the actual certification can be attained in one weekend following a series of self paced preparatory steps. Phase One: The following needs to be completed within six months. Send in NARHA Instructor Certification application and fee. Join NARHA with individual membership of $45. Complete the NARHA Center Accreditation Training Course (CAT) in person or on-line at the NARHA Campus. Complete NARHA Instructor Self-Study on-line or via hard copy. Achieve First Aid/CPR certification. Request open book exam from NARHA (hard copy or electronically). Applicant has now achieved Instructor-in-Training status and has twelve months to complete the next part of the process. Phase Two: A) Accumulate and record 25 hours of practice teaching in therapeutic horsemanship under the guidance of a NARHA Certified Instructor. B) Attend and successfully pass NARHA Registered On-Site Workshop and Certification.

**Facilities:** Across the U.S.A; centers located in California, Connecticut, New Jersey, North Carolina, and Texas

## Northeastern Junior College

Equine Department, Northeastern Junior College, 100 College Drive, Sterling, CO 80751. Phone: (970) 522-6931. Contact: Ken Amen, Director of Equine Sciences. Email: Ken.Amen@njc.cccoes.edu.

**Accreditation:** North Central Association of Colleges and Schools.
**Degrees Offered:** Associate of Applied Science, Associate of Science
**Majors Offered:** Equine Management (A.A.S.), Equine Science (A.S.)
**Tuition Costs:** In-state: $67/unit; out-of-state: $238/unit; room and board: $2,600
**Description of Program:** Five instructed rides per week. The Equine Management program is designed to provide the students with the basic skills and background knowledge necessary for entry-level employment as trainers and assistant trainers in the horse industry. This two-year program provides students access to the business, economic, technical, and general education classes necessary to become competent managers. Practical experience is provided in many of the classes as well as in the internship portion of the program. The Equine Science program has two concentrations: the Industry Concentration and the Science Concentration. The Industry Concentration prepares students to transfer and prepare for careers in the training and production sectors of the industry. The Science Concentration is designed to prepare students for graduate degrees after they have completed their bachelor-level program.
**Facilities:** The equestrian center is one mile from campus. Forty school horses, one indoor arena (280ft x 140ft), two outdoor arenas (300ft x 150ft), track, three round pens.
**Classroom/Hands-On Equine Courses:** 2:1
**Showing:** Judging Team

**Website:**
www.nejc.cc.co.us

**Type of School:**
Community College

## Pat Parelli International Study Center

P.O. Box 3729, Pagosa Springs, CO 81147. Phone: (800) 642-3335 or (970) 731-9400. Email: pnhusa@parelli.com
**Degrees Offered:** Certificate
**Majors Offered:** Level 1: Partnership; Level 2: Harmony; Level 3: Refinement; Level 4: Versatility

**Website:**
www.parelli.com

**Type of School:**
Specialty School

**Tuition Costs:** Courses taught by Parelli range from $2,500-$10,000. Courses taught by a PNH Instructor range from $1,300-$3,500. Course fees include feed and pen for one horse. All meals and housing included in course fee.

**Description of Program:** Young Horses & Difficult Horses; the Horsemanship Experience. Level 1: Partnership: Seven Games, Zone-ology, The Four Phases, Independent Seat, Focus, Lateral Flexion, Direct/Indirect Rein, Ground Skills, Trailer Loading, Challenge Course, Equine Psychology, Natural Riding Principles. Level 2: Harmony: The Four Savvys, On Line (22'), Liberty, Freestyle, Finesse, Equine Relationship Skills, Natural Riding Principles, Four Responsibilities of the Horses, Achieving True Impulsion, Harmony, Positive Reflexes, Canter Leads, Simple Lead Changes, Flying Lead Changes, Supporting Rein, Diagonals, The Soft Feel, Beginning Bridle-less Riding, Bit and Spur Savvy, Trailer Loading, Challenge Courses, Lectures, Demonstrations, Riding Sessions. Level 3: Refinement: The Four Savvys, On Line (45'), Advanced Liberty, FreeStyle, Finesse, Refinement, The Soft Feel, Bridle-less Riding, Refined Simple and Flying Lead Changes, Lateral Maneuvers, Lateral Skill, Vertical Flexion, Foundations for Cow-Working, Jumping, Dressage, Reining, Advanced Trailer Loading, Horse Psychology and Behavior, Challenge Course, Tournaments, Demonstrations, Riding Sessions. Level 4: Versatility: Advancing the Four Savvys, One Line, Liberty, FreeStyle, Finesse Exploring Collection and Engagement, Performance Patterns, Laying Horses Down, Flexion Zone by Zone. The Savvy Forum, Horseman's Savvy Conference. PNH Instructors teach the one- and two-week lower level courses. Parelli teaches the higher-level courses.

**Facilities:** Main lodge with dining rooms, bathrooms, shared cabins, horse pens, tack barns, challenge course, obstacles, 90 acres of riding meadows, arenas, playground, liberty complex, round corrals, ponds, and water challenges. You can bring your own horse or lease a horse from the study center. You must bring your own PNH equipment.

**Website:**
www.ppcc.edu

**Type of School:**
Community College

## Pikes Peak Community College

5675 South Academy Boulevard, Colorado Springs, CO 80906. Phone: (800) 456-6847. Fax: (719) 540-7092. Email: admissions@ppcc.cccoes.edu.

**Accreditation:** North Central Association (NCA) of Colleges and Schools
**Degrees Offered:** Certificate
**Majors Offered:** Farrier, Master Farrier
**Tuition Costs:** In-state: $64.05/credit; out-of-state: $319.40/credit
**Description of Program:** This program is designed for military personnel and private horse owners, as well as those aspiring to become commercial farrier. Enrollment is open to the general public. Students must have average skill in handling horses, and possess a general knowledge of using ordinary hand tools. The master farrier option is open to qualified farriers who wish to become exceptionally proficient in this occupation. Students must possess qualities that assure future success as a craftsman in the field.
**Facilities:** Local stables and ranches
**Classroom/Hands-On Equine Classes:** 15/67.5 hours per class

**Website:**
www.equinemassagecollege.com

**Type of School:**
Specialty School

## Prairie Winds Equine Massage Therapy College

Contact: Sara or Michael Stenson. Phone: (970) 568-3986. Fax: (970)568-3987. Email: mstenson@prairiewinds.com.
**Accreditation:** Colorado Department of Higher Education Division of Private Occupational Schools

**Degrees Offered:** Certificate
**Majors Offered**: Equine Massage Therapy
**Tuition Costs:** Contact school
**Description of Program:** Certified Equine Massage Therapist program (320 hours): To start and grow an equine massage practice you must be able to make demonstrable changes, speak intelligently with customers, vets, trainers and other equine professionals and have sound business and effective marketing plans. The curriculum includes: Shiatsu & Myofascial Release Massage taught by Sara Stenson (CMT), Anatomy taught by Harline Larkey (ESMT), Anatomy of Equine Movement by both Sara & Harline, Pathophysiology of Pain co-taught by Pam Muhonen (DVM, Faculty Colorado State University Veterinarian College Alternative Therapies Program) and Karen Riedlinger (DVM), Hoof Anatomy & Care by a Brian Buckner (Certified Journeyman Farrier), Horse Quieting by Rick Noffsinger (horse trainer), and How To Start & Grow Your Equine Business by Michael Stenson, who teaches students to apply management and marketing principles so graduates finish the program with personal entrepreneurial spirit development, business and marketing plans in hand. Prairie Winds also offers Professional Development classes for farriers, barn managers, veterinarians & assistants, horse trainers, chiropractors, massage therapists and other equine professionals in courses such as Saddle Fitting, Homeopathy, Hoof Care & Anatomy, and Business, etc.
**Facilities:** Classes are held in a variety of regional barns and in classrooms adjoining a veterinarian clinic near Wellington, Colorado, some of the most scenic territory in the state.
**Classroom/Hands-On Equine Classes:** 30/70 theory to practice

# CONNECTICUT

## Ethel Walker School

Riding Program, Ethel Walker School, Bushy Hill Road, Simsbury, CT 06070. Contact: Rick Caldwell. Phone: (860) 658-4467. Fax: (860) 658-6763.
**Degrees Offered:** High School Diploma

**Website:**
www.ethelwalker.org

**Type of School:**
Private 7-12 All-Girls Grade School

## Equi-Myo Training Program

249 Mountain Rd., North Granby, CT 06060. Contact: Margie Amster-Herr or Charles E. Herr. Phone: (800) 523-2876. Fax: (860) 653-4224. Email: info@equimyo.com.
**Degrees Offered:** Certificate
**Majors Offered:** Trigger Point Myotherapy

**Website:**
www.equimyo.com

**Type of School:**
Specialty School

## Kent School

P.O. Box 2006, Kent, CT 06757. Phone: (800) 538-5368 or (860) 927-6111. Fax: (860) 927-6109.
**Degrees Offered:** High School Diploma
**Tuition Costs:** $25,000 day school; $31,900 boarding school; $2,200 per term (3 terms per year) for Riding Lesson Program using Kent School Horses; $1,100 per term for Board/Lesson Program; $800 per month board
**Description of Program:** Maximum program size is 28 students. The program is filled

**Website:**
www.kent-school.edu

**Type of School:**
Private Secondary School

on a first come first serve basis and students ride six afternoons per week. The program fulfills the athletic requirement.

**Facilities:** Large heated indoor arena (100ft x 200ft), small attached heated indoor (50ft x 100ft), two sand/rubber footing outdoor rings, one grass hunter field, and one grass grand prix field.

**Showing:** Three USEA rated events per year hosted on grounds.

## The Taft School

Watertown, CT 06795. Contact: Frederick H. Wandelt III, Director of Admissions. Phone: (860) 945-7777. Fax: (860) 945-7808. Email: admissions@taftschool.org.
**Degrees Offered:** High School Diploma

## Teikyo Post University

Equine Department, Teikyo Post University, 800 Country Club Rd., P.O. Box 2540, Waterbury, CT 06723. Contact: Carole Baker, Director of Equine Programs.
Phone: (800) 345-2562 x4631 or (203) 596-4631. Fax: (203) 596-4695.
Email: cbaker@teikyopost.edu or equine@teikyopost.edu.
**Accreditation:** North Eastern Association of Schools and Colleges, Inc., Connecticut Department of Higher Education.
**Degrees Offered:** Certificate, Minor, Associate of Science, Bachelor of Science
**Majors Offered:** Equine Law (C), Equine Studies (C, A.S.), Equine Management (B.S.), Therapeutic Riding Instructor (C), Trigger Point Equine Myotherapy (C)
**Tuition Cost:** $565 per credit; $7,375 room and board; $550 student service fee; $975 per riding course
**Description of Program:** English: Balanced seat, dressage, and combined training styles taught. Equine Management Degree combines equine studies with course work in business administration to teach students the skills required for the care and management of horses and the efficient running of an equine-related business. Equine subjects include all aspects of proper horse care and stable management, anatomy and nutrition, ethical treatment of horses, up-to-date veterinary information, instructor training, and hands-on opportunities for each student. A variety of business courses provide a solid grounding in management. ◆ Equine Studies Degree prepares students for a career in the equine field. They learn the specialized knowledge and practical skills required to safely and competently care for and manage horses. Students improve their own skills while learning to teach basic horsemanship and riding skills to others effectively and safely. Basic educational concept courses complement this program. Study Abroad: Juniors and seniors who opt for this excellent addition to the program will spend four months (from end of August to middle of December) at one of England's top colleges or equestrian centers specializing in preparing students for internationally recognized professional examinations run by the British Horse Society.
**Facilities:** Equestrian center is ten miles from campus. Nine school horses, one indoor arena (80ft x 100ft), one outdoor arena (200ft x 100ft), grass turnout, trails.
**Classroom/Hands-On Equine courses:** 9/8, plus Internships/Co-ops
**Showing:** IHSA and IDA

## University of Connecticut

Animal Science, University of Connecticut, 3636 Horsebarn Road Ext., Box U- 4040,

Storrs, CT 06269-4040. Contact: Jennifer Simoniello. Email: anscimail@uconn.edu.
**Accreditation:** New England Association of Schools and Colleges
**Degrees Offered:** Associate of Applied Science, Bachelor of Science, Master of Science, Doctor of Philosophy
**Majors Offered:** Animal Science with Equine option
**Tuition Costs:** In-state: $13,688/year; out-of-state: $24,472/year; horse activities and teams extra
**Description of Program:** Animal Science students work with animals and learn the basic sciences of genetics, physiology, nutrition, health, and behavior. Courses offered: Developing the Driving Horse, Pleasure Horse Appreciation and Use, Horse Science, Light Horse Training and Management, Methods of Equitation Instruction, Horse Breeding Farm Management, Horse Selection and Evaluation, Advanced Animal and Product Evaluation, Equine Podology, and Farrier Science. Because the department believes that practical experience is important for professional development and educational improvement, there are many activities available to students. The Horse Practicum is a professional improvement, non-credit activity designed to increase the total experience and job competitiveness of Animal Science and other UConn majors with a strong interest in horses. Students ride hunt seat, Western, dressage and saddle seat, from beginner to advanced levels. Students are required to attend monthly meetings where guest speakers and demonstrations expose students to various aspects of the horse industry. The Polo Practicum is a non-credit, extracurricular riding program that offers beginner through advanced lessons in polo techniques and strategy. Students can ride at least once a week in the indoor arena. Students can also participate on the Polo Team, the Equestrian Team, the Drill Team, and the Horse Judging Team.
**Facilities:** Approximately 85 horses; the school specializes in the breeding of Morgans. Horse Unit I: Main horse barn with 55 stalls and a classroom. Horse Unit II: Research barn with classroom, laboratory and stalls, lighted outdoor arena (100ft x 220ft), Ratcliffe Hicks heated indoor arena (60ft x 120ft), large indoor arena (120ft x 220ft), outdoor training arena, turnout sheds, and paddocks. UConn maintains more than twenty polo horses, with tack and equipment provided for students participating in the Polo Practicum.
**Classroom/Hands-On Equine Classes:** 40:60
**Showing:** IHSA, Polo Team, Judging Team, Show Team, Drill Team, Vaulting Team, and Eventing Team

## Woodcock Hill Riding Academy, Inc.

17 Marsh Road, Willington, CT 06279. Phone: (860) 487-1686.
**Degrees Offered:** Certificate
**Majors Offered:** Instructor

**Type of School:**
Specialty School

# *DELAWARE*

## University of Delaware

Department of Animal and Food Science, Townsend Hall, Newark, DE 19717-1303.
Contact: Dr. David Marshall. Phone: (302) 831-2524 or (302) 831-1340.
Email: 93564@udel.edu.

**Website:**
www.udel.edu

**Type of School:**
Public Land Grant University

**Accreditation:** Middle States Association of Colleges and Secondary Schools
**Degrees Offered:** Bachelor of Science, Master of Science, Doctor of Philosophy
**Majors Offered:** Animal Science
**Tuition Costs:** Resident: $5,890/year; nonresident: $15,420/year
**Description of Program:** UD has several equine courses as part of the Animal Science major including courses in equine reproduction, health, lameness and management. The University has a nationally-ranked equestrian team—English and western.
**Facilities:** Indoor arena. There is a 350-acre teaching and research complex right on campus; classes can move from classroom to farm, from laboratory to barn in a matter of minutes. The "resident animals" include poultry, horses, sheep, swine, beef cattle, and a dairy herd, all of which are used regularly in teaching and research. The equine herd includes fifteen to twenty Haflinger mares and foals that are used in courses and laboratories.
**Showing:** IHSA, open shows

# FLORIDA

**Website:**
www.americanhorsepubs.org

**Type of School:**
Internship

## American Horse Publications Internship Program

AHP, 49 Spinnaker Circle, South Daytona, FL 32119. Contact: Christine W. Brune, Executive Director. Phone: (386) 760-7743. Fax: (386) 760-7728.
Email: ahorsepubs@aol.com.
**Degrees Offered:** Internship
**Description of Program:** Established in 1970, American Horse Publications is a national professional association of more than 300 publishers, individuals, businesses, and organizations serving the equine publishing industry. The AHP Internship Program is designed specifically for college students who have an interest in horses and seek a career in equine publishing. This program offers opportunities for students to work at equine publications and businesses throughout the country, and the opportunity for AHP members to utilize the talents of students with an interest in equine publishing. The AHP Internship Handbook includes a directory of AHP members participating in the AHP Internship Program. Each listing includes the types of internships offered, availability throughout the year and duration, selection requirements, and duties involved. These may vary according to each AHP member's needs. Some offer salaries, stipends, or college credit as compensation. Most do not provide housing for interns, although some do offer housing search assistance. In all cases, transportation, as well as room and board. are the responsibility of the intern. AHP functions solely as the umbrella organization for the internship program. Interns must apply to the individual AHP member, and each participating AHP member will choose its own interns based on its needs and the intern's completed application package. In every case, however, strong consideration is given to publication journalism or production experience, as well as an interest in the horse industry. The 2004 AHP Handbook and application are available at the AHP website.

**Website:**
www.riding-instructor.com

**Type of School:**
Specialized Certification Process

## American Riding Instructor Certification Program (ARICP)

The American Riding Instructors Association (ARIA), 28801 Trenton Ct., Bonita Springs, FL 34134. Contact: Charlotte Kneeland. Phone: (239) 948-3232. Fax: (239) 948-5053. Email: aria@riding-instructor.com.

**Accreditation:** American Riding Instructors Association

**Degrees Offered:** Certificate

**Majors Offered:** Level 1: Instructor in Training; Level 2: Instructor of Beginner through Intermediate; Level 3: Instructor of Beginner through Advanced. Specializations available in Eventing, Distance Riding: Endurance, Dressage, Driving, Hunt Seat, Mounted Patrol Training, Show Jumping, Recreational Riding, Saddle Seat, Side-Saddle, Stock Seat, Stable Management, Reining and Riding to Hounds.

**Tuition Costs:** $395: one-day test center; $595 four-day seminar and testing; $595 individual testing

**Description of Program:** The American Riding Instructor Certification Program (ARICP) was established in 1984 to validate the qualifications of riding instructors. The major objective of the program is to identify riding instructors who teach in a safe, competent, and professional manner, and who possess a high degree of knowledge and integrity. Since the establishment of the ARICP, many teaching facilities and insurers are requiring that their instructors be ARICP-certified. ARICP's emphasis on safe teaching practices has resulted in some of the major insurance companies who write equine policies giving ARICP- certified instructors a substantial reduction on their liability insurance. The ARICP offers certification to instructors of all levels of experience and in virtually all teaching specialties. If you are an instructor who would like to further your career, apply for ARICP certification at one of the ARICP one-day test centers or at the annual four-day ARICP National Riding Instructors Seminar and testing center. The seminar provides lectures, roundtable discussions, and networking sessions by some of the country's top horsemen, as well as the certification tests. One-day test centers are held at various locations around the country throughout the year.

**Facilities:** Testing cities are located across the U.S.

## Austin Education Center

**Website:**
www.horsecoursesonline.com

**Type of School:**
Non-profit Foundation, Independent Study

Austin Education Center, PO Box 318, 3000 Marion County Road, Weirsdale, FL 32195. Contact: Cecile Dunn or Don Blazer. Phone: (352) 750-0271 (Dunn) or (602) 689-6171 (Blazer). Fax: (480) 219-6873. Email: donblazer@donblazer.com.

**Majors Offered:** Professional Designation in Horse Training

**Tuition Costs:** $75 to $200 per course

**Description of Program:** Austin Education Center is a nonprofit foundation dedicated to the advancement of education for horses and horsemen. Professional Designation in Horse Training is awarded when a student completes 9 required courses. Austin is the host for clinics, seminars and horse shows and is the location of the Austin Carriage Museum. Students are in email contact with nationally recognized "celebrity" instructors. Students get one-on-one assistance with any specific questions or problems at any time. Start a course anytime; take one course or several at a time. Work at your own pace and complete courses at your convenience. All of the AEC courses are online. However, Austin does make recommendations for hands-on training with stables in various parts of the country. AEC also has a job placement network for program graduates.

## Central Florida Community College

**Website:**
www.cfcc.cc.fl.us

**Type of School:**
Community College

Ocala Campus, Continuing Education, P.O. Box 1388, Ocala, FL 34478-1388. Contact: Sheila Ramos. Phone: (352) 854-2322 ext. 41496. Fax: (352) 237-0139. Email: ramoss@cf.edu.

**Accreditation:** University of Florida and Central Florida Community College joint partnership
**Degrees Offered:** Certificate
**Majors Offered:** Basic Equine Care and Technology, Intermediate Equine Care and Technology, Advanced Equine Care and Technology, Groom School, Equine Foaling
**Tuition Costs:** $55 per class for Basic, Intermediate, and Advanced Care and Technology; $999 for groom school; $199 for equine foaling
**Description of Program:** The Groom School includes basic handling and showmanship techniques, care of the horse's environment, grooming, leg care, and the horse's digestive system. In Equine Foaling, learn how to care for the pregnant mare and foal through lectures, hands-on demonstrations, and tours to nearby farms. Basic ECT covers basic care of the horse, including feeding, foaling, first aid, herd management, breeding, and equipment maintenance. Advanced ECT covers nutrition (deficiencies, supplementation, digestive system), hoof care, parasitology, immunology, animal welfare, government rules and regulations for the equine industry, limb deformities, advanced reproduction, pharmacology, dentistry, and horse farm economics.
**Facilities:** Class is held at CFCC, and field trips to local farms are included.

## Don Doran's Equine Sports Massage Program

9791 NW 160th Street, Reddick, FL 32686. Phone: (352) 591-4735. Fax: (352) 591-0988. Email: equinesportsmassage@equinesportsmassage.com.
**Degrees Offered:** Certificate
**Majors Offered:** Massage Therapy

## Grand Cypress Equestrian Center

Grand Cypress Resort, One Equestrian Drive, Orlando, FL 32836. Phone: (407) 239-1938. Email: kfiske@grandcypress.com.
**Accreditation:** British Horse Society
**Degrees Offered:** Certificate, Apprentice
**Majors Offered:** Stages I, II, III, and Preliminary Teaching Test
**Description of Program:** A multi-discipline facility. Instruction is offered for all ages in dressage, jumping, hunt seat and equitation, and basic Western riding. Lessons are available in trail riding and novice Western trail. The junior riding academy includes Progressive Riding Tests, and there is a live-in apprentice BHS preparatory program.
**Facilities:** The main facility has a 44-stall barn; lighted, covered arena; lighted outdoor jumping ring; regulation dressage ring; exercise track; turnout paddocks; tack rooms; indoor washing and grooming stalls; clubhouse with locker rooms; and the Tack & Gift Shop. The Western Trail Barn is a small auxiliary barn, reminiscent of the Old West. Picturesque trails wind through a "real Florida forest" and past beautiful scenery and wildlife. The cross-country course is the site of our exciting competitions and clinics.

## Horsemanship Safety Association, Inc.

P.O. Box 2710, Lake Placid, FL 33862. Contact: Steve Bennett. Phone: (800) 798-8106 or (863) 465-0289. Fax: (863) 699-5577. Email: HSANews@juno.com.
**Accreditation:** Horsemanship Safety Association
**Degrees Offered:** Certificate
**Majors Offered:** Instructor, Assistant Instructor, Trail Guide

**Tuition Costs:** Four-day seminar: $395; on-site, housing and meals: $100
**Description of Program:** "Equestrian Lifeguard" training. The goal is to train competent equestrians to be able to maintain a safe environment for both horse and rider. In the form of four-day clinics. The Instructor Certification Course focuses on safety awareness and teaching techniques.
**Facilities:** Clinics at headquarters in Florida and at sites nationally. Hosting facilities will have at least four beginner level "school horses," fenced riding arenas, and classroom/meeting space.
**Classroom/Hands-On Equine Classes:** 50:50

## Rancho Del Castillo

**Website:**
www.backyardracehorse.com

**Type of School:**
Specialty School

3708 Crystal Beach Rd., Winter Haven, FL 33880. Contact: Janet Del Castillo.
Phone: (863) 299-8448. Fax: (863) 294-9401. Email: delcastilo@aol.com.
**Degrees Offered:** Certificate
**Majors Offered:** Race Horse Training
**Tuition Costs:** $350 plus $150 for partner or significant other; $25 per night, including breakfast. If you travel overnight to tracks, there will be additional hotel room charges.
**Description of Program:** Hands-on seminars are held at Rancho Del Castillo year-round. Seminars are typically held on the weekends; participants arrive Friday night and depart Sunday night. However, seminars can be held at any time, depending on the racing schedule. Ms. Del Castillo tries to schedule seminars so that a race or workout is available for observation at the track; this allows participants to see and understand the logical transition from the farm to the racetrack. Horses are turned out to graze for a portion of every day at the farm; then they are loaded into the van and taken to the track to gallop, work, or race. Students are involved in every part of the process, allowing them to determine how to adapt their own circumstances to racing off the farm. The fourth edition of *Backyard Race Horse* is now available and covers all the information that is presented during the seminars.
**Facilities:** Training centers and stud farms in Ocala; Miami or Tampa racetracks

## University of Florida

**Website:**
www.vetmed.ufl.edu

**Type of School:**
Public University

The College of Veterinary Medicine at the University of Florida, Campus Box 100125, 2015 SW 16th Ave., Gainesville, FL 32610. Phone: (352) 492-4700.
Email: admissions@vetmed.ufl.edu.
**Degrees Offered:** Master of Science, Doctor of Philosophy, Doctor of Veterinary Medicine
**Majors Offered:** Physiological Sciences (M.S., Ph.D.), Infectious Disease and Experimental Pathology (M.S., Ph.D.), Veterinary Medical Sciences (M.S., Ph.D.), Veterinary Medicine (D.V.M.)

# *GEORGIA*

## Berry College

Animal & Plant Sciences Department, Berry College, 2277 Martha Berry Blvd., Mount Berry, GA 30149-5003. Contact: Dr. Judy Wilson, Director, Gunby Equine

Center or Marvin Howlett. Phone: (706) 238-7736. Fax: (706) 236-2233. Email: jwilson@berry.edu or mhowlett@berry.edu.

**Accreditation:** Southern Association of Colleges and Schools

**Degrees Offered:** Bachelor of Science

**Majors Offered:** Animal Science with emphasis in Equine Science

**Tuition Cost:** $7,590/semester; room and board: $2,915/semester; horse board: $300/month

**Description of Program:** Three instructed rides per week; riding class size averages four students. Hunt and stock seat riding styles taught. The Animal Science program is designed for the student interested in professional careers related to horses or other animal species. Students in many academic areas of liberal arts and sciences take advantage of Animal Science courses as electives to enhance their knowledge and skills with horses or other animals. An Animal Science minor is available, and students may emphasize equine courses within this minor. Equine courses include Horse Systems and Management, Equine Health, Equine Evaluation, and Comparative Exercise Physiology and Stable Management. The primary uses of the Gunby Equine Center are for training, research, development of the equestrian team, and educating students in various areas of the equine and animal industry. A wide variety of courses are available through the Animal Science/Pre-Veterinary major. Guided trail rides and equine-related events enhance student and community involvement at the equine center.

**Facilities:** Equestrian center is three miles from campus and has 55 school horses, one outdoor arena (120ft x 200ft), one covered arena (125ft x 250ft), three barns, pasture, and trails.

**Classroom/Hands-On Equine Courses:** Each course is a combination of classroom and laboratory work.

**Showing:** IHSA

## Casey & Son Horseshoeing School

14013 East Highway 136, LaFayette, GA 30728 U.S.A. Phone: (706) 397-8909. Fax: (706) 397-8047. Email: rcaseysch@aol.com.

**Accreditation:** Brotherhood of Working Farriers Association (BWFA) affiliated

**Degrees Offered:** BWFA Farrier Certification

**Majors Offered:** Apprentice Farrier

**Tuition Costs:** $1,395/two weeks; $2,995/six weeks; $4,880/twelve weeks; $545 tools; housing included

**Description of Program:** Two-week (ten days) course is designed to teach the student how to properly shoe a normal horse for his/her own personal use or as a beginner course as a prelude to the six- or twelve-week course. Your training will consist of time in the classroom, shoeing live horses, and learning the necessary forging techniques. Six-week course will teach you how to change the horse's mode of travel caused by poor leg and hoof conformation or previous improper shoeing; how to recognize, prevent, and correct lameness; and provide you with an in-depth study of the anatomy related to proper balance and shoeing of all breeds and types of horses. You will learn how to set up your own business and shoeing rig, receive business strategy lectures; with plenty of classroom time, and extensive live shoeing and forging. Twelve-week course prepares the student further to be a professional farrier. You will work with professional farriers in the Farrier Research Laboratory. You will learn to use the arc welder in making more professional corrective shoes. You will learn advanced shoeing techniques for lameness of the leg, hoof repair, and leg braces; you will also participate in live shoeing, classroom work, and forging each day.

**Facilities:** 80ft x 130ft indoor and outdoor arenas

**Classroom/Hands-On Equine Classes:** 20:80

## University of Georgia

Animal & Dairy Science Dept., Edgar L. Rhodes Center for Animal & Dairy Science, Athens, GA 30602-2771. Contact: Dr. Josie Coverdale. Phone: (706) 583-0398. Fax: (706) 542-0399. Email: jcover@.uga.edu.

**Degrees Offered:** Bachelor of Science, Master of Science, Master of Animal and Dairy Science, Doctor of Philosophy, Doctor of Veterinary Medicine

**Majors Offered:** Animal Science (B.S.) with equine classes in Pre-Veterinary, Business, or Production; Equine Topics (M.S., M.A.D.S., Ph.D.), Veterinary Medicine (D.V.M.)

**Tuition Cost:** In-state: $2,039; out-of-state: $7,427; housing: $1,591/semester; meal plan: $1,287/semester; horse board: $225/month

**Description of Program:** Equine courses include two courses in production and management and live evaluation. Upon completion of the advanced evaluation course, students have the opportunity to compete on the judging team. In addition, courses in breeding and training/conditioning are offered. These courses allow students to develop specialized skills through exposure to breeding techniques and training of two-year-olds. All courses emphasize hands-on learning with weekly laboratory periods. Class size averages 35 students, and both Western and hunt seat styles are taught.

**Facilities:** Modern classroom and animal facilities facilitate learning. The new office complex has five classrooms, computer lab, study lounge, and many research and extension activities to involve students. Teaching arena is three miles from campus and has an indoor, air-conditioned arena, and a covered arena for riding. The breeding herd maintained at a separate facility near campus offers further opportunity for student involvement.

**Classroom/Hands-On Equine Courses:** One lab, per week, per class

**Showing:** NCAA, judging, rodeo, breed and open shows

**Website:**
www.uga.edu

**Type of School:**
Public University

## Wesleyan College

Wesleyan College Equestrian Center, 4760 Forsyth Rd., Macon, GA 31210-4462. Contact: Mrs. Barbara Exum, Equestrian Center Director, Head Instructor and IHSA Team Head Coach. Phone: (478) 757-5103 or (478) 757-5111.

**Accreditation:** Southern Association of Colleges and Schools, National Association of Schools of Music (NASM), Georgia Professional Standards Commission

**Degrees Offered:** Baccalaureate, Master of Arts, Master of Business Administration

**Majors Offered:** No equine degrees

**Tuition Cost:** Full time: $9,570; part time: $360 per semester hour

**Description of Program:** HPE Equestrian courses at progressive levels for credit in Hunter Seat Equitation and Western Horsemanship. Classes meet hourly, twice a week with two to six students in each class. IHSA Show Teams compete at regional, zone and national competitions. Independent field studies and internships in areas of equine education can earn college credits. Clinics and seminars are regularly scheduled with leaders in the horse industry and cover a wide range of subjects.

**Facilities:** Equestrian Center on campus has 30 horses, including school horses, and student and alumni boarders. Lighted oval ring (150ft x 225ft), Hunter Trial field, trails, 24 stall barn adjacent to classroom, meeting and office space, eight-stall Com-

**Website:**
www.wesleyan-college.edu

**Type of School:**
Private Women's College

munity Lesson barn with adjoining ring, and large paddocks for daily turnout rotation.

**Showing:** IHSA, ANRC, invitational, local and open shows, foxhunting with Belle Meade Hunt

# *HAWAII*

**Website:**
www.hpa.edu

**Type of School:**
K-12 Day School,
6-12 Boarding School

## Hawaii Preparatory Academy

65-1692 Kohala Mountain Road, Kamuela, HI 96743-8476. Phone: (808) 885-7321.
**Accreditation:** Western Association of Schools and Colleges
**Degrees Offered:** College Preparatory Diploma
**Majors Offered:** Horse Program
**Tuition Costs:** Seven-day boarding: $23,800; five-day boarding: $18,700; day school grades 9-12: $11,000; day school grades 6-8: $9,350; horse program: $600/ten weeks, $60/one week
**Description of Program:** The horse program at HPA is available to every student at the school, regardless of expertise or experience. The staff is just as attuned to the needs of the rank beginner as they are to the requirements of the most experienced and motivated riders. Instruction is based on the Pony Club format, and students are encouraged to work at the various levels. The program offers instruction to prepare for showing, both English and Western, as well as polo instruction with scrimmages and club play appropriate to the students' skill levels. HPA stages a major combined training event every year, and students are encouraged to work towards participating in this effort at all levels. The regular program offers the only varsity regimen in the state of Hawaii for students who wish to earn their letter. HPA also offers a special intensive session for riders each summer. Occasionally, students ride on overnight pack trips to remote locations–excursions that are a highlight of the equestrian experience at HPA. Students have opportunities to go beyond the requirements. The school regularly participates in horse shows, and students are encouraged to get involved in these weekend activities. Student instructors receive credit for help with an elementary program on Friday afternoons.
**Facilities:** Equestrian facilities at HPA include a polo field, stadium jumping area, dressage area, and cross-country course. The school herd consists of 30 animals, including registered Thoroughbreds, Warmbloods, Arabs, and Quarter Horses. The school has its own breeding program.
**Showing:** English shows, Western shows, combined training, polo

# *IDAHO*

**Website:**
www.equinedentalacademy.com

**Type of School:**
Specialty School

## Academy of Equine Dentistry

242 E. 1st Ave. , P.O. Box 999, Glenns Ferry, ID 83623. Contact: Dale Jeffrey, President. Phone: (208) 366-2315. Fax: (208) 366-2340. Email: academy@equinedentistry.com.
**Accreditation:** Compliance with the Idaho State Board of Education as a private technical  school in the state of Idaho.

**Degrees Offered:** Certificate
**Majors Offered:** Equine Dentistry
**Tuition Costs:** $6,880.32
**Description of Program:** One, two, and four-year programs featuring equine dental and anatomy courses. Classroom time and lab hands-on time is 50 hours per session. During lab time, approximately 150 horses are worked on in a ten-day period.
**Facilities:** Separate classroom and lab facilities with 25 horse bays (stalls) and one certified instructor per group of two to four students. Housing can be provided.
**Classroom/Hands-On Equine Classes:** 50:50

## College of Southern Idaho

Agriculture Department, College of Southern Idaho, 315 Falls Ave., P.O. Box 1238, Twin Falls, ID 83303-1238. Contact: Jim Knight. Phone: (208) 733-9554 x 2414. Fax: (208) 736-2136.
**Degrees Offered:** Associate of Applied Science
**Majors Offered:** Horse Management

**Website:**
www.csi.edu

**Type of School:**
Community College

## University of Idaho

Animal and Veterinary Science Department, Ag Science Building, Room 213, University of Idaho, Moscow, ID 83844-2330. Phone: (208) 885-6345 or (888) 8UIDAHO (ask for AVS).Fax: (208) 885-6420. Email: avs-student@uidaho.edu.
**Degrees Offered:** Bachelor of Science, Doctor of Veterinary Medicine
**Majors Offered:** Animal Science (B.S.), Veterinary Science (B.S.), Range Livestock Management (B.S.), Veterinary Medicine (D.V.M.)
**Description of Program:** No riding. The B.S. in Animal Science can be taken with options in Business, Dairy, Production, or Science Pre-Veterinary. The B.S. in Veterinary Science is a three-year program with one year spent at an accredited veterinary school equaling the first year of a D.V.M. degree.

**Website:**
www.uidaho.edu

**Type of School:**
Public University

# *ILLINOIS*

## Black Hawk College

Applied Science Department, Black Hawk College, 1501 State Hwy. 78, Kewanee, IL 61443-8630. Contact: Jon R. Wolf. Phone: (309) 852-5671 x 6264. Fax: (309) 856-6005. Email: wolfj@bhc.edu.
**Accreditation:** North Central Association of Colleges and Schools
**Degrees Offered:** Associate of Science, Associate of Applied Science, Certificate
**Majors Offered:** Equestrian Science (A.S.), Horse Science (A.A.S., C)
**Tuition Costs:** $53 per credit hour
**Description of Program:** Hunt, stock, and saddle seat riding styles taught. The program's goal is to provide the equine students with the necessary education and hands-on experience to gain employment in an ever-changing world. This is accomplished through lectures, labs, field trips, guest speakers, clinics, and seminars. The students ride on a daily basis in the newly constructed 100ft x 250ft heated indoor arena. Students also have an opportunity to compete on the Horse Judging Team and/or the

**Website:**
www.bhc.edu

**Type of School:**
Community College

IHSA Team, and rope two evenings each week.
**Facilities:** 102 acres, indoor and outdoor arenas and stalls
**Showing:** IHSA, Horse Judging Team, Roping, Agri-Business Club

## Equine Education Institute

P.O. Box 68, Ringwood, IL 60072-0068. Phone: (815) 653-2382. Fax: (815) 653-9496. Email: info@equus.com.
**Majors Offered:** Basic Horseshoeing, Trimming the Foot
**Tuition Costs:** $150 per set of books and tapes
**Description of Program:** Independent study program that includes books and videos.

## Kishwaukee College

21193 Malta Road, Malta, IL 60150 Phone: (815)825-2086 x296. Fax: (815) 825-2072.
**Accreditation:** North Central Association of Colleges and Schools
**Degrees Offered:** Certificate
**Majors Offered:** Equine Science
**Tuition Costs:** $56 per credit
**Description of Program:** The equine certificate program is designed for the student interested in equine care, selection, and training. Students may enroll in single courses or complete all eighteen credit hours of the certificate. Equine instructors are professionals in their trade.
**Facilities:** Classrooms and private farm facilities. No housing supplied.
**Classroom/Hands-On Equine Classes:** 50:50

## Midwest Horseshoeing School

2312 South Maple Avenue, Macomb, IL 61455. Phone: (309) 833-4063.
Email: royevans@macomb.com.
**Accreditation:** Approved by the State of Illinois and the Job Training Partnership Act, Department of Vocational Rehabilitation, and Veterans Administration
**Degrees Offered:** Certificate, Diploma
**Majors Offered:** Beginning Two-Week (C), Basic Four-Week (C), Intermediate Six-Week (C), Twelve-Week Advanced Farrier (D)
**Tuition Costs:** Two-week course: $800 for tuition, $100 for housing; four-week course: $1,200 for tuition, $200 for housing; six-week course: $1,600 for tuition, $300 for housing; twelve-week course: $2,500 for tuition, $550 for housing
**Description of Program:** Two instructors. Through a carefully structured combination of lecture, laboratory, and practical experience, you will learn the proper use of all blacksmithing tools and equipment, forging techniques, and the correct methods of shoeing a horse. This includes cold shoeing, hot shoeing, and corrective shoeing. As a student, you will also learn how to make some of your own tools, how to set up your equipment, and examine successful ways to set up your own business.
**Facilities:** There is a classroom for lectures, a modern shop area, and a large shoeing area. Hand tools, a workbench, a forge, an anvil, and a textbook will be assigned to each student for personal use throughout the term of the course. Furnished rooming houses with kitchen facilities are available
**Classroom/Hands-On Equine Classes:** Lecture one hour a day, hands-on the rest of the day

## Parkland College

**Website:**
www.parkland.edu

**Type of School:**
Community College

Business & Agri-Industries Department, Parkland College, 2400 West Bradley Ave., Champaign, IL 61821-1899. Contact: Bruce Henrikson, Chair. Phone: (217) 351-2213 or (800) 346-8089. Fax: (217) 373-3896. Email: bhenrikson@parkland.edu.

**Degrees Offered:** Certificate, Associate of Applied Science

**Majors Offered:** Equine Management (A.A.S.), Equine (C)

**Description of Program:** Equine students in the A.A.S. program study nutrition and ration formulation, genetics, horse selection, equitation skills, breeding, stallion and broodmare management, horse health, and young stock training, as well as two cooperative education work experience courses in a local equine farm or business. Certificate students cover the same equine studies areas, but without the cooperative education experience or as many general education courses. Stock seat and hunt seat riding styles are included.

**Facilities:** Local stable owners provide indoor arenas and other facilities needed for courses.

**Showing:** IHSA Riding Team, Judging Team

## Southern Illinois University–Carbondale

**Website:**
www.siu.edu

**Type of School:**
Public University

Department of Animal Sciences, Southern Illinois University, Carbondale, IL 62901. Contact: Dr. Sheryl King, Director of Equine Studies or Stephanie Speiser, Instructor. Phone: (618) 453-2329 or (618) 453-1771. Fax: (618) 453-5231. Email: sking@siu.edu or sspeiser@siu.edu.

**Accreditation:** North Central Association of Colleges and Schools

**Degrees Offered:** Minor, Bachelor of Science, Master of Science, Doctor of Philosophy

**Majors Offered:** Equine Studies (M), Animal Science with equine specialization (B.S.), Pre-Veterinary Medicine (B.S.), Animal Science with Equine Reproduction (M.S.), Physiology with Equine Reproduction (Ph.D.)

**Tuition Costs:** In-state: $141.50/credit; out-of-state: $283/credit; room and board: $4,974; student fee: $638.15/semester; riding classes: $300/semester

**Description of Program:** Two instructed rides per week; riding class size maximum of twelve students. Two instructors for Equine Science classes. Undergraduate curriculum emphasis is on animal and facilities management with a scientific emphasis. All courses have laboratories, with a heavy hands-on component. More than a dozen equine-related courses are offered. Approximately 50 students are enrolled in Equine Science. Riding instruction is in balance seat and available at all levels; advanced riding students can specialize in hunt, stock, dressage and saddle seat. Riding is conducted on campus. There are currently no facilities for boarding student's horses, although construction plans are underway. Extracurricular horse activities include the service-oriented SIUC Equine Science Club, which sponsors seminars, open houses and promotional events. The SIUC Riding Club/Equestrian Team is a sports club offering involvement with riding and competition. The Equestrian Team competes at Intercollegiate Horse Show Association-sponsored events. The SIUC also sponsors a Rodeo Club, which competes on the intercollegiate level.

**Facilities:** Equestrian center is three miles from campus and has 50 school horses, one indoor arena (70ft x 70ft), one outdoor arena (100ft x 200ft), four round pens (60ft), lab, more than 100 acres of pasture, and an on-farm classroom.

**Classroom/Hands-On Equine Courses:** All equine classes have a mandatory hands-on component. Scheduled on-farm hours per class increase with class level. Mandatory horse industry internship follows on-campus curriculum.

**Showing:** IHSA, equestrian team, local and open shows, rodeo

## University of Illinois at Urbana–Champaign

**Website:**
www.uiuc.edu

**Type of School:**
Public University

University of Illinois at Urbana–Champaign, 901 West Illinois Street, Urbana, IL 61801. Phone: (217) 333-0302. Email: ansci@uiuc.edu.

**Degrees Offered:** Bachelor of Science, Master of Science, Doctor of Philosophy, Doctor of Veterinary Medicine

**Majors Offered:** Animal Sciences (B.S. M.S., Ph.D.), Veterinary Medicine (D.V.M.)

# INDIANA

## The Culver Academies

**Website:**
www.culver.org

**Type of School:**
Private Secondary Boarding and Day Schools

1300 Academy Road, Culver IN 46511-1291. Contact: Ed Little. Phone: (219) 842-7000. Email: littlee@culver.org.

**Accreditation:** Independent Schools Association of the Central States (ISACS), Indiana Department of Education, National Association of Independent Schools (NAIS), North Central Association of Colleges and Schools (NCA)

**Degrees Offered:** High School Diploma

**Majors Offered:** Basic Equine Science, Advanced Equine Science, Honors in Equitation

**Tuition Costs:** $25,400 boarding; $17,500 day; $1,500 uniform for boys; $850 uniform for girls; $600 equitation clothing/equipment for boys; $400 equitation clothing/equipment for girls; $3,500 Black Horse Troop and Equitation fee

**Description of Program:** Culver's equitation program is based on the methodologies of schooling riders and horses developed by the U.S. Cavalry that is a direct descendant of the cavalry schools of Europe. All equitation classes are held during the academic day. In BES, a two-semester course, students are evaluated and placed in classes with comparable riding experience. Lessons are conducted in the "Balance Seat." Activities include an introduction to mounted drill, vaulting, dressage, jumping, polo, cross-country, and trail rides. Booklet instructions include basics in horse care, feeds, diseases, wounds, treatments, anatomy, and more. AES, a six-semester course, is a continuation of advanced instruction in the "Balance Seat." Foxhunting, dressage, *pas de quatre*, polo, jumping, polocrosse, and cross-country are a few of the riding activities. Notebook topics include history of the horse and cavalry, breeds, conformation, age by teeth, horse identification, horse shoeing, and hoof care. Honors in Equitation is a project offered to seniors enrolled in AES. It is designed to provide a strong foundation for those who choose to pursue a career in the equine industry. Three portfolios are compiled on subjects such as training and schooling the horse, stable management, teaching, horse sports, and vet work.

**Facilities:** The Vaughn Equestrian Center features 130 stalls, a riders' lounge, offices for instructors, and a 90ft x 300ft heated indoor riding arena with seating for 750 spectators. This arena allows students to continue their riding classes throughout the winter months. Culver's campus also includes a 600-acre bird sanctuary with ten miles of trails suitable for the novice or advanced rider.

**Classroom/Hands-On Equine Classes:** 1:5 hours

**Showing:** Hunter/jumper, polo, combined training, dressage, drill team, vaulting

## Purdue University

Animal Science, 1151 Lily Hall, West Lafayette, IN 47907. Phone: (765) 494-1776 or (765) 494-7677 or (765) 494-4808. Fax: (765) 494-0544.
Email: horses@vet.purdue.edu.
**Degrees Offered:** Bachelor of Science, Doctor of Veterinary Medicine
**Majors Offered:** Animal Science (B.S.), Agriculture (B.S.), Veterinary Medicine (D.V.M.)

**Website:**
www.purdue.edu

**Type of School:**
Public University

## Saint Mary-of-the-Woods College

Equine Studies Department, Saint Mary-of-the-Woods College, Saint Mary-of-the-Woods, IN 47876-1099. Contact: Christine S. Marks, Chair. Phone: (812) 535-5106 or (812) 535-5190. Fax: (812) 535-5010. Email: cmarks@smwc.edu.
**Accreditation:** North Central Association of Colleges and Universities
**Degrees Offered:** Minor, Associate of Science, Bachelor of Science
**Majors Offered:** Equine Science (M), Equine Business Management (B.S.), Equine Studies (A.S., B.S.), Equine Training and Instruction (B.S.). Therapeutic Riding is offered as an emphasis in Equine Studies (B.S.)
**Tuition Costs:** $15,500/year plus $5,500-6,500 housing/year
**Description of Program:** SMWC offers three majors in the department of equine studies. The general equine studies degree is the most flexible, allowing the students to choose from a variety of equine studies electives while taking the equine science and business core courses. The training and instruction major incorporates many training courses, as well as courses designed for those who wish to become instructors. The equine business management major, while still requiring a thorough grounding in horse care and management, relies heavily on business course offerings to prepare students for a career in an equine-related business. The facilities at SMWC are state-of-the-art and are located right on campus. The equestrian team is highly competitive in both English and Western disciplines; athletic scholarships are available. The modern classroom/laboratory facility is comfortable and workable. Students learn from highly-trained faculty in small classes (most have twelve or fewer students). Job placement of graduates is excellent. The Equine Business Management degree will soon be offered as a distance degree with some residency requirements.
**Facilities:** There are 52 stalls, large indoor and outdoor arenas, turnout, a classroom and a laboratory.
**Classroom/Hands-On Equine Classes:** 1/3 of courses are mostly classroom, 2/3 mostly hands-on
**Showing:** IHSA

**Website:**
www.smwc.edu

**Type of School:**
Private Women's College, Independent Study

# *IOWA*

## Ellsworth Community College

Equine Management Program, Ellsworth Community College, 1100 College Ave., Iowa Falls, IA 50126. Contact: Judy Miller, Director Equine Management. Phone: (800) ECC-9235 or (515) 648-4611. Fax: (515) 648-2809. Email: judymill@iavalley.cc.ia.us.
**Degrees Offered:** Diploma, Associate of Applied Science
**Majors Offered:** Equine Management

**Website:**
www.iavalley.cc.ia.us

**Type of School:**
Community College

## Iowa State University of Science and Technology

**Website:** www.iastate.edu

**Type of School:** Public University

Animal Science Department, 119 Kildee Hall, Ames, IA 50011-3150. Contact: Dr. Peggy Miller. Phone: (515) 294-5260. Fax: (515) 294-0018. E-mail: peggy@iastate.edu.

**Degrees Offered:** Bachelor of Science, Master of Science, Doctorate of Philosophy, Doctor of Veterinary Medicine

**Majors Offered:** Animal Science (B.S.), Animal Physiology (M.S., Ph.D.), Animal Nutrition (M.S., Ph.D.), Pre-Veterinary (B.S.), Veterinary Medicine (D.V.M.)

**Tuition Costs:** In-state: $1654/semester; out-of-state: $4872/semester

**Description of Program:** Hunt and stock seat riding styles taught. The horse program is within the Animal Science Department. Current horses consist of Quarter Horses, Paints, and Thoroughbreds. All horses are used in the curriculum. Stallions are stood to University and privately owned mares. Students are involved in learning breeding techniques. Hands-on activities are utilized as much as possible. These activities include handling horses, breeding horses, foaling mares, training horses, sales preparation, and much more.

**Facilities:** Outdoor arena, breeding lab

**Showing:** Intercollegiate shows, rodeos

## Kirkwood Community College

**Website:** www.kirkwood.cc.ia.us

**Type of School:** Community College

Agricultural Technologies - Horse Science, Kirkwood Community College, 6301 Kirkwood Blvd. SW, PO Box 2068, Cedar Rapids, IA 52406-2068. Contact: Dale McNeeley. Phone: (319) 398-5411 or (319) 398-4950. Fax: (319) 398-5611. Email: dmcneel@kirkwood.cc.ia.us.

**Accreditation:** North Central Association of Colleges and School

**Degrees Offered:** Certificate, Associate of Applied Science

**Majors Offered:** Horse Science Technician (A.A.S.), Horse Show (C)

**Tuition Costs:** $1080 per semester; $250-275 per month for student apartments

**Description of Program:** English and Western riding styles taught. The Horse Science Technology Program prepares you for a variety of positions in equine enterprises. During the first year, you'll study genetics, breeding, horsemanship, training, nutrition, management, and judging. You'll also take courses in communication, accounting, human relations, computer science, math, and merchandising to become a well-rounded professional. More than 50 percent of instruction takes place in a laboratory setting using Kirkwood-owned horses or horses from outside the campus. Advanced students train their own horses or horses sponsored for training. Horse Science students complete an eight-week, paid internship during their final semester at Kirkwood. Students work 40 hours each week at a breeding farm, dude ranch, trail riding establishment, breed association, or training stable for race or performance horses. During your internship, you will apply your lab and classroom skills in an actual work setting. Plus, you'll make some great industry contacts that could lead to a position after graduation. Instructors will help you find an internship site, in Iowa or out-of-state.

**Facilities:** Indoor arena, 30 school horses

**Classroom/Hands-On Equine Classes:** 50:50

**Showing:** Judging, local and open shows

# KANSAS

## The Arabian Riding School

**Website:**
hometown.aol.com/tars1al/
Arabian-Riding-Schoolindex.htm

**Type of School:**
Specialty School

302 Washington Street, Baldwin City, KS 66066. Phone: (785) 594-6618.
Email: DirectorARS@aol.com.
**Degrees Offered:** Diploma, Associate, Bachelor, Master, Doctorate
**Majors Offered:** Equestrian Instructor
**Tuition Costs:** Contact school
**Description of Program:** The riding school is intended as a teaching institution for those students who have a desire to learn how to school horses and riders up to the highest levels possible, using kindness, understanding, and clear, precise detailed instructions, from the simplest movements to the most advanced exercises that a horse and rider can perform together. A basic requirement of the art of riding and teaching is that no harm, either physical or mental, comes to the horse or student during their schooling. Thus, the result of the schooling is a quiet, reliable riding horse that is pleasant in all of its movements, and the rider or teacher is comfortable with teaching horses and students.
**Facilities:** The facility is located on seventeen acres and consists of a riding hall that is 84ft x 180ft; this includes the classroom area where students can study, attend lectures, and have progress reviews. Housing is not provided.
**Classroom/Hands-On Equine Classes:** 50:50

## Colby Community College

**Website:**
www.colbycc.edu

**Type of School:**
Community College

1255 South Range Ave., Colby, KS 67701. Contact: Kelly R. Riccitelli, Ph.D., Horse Program Director. Email: kelly@colbycc.edu.
**Accreditation:** North Central Association of Colleges and Schools
**Degrees Offered:** Associate of Applied Science, Associate of Science
**Majors Offered:** Equine Science
**Tuition Costs:** $56 per credit/in-state; $95 per credit/out-of-state (except Colorado and Nebraska residents: $66 per credit); $3,314 room and board per year
**Description of Program:** This course of study is designed for students who wish to pursue careers in the equine industry or for those who desire to pursue advanced study in equine science or veterinary medicine. The curriculum involves both classroom and applied study, primarily aimed at the production aspects of the horse industry. Students pursuing direct entry into the equine industry are expected to complete an 8- to 26-week internship in their chosen field of equine production. The Associate in Applied Science Program electives are selected to meet the specific needs of the individual student and his/her career objectives. The primary focus of the program is to prepare students to work on a horse breeding farm or horse training operation. Students learn the latest techniques in managing stallions and mares for optimum production efficiency. Instruction includes hands-on activities including handling and collecting stallions, preparing semen for insemination and cold storage, inseminating and foaling-out mares. Students may also emphasize training and showing by selection of electives including horsemanship and horse training. Degree is awarded to students who fulfill the program requirements.
**Facilities:** Equestrian Center is five miles from campus and has 50 school horses and two arenas (100ft x 180ft, 120ft x 215ft).
**Classroom/Hands-on Equine Courses:** 50:50
**Showing:** IHSA

**Website:**
www.dc3.edu

**Type of School:**
Community College

## Dodge City Community College

Agriculture, Dodge City Community College, 2501 N. 14th Ave., Dodge City, KS 67801. Contact: Dave McCollum, Assoc. Prof. Equine Science. Phone: (620) 225-1321 x 288. Fax: (620) 227-9380. Email: mac@dc3.edu.

**Degrees Offered:** Certificate, Associate of Applied Science

**Majors Offered:** Horse Science

**Tuition Costs:** In-state: $35/credit; out-of-state: $35/credit; international: $90/credit

**Description of Program:** Western, roping, reining and cutting are taught.

**Facilities:** Outdoor arena

**Showing:** Open and local rodeos

**Website:**
www.ksu.edu or www.vet.ksu.edu

**Type of School:**
Public University

## Kansas State University

Dept. of Animal Sciences and Industry, Equine Section, Kansas State University, 128 Weber Hall, Manhattan, KS, 66506-0201. Contact: Dr. Joann Kouba, Equine Teaching and Research Specialist. Phone: (785) 532-1240. Fax: (785) 532-7059. Email: jkouba@oznet.ksu.edu.

**Accreditation:** North Central Association of Colleges and Schools

**Degrees Offered:** Bachelor of Science, Master of Science, Doctor of Philosophy, Doctor of Veterinary Medicine

**Majors Offered:** Animal Science (B.S., M.S., Ph.D.), Graduate Program in Equine Reproduction, Veterinary Medicine (D.V.M.)

**Tuition Costs:** Resident: $106/credit; nonresident $369/credit; room and board: $2,400/semester

**Description of Program:** Numerous courses focusing on all aspects of horse management and care, including nutrition, breeding, health care, business management, and training. Additional courses focus on conformation and performance appraisal, and anatomy and physiology. Program does not currently have horsemanship courses; however, students can receive instruction in Western and English riding through involvement with the Women's Equestrian Team. Extracurricular activities include Rodeo Club, Horseman's Association, Block and Bridle, and Pre-Vet Club. KSU sponsors several teams, including the NCAA Women's Equestrian Team, Rodeo Team, and Horse Judging Team, all of which participate in and host regional and national intercollegiate competitions.

**Facilities:** Horse Teaching and Research Unit is located two miles from campus and maintains a herd of about 60 Quarter Horses, including several stallions, 20-25 broodmares, and 15-20 weanlings, yearlings, and two-year-olds. Facilities include several barns, paddocks, round pens, pasture, and an outdoor arena. Connected to the Animal Science building on campus is a multi-purpose indoor arena. Fundraising will soon start for a new multi-million dollar equine education and performance complex. The Equestrian Team leases a private facility about ten minutes from campus and maintains a separate horse herd.

**Classroom/Hands-On Equine Classes:** Almost all equine courses involve hands-on activities.

**Showing:** IHSA, NCAA

# KENTUCKY

## American Academy of Equine Art Workshops

Kentucky Horse Park, 4089 Iron Works Parkway, Lexington, KY 40511.
Contact: Julie Buchanan, Director. Phone (859) 281-6031 and Fax (859) 281-6043.
Email: julieb@aaea.net.
**Accreditation:** American Academy of Equine Art
**Majors Offered:** Drawing, Painting, Sculpture
**Tuition Costs:** $400 per workshop
**Description of Program:** Academy workshops are open to anyone interested in equine art, including beginners and more experienced artists who wish to sharpen their skills. Instruction is offered in drawing, painting, and sculpting. Workshops fill a void that is not addressed by existing art schools today. They provide the opportunity for students to exchange ideas with a group of artists who share similar creative goals. Academy instructors are nationally renowned professionals selected for their merit as equine artists. The year 2003 marked the American Academy of Equine Art's thirteenth year of workshops at the Kentucky Horse Park. The park is one of the most complete equine facilities in the world, with more than 1,200 acres dedicated to the horse and to mankind's long-standing relationship with him. It is home to outstanding examples of more than 50 breeds of horses, and hosts some of the world's finest equestrian events. The park provides an ideal setting for students to observe equine nature and to work first-hand from live models. Located within the park, the International Museum of the Horse presents dynamic exhibitions on all facets of the world of horses. On the museum's lower level, the William G. Kenton Gallery features changing exhibitions of equine art.
**Facilities:** The Kentucky Horse Park. Housing and meals not provided.

**Website:**
www.aaea.net
**Type of School:**
Specialty School

## Asbury College

One Macklem Dr., Wilmore, KY 40390-1198. Contact: Harold Rainwater.
Phone: (606) 858-3511. Email: admissions@asbury.edu.
**Accreditation:** Southern Association of Colleges and Schools
**Degrees Offered:** Minor, Bachelor of Arts
**Majors Offered:** Equine Management Minor, Recreation Major (B.A.)
**Tuition Costs:** $14,624 per year
**Description of Program:** The program seeks to bring glory and praise to God as it ministers through the horse in an educational, safe, and fun atmosphere. The equine program began in 1997 on 341 acres owned by Asbury College. At present, there are 30 horses, representing most major breeds and offering a new forum of learning and ministry at the college.
**Facilities:** Equestrian center is located on over 300 acres and includes a riding area provided for ring work, and two small barns housing seventeen stalls and several tack rooms. Future plans include an indoor arena.
**Classroom/Hands-On Equine Classes:** 15:85
**Showing:** Students are given the opportunity to show at local shows during spring, summer, and fall.

**Website:**
www.asbury.edu
**Type of School:**
Private Christian University

## Kentucky Equine Management Internship Program

P.O. Box 910628, Lexington, KY 40591-0628. Contact: Leslie Janecka. Phone: (859) 277-2512 or (877) 644-KEMI. Fax: (859) 277-2753. Email: lesliej@kemi.org.

**Degrees Offered:** Internship

**Tuition Costs:** $1085/semester; includes housing and books

**Description of Program:** KEMI is a curriculum intended to recruit an educated, enthusiastic work force with an affirmative, lifelong participation in the equine industry. The internship program is designed by educators and farm managers with the purpose of providing a unique "hands-on" theoretical training for students. These internships are intended to attract presently enrolled or recently graduated college or university students who are interested in pursuing a career in the equine industry. The internships convene for periods, covering the 22 week breeding season (January to June) or performance season (July to December). The program tuition covers the costs of speaker's fees, course text and a membership to the Kentucky Thoroughbred Farm Manager's Club (KTFMC) during the internship period. Each intern will be placed on a horse farm as a full-time employee and working in multiple specialty areas. The KEMI curriculum complements the practicum by providing weekly lectures and occupational learning experiences. One meeting each month includes a reservation to attend the KTFMC's meeting, including a meal and a guest speaker. This unique opportunity enables the interns to interact with industry professionals and form network affiliations that enhance future employment opportunities. The course curriculum prepares the interns for the individual responsibilities that accompany the internship, including relevant expectations and demands of employment.

**Facilities:** Various farms

**Classroom/Hands-On Equine Classes:** 2 1/2 hours : 48-52 hours per week

**Showing:** Depends on previous experiences and ability.

## Kentucky Horse Park Education Program

4089 Iron Works Parkway, Lexington, KY 40511. Contact: Margi Stickney. Phone: (859) 259-4206 or (800) 568-8813 ext. 206. E-mail: education@kyhorsepark.com.

**Degrees Offered:** Certificate

**Majors Offered:** Equine Management Program

**Tuition Costs:** $1,200 plus books

**Description of Program:** Using representatives of 40 different breeds of horses and world-class equine facilities, the Kentucky Horse Park's Education Department coordinates a long term equine program, workshops and weekend classes. These programs also incorporate the resources of the Bluegrass equine industry. The Equine Management Program is a six month work/study program. Participants spend approximately two hours a day in lecture. The remainder of the day is spent caring for horses and practicing related skills. Included in the program are the Park's mares and foals and mustangs. The curriculum covers stable management, grooming, horse handling, anatomy and physiology, herd health, reproduction, mare and foal care, and riding opportunities. Single-day Community Education classes held on Saturdays cover topics such as basic care and handling, health care, foal care, and handling, and single horse or team driving.

**Facilities:** All programs are held at the Kentucky Horse Park. Student housing is not furnished, but it is available in the nearby areas.

**Classroom/Hands-On Equine Classes:** 2-3 hours per day in lecture, the rest in hands-on activities

# Kentucky Horseshoeing School

**Website:**
www.kyhorseshoeing.com

**Type of School:**
Specialized Vocational School

Highway 53, P.O. Box 120, Mt. Eden, KY 40046. Phone: (502) 738-5257 or (800) 626-5359. Email: kyhorseshu@aol.com.

**Accreditation:** Approved and licensed by the Kentucky State Proprietary Board of Education, approved for funding through the Veterans Administration, Workforce Investment Act, and Vocational Rehabilitation

**Degrees Offered:** Certificate, Internship, Apprenticeship

**Majors Offered:** Specialized Course, Basic Farrier Course, Master Farrier Course

**Tuition Costs:** $1,100/Specialized Course; $4,400/Basic Farrier Course; $6,500/Master Farrier Course; housing included

**Description of Program:** Four instructors. Two-Week Specialized Course: This course is designed for those people who are interested in trimming and flat-shoeing their own horses. The emphasis will be placed on balanced trimming and applying ready-made shoes. Eight-Week Basic Farrier Course: This course will include proper horse handling, trimming, shoeing, intermediate anatomy and physiology, and equine biomechanics. Twelve-Week Master Farrier Course: This is the course for individuals who desire to be professional farriers. The Farrier Internship Program requires the completion of the Sixteen-week Master Farrier Course. Each student will then be placed with a master farrier under contract for a minimum six-month training term. During the internship, students will follow a syllabus prescribed by the KHS, which includes forging and field assignments. Each student's progress will be monitored monthly by KHS throughout the six months.

**Facilities:** The training facility is housed in two buildings; there are two forge rooms, both equipped with propane and coal forges, and a separate building for advanced forging classes and continuing education clinics. There are sufficient forge stations to allow each student to be assigned his or her own, thus maximizing safety, efficiency, and hands-on experience. The shops are equipped with the necessary tools and equipment for all case studies.

**Classroom/Hands-On Equine Classes:** 25:75

# Midway College

**Website:**
www.midway.edu

**Type of School:**
Private University

Equine Studies, Midway College, 512 E. Stephens St., Midway, KY 40347. Contact: Dr. Sally Haydon, Chair, Equine Studies Program. Phone: (859) 846-4421 or (859) 846-5372. Fax: (859) 846-5349. Email: shaydon@midway.edu.

**Accreditation:** Southern Association of Colleges and Schools

**Degrees Offered:** Minor, Associate of Arts, Bachelor of Arts, Bachelor of Science

**Majors Offered:** Equine Studies with concentration in Management or Instruction (B.A.), Equine Science or Equine Therapy (B.S.), Equine Management (A.A.), Business Administration with concentration in Equine Business (B.A.), Horsemanship (Minor)

**Tuition Costs:** $11,700/year; room and board: $5,800; horse board: $400/month; Equine Program fee: $390/course; Equine Therapy Tuition Premium: $210/credit hour

**Description of Program:** Three majors are organized within the equine studies program: the Associate of Arts in equine management, the Bachelor of Arts in equine studies, and the Bachelor of Science in equine therapy or equine science. Students seeking the Bachelors of Arts degree in equine studies may choose a concentration in equine management or equitation instruction. The general education component of each major assures a fundamental understanding of the humanistic, mathematical, and communication aspects of learning, which are critical to career and life planning and the understanding of others. Courses in accounting, marketing, management, and economics prepare the student for the management of a horse farm. Required equine courses common to all majors provide the student with general knowledge of equine breeds, anatomy and physiology, diseases and unsoundness, treatments and prevention of illnesses, nutrition and feeding, farm management, and record keeping systems. In addition, courses in horse training and schooling, hunt and stock seat equitation, and equitation teaching are available. In order to graduate with a A.A., B.A., or B.S. degree in equine studies, the student must also complete four hours per week of an equine practicum at the college stables.

**Facilities:** Equestrian center is on campus and has 57 school horses, 65 acres, two indoor arenas (80ft x 220ft, 105ft x 320ft), and one large outdoor arena.

**Classroom/Hands-On Equine Classes:** Both classroom and hands-on experience.

**Showing:** IHSA (hunt and Western), local and open hunter shows, combined training

## Morehead State University

Agriculture, Morehead State University, U.P.O. 702, Morehead, KY 40351. Contact: Dr. Judy Willard, Coordinator, Equine Program. Phone: (606) 783-2662.
Fax: (606) 783-5067. Email: j.willard@morehead-st.edu.

**Accreditation:** Southern Association of Colleges and Schools

**Degrees Offered:** Minor, Associate of Applied Science, Bachelor of Science

**Majors Offered:** Agricultural Technology with concentration in Equine Technology (A.A.S.), Equine Science (B.S.), Horsemanship (M)

**Tuition Costs:** Residents: $1,682; nonresidents: $4,474; housing: $1,000-1,200/semester; horse board: $100/part care, $200/full care; riding fee: $10

**Description of Program:** Two to four instructed rides per week; riding class size averages ten students. Two instructors. The Equine Technology program, which prepares students for entry into the equine industry, includes the production, care, and management aspects of horses, as well as equitation. The Animal Science major program focuses on the scientific principles that underlie the breeding and husbandry of agricultural animals, and the production, processing, and distribution of agricultural animal products. This program is broad enough to allow students to select courses related to equines, or food animal production. The horsemanship minor consists of 21 semester hours of equine or equitation courses. Some of these courses are specified requirements, the other courses count as elective hours. General course electives may also be taken in horsemanship, agriculture, and related areas.

**Facilities:** Equestrian center is five miles from campus with 45 school horses, two indoor arenas (170ft x 250ft, 84ft x 84ft), and one outdoor arena (150ft x 300ft).

**Classroom/Hands-On Equine Classes:** Classroom 1-2 hours per week, labs 2-4 hours per week

**Showing:** IHSA, local and open shows

**Website:**
www.morehead-st.edu

**Type of School:**
University

## Murray State University

Agriculture, Murray State University, 103 S. Oakley Applied Science Bldg., Murray, KY 42071-3345. Contact: Dr. James Rudolph. Phone: (270) 762-3328.
Fax: (270) 762-5454. Email: ag@murraystate.edu.

**Accreditation:** Southern Association of Colleges and Schools

**Degrees Offered:** Minor, Bachelor of Science, Master of Science

**Majors Offered:** Equine Science (M), Animal/Equine Science (B.S.), Pre-Veterinary Medicine (B.S.), Animal Health Technology (B.S.), Agriculture with equine research/theory (M.S.)

**Website:**
www.murraystate.edu

**Type of School:**
Public University

**Tuition Costs:** Undergraduate residents: $1,718/semester; undergraduate nonresidents: $4,662/semester; graduate residents: $1,801.50/semester; graduate nonresidents: $5,035.50/semester; room and board: approximately $2,190; horse board: $300/semester; tuition discount available to residents of Tennessee, Indiana, Illinois, and Missouri

**Description of Program:** Hunt seat and stock seat styles taught. Animal Agriculture is specific, specialized, mechanized, computerized, and industrialized. Students enrolled in the animal sciences have an opportunity to study in the many areas of subject matter associated with animal agriculture. Students receive scientific training in animal breeding and genetics, nutrition, physiology, management, animal evaluation and selection, disease control, and sanitation. More than ever, students must be well-grounded in the biological and physical sciences. It is recognized that many animal science students today do not have the practical experience necessary for many positions requiring a combination of technical and practical training. Practical experience in animal science is attained through laboratories and summer internships. The Master of Science degree in Agriculture offers the opportunity for professional agriculture personnel to obtain an education at the graduate level and provides students with the opportunity for graduate study in the various disciplines of agriculture. Students who wish to be considered for admission to graduate study leading toward the Master of Science degree must have completed the equivalent of an undergraduate major or minor in Agriculture, in addition to meeting all the general requirements for graduate studies.

**Facilities:** The MSU Equine Center consists of several facilities, including the newly constructed Equine Instructional Facility, a stall barn for boarding student-owned horses, and a mare-and-foal facility. Also features barns for boarding horses; a 40,000-square-foot lighted outdoor arena for equine academic training and team practice; a 20,000-square-foot outdoor arena for equestrian team practices; a 6,000-square-foot outdoor arena; a hay storage facility; a treadmill; round riding pens; and a pasture riding area.

**Classroom/Hands-On Equine Classes:** 50:50

**Showing:** IHSA, NIRA, Rodeo Club, Rodeo Team, Equestrian Team, Horseman's Club Equine Judging Team, Block and Bridle Club

# United States Dressage Federation, Inc.

220 Lexington Green Circle, Suite 510; Lexington, KY 40503.
Phone: (859) 971-2277. Fax: (859) 971-7722. Email: usdressage@usdf.org.
**Degrees Offered:** Certificate
**Majors Offered:** Instructor Certification (C), USDF University Program (C), "L" Education Program for Judge Training (C)
**Tuition Costs:** $475 Instructor Certification Testing T-2; $415 Instructor Certification Testing 3-4; approximately $1,045 "L" Education Program Judge Training
**Description of Program:** USDF Instructor Certification is offered in two categories: Training through Second Level and Third through Fourth Level Certification. A candidate must achieve Training-Second Level certification before achieving Third-Fourth Level certification; however, a candidate may be tested for the entire Training-Fourth level at one testing site if the applicant has demonstrated an appropriate level of experience to the office. The "L" Education Program for Judge Training will help you to evaluate dressage performance at Training through Second Level. Gaits, paces, movements, and figures, as well as collective marks and basics, are covered. You will learn the judge's role and responsibility, as well as judging methodology. Biomechanics and Musical Freestyle will also be discussed. By the end of the program, partici-

**Website:**
www.USDF.org

**Type of School:**
Specialty Program

pants will be asked to judge full tests, giving scores and appropriate comments in a show-like atmosphere. Programs with a wide range of subject matter are eligible for USDF University accreditation. Topics can include those of a general equestrian nature to further a member's education in equine anatomy, health, feeding, care, etc. More specific programs related to dressage theory and practice and to furthering the abilities in the dressage arena, such as adult camps, can also be included.

**Facilities:** Vary. Housing is not supplied.

**Classroom/Hands-On Equine Classes:** Vary

## University of Kentucky

**Website:**
www.uky.edu

**Type of School:**
Public University

Animal Sciences, University of Kentucky, Lexington, KY 40546. Contact: Laurie Lawrence. Phone: (859) 257-7509. Email: llawrenc@uky.edu. College of Law, Office of Continuing Legal Ed., Suite 260, Law Building, Lexington, KY 40506-0048. Contact: Equine Law Senior Organizer. Phone: (859) 257-2921. Fax: (859) 323- 9790. Email: meraw10@uky.edu.

**Accreditation:** Southern Association of Colleges and Universities

**Degrees Offered:** Bachelor of Science, Master of Science, Doctor of Philosophy

**Majors Offered:** Animal Science with Equine Option (B.S.), Equine Nutrition (M.S., Ph.D.), Pre-Veterinary (B.S.), Veterinary Science (M.S., Ph.D.)

**Tuition Costs:** $2,274 in-state; $5,613 out-of-state

**Description of Program:** No riding classes. The animal science undergraduate program focuses on the management and production aspects of animals; the horse-specific courses include Equine Anatomy and Conformation, Advanced Equine Evaluation, Equine Nutrition, Equine Management and Horse Science. The "Horse Industry Study Course" provides students with an overview of current issues in the horse industry and introduces them to a variety of career options. The farm maintains about 20 broodmares and two or three stallions. Students utilize the farm for demonstrations and hands-on laboratories in areas such as breeding and teasing mares, teaching foals to lead, conformation evaluation, first aid, and health care procedures. The Graduate Program in Animal Sciences provides the opportunity for advanced study in the discipline of animal sciences. The aim of the program is to develop animal science specialists who are able to function in a variety of sophisticated academic, industrial, and professional settings. Research work in the broad areas of nutrition and management, reproductive and lactational physiology, genetics, and nutritional/anaerobic microbiology may be conducted with beef cattle, dairy cattle, horses, poultry, sheep, swine, or laboratory species, either individually or in suitable combinations. Continuing Legal Ed credit is available for annual Equine Law Seminar on Derby weekend. The seminar covers business structures, taxation, and racing issues.

**Facilities:** Breed farm, nutrition lab, treadmill, round pen

**Classroom/Hands-On Equine Classes:** 85:15

**Showing:** IHSA

## University of Louisville

**Website:**
www.louisville.edu

**Type of School:**
Public University

Equine Industry Program, CBPA, Louisville, KY 40292. Contact: Robert Lawrence, Director. Phone: (502) 852-7617 or (800) 334-8635. Fax: (502) 852-7672. Email: tjburc01@cbpa.louisville.edu.

**Degrees Offered:** Certificate, Bachelor of Science

**Majors Offered:** Business Administration with Equine Business (B.S.), Equine Business Administration (C)

**Tuition Costs:** $8,102 resident; $14,780 nonresident; includes room and board

**Description of Program:** No riding courses. The Equine Industry Program offered by the University of Louisville's College of Business and Public Administration is an educational opportunity unlike any other in North America. For students pursuing careers involving the business of horses, few degrees are as practical. Yet, because the curriculum demands more than merely a love of horses, this program is not suited for all students. Students enrolled in equine business gain their foundation in business disciplines from one of the nation's top business colleges. In addition, they take an entire core (more than 30 hours) of specialized courses, each related directly to the business of horses. Classroom attendance is supplemented by trips, guest lecturers, and internships at tracks (Churchill Downs is only a mile away), Bluegrass breeding farms, bloodstock agents, associations, even banks. Those who already have degrees in other fields, from agriculture to equitation, can earn a postgraduate certificate in equine business by spending one year (if qualified) taking the entire curriculum of the university's specialized courses related to the business of horses.

**Showing:** IHSA

## Western Kentucky University

Agriculture Department, Bowling Green, KY 42101. Contact: C.E. Anderson Ph.D. Phone: (270) 745-5958. Fax: (270) 745-5972. Email: charles.e.anderson@wku.edu.

**Accreditation:** Southern Regional Education Board

**Degrees Offered:** Minor, Bachelor of Science, Master of Science

**Majors Offered:** Agriculture with Horse Science option (M, B.S., M.S.), Business (M, B.S., M.S.), Pre-Veterinary (B.S.), Public Relations (M), Journalism (M)

**Tuition Costs:** Residents: $2,520/year; nonresidents: $6,820/year; room and board: $3,530

**Description of Program:** Four-year program, encompassing primarily practical, applied, hands-on horse science and related agriculture and business support courses. Multiple stock seat equitation courses, hunt seat equitation, multiple horse training courses, horse production and management, multiple horse judging courses, numerous support business, and agriculture courses.

**Facilities:** The farm is on 900 acres with two indoor arenas, covered outdoor arena, open outdoor arena, 200 rental stalls, two student stall barns, and a herd of school-owned horses.

**Classroom/Hands-On Equine Classes:** Primarily hands-on

**Showing:** Intercollegiate Horse Show Teams, Collegiate Horse Judging Teams, AQHA Showing

**Website:**
www.wku.edu

**Type of School:**
State University

# *LOUISIANA*

## Academy of the Sacred Heart

1821 Academy Road, Grand Coteau, LA 70541. Contact: Admissions. Phone: (337) 662-5275, Equestrian Program Director Jolene Ridenoure. Phone: (337) 662-3920. Fax: (337) 662-3011. Email: admissions@ashcoteau.org.

**Accreditation:** Southern Association of Colleges and Schools, Louisiana State Department of Education, Independent Schools Association of the Southwest, Network of Sacred Heart Schools member

**Website:**
www.ashcoteau.org

**Type of School:**
PreK-12 Private Day and Boarding School

**Degrees Offered:** High School Diploma

**Tuition Costs:** $5,450-$8,050/day students; $19,050/resident students; $20,350/international students; $1,500 activity fee for boarding students; scholarships and financial aid available

**Description of Program:** The Academy's equestrian program is designed to provide students from kindergarten through twelfth grade with life skills as well as a strong foundation in hunt seat. Responsibility, overcoming fear, adaptability, and setting and reaching goals are just a few of the life lessons learned through riding at the academy. The emphasis is on safety, fun, and good, solid form. Content includes equine behavior, stable care, grooming, first aid, anatomy, nutrition, and the fundamentals of riding from beginner through advanced. Grades K-4 meet one day a week after school; grades 5-8 meet during the regular school day three times per week, with one day dedicated to classroom instruction and two days of mounted classes. Grades 8-12 meet during the regular school day four times per week, with one day dedicated to classroom instruction and three days of mounted classes. Private lessons are available. Students have the option of taking horsemanship in place of other P.E. courses. Students may board their horses at the school or use a school horse for lessons and shows.

**Facilities:** Academy's 250-acre campus includes horse boarding, dressage and jump arenas, trails, and a cross-country course.

**Showing:** Interscholastic Equestrian Team, rated and non-rated hunter shows, on-site schooling shows

## Louisiana State University

**Website:**
www.lsu.edu

**Type of School:**
Public University

Animal Science, 105 J.B. Francioni Building, Baton Rouge, LA 70803-4210. Contact: Dr. Don Thompson. Phone: (225) 388-3445. Fax: (225) 388-3279. Email: dthompson@agctr.lsu.edu.

**Degrees Offered:** Bachelor of Science, Master of Science, Doctor of Philosophy, Doctor of Veterinary Medicine

**Majors Offered:** Animal Science (B.S.), 3+1 Pre-Vet option, Equine Research options (M.S., Ph.D.), Veterinary Clinical Sciences (M.S., Ph.D.), Veterinary Medicine (D.V.M.)

**Tuition Costs:** $1,988 resident/semester; $4,638 nonresident/semester

**Description of Program:** Equestrian Team (club), and Block and Bridle Club

**Facilities:** Facility on 150 acres with breeding shed and lab.

**Showing:** Student rodeos, open shows

## Louisiana Tech University

**Website:**
www.latech.edu

**Type of School:**
Technical University

Agricultural Sciences, Louisiana Tech University, P.O. Box 10198, Ruston, LA 71272. Contact: Gary Kennedy, Department Head. Phone: (318) 257-3275. Fax: (318) 257-4288. Email: ANSmail@ans.latech.edu.

**Degrees Offered:** Bachelor of Science

**Majors Offered:** Animal Science with Equine or Pre-Veterinary option

## University of Louisiana–Monroe

**Website:**
www.ulm.edu

**Type of School:**
Public University

Agriculture Department, 700 University Ave., Monroe, LA 71209-0510. Contact: Tami Lewis. Phone: (318) 342-1766. Fax: (318) 342-1779. Email: schmeer@ulm.edu.

**Degrees Offered:** Bachelor of Science

**Majors Offered:** Agribusiness with concentration in Equine Science or Pre-Vet (B.S.)

# MAINE

## Gould Academy

P.O. Box 860, Bethel, ME 04217. Phone: (207) 824-7777. Fax: (207) 824-2926. Email: admissions@gouldacademy.org.

**Accreditation:** New England Association of Schools and Colleges, National Association of Independent Schools member, Independent Schools Association of Northern New England, Secondary School Admission Test Board, Educational Records Bureau

**Degrees Offered:** High School Diploma

**Tuition Costs:** Boarding: $32,100; day: $19,500; riding lessons: $525/trimester; show fees: roughly $75/trimester

**Description of Program:** The equestrian program at Gould is an afternoon activity satisfying the school's competitive sport requirement. The focus is on dressage, and no previous riding experience is necessary. It is offered during the fall and spring trimesters for a seven-week period. Participants ride every day in small groups for 45-60 minutes. There is a beginner group and a more advanced group. While one group is riding, the other group is engaged in caring for horses and equipment. Often, one afternoon per week is set aside for trail riding. Lessons are taken at a private, off-campus facility. Students may arrange private lessons to be taken on the weekend. Payment for private lessons is separate from the fees already mentioned.

**Facilities:** Gould Academy is fortunate to have Deep Wood Farm, owned by Dianne and Wyatt Ward, only fifteen minutes from campus. They own approximately twelve horses and board several others, including some Gould students' horses. There is a 66ft x 131ft (20m x 40m) outdoor ring where lessons are taken. The farm is in a heavily wooded area near the White Mountain National Forest, providing many miles of trails.

**Showing:** There are two shows in the fall and two in the spring. Students must ride two tests in each show in order to receive competitive sport credit, and some choose to ride additional tests.

> **Website:**
> www.gouldacademy.org
>
> **Type of School:**
> Secondary School

## Kents Hill School

Kents Hill, ME 04349-0257. Phone: (207) 685-4914 or 4965. Fax: (207) 685-9529. Email: info@kentshill.org.

**Accreditation:** New England Association of Schools and Colleges, Cum Laude Society member, National Association of Independent Schools, College Board, Secondary School Admission Test Board, Independent Schools Association of Northern New England, Council for the Advancement and Support of Education, Council for Religion in Independent Schools, Association of Boarding Schools

**Degrees Offered:** High School Diploma

**Tuition Costs:** $31,850 boarding; $18,400 day

**Description of Program:** The Kents Hill School Equestrian program is located at Meadow View Equestrian Center, just a half-mile mile from campus. The school's focus is turning-out safe and confident riders. Brochures on the riding program and facility are available upon request.

**Facilities:** The Meadow View Equestrian Center is a half-mile from campus and includes an indoor arena (72ft x 150ft), outdoor sand arena (100ft x 200ft), grass arena (200ft x 300ft), heated wash stall, two heated tack rooms, 15 matted stalls (12ft x 12ft), washer/dryer, restrooms, and much more.

> **Website:**
> www.kentshill.org
>
> **Type of School:**
> Secondary School

## University of Maine–Orono

**Website:**
www.umaine.edu

**Type of School:**
Public University

Dept. of Animal and Veterinary Sciences, 132 Hitchner Hall, Orono, ME 04469. Contact: Dr. Martin Stokes, Dept. Chair. Phone: (207) 581-2770. Fax: (207) 581-2729. Email: stokes@maine.edu.

**Accreditation:** New England Association of Schools and Colleges

**Degrees Offered:** Minor, Master of Science, Doctor of Philosophy

**Majors Offered:** Animal Sciences (M.S., Ph.D.), Equine Studies (M)

**Tuition Costs:** Resident undergraduate: $12,998; nonresident undergraduate $20,738; resident graduate: $14,848; nonresident graduate: $21,796; books, room and board included

**Description of Program:** While a major in Equine Business Management is not on the books yet, students can prepare for it by taking the Agriculture Business Management and the Equine Minor.

**Facilities:** A 30-box-stall horse barn, turn out paddocks, outdoor riding arena, nine miles of trails

**Classroom/Hands-On Equine Classes:** 2 classroom equine courses and 3 hands-on

**Showing:** Students compete in local fairs and the equestrian team competes within the region.

# *MARYLAND*

## Garrison Forest School

**Website:**
www.gfs.org

**Type of School:**
Coed Preschool, All-Girls
K-12 School

300 Garrison Forest Rd., Owings Mills, MD 21117. Phone (410) 363-1500. Fax (410) 363-8441. Email: gfs_info@gfs.org.

**Accreditation:** The Middle States Association of Colleges and Schools, the Association of Independent Maryland Schools

**Degrees Offered:** High School Diploma

**Tuition Costs:** Three-year-old program: $3,900/two days per week; $5,750/three days per week; Prekindergarten: $8,450; Kindergarten/Pre-First Grade: $14,800; Grades 1-5: $15,400; Grades 6-8: $16,300; Grades 9-12 (day school): $17,300; Grades 8-12 (boarding): $31,650

**Description of Program:** The Garrison Forest Riding Program welcomes riders with any amount of experience. The primary focus of the riding program is Hunter Seat Equitation. The program is very broad-based with riders participating in Show-Jumping, Eventing, Hunter Trials, Hunter Pace, and Polo on all levels. The aim is teach girls to become self-sufficient riders; they do all of their own tacking up, grooming and preparation for competition and daily riding. Competitive Riding: Students who have achieved a basic competence over fences and flat work but wish to refine their skills, take part in the competitive side of riding. Advanced Riding: Highly experienced riders concentrate on perfecting their equitation, hunter and jumper skills. Intermediate Riding: Riders continue to review the fundamentals of position and control. Beginning Riding: Students may start their instruction on the fundamentals of riding and horse care at any point in the Upper School. There are three levels of polo: Varsity, Junior Varsity, and Third Team. In the polo program, riders at every level have the opportunity to experience the dynamics of developing a partnership with a horse and working as a team, while learning the rules and skills required as part of the game.

**Facilities:** Equestrian center is located on the 115-acre campus and has 90 stalls, two indoor arenas (110ft x 200ft, 225ft x 120ft), two large outdoor sand rings, a dressage ring, a 30-acre field for cross-country schooling, tack rooms, wash stalls, laundry rooms, offices, bathrooms, changing rooms, and a lounge/classroom area. The school owns and operates a four-horse rig and a six-horse van.

**Showing:** Local and A level shows, foxhunting with Greenspring Hounds, hunter trials, hunter paces, eventing, polo

## Maryland Horseshoeing School

11200 Wolfsville Rd., Smithsburg, MD 21783. Phone: (301) 416-0800. Email: horseshoe@frederickmd.com.

**Degrees Offered:** Certificate

**Majors Offered:** Apprentice I, Apprentice II, Journeyman I, Journeyman II, Master Farrier

**Website:**
www.lrn2shoe.com

**Type of School:**
Specialty School

## Oldfields School

1500 Glencoe Rd., Glencoe, MD 21152. Phone: (410) 472-4800. Fax: (410) 472-6839. Email: Admissions@oldfieldsschool.org.

**Degrees Offered:** High School Diploma

**Tuition Costs:** Boarding school: $31,200; day school: $20,000; riding tuition for boarding students: $1,900; riding tuition for day students: $2,000; horse board: $15/day

**Description of Program:** All-girls day and boarding school. The riding program is designed to educate the rider individually in the realm of overall horsemanship. To this end, one day each week is devoted to stable management and veterinary science lessons, and instructors reserve the early morning and evening hours for individual instruction. Overall instruction and competition are offered at a variety of levels. At the beginning and intermediate levels, students are grouped according to ability into classes of six or fewer. The more advanced riders gravitate towards the type of competition in which they are most interested, and are loosely divided into show riders and event riders. The show riders train for equitation, hunter, and jumper classes at shows in the Maryland-Virginia area, and the event riders work in the disciplines of dressage, cross-country, and show jumping to achieve the all-around competency required at combined training competitions. This division is very flexible and riders often switch from one group to another as they prepare for different events. Oldfields teams are exceptionally strong, and it is considered an honor to be a team member.

**Facilities:** Indoor riding arena, two show rings, a cross-country course, and miles of trails in the heart of Maryland's foxhunting countryside

**Showing:** Equitation, hunter/jumper, combined training events, foxhunting on weekends

**Website:**
www.oldfieldsschool.com

**Type of School:**
Private 8-12 Girls Boarding School

## Potomac Polo School

Red Eagle Ranch, P.O. Box 447, Poolesville, MD 20837. Phone: (301) 972-7303. E-mail: info@redeagleranch.com.

**Degrees Offered:** Certificate, Award

**Majors Offered:** Polo

**Tuition Costs:** $250/three-lesson beginner package

**Description of Program:** PPS is the oldest polo school in the United States, first intro-

**Website:**
www.redeagleranch.com

**Type of School:**
Specialty School

ducing residents of the Washington, D.C., area to polo more than 20 years ago. Beginner, intermediate, and advanced polo players have found that PPR's instructors provide the level of quality and personalized instruction that brings out the best in any competitor. The instructors enjoy teaching as much as playing! Classes cover the basics of the rules, strokes, and the strategy of the game, combining lectures and hands-on experience. Students begin with the essentials of horsemanship and progress to the intermediate level of stick-and-ball practice. Then they go on to specially scheduled student games. A strong grounding in the fundamentals, backed up by hard-hitting field experience, turns determined riders into rated players. The polo school is fun and addictive! Students routinely arrive early and hang around after to socialize and discuss the day's play.

**Facilities:** Red Eagle Ranch

**Showing:** Chukkers

## St. Timothy's School

**Website:**
www.sttims-school.org

**Type of School:**
Private Secondary School

8400 Greenspring Ave., Stevenson, MD 21153. Phone: (410) 486-7401. Fax: (410) 486-1167. Email: admis@sttimothysschool.com.

**Degrees Offered:** High School Diploma

**Tuition Costs:** $30,725 Boarding; $17,750 Day

**Description of Program:** Almost a quarter of the students at St. Tim's participate in the riding program, whether they are competitive riders or riding for pleasure. Most girls ride the school horses, but some bring their own to board at the school. Several students enjoy foxhunting with the Carrollton Hounds, and many take advantage of ample opportunities in the area to compete. St. Timothy's sponsors a horse show each fall and spring and a series of winter indoor schooling shows. The Varsity and Junior Varsity teams compete with other schools, and riders participate in the Maryland Interschool Horse Show and Event, as well as the Mid-Atlantic Interschool Horse Show. The Equestrian Club organizes a riding trip to Europe each summer, sponsors clinics, and has hosted workshops run by well-known professionals including Frank Madden, Steve Bradley, and Phillip Dutton.

**Facilities:** The Hamilton-Ireland equestrian center located on the school's campus includes a 24-stall barn with two tack rooms and a wash stall, 70ft x 200ft indoor riding arena, 150ft x 300ft outdoor sand arena, double-fenced turnout paddocks, two fenced ten-acre fields, and three fenced five-acre fields, plus wooded trails.

**Showing:** Varsity and Junior Varsity inter-school competition, Maryland National "A" Horse Show, McDonogh School Horse Shows, Quentin "A" Horse Show, Baltimore and Harford County Horse Shows, Menfelt Horse Trials, Olde Hope Horse Trials, Olney Farm Horse Trials, Plantation Field Horse Trials, Maryland Combined Training Horse Trials at Shawann Downs

## University of Maryland

**Website:**
www.umd.edu

**Type of School:**
Public University

Animal & Avian Science, 1415 Animal Sciences Center, College Park, MD 20742-2311. Contact: Undergraduate Program Coordinator. Phone: (301) 405-1374 or (301) 405-1373. Fax: (301) 314-9059. Email: cdingess@umd.edu.

**Accreditation:** Middle States Association of Colleges and Schools

**Degrees Offered:** Certificate, Bachelor of Science, Master of Science, Doctor of Philosophy

**Majors Offered:** Animal Science with Equine option (B.S., M.S., Ph.D.), Equine Business Management (C), Pre-Vet (B.S.), Veterinary Medical Science (M.S., Ph.D.)

**Tuition Costs:** Resident: $5,136/year; nonresident: $12,668/year

**Description of Program:** Courses taught: Horse Management, Horse Management Practicum, Equine Science, Pasture Management/Hay Production, Equine Business Management, Equine Health Management, Equine Nutrient Management. Dressage quadrille, jumping, pleasure, and combined training riding styles taught. Extracurricular activities: Equestrian Club, Equestrian Team, and Veterinary Science Club.

**Facilities:** A ten-stall barn on the main campus houses the Equestrian Club horses. Riding venues include two outdoor rings on campus, plus trails on campus and in adjacent parkland. The equestrian team rides and competes out of Clay Hill Stables in nearby Springdale, Maryland.

**Classroom/Hands-On Equine Classes:** Most courses have a hands-on component.

**Showing:** IHSA

# MASSACHUSETTS

## Cushing Academy

39 School Street, P.O. Box 8000, Ashburnham, MA 01430-8000.
Phone: (978) 827-7300. Fax: (978) 827-6253. Email: admission@cushing.org.
**Degrees Offered:** High School Diploma
**Tuition Costs:** Boarding: $33,285; Day: $23,250
**Description of Program:** Cushing Academy is an independent, co-educational boarding school located about an hour west of Boston, Massachusetts. Horseback riding is offered as a minor afternoon activity during spring term. Participants are of varying levels of ability and experience. Students travel to stables that are located approximately 20 minutes from campus.

**Website:**
www.cushing.org

**Type of School:**
Secondary School

## Dana Hall School

45 Dana Road, Wellesley MA 02482. Phone: (781) 235-3010. Fax: (781) 235-0577. Email: admission@danahall.org.
**Degrees Offered:** High School Diploma
**Tuition Costs:** $32,475: Upper School Boarder and International; $24,600: Upper School Day; $24,600: Middle School Day
**Description of Program:** Grades 6-12 Day School, Grades 9-12 Boarding School. The Dana Hall School Riding Centre gives priority to Dana Hall students in its lesson program for beginning through advanced students. The riding center offers a hunt seat equitation program for beginning through advanced students. All students may ride for physical education credit, which requires lessons twice a week per trimester. Students may also choose to ride one or twice a week per trimester for non-credit physical education. Riding instruction is typically offered in hour-long group lessons, and half-hour private or semi-private lessons on a more limited basis. Students are grouped according to ability and a strong emphasis is placed on safety for horse and rider. The program focuses on teaching control, correct position, and strives to develop confidence at the walk, trot, canter, and over jumps. Good horsemanship, including basic care and preparation of the horse is stressed. In addition to its lesson program, the Center has a strong horse show program. Students can join the interscholastic riding team where they compete with other schools in the area without having to own a horse. Students may also participate in the regular horse show program, year-round.

**Facilities:** Two indoor riding rings and one outdoor ring; two enclosed observation

**Website:**
www.danahall.org

**Type of School:**
Secondary Private Boarding School

areas; two wash stalls and seven turnout paddocks; stable accommodates 46 horses; 24 school horses.

**Showing:** Interscholastic, National Pony Finals, Regional and National Equitation Finals, Local Shows, East Coast "A" Circuit, Florida "A" Circuit during the winter

## Institute of Equine Podiatry

Institute of Equine Podiatry, Inc., 19 Woodchuck Lane, Spencer, MA 01562. Phone/Fax (508) 248-4444 (MA) (518) 993-2074 (NY). Email: kc@thenaturalequine.com.
**Degrees Offered:** Certificate, Workshops
**Majors Offered:** Equine Podiatrist (C), High Performance Trim Method (W)

## Lucky Braids™ Top Turnout™ Clinics with Ruthann Smith

Phone: (781) 665-5988 or (877) 272-4337
**Description of Program:** Ruthann Smith teaches how to groom horses to win. Topics include: horse care myths and tips, braiding, barn management, achieving the shiniest coat, stress-free mane pulling, and safety. Two-day workshops include engaging demonstrations and individualized hands-on segments.
**Facilities:** Various international locations

## Mount Holyoke College

50 College St., South Hadley, MA 01075-1430. Contact: Joanne Bonano.
Phone: (413) 538-2000. Email: jbonano@mtholyoke.edu.
**Degrees Offered:** Bachelor of Science
**Majors Offered:** No equine major offered, Pre-Veterinary (B.S.)
**Tuition Costs:** Riding classes: $500/semester; horse board: $550/month
**Description of Program:** Riding classes meet twice weekly to earn physical education credits. The program offers classes and private lessons in hunt seat equitation, dressage, and jumping. In addition, the program offers clinics with international competitors, seminars, and horse shows. Both the IHSA hunt seat team and the IDA dressage team are highly competitive and nationally renowned.
**Facilities:** The state-of-the-art facility includes 60 airy, rubber-matted stalls, two heated tack rooms, two heated wash stalls, turnout paddocks, and an overnight security system. The large 100ft x 256ft indoor riding arena is connected to the stable by another 100ft x 70ft indoor arena. There is a Fibar dressage arena, a large outdoor jumping area, cross-country courses, and more than 120 acres of woods, fields, and streams for trail riding. Students may stable their privately owned horses at the equestrian center.
**Showing:** In addition to the IHSA and IDA competitions, the equestrian center hosts monthly hunter/jumper schooling shows and an annual dressage and combined test schooling show. Students are encouraged to participate on their own horses, or they may use a school horse.

## Mount Ida College

Mount Ida College, Office of Admissions, 777 Dedham St., Newton Centre, MA 02459. Phone: (617) 928-4553. Fax: (617) 928-4507. Email: admissions@mountida.edu.
**Accreditation:** New England Association of Colleges and Schools
**Degrees Offered:** Associate of Arts, Bachelor of Science

**Majors Offered:** Veterinary Technician (A.A.), Veterinary Technology (B.S.), Equine Management (B.S. in Business Administration)

**Tuition Costs:** $16,100 per year; $9,000 room and board

**Description of Program:** The Equine Studies Program prepares student in all facets of horse care, stable management, competition preparation, and riding and training through continual hands-on practice taught by a professional faculty. Teaching is geared towards today's hunt seat riders, focusing on the "A" circuit hunter/jumper shows in the Northeast region of the country as well as on the Florida circuit. The students can tailor their programs to their career goals by selecting courses from other areas such as journalism, photography, merchandising, and psychology. Students can spend a semester of their junior year abroad. The program includes internships that provide an opportunity to gain outside experience, acquire references, and network. Our students have trained with equine message therapists, worked on breeding farms with foals, helped prepare young horses for the race track, learned to groom on the "A" circuit in Florida, and competed during winter break on the Florida circuit. The Veterinary Technician and Veterinary Technology Programs focus almost exclusively on working with animals in medical and laboratory settings. Students participate in hands-on learning at onsite facilities, including a kennel and clinic, radiography area, animal runs, a grooming center and a stable. Practical learning is also emphasized though off-site internships, opening doors to future employment opportunities.

**Facilities:** Students take their equitation and other hands-on classes at River Wind Farm, a lovely equestrian facility in Pembroke, MA, specializing in Hunter, Jumper and Equitation.

**Showing:** Mount Ida Equestrian Team (IHSA), local, open, and "A" shows

## Stockbridge School of Agriculture

115 Stockbridge Hall, University of Massachusetts Amherst, Amherst, MA 01003. Contact: Ms. Suzanne Mente, Equine Industries Program Coordinator. Phone: (413) 549-3250. Email: mente@vasci.umass.edu. Admissions Contact: Kathy Conway, Phone: (413) 545-2222. Email: kmconway@nre.umass.edu.

**Accreditation:** New England Association of Schools and Colleges

**Degrees Offered:** Associate of Science

**Majors Offered:** Equine Industries

**Tuition Costs:** $8,982 resident; $17,836 nonresident; $5,748 room and board

**Description of Program:** Stockbridge School of Agriculture, founded in 1918, is the two-year component of the College of Natural Resources and the Environment at the University of Massachusetts—Amherst. The Equine Industries major was established in 1989. It is a horse management program with emphasis on the care, breeding, and training of horses. Business and financial aspects of the industry are also covered. Hands-on experience is gained by working with the University's 70-horse herd, which includes 30 registered Bay State Morgans. The offspring of the Morgan breeding program provide animals for training classes and school horses for the riding program. Courses include Anatomy & Physiology; Handling Horses; Equine Skills; Horse Breeds, Types and Selection; Stud Farm Management; Equine Business; Equine Management; Animal Care & Welfare; Nutrition & Feeding; Equine Diseases; Equitation; Practice Teaching Equitation; Breaking & Training; English; Math; Biology; Chemistry; Marketing.

**Facilities:** Farm on 138 acres, three spacious barns, indoor arena, dressage arenas, 5/8-mile track

**Classroom/Hands-On Equine Classes:** 40:60

**Showing:** IHSA, Interscholastic Dressage Association, horse trials

**Website:**
www.umass.edu/stockbridge/

**Type of School:**
Two-Year School at State University

## Stoneleigh-Burnham School

574 Bernardston Road, Greenfield, MA 01301. Contact: George Halkett, Riding Director. Phone: (413) 773-8333. Fax: (413) 772-2602. Email: ghalkett@sbschool.org.
**Degrees Offered:** High School Diploma
**Tuition Costs:** Boarding students: $29,700/year; Day students: $18,800/year
**Description of Program:** Instruction is offered in hunters, jumpers, equitation, dressage and combined training. The program accommodates students of all levels, from the experienced competitor to the recreational rider to the absolute beginner. Equine science provides an in-depth coverage of various breeds, the anatomy and physiology of the horse, and horse management. The course considers the relationship of conformation, proper function, and the development of unsoundness. Disease, preventative health care, and nutrition are studied in detail. Practical subjects, such as principles of training, medications, stable management, and facility design are covered. There are class practicals on a variety of topics, with regular sessions at the school's barn and with the school's veterinarian. Stoneleigh-Burnham riders find numerous opportunities to improve their riding skills, learn about the operation and organization of horse trials and horse shows, and have fun through lessons, competitions, clinics, volunteerism, and the riding club.
**Facilities:** Two barns house 45 school horses with stabling for 66 horses available in total. Each barn has its own wash stall, tack room, lounge, and tack cleaning room. The indoor riding arena complex features a 100ft x 200ft indoor competition arena with a heated viewing lounge, and an adjacent 70ft x 120ft indoor warm-up arena. The outside facilities include two sand rings, a derby field consisting of permanent European-style derby jumps, a cross-country course for novice, training, and preliminary levels, and a bridle path surrounding the school's 100-acre campus.
**Showing:** AHSA, USCTA, USDF, interscholastic competitions on and off campus

## Tufts University

School of Veterinary Medicine, 200 Westboro Road, North Grafton, MA 01536.
Phone: (508) 839-5302.
**Degrees Offered:** Master of Science, Doctor of Philosophy, Doctor of Veterinary Medicine
**Majors Offered:** Animals and Public Policy (M.S.), Comparative Biomedical Sciences (Ph.D.), Veterinary Medicine (D.V.M.)

## University of Massachusetts–Amherst

Animal Science, University of Massachusetts, 115 Stockbridge Hall, Amherst, MA 01003. Phone: (413) 545-2371. Fax: (413) 577-1150. Email: sde@vasci.umass.edu.
**Degrees Offered:** Associate of Science, Bachelor of Science, Doctor of Veterinary Medicine (through Tufts University School of Veterinary Medicine)
**Majors Offered:** Equine Industries (A.S.) [through Stockbridge School of Agriculture], Animal Science (B.S.) with emphasis in Equine Studies in Horsemanship Skills or Equine Studies Management, Animal Science B.S./ D.V.M. Dual Degree

# MICHIGAN

## Michigan State University

Animal Science, Michigan State University, 124 Anthony Hall, East Lansing, MI, 48824-1225. Contact: Dr. John Shelle. Phone: (517) 353-9227 or (517) 355-8383. Fax: (517) 353-1699. Email: shelle@msu.edu.
**Degrees Offered:** Certificate of Completion, Bachelor of Science, Master of Science, Doctorate of Philosophy, Doctor of Veterinary Medicine
**Majors Offered:** Horse Management (C.C.), Animal Science with Equine emphasis (B.S.), Animal Science with Equine concentration (M.S., Ph.D.), Veterinary Medicine (D.V.M.)
**Description of Program:** Dressage, hunt seat, and Western riding taught.
**Facilities:** Indoor arena, breeding program
**Showing:** IHSA, open dressage shows, Arabian shows, rodeo

**Website:**
www.msu.edu

**Type of School:**
Public University

## Schoolcraft College

CES Department, 18600 Haggerty Road, Livionia, MI 48152. Contact: Diane Burns. Phone: (734) 462-4448. Fax: (734) 462-4538. Email: admissions@schoolcraft.edu.
**Accreditation:** North Central Association of Colleges and Schools
**Degrees Offered:** Certificate
**Majors Offered:** Equine Arts & Science
**Tuition Costs:** Vary
**Description of Program:** The Equine Arts & Science Program at Schoolcraft College is offered through Continuing Education. The program has more than 60 different courses to offer, ranging from horse care to conditioning, from training to breeding. These courses are taught by veterinarians, trainers, and respected equine professionals. Students may take individual courses, or they may work towards a certificate. Some of the courses are held at local farms, but the majority are held in a classroom setting on campus. The Equine Arts & Science Program is offered during the fall and winter semesters. Admission to the college is not necessary. No riding.
**Facilities:** Some courses are held at local farms, but the majority are held in a classroom setting on campus. No housing provided.
**Classroom/Hands-On Equine Classes:** Only a few hands-on courses available.

**Website:**
www.schoolcraft.edu

**Type of School:**
Community College

## Wolverine Farrier School

3104 E. Stevenson Lake Rd., Clare, Michigan 48617. Phone: (989) 386-7430. Email: ggray@journey.com.
**Degrees Offered:** Certificate
**Majors Offered:** Basic Farrier Course

**Website:**
www.wfschool.com

**Type of School:**
Specialty School

# MINNESOTA

## Minnesota Horse Training Academy

1253-210th Avenue, Ogilvie, Minnesota 56358. Contact: Larry Surrett, Head Instructor. Phone: (320) 272-4199. Email: mntrainingacademy@hotmail.com.

**Degrees Offered:** Diploma

**Majors Offered:** Horse Training

**Description of Program:** This course runs 40 hours per week for three weeks. Training takes place during the morning, with hands-on experience provided afterwards. Each is designed to teach you everything from cutting cows to taking bows. Each student trains a horse to neck rein, back, perform a sliding stop without a bridle, and stand quietly while the rider fires a gun. Students also learn basic handling, halter training, gentling, sacking, controlled and free longing, ground driving, bitting and flexing, changing leads, and using leg aids. Each class will train a trick horse and learn the mechanics of teaching a horse to do anything physically possible, including bow, sit, play dead, have a gun fired overhead, count, say yes or no, smile, give kisses, etc. Each class will also train a special performance horse, such as a calf roping horse. Students will also learn to teach horses to sidepass, give to pressure, turn on the forehand and hindquarters, advance under saddle, load in a trailer, perform in a trail class, drive single and double, etc. Students will be taught how to correct problems such as kicking, rearing, bucking, and shying. Students are given more knowledge for less money.

**Facilities:** Box stalls, automatic waterers, bedding, and feed supplied. Lodging includes bedroom, sitting room, bathroom, huge kitchen with all the appliances needed, TV and VCR.

**Showing:** There is a competition at the end of each course for a trophy and "head of the class" honors.

## Minnesota School of Horseshoeing

6250 Riverdale Drive, N.W., Ramsey, MN 55303. Contact: Richard T. Duggan, Owner. Phone: (763) 427-5850 or (800) 257-3395. Fax: (763) 427-3395. Email: nancy.duggan@worldnet.att.net.

**Accreditation:** Licensed by State of Minnesota

**Degrees Offered:** Diploma

**Majors Offered:** Farrier Program, Apprenticeship Program

**Tuition Costs:** $3,800 plus $950 for books and tools

**Description of Program:** The Farrier Science Program is a ten-week, complete course designed to provide you with entry-level skills in the art and science of horseshoeing. Together with the optional apprenticeship program, this is the most comprehensive source of its kind offered by a private institution in the United States. The primary purpose of this in-depth approach is to prepare students who wish to practice horseshoeing professionally. This is a forge-based program, with the major emphasis on balancing horses, or corrective shoeing. Because of the great responsibility farriers have to the well-being of horses, and the high degree of skill necessary to succeed, it is this program's desire to develop technical excellence and instill strong professional attitudes in its graduates. Though not all students may have this professional goal as their personal objective, all students must demonstrate progress in the development of their academic and physical skills.

**Facilities:** The school is housed in a well-maintained modern building. The shop is fully equipped and designed with ample room for shoeing horses and working at the forge. The classroom and offices are electrically heated and carpeted for the students' comfort. Students work on horses from outside stables. Housing is not provided, though the school will help to make arrangements.

**Classroom/Hands-On Equine Classes:** 20:80

## University of Minnesota College of Veterinary Medicine

1365 Gortner Avenue, St. Paul, MN 55108. Phone: (612) 624-4747.
Email: dvminfo@umn.edu.
**Degrees Offered:** Doctor of Philosophy, Doctor of Veterinary Medicine
**Majors Offered:** Molecular Veterinary Biosciences (Ph.D.), Veterinary Medicine (Ph.D., D.V.M.)

**Website:**
www.cvm.umn.edu

**Type of School:**
Veterinary School in
Public University

## University of Minnesota–Crookston

Equine Industries Management Program, University of Minnesota–Crookston, 2900 University Avenue , Crookston, MN 56716. Contact: Cheryl Byrne, Assistant Professor. Phone: (218) 281-8111. Email: byrne038@umn.edu.
**Accreditation:** North Central Association of Colleges and Schools
**Degrees offered:** Associate of Applied Science, Bachelor of Science
**Majors offered:** Agriculture with emphasis in Animal/Dairy/Equine Science (A.A.S.), Equine Industries Management (B.S.) with emphasis in Pre-Veterinary study
**Tuition Costs:** $162.38/credit; $2,642 room and board/semester
**Description of Program:** Two to ten instructed rides per week; riding class size limit of ten students. Specialty riding classes include: hunt, saddle and stock seat; light horse driving, breaking and training. Equine and animal science courses in equine reproduction with emphasis on assisted reproductive techniques, production, exercise physiology, management and evaluation include lab practicals. Stallions and broodmares on premise. Mandatory internship experience. Equine Industries Management degrees prepare students with the hands-on experience and theoretical background to enter the horse industry as farm managers for breeding/training/boarding facilities, trainers/instructors, feed/pharmaceutical/tack sales, breed organization administration. Pre-vet concentration fulfills requirements for application to the University of Minnesota—College of Veterinary Medicine.
**Facilities:** State-of-the-art equestrian facility, barn, indoor ring with bleachers, round pen, classrooms, reproduction lab, breeding phantom, stocks, outdoor ring, 40 school horses
**Showing:** Horseman's Association, IHSA, Rodeo Association, student-run horse shows

**Website:**
www.crk.umn.edu

**Type of School:**
Public University

# *MISSISSIPPI*

## Mississippi State University

Animal & Dairy Sciences, Mississippi State University, P.O. Box 9815, Mississippi State, MS 39762. Contact: Terry Kiser, Dept. Head. Phone: (662) 325-2802. Fax: (662) 325-8873. Email: tkiser@ads.msstate.edu.
**Degrees Offered:** Bachelor of Science, Doctor of Veterinary Medicine
**Majors Offered:** Animal Science with equine emphasis (B.S.), Animal Science with Pre-Vet science option (B.S.), Veterinary Medicine (D.V.M.)
**Tuition Costs:** Resident: $1,937/semester; nonresident: $2,453/semester; housing: $1,270/semester
**Description of Program:** Western and English riding styles taught

**Website:**
www.msstate.edu

**Type of School:**
Public University

**Website:**
www.mofoxtrot.com/heartland/ or
www.ruralheritage.com

**Type of School:**
Specialty School

## Heartland Horseshoeing School

327 SW 1st Lane, Lamar, MO 64759. Phone: (417) 682-6896. Fax: (417) 682-6394. Email: anvil@earthlink.net.
**Degrees Offered:** Certificate of Completion
**Majors Offered:** Practical Farrier Course, Advanced Farrier Course, Journeyman Farrier Course, Farrier Blacksmith Course, National Certification Course

**Website:**
www.sankeyrodeo.com

**Type of School:**
Specialty School

## Sankey Rodeo Schools

3943 Sycamore Church Road, Branson, MO 65616. Phone/Msgs.: (417) 334-2513. Fax: (417) 332-0676. Email: info@sankeyrodeo.com.
**Degrees Offered:** Certificate
**Majors Offered:** Bareback, Saddle Bronc, Bull Riding, Junior Bull Riding, Clown-Bull-fighting
**Tuition Costs:** $250 to $380, depending on location and session length
**Description of Program:** Bareback, Saddle Bronc, Bull Riding, and Junior Bull Riding (age fourteen and under), along with Clown-Bullfighting. The perfect place for beginners to get the right start or for veterans to polish up. Sankey Rodeo Schools are designed to provide physical and mental training techniques essential to success in the sport, a solid foundation for beginner or novice athletes, and fine tuning for advanced competitors ready to take it to the next level. Classroom sessions go beyond technical skills and give you an in-depth look at other important issues of successful rodeo competition, such as rodeo business, building winning attitude, getting sponsorships, animal rights concerns, rodeo training, conditioning, injury response, rule book review, realizing your potential, goal setting, motivation, safety considerations, how to get started, rodeo travel tips, learning how to win, and becoming consistent.
**Facilities:** Rodeo facilities with classroom nearby. Housing is typically not supplied.
**Classroom/Hands-On Equine Classes:** Classroom is two hours, and the rest of the day is hands-on.
**Showing:** End-of-course competition

**Website:**
www.shurshod.com

**Type of School:**
Specialty School

## Shur Shod Horseshoeing School

2900 Bluebird Drive, Grovespring, MO 65662. Phone: (417) 462-7848.
Email: kelly@shurshod.com or max@shurshod.com.
**Degrees Offered:** Certificate
**Majors Offered:** Horseshoeing, Blacksmithing
**Tuition Costs:** $2,100; includes housing and tools
**Description of Program:** Six students per class with two instructors. Each session is four weeks in length, with a total of 160 structured class hours. Students are allowed additional practice time before and after class hours to further develop their skills. Prior experience in handling horses is helpful, but not required. Instruction begins with the basics and consists of demonstrations, lectures, hands-on trimming and shoeing, and hands-on training in forge work. Students learn to make basic, corrective, pathological, and special-breed types of shoes. Additional topics covered in the program are horsemanship, anatomy and physiology, lameness, gaits, operation of a

horseshoeing business, and public relations.

**Facilities:** Students are furnished anvils, forges, and the necessary tools needed for forge work. The tuition also includes tools needed for trimming and shoeing. The students will have individual sleeping rooms with a communal kitchen and living room area.

**Classroom/Hands-On Equine Classes:** 99 percent hands-on

## Southwest Missouri State University

Agriculture Department, Southwest Missouri State University, 901 S. National Ave., Springfield, MO 65804-0094. Contact: Dr. Gary Webb. Phone: (417) 836-5638. Fax: (417) 836-6979. Email: agriculture@smsu.edu or gww454f@smsu.edu.
**Degrees Offered:** Minor, Bachelor of Science, Master of Science
**Majors Offered:** Animal Science or Agricultural Business (B.S.), Equine Science (M), Natural and Applied Science with concentration in Reproduction, Nutrition, or Management (M.S.)

**Website:**
www.smsu.edu

**Type of School:**
Public University

## Stephens College

Stephens College, 1200 East Broadway, Columbia, MO 65215. Contact: Admissions or Michelle Smith, Chair of the Equestrian Department. Phone: (573) 876-7207 or (800) 876-7207 (admissions office). Fax: (573) 876-7237. Email: apply@stephens.edu or mpsmith@stepherns.edu.
**Accreditation:** North Central Association of Colleges and Schools
**Degrees Offered:** Minor, Bachelor of Science
**Majors Offered:** Equestrian Business Management (B.S.), Equestrian Science (M)
**Tuition Costs:** $17,360 per year; $6,900 room and board per year; $275 horse board per month; $440 riding class fee
**Description of Program:** Two instructed rides per week; riding class size averages six students. Three instructors. Hunt seat, stock seat, saddle seat, and dressage riding styles taught. The Stephens College Equestrian Program, in conjunction with the Business Administration Program, offers an interdisciplinary program in Equine Business Management. A minor in Equestrian Sciences is also offered. The College's riding program began in 1925. The program maintains numerous horses of various breeds that have been donated for educational purposes. Each year, equestrian students and faculty participate in schooling through A-rated shows and host the Prince of Wales Charity Horse Show. Stephens' Prince of Wales Club was established in 1926 and is one of the oldest continually active riding clubs in the nation.
**Facilities:** Indoor arena, a lighted outdoor arena, seven turn-out paddocks, two stables, and a cross-country course on eighteen acres.
**Classroom/Hands-On Equine Classes:** Vary
**Showing:** AHSA, AQHA, USEA, USDF, IAHA, open, and local

**Website:**
www.stephens.edu

**Type of School:**
Private College

## Truman State University

158 Barnett Hall, Kirksville, MO 63501. Contact: Dr. Charlie Apter, Assistant Professor and University Farm Director. Email: capter@truman.edu.
**Degrees Offered:** Minor, Bachelor of Science
**Majors Offered:** Agricultural Science with Equine Science emphasis, Ag Science Pre-Vet

**Website:**
http://agriculture.truman.edu

**Type of School:**
Public Liberal Arts and Sciences University

**Tuition Costs:** In-state: $104/credit; out-of-state: $186/credit; room and board: $4,400/year; horse board: $225/month; riding class: $50-$75

**Description of Program:** Two instructed rides per week; riding class size averages ten students. Two instructors. Truman State University has been ranked for five consecutive years as the number-one public university in the Midwest. The equine program at Truman provides the student with technical and hands-on training in the three major scientific areas related to horses: equine reproduction, equine nutrition, and equine exercise physiology. Courses in these three areas include both theory and the practical application of theory in hands-on exercises and experiences. Students may pursue a B.S. in agriculture with a pre-veterinary or equine emphasis, or may pursue a minor in Equine Science combined with any non-agriculture major offered at Truman. There are three avenues for pursuing and improving riding skills: horsemanship classes (3 levels), the Equestrian Team (IHSA-affiliated), and the Horseman's Association. Boarding for student-owned horses is available at Truman's farm. The farm is an integral part of the program; both a cattle and horse herd are housed there. Employment opportunities are available at the farm, as is limited on-farm housing for undergraduate students.

**Facilities:** Equestrian center is on 400 acres, located about one mile from campus at the edge of Kirksville. Facilities include a lighted indoor arena, three outdoor arenas, round pens, and 30 stalls in the stallion barn, mare motel, and breeding barn. Limited on-farm housing for students is also available rent-free in return for ten hours of work per week. Classrooms, teaching laboratories, and research laboratories are located on campus.

**Classroom/Hands-On Equine Classes:** 70:30

**Showing:** Equestrian Team, IHSA

## University of Missouri–Columbia

**Website:**
www.cvm.missouri.edu

**Type of School:**
Public University

Columbia, MO 65211. Phone: (573) 882-2121. E-mail: webeditor@missouri.edu.

**Degrees Offered:** Master of Science, Doctor of Philosophy, Doctor of Veterinary Medicine

**Majors Offered:** Biomedical Sciences with an emphasis in Veterinary Clinical Science (M.S.), Pathobiology (Ph.D.), Veterinary Medicine (D.V.M.)

## William Woods University

**Website:**
www.williamwoods.edu

**Type of School:**
Private Liberal Arts University

Equestrian Studies Division, William Woods University, One University Ave., Fulton, MO 65251-1098. Contact: Laura Ward, Program Director. Phone: (573) 592-1153 or (573) 642-2251. Fax: (573) 592-1196. Email: lward@williamwoods.edu.

**Accreditation:** North Central Association of Colleges and Schools

**Degrees Offered:** Minor, Bachelor of Science, Bachelor of Arts

**Majors Offered:** Equestrian Science (B.A., B.S., M), Equine Administration (B.A., B.S., M)

**Tuition Costs:** $14,000/year; $6,120 room and board

**Description of Program:** Applied instruction in dressage, hunter/jumper, saddle seat, and Western. The Equestrian Science degree is especially designed for the student interested in pursuing a career in training and managing horses, and/or teaching equitation. Students enrolled in the program receive both theoretical and applied "hands-on" experience through required course work. Equine Administration is the major for students who wish to pursue a career in equestrian business, equestrian organizations, breed associations, or facility and event management. Courses cover such topics as economics, entrepreneurship, promotion and public relations, law, and taxation in equine-specific formats. Five additional business and computer courses are required to intensify the major.

**Facilities:** Two heated indoor arenas, one lighted outdoor arena, cross-country course, 110 stalls for 110 school horses.

**Classroom/Hands-On Equine Classes:** 60:40

**Showing:** USAE, USDF, AQHA, open, schooling, judging

# MONTANA

## Cowtown Horseshoeing School

P.O. Box 841, Miles City, MT 59301. Contact: Merlin Anderson, Director.
Phone: (406) 232-3362. Fax: (406) 232-6656. Email: horseshoe@mcn.net.

**Accreditation:** Approval with Veterans Administration

**Degrees Offered:** Certificate

**Majors Offered:** Ten-week Horseshoeing Class

**Tuition Costs:** $5,000/ten-week course; includes housing

**Description of Program:** Classes are limited to six students so we can offer each student an intensive learning experience with close, individualized instruction. The primary emphasis of this course is the use of the Natural Balance method of trimming and shoeing. This method is proven to produce comfortable, sound horses. The course also includes forge work, basic corrective shoeing, and tool fabrication. The course's main goal is to provide you with the skills needed to become a competent farrier. Individualized instruction is offered using an unlimited number of live horses. Students are placed under the horse right away, and all available time is used for learning. The school is kept small by design. This ensures that teaching and learning are achieved and the best possible training is provided.

**Facilities:** The training facility is a 30ft x 40ft blacksmith shop and shoeing facility. Training will be conducted in real-world situations as often as possible. Some training will be conducted at local ranches. Student housing provided with laundry and cooking facilities at no additional charge.

**Classroom/Hands-On Equine Classes:** 40:60

**Type of School:**
Specialty School

## Dawson Community College

Agriculture, Dawson Community College, P.O. Box 421, Glendive, MT 59330. Contact: Tom Ree, Director of Agriculture. Phone: (406) 377-3396. Fax: (406) 377-8132. Email: WebMaster@dawson.cc.mt.us.

**Degrees Offered:** Associate of Applied Science

**Majors Offered:** Agricultural Business Technology with Equitation option

**Tuition Costs:** In-state: $59.50/credit; out-of-state: $179/credit; room and board: $4,350

**Description of Program:** Two instructed rides per week; riding class size averages twelve students. Dawson's two-year Agri-Business Technology degree program is intended to give students a broad business background, as well as the basic skills necessary for interpreting recent advances in agriculture technology. The program is

**Website:**
www.dawson.cc.mt.us

**Type of School:**
Community College

designed for students to pursue a four-year bachelor's degree. Those wishing to transfer after completing coursework at Dawson should work closely with an advisor and plan their work according to the most recent catalog of the transfer institution.

**Facilities:** Equestrian center is three to five miles from campus and has 23 school horses, one indoor arena, and one outdoor arena.

**Showing:** NIRA

## Equestrian Education Systems

**Website:**
www.equestrianeducation.org

**Type of School:**
Specialty School

P.O. Box 460125, Huson, MT 59846. Phone: (406) 626-1947 and (360) 675-3474. Fax: (406) 626-5774. Email: EquestrianEdu2@aol.com.

**Majors Offered:** Individualized Programs

**Tuition Costs:** Vary

**Description of Program:** EES offers a unique riding, teaching, and learning system designed for riders and instructors. The system blends modern and classical approaches to horsemanship. It combines educational theory, sports psychology, and exercise techniques from the fields of tai chi, yoga, and Pilates, as well as massage and relaxation therapy. EES promotes lifelong learning through a variety of programs, clinics, internships, workshops, seminars, and support materials.

## Montana State University

**Website:**
www.montana.edu

**Type of School:**
Public University

Department of Animal & Range Sciences, 119 Linfield Hall, P.O. Box 172900, Bozeman, MT 59717-2900. Contact: L.C. (Sandy) Gagnon, Equine Director or Mary Huenergardt, Administrative Assistant, Horseshoeing. Phone: (409) 994-6623 Gagnon or (409) 994-3722 Huenergardt. Email: gagnon@montana.edu or maryh@montana.edu.

**Degrees Offered:** Certificate, Bachelor of Science, Master of Science, Doctor of Philosophy, Doctor of Veterinary Medicine

**Majors Offered:** Horseshoeing (C), Animal Science (B.S., M.S., Ph.D.), Veterinary Medicine (D.V.M.)

**Tuition Costs:** Contact School

**Description of Program:** The Animal Science curriculum provides students with a firm foundation in biological and natural sciences, animal breeding and genetics, reproductive physiology, nutrition, and livestock production and management. The horse science program has been designed to give students an opportunity to study horse science and management, including the breaking and training of horses. Equitation classes in stock seat and English are taught. The emphasis in this horse science program has been placed on teaching rather than research. The Horseshoeing School offers an eleven-week program designed specifically for those who wish to pursue careers as farriers. This professional course provides students with the opportunity to obtain a solid background in the field of farrier science through the application of sound principles in a practical hands-on setting. Students will have the opportunity to obtain the knowledge and develop the skills necessary to establish their own practice, qualify for licensing at major race tracks, and prepare for the American Farrier Association Certification exam. Further study in an advanced class is also offered.

**Facilities:** Indoor arena. University maintains a herd of 40 equitation horses for class use, along with a small breeding herd of mares.

**Classroom/Hands-On Equine Classes:** 1:15 (Equine); 1:7 (Horseshoeing)

**Showing:** Rodeo, local, open

## Rocky Mountain College

Equestrian Department, Rocky Mountain College, 1511 Poly Dr., Billings, MT 59102-1796. Contact: Scott Neuman, Equestrian Director. Phone: (406) 657-1025. Fax: (406) 259-9751. Email: neumans@rocky.edu.
**Degrees Offered:** Minor, Bachelor of Science
**Majors Offered:** Equestrian Studies with emphasis in Equitation and Training, Equine Business, Equine Writing and Publications, Riding Instructor, or Therapeutic Riding

**Website:**
www.rocky.edu

**Type of School:**
Private University

# NEBRASKA

## University of Nebraska–Lincoln

A224 Animal Science, University of Nebraska–Lincoln, Lincoln, NE 68583. Contact: Kathy Anderson. Phone: (402) 472-6411. Email: kanderson1@unl.edu.
**Degrees Offered:** Bachelor of Science, Master of Science, Doctor of Philosophy
**Majors Offered:** Animal Science (B.S., M.S., Ph.D.), Pre-Vet (B.S.), Veterinary Science (M.S.)
**Tuition Costs:** $10,043 resident; $17,626 nonresident; includes room and board
**Description of Program:** The major in animal science is designed for students pursuing a career in the livestock, horse, poultry, or meat industry. There are five areas of the program, each focusing on a specific career objective: (1) Management positions with companies serving animal agriculture through the manufacture and distribution of feed, pharmaceuticals, equipment, and other products. (2) Animal production in beef, dairy, horses, poultry, sheep, and swine. (3) The processing of animals and their products (e.g., meat, eggs, wool). (4) Teaching animal science to youth and adults in formal education and extension. (5) Research and teaching in universities and in the industry. There are five options offered to Animal Science majors: Animal Biology, Animal Production, Animal Products, Business, Pre-Veterinary. In consultation with an animal science advisor, each student prepares a plan of study early in the four-year program. The Equine Emphasis may be used within any of the five Animal Science options. Students with an interest in the horse area are able to enroll in numerous courses dealing specifically with various aspects of horse production, equitation and evaluation. In addition, students majoring in a degree program other than Animal Science may choose a minor with the Equine Emphasis.
**Facilities:** On-campus equestrian center, one arena (80ft x 215ft), fourteen box stalls

**Website:**
www.unl.edu

**Type of School:**
Public University

# NEVADA

## University of Nevada–Reno

Department of Animal Biotechonology/School of Veterinary Medicine, Mail Stop 202, University of Nevada–Reno, Reno, NV 89557-0104. Contact: A. A. Cirelli, Jr. Phone: (775) 784-1635. Fax: (775) 784-1375. Email: acirelli@cabnr.unr.edu.
**Accreditation:** Northwest Association of Schools and Colleges
**Degrees Offered:** Bachelor of Science, Master of Science

**Website:**
www.unr.edu

**Type of School:**
Public University

**Majors Offered:** Animal Science with Equine option (B.S.), Animal Science (M.S.).

**Tuition Costs:** Undergraduate residents: $80.50/credit; undergraduate nonresidents: $85/credit; graduate residents: $107.50/credit; graduate nonresidents: $109/credit; room and board: $6,090

**Description of Program:** This major offers options emphasizing livestock management, biotechnology, and range livestock operations. Areas of study include, but are not limited to, the interaction of animals with their environments, meat technology, the nutritional requirements of animals, and reproductive physiology. The equine option curriculum is sequenced to provide progressive advancement through theory and technique. Equine anatomy and physiology, behavior, conformation, riding, training and conditioning, nutrition, reproduction, farm business management, and health management are a few of the topics examined at each level. Emphasis is placed on problem solving and learning-by-doing. All classes include hands-on sessions in a practical environment. Hunt seat and stock seat riding styles taught. The graduate program focuses on two major areas of research: animal nutrition and animal physiology. The animal nutrition option focuses on the utilization of forages by ruminants. The animal physiology option focuses mainly on reproduction, and emphasizes improving the efficiency of livestock production through new biotechnology.

**Facilities:** The equestrian center, an eighteen-acre facility, is located within walking distance of the main campus. It has indoor, outdoor, and dressage arenas, stalls, and pastures.

**Classroom/Hands-On Equine Classes:** 60:40

**Showing:** Intercollegiate riding team

# *NEW HAMPSHIRE*

## Brewster Academy

**Website:**
www.brewsteracademy.org

**Type of School:**
Secondary School

80 Academy Drive, Wolfeboro, NH 03894. Phone: (603) 569-7200. Fax: (603) 569-7272. Email: admissions@brewsteracademy.org.

**Degrees Offered:** High School Diploma

## New England Academy of Therapeutic Sciences

**Website:**
www.neats.com

**Type of School:**
Specialty School

402 Amherst Street, Nashua, NH 03063. Phone: (603) 886-8433. Fax: (603) 880-8654. Email: equineinfo@neats.com

**Degrees Offered:** Certificate

**Majors Offered:** Equine Bodywork Professional

## Proctor Academy

**Website:**
www.proctoracademy.org

**Type of School:**
Secondary School

P.O. Box 500, Andover, NH 03216. Contact: Christopher Bartlett, Director of Admission. Phone: (603) 735-6000. Fax: (603) 735-6284.
Email: admissions@proctornet.com.

**Accreditation:** New England Association of Schools and Colleges, National Association of Independent Schools member, Educational Records Bureau, Association of Boarding Schools, Council for Advancement and Support of Education

**Degrees Offered:** High School Diploma

**Tuition Costs:** Boarding: $32,700; Day: $20,100

## Thompson School of Applied Science

**Website:**
www.unh.edu/thompson-school/

**Type of School:**
Public University

Cole Hall, 291 Mast Rd., Durham, NH 03824-3562. Phone: (603) 862-1025. Fax: (603) 862-2915. Email: tsas.admit@unh.edu.

**Accreditation:** Affiliated with the University of New Hampshire

**Degrees Offered:** Associate of Applied Science

**Majors Offered:** Applied Animal Science, Equine Management

**Description of Program:** The riding focus at UNH is balance seat, with schooling in dressage, cross-country, and stadium jumping. Thompson School students in horsemanship classes ride in the UNH program and have the opportunity to compete in intercollegiate shows. The equine management specialization provides the most recent technical information, as well as related practical experience. The hands-on learning provides opportunities for bandaging, selection, ration-balancing by computer, fitting and care of equipment, and farm and barn analysis. The program emphasizes decision-making and managerial skills. The curriculum offers a solid basis for direct employment opportunities, yet affords enough flexibility for the students to further their education.

**Facilities:** On-campus equestrian center is on campus, one outdoor arena (85ft x 150ft), one indoor arena, a two-mile cross-country course (novice to preliminary)

**Showing:** Intercollegiate shows

## University of New Hampshire

**Website:**
www.unh.com

**Type of School:**
Public University

Animal & Nutritional Sciences, University of New Hampshire, Kendall Hall, Durham, NH 03824-3590. Contact: Dr. Tom Foxhall. Phone: (603) 862-1000. Fax: (603) 862-3758. Email: tf@christa.unh.edu.

**Accreditation:** New England Association of Schools and Colleges

**Degrees Offered:** Associate, Bachelor of Science

**Majors Offered:** Animal Science (B.S.), Equine (A)

**Tuition Costs:** $7,400 in-state; $5,100 room and board; $425/month horse board; $400/semester horsemanship lab fee

**Description of Program:** Two to three instructed rides per week; riding class size averages seven students. Three instructors. Balance seat, dressage, and combined training riding styles taught. The UNH Equine Program is proud to offer a unique and well-rounded program of study to students pursuing careers in the horse industry. The equine program's outstanding physical facilities are complemented by a strong science-based curriculum taught by a six-member faculty, all with years of experience in the equine industry. Small class size, an experienced faculty, and approximately 30 school horses enable students to gain practical hands-on experience in many areas of equine specialization. The core curriculum provides students with a solid background in the biological and equine sciences.

**Facilities:** On-campus equestrian center on campus, 40 school horses, one indoor arena (80ft x 160ft), one outdoor arena (100ft x 200ft), three dressage arenas, cross-country course, turnout, pasture facilities

**Classroom/Hands-On Equine Classes:** 50:50

**Showing:** IHSA, IDA, combined training, dressage

www.centenarycollege.edu

**Type of School:**
Private College

## Centenary College

Equine Studies, Centenary College, 400 Jefferson St., Hackettstown, NJ 07840-2100. Contact: Jane Ozga, Admissions. Phone: (800) 236-8679. Fax: (908) 852-3454. Email: admissions@centenarycollege.edu.

**Accreditation:** Middle States Association of Colleges Schools, National Association of State Directors for Teacher Education and Certification (NASDTEC)

**Degrees Offered:** Certificate, Associate of Science, Bachelor of Science

**Majors Offered:** Equine Studies (A.S., B.S.) with concentration in Equine Business Management, Communication for Equine Industry, or Riding Instruction and Training; Teaching Therapeutic Riding (C)

**Tuition Costs:** $17,820; room and board: $3,575; Equine Studies fee: $800/semester; horse board: $500/month

**Description of Program:** The curriculum is designed to meet the needs of today's fast-growing equine industry. Fully integrated into the college's liberal arts core curriculum, Equine Studies ensures a well-balanced and practical education, with a strong background in critical thinking and communication. The Equine Studies program was established in the early 1970s and currently has 140 full-time equine majors and 20 equine minors, part-time majors, and equine elective students. Major riding emphases are on hunt seat equitation, dressage, hunters, and jumpers. The four degrees lead students to careers in a variety of areas in the equine industry, including riding instruction, training, professional groom, barn management, advertising, marketing, public relations, journalism, therapeutic riding instruction and management, breeding, and veterinary-related positions. Class size is small. Internships are encouraged. The Career Center offers a variety of jobs to graduates and alumni. Horses are mostly Thoroughbred type, Warmbloods, and Quarter Horses. Each student is encouraged to ride every semester, but only the Riding Instruction & Training major requires this. Other majors require four semesters of riding. Other hands-on classes are Training the Green Horse, Course Design, Training Theory Applied, and Teaching Practicum. Every student is responsible for the care of a school horse three days per week.

**Facilities:** Two indoor arenas, one outdoor arena, fields to ride in, 80 stalls

**Classroom/Hands-On Equine Classes:** (Freshman) 75:25; (Upperclassman) 60:40

**Showing:** IHSA, Intercollegiate Dressage, Hunter/Jumper

**Website:**
www.rutgers.edu

**Type of School:**
State Agricultural College

## Cook College, Rutgers University

Department of Animal Science, Cook College, Rutgers University, 84 Lipman Dr., New Brunswick, NJ 08901. Contact: Dr. Sarah Ralston. Phone: (732) 932-9404. Fax: (732) 932-6996. Email: ralston@aesop.rutgers.edu.

**Accreditation:** Middle States Association of Colleges and Schools

**Degrees Offered:** Bachelor of Science, Master of Science, Doctor of Philosophy

**Majors Offered:** Animal Science with Equine specialty in Animal Industries (B.S., M.S., Ph.D.), Pre-Veterinary Sciences (B.S.)

**Tuition Costs:** Residents: $7,927; non-residents: $12,804; housing not included

**Description of Program:** The emphasis is on the science, giving the "why" not just "how to" information to our students. Many of our students go on to veterinary school. Three didactic courses (Horse Management, Nutrition, and Exercise Physiology) are devoted solely to equine issues; other courses, such as Animal Reproduction and Animal Nutrition, include equine topics. A practicum course and a fitting and handling class offer "hands-on" experience, and there are many opportunities for independent study and more "hands on" experience in equine research and cooperative education. A cooperative agreement with Delaware Valley College allows students to take some of their courses and vice versa. There are no riding programs on campus, only equine research activities and a limited Student Mounted Patrol, that uses 3 college-owned horses. There is a very active Equestrian Team, which trains at a local stable, and an Equine Science Club that organizes a wide variety of activities throughout the school year. 60 to 90 percent of pre-vet majors that apply to veterinary school after graduation are accepted. There is a strong Pre-Vet Club on campus for interested students.

**Facilities:** Two research barns, high-speed treadmill, "Equicizer," multiple turnout pastures, fully equipped research labs

**Classroom/Hands-On Equine Classes:** 50:50

**Showing:** IHSA

## Far Hills Forge

7 Timberline Road, Asbury, NJ 08802. Phone: (908) 537-9041.
Email: farhillsforge@hotmail.com.

**Accreditation:** AFA and the BWFA

**Degrees Offered:** Certificate

**Majors Offered:** Six-Month Horseshoeing Course

**Description of Program:** Video available on website with details

**Facilities:** The course is hands-on, and students travel to ranches to shoe horses.

**Website:**
www.farhillsforge.com

**Type of School:**
Specialty School

## Purnell School

Pottersville, NJ 07979. Contact: Darlene Snell, Director of Admission and Financial Aid. Phone: (908) 439-2154. Fax: (908) 439-4088. Email: info@purnell.org.

**Accreditation:** Middle States Association of Colleges and Schools, National Association of Independent Schools member, New Jersey Association of Independent Schools, National Association of Principals of Schools for Girls, National Coalition of Girls' Schools, Alumni Presidents' Council

**Degrees Offered:** High School Diploma

**Tuition Costs:** Boarding: $32,975; Day: $23,100; riding lessons not included

**Description of Program:** As a Purnell Student, you can take lessons, from beginning to advanced hunt seat equitation, with skilled instructors and classmates who are as enthusiastic about riding as you. Purnell is located in the heart of a peaceful and picturesque valley dotted with horse farms and estates, hunt courses and trails. Horse shows and trials, the Far Hills Race, and Pony Club events draw crowds of participants and spectators. The U.S. Equestrian Team is a neighbor, and the Essex Fox Hounds often meet on campus. The school's prime location has enabled it to be associated with one of the area's leading horse farms and instructional facilities: Fieldsteps Farm, in nearby Fairmount. The Purnell Equestrian Program is based here, on 40 scenic, well-groomed acres. Fieldsteps was chosen because of its outstanding indoor and outdoor facilities, well-regarded riding program, and close proximity to Purnell. It is also important that Fieldsteps, a family owned and operated farm, provides the same friendly and supportive learning that students experience at Purnell. Fieldsteps' highly qualified teaching staff has earned a reputation for inspiring and empowering young students.

**Website:**
www.purnell.org

**Type of School:**
All-Girls Secondary School

## Mesalands Community College

**Website:**
www.mesalands.edu

**Type of School:**
Community College

911 South Tenth St., Tucumcari, NM 88401. Contact: Nathan Allen, Div. Chair Applied Science. Phone: (505) 461-4413 x158. Fax: (505) 461-1901. Email: natea@mesatc.cc.nm.us.
**Degrees Offered:** Certificate, Diploma, Associate of Applied Science
**Majors Offered:** Agri-Business, Animal Science (A.A.S.) with concentration in Equine Science, Farrier Science (C)

## New Mexico State University

**Website:**
www.nmsu.edu

**Type of School:**
Land Grant University

Animal & Range Sciences, PO Box 30003 MSC 3-I, Las Cruces, NM 88003.
Contact: Dr. Jason Turner. Phone: (505) 646-1242. Email: jlturner@nmsu.edu.
**Accreditation:** North Central Association of Colleges and Schools
**Degrees Offered:** Minor, Bachelor of Arts, Bachelor of Science, Master of Science, Doctor of Philosophy
**Majors Offered:** Horse Management (M), Animal Science (B.S., M.S., Ph.D.), Pre-Veterinary Science
**Tuition Costs:** Undergraduate resident: $1,686/semester; undergraduate nonresident: $5,625/semester; housing: $1,220-1,877
**Description of Program:** NMSU offers intercollegiate competition in equestrian, horse judging, polo, and rodeo. NMSU offers Equitation I, II, III for both English and Western Equitation and a two-year-old training class. Care and Management courses address: health, nutrition, marketing, business management, reproduction, behavior, selection, and sales prepping. The NMSU Horse Program routinely maintains 30 to 40 horses for use in the equitation teaching program. While this herd is predominately Quarter Horses, there are some Arabians, Paints, and Thoroughbreds. The NMSU Horse Center has a well established Quarter Horse breeding program. The center maintains approximately 25 brood mares and three stallions. The foals produced by the program are extensively used in the "hands-on" teaching program, and sold as yearlings or two-year-olds in the April sale. The NMSU Polo Team routinely keeps approximately fifteen horses for use in daily practices and regional matches.
**Facilities:** The NMSU Horse Center is located one mile south of the main campus. It consists of 50 acres of irrigated pastures, four round pens, a polo arena, sale ring, and a yearling barn. The main barn contains offices and a reproduction laboratory. The Equine Education Center was opened in April 2003. It is located on the main campus and offers modern classroom facilities, offices, a spacious tack room, dressing rooms, and lockers. Adjacent to the center are two riding arenas, a round pen, and several pens for maintaining riding horses. The Aggie Rodeo Association has a large practice arena located five miles east of the main campus. There are approximately 60 outdoor stalls provided for NMSU Rodeo Team members.
**Classroom/Hands-On Equine Classes:** 50:50
**Showing:** IHSA

## Taos School of Equine Art

PO Box 2588, Taos, NM 87571. Phone: (505) 758-0350. Email: tas@laplaza.org.
**Majors Offered:** Drawing, Painting, Photography, Sculpting, Expeditions

**Tuition Costs:** $400/week-long workshop

**Description of Program:** The Taos School of Equine Arts offers the largest and most innovative selection of workshops on art and horses anywhere! The school specializes in a truly immersive experience: after a day of painting, sculpting, or drawing magnificent equine models all day, you can rent horses from a neighboring ranch and go riding in the nearby mountains for a few hours until sunset. All classes are held in the covered arena of a local barn with a horse in every class at all times—pats are encouraged! Weekly workshops include: Horse Painting for Beginners; A Horse of a Different Color; Equine Sculpture; Equine Photography; Painting the Arabian; Drawing the Dynamic Horse; The Spirit of the White Horse; Drawing Navajo Ponies; Canyon de Chelly Riding and Painting Expedition. College credit available.

**Facilities:** Housing not supplied

**Website:**
www.taosartschool.org

**Type of School:**
Specialty School

## Tellington Method Training

**Website:**
www.tellingtontouch.com

**Type of School:**
Specialty School

TTEAM and TTouch International
P.O. Box 3793, Santa Fe, NM 87506
Tel: 1-800-854-8326; Fax: 1-505-455-7233; Email: info@TTouch.com

**Degrees Offered:** Certification as a Tellington Method TTEAM Practitioner

**Tuition Costs:** From $650 to $800 per weeklong session

**Description of Program:** Linda Tellington-Jones, a pioneer in the arena of non-traditional horse training since 1965, has combined classical horsemanship with a scientific approach to training, while acknowledging the spiritual connection between horses and humans. The Tellington Method is a gentle, non-confrontational system of training that fosters a deep respect and relationship between horses and their people; enhances a horse's health and well-being, and resolves behavioral and performance challenges. This training approach recognizes the horses' individuality and can be customized to fulfill unique training needs and circumstances. Through the combination of gentle, directed touch, (Tellington TTouch) creative movement exercises (in hand and under saddle), and innovative training tools and equipment, the Tellington Method increases relaxation, promotes body awareness, improves athletic ability and accelerates a horse's willingness and ability to learn. The Tellington Method affects the whole being at the cellular level. The work is shown to affect a positive change in the trainer as well as the horse. Working with the body, mind, and spirit of horse and rider is a primary goal of the work.

To earn certification as a Practitioner of TTEAM (Tellington TTouch Equine Awareness Method), candidates must satisfactorily complete four week-long workshops, compile and present ten case studies for review, and complete a written exam. During the four trainings, a Practitioner level student will: learn and practice the TTouches and discuss their application; work with the TTEAM Confidence Course; learn and practice TTEAM leading positions and discuss their application; learn and practice the TTEAM method of ground driving; gain proficiency in use of TTEAM equipment under saddle, including the Lindell sidepull, TTEAM roller bit, neck ring, balance rein and body wraps, and learn the steps of riding bridleless; discuss saddle fit, equine dentistry and complementary veterinary modalities. Included are such specialty programs such as "Starting Young Horses", Peggy Cummings' Connected Riding, and Sally Swift's Centered Riding.

The TTEAM program is suitable for and highly popular with both beginners and professionals. Students gain valuable training tools in a supportive, non-judgemental learning environment. Problem-solving and independent thought are an integral part of the program.

As a Practitioner, individuals are qualified to work one-on-one with clients. To move up to higher levels, Practitioner 1, 2, and 3 candidates must complete additional workshops and fulfill further requirements. For a complete review of requirements for each level, visit the TTEAM website. Certification trainings are available in the United States, Canada, Germany, Switzerland, Austria, South Africa, and Australia, and weekend workshops taught by TTEAM practitioners are offered in 17 countries.

The Tellington Method sets high standards for TTEAM Practitioners. The basic tools of TTEAM are simple to learn, but it is the knowledge of the details that makes TTEAM so effective in a wide range of training situations.

**Facilities:** Facilities vary depending on workshop location.

**Classroom/Hands-On Equine Classes:** 20 percent classroom, 80 percent hands-on

# NEW YORK

## Alfred University

**Website:**
www.alfred.edu

**Type of School:**
Private University

Admissions, Alfred University, Alumni Hall, Saxon Dr., Alfred, NY 14802. Phone: (800) 541-9229 or (607) 871-2115. Fax: (607) 871-2712. Email: admwww@alfred.edu.

**Degrees Offered:** Minor

**Majors Offered:** Equestrian Studies

**Description of Program:** The program at Alfred provides students with several different opportunities to ride. Physical Education credit: class size is three to six students, with instruction in riding as well as in ground care. Equestrian Minor: students may earn 16 to 24 credits, with the opportunity for independent study in virtually any area. Varsity Intercollegiate Equestrian Team: the team attends three practices per week and eight competitions per year. There is no extra charge for students to participate on the team.

**Facilities:** The equestrian center is located off-campus, but transportation is provided by the school. Facilities include an indoor arena (80ft x 200ft), heated lounge, outdoor arena (150ft x 250ft), and 30 lesson horses of varying levels.

**Classroom/Hands-On Equine Classes:** 30:70

**Showing:** IHSA

## Cazenovia College

**Website:**
www.cazenovia.edu

**Type of School:**
Private College

Cazenovia College, 22 Sullivan St., Cazenovia, New York 13035. Contact: Barbara Lindberg, Associate Professor. Phone: (800) 654-3210. Email: belindberg@cazenovia.edu.

**Accreditation:** Middle States Association of Colleges and Schools

**Degrees Offered:** Certificate, Bachelor of Professional Studies

**Majors Offered:** Equine Reproduction Management (C), Professional Studies in Management with emphasis in Equine Business Management (B.P.S.)

**Tuition Costs:** $16,730/year; $6,960 room and board

**Description of Program:** Five full-time and thirteen adjunct instructors. The Equine Studies Degree Program blends the science of horse care with practical management skills necessary in all aspects of work within the horse industry. Application of learning through hands-on experience is a significant part of the coursework. The program involves some physically demanding work. Formal and informal laboratories are found in most of the courses and are heavily represented in the first two years of study. The college teaches a variety of riding and driving courses: hunter seat (flat and over fences), stock seat, reining, dressage, and pleasure driving. The riding and driving classes are hour-long instruction periods twice a week with an average of five students per class. The Equine Reproduction Management Certificate Program provides students with an opportunity to receive specialized training in the area of equine reproduction management. The program is designed to complement the baccalaureate degree.

**Facilities:** The equestrian center is located less than five miles from campus. The 243-acre farm houses 75 horses and includes one indoor arena (100ft x 300ft) with an enclosed second-floor viewing area, and three outdoor riding arenas, which include a dressage arena and a Grand Prix show jumping ring. Facilities also include classrooms, lockers for students, a student lounge, and a breeding barn, which has its own breeding lab.

**Showing:** IHSA Hunter Seat and Western Riding Team, IDA Dressage Team, Judging Team, recognized and local shows

## Cornell University

**Website:**
www.cornell.edu

**Type of School:**
Public University

Animal Science Department, Morrison Hall, Ithaca, New York 14892. Contact: Jean Griffiths or Harold Hintz. Phone: (607) 255-2857 or (607) 255-7191. Fax: (607) 255-9829. Email: jtg4@cornell.edu or hfh1@cornell.edu. Farrier Courses, College of Veterinary Medicine, Veterinary Medical Teaching Hospital, Cornell University, Ithaca, NY 14853. Contact: Mike Wildenstein. Phone: (607) 253-3127. Email: cms22@cornell.edu.

**Degrees Offered:** Certificate, Bachelor of Science, Doctor of Veterinary Medicine

**Majors Offered:** General Farrier (C), Advanced Farrier (C), Animal Science with three horse courses (B.S.), Veterinary Medicine (D.V.M.)

**Tuition Costs:** Contact School

**Description of Program:** Hunt seat, Western, dressage, and polo riding styles taught, as well as Animal Science, Agriculture, Farm Business Management, and Biological Sciences. The General Farrier Short Course is designed for persons who have demonstrated an interest in farriery and who have independently acquired some of the basic skills of the farrier trade. The sixteen-week Short Course provides students with general classroom and practical knowledge of related anatomy and the fundamental aspects of shoeing and fabrication of shoes. The Advanced Farrier Course is a one-week course available to practicing farriers with at least two years of experience and to active veterinarians interested in the latest advances in farriery techniques. This course will also provide advanced training for those interested in pursuing certification through the American Farriers Association.

**Facilities:** Indoor and outdoor arenas

**Classroom/Hands-On Equine Classes:** Depends on course

**Showing:** IHSA, Polo Team, open horse shows

## Houghton College

**Website:**
www.houghton.edu

**Type of School:**
Private Liberal Arts College

1 Willard Avenue, Houghton, NY 14744. Contact: Jo-Anne Young, Equestrian Program Director. Email: Joanne.Young@houghton.edu.

**Accreditation:** Middle States Association of Colleges and Schools, Regents of the University of the State of New York, Certified Horsemanship Association, Wesleyan Church affiliation

**Degrees Offered:** Minor, Bachelor

**Majors Offered:** Equestrian Studies (M), Pre-Veterinary (B)

**Tuition Costs:** $750 per credit (flat rate: $8,992/12-18 hours per semester plus $420/hour over 18); $3,000/year room and board; $170/month horse board; $135 riding lab fee; $300/year health coverage

**Description of Program:** One to six instructed rides per week; riding class size averages nine students. Two instructors. Courses taught: Horsemanship 1 (Beginners), Horsemanship 2 (Stable Management), Jumping 1, Jumping 2, Eventing, Dressage, Principles of Training, CHA Riding Instructor Certification, CHA Instructor of Riders with Disabilities Certification, Judging, Mini-Prix Jumping Equitation. Independent Studies in Driving, Pack and Trail, Endurance Riding, Reining, and more. Outstanding internationally-recognized clinicians teach clinics several times per year at the college. The college also hosts functions for WNYDA, such as "L" Judge programs and USDF Instructor Certification workshops. Pre-Veterinary Science (Biology Major) Program has a DVM on faculty.

**Facilities:** Equestrian center is 2 1/2 miles from campus with 20 school horses, one jumping arena (120ft x 240ft), one all-purpose arena (90ft x 220ft), one indoor arena (60ft x 145ft), one standard dressage arena, cross-country courses, and trails.

**Classroom/Hands-On Equine Classes:** 50:50

**Showing:** Students show at local and recognized competitions in hunters, jumpers, dressage, and eventing. The college provides coaching and transport of students and horses; students pay their own entry fees. The college also hosts several competitions each semester, as well as recognized dressage competitions in the spring.

## The Kildonan School

**Website:**
kildonan.org

**Type of School:**
Elementary, Middle and Secondary School

425 Morse Hill Road, Amenia, NY 12501. Contact: Bonnie A. Wilson, Director of Admissions. Phone: (845) 373-2013. Fax: (845) 373-2004.
Email: admissions@kildonan.org.

**Accreditation:** New York State Association of Independent Schools, National Association of Independent Schools member, chartered by New York State Board of Regents

**Degrees Offered:** High School Diploma

**Tuition Costs:** Boarding: $40,800; Five-Day Boarding: $38,800; Day: $28,000. Elementary: $23,000

**Description of Program:** Serves the needs of dyslexic students of average to above-average intelligence.

## The Knox School

**Website:**
www.knoxschool.org

**Type of School:**
Co-ed College Preparatory 6-12 School

541 Long Beach Road, St. James, NY 11780. Contact: Joanna Hulsey, Director of Admissions. Phone: (631) 584-6562. Fax: (631) 584-2022.
Email: jhulsey@knoxschool.org.

**Accreditation:** Middle States Association of Colleges and Schools, New York State Board of Regents, National Association of Independent Schools member, New York State Association of Independent Schools, Association of Boarding Schools, Secondary School Admission Test Board, National Association for College Admission Counseling

**Degrees Offered:** High School Diploma

**Tuition Costs:** $27,200/Boarding; $13,800/Day

**Description of Program:** The Knox Riding Program is offered during each of the three terms of the school year. Riding takes place each afternoon in a formal lesson with instructors. Weekend recreational riding is also available for all riders. The program is coeducational, and many students have found success in it. Instruction is given for hunters, jumpers, and hunter seat equitation. Showing is possible for those who wish to compete and are prepared to do so, but the riding program is accessible for beginning riders as well. Students may bring their own horses or may use the horses belonging to the school. Many of the horses presently housed on campus were donated to the school.

**Facilities:** The Phillips Equestrian Center is a unique horseshoe-shaped barn with 25 box stalls.

**Showing:** Varies

## Millbrook School

School Road, Millbrook, NY 12545. Phone: (845) 677-6873.
Email: admissions@millbrook.org.
**Degrees Offered:** High School Diploma

**Website:**
www.millbrook.org

**Type of School:**
Secondary School

## North Country School

Director of Admissions, North Country School-Camp Treetops, P.O. Box 187, Lake Placid, NY 12946. Phone: (518) 523-9329. Fax: (518) 523-4858.
Email: admissions@nct.org.
**Accreditation:** New York State Association of Independent Schools, American Camping Association, Secondary School Admission Test Board member, Educational Records Bureau, National Association of Independent Schools
**Tuition Costs:** $35,000
**Description of Program:** Students in grades 4-9 learn how to manage a horse from the saddle and from the ground during twice-daily barn chores. Horse care, tacking up, and English equitation are all part of the program of instruction. All children have riding lessons in the fall and spring. The goal of the North Country School Riding Program is not the show circuit (though a number of students each year are inspired to pursue riding at this level during their summers at home), but to expose students to the sport and (incidentally) to teach self-control, responsibility, and confidence through mastery of an animal far larger and stronger than themselves. The school has two riding rings and typically houses about a dozen horses. After sufficient skill is acquired through ring work, children may participate in rides over wooded trails on NCS property and in the surrounding wilderness. Stable management classes are frequently held for interested students. There is an annual horseback overnight camping trip, and a drill team is open to advanced riders.
**Facilities:** Two riding rings, twelve horses

**Website:**
www.nct.org

**Type of School:**
Elementary, Middle, and Secondary Boarding School

## State University of New York–Cobleskill

Animal Sciences Department, College of Ag. & Technology, State University of New York–Cobleskill, Cobleskill, NY 12043. Contact: Dr. Lynn Dunn.
Phone: (518) 255-5670. Fax: (518) 255-6025. Email: dunnl@cobleskill.edu.
**Degrees Offered:** Associate of Applied Science, Bachelor of Technology
**Majors Offered:** Agricultural Business Management with emphasis in Equine Business Management (B.T.), Animal Science with emphasis in Equine Studies (A.A.S. or B.T.) or Thoroughbred Management (A.A.S.), Pre-veterinary Studies
**Tuition Costs:** In-state: $5,689/year; out-of-state: $8,339/year; room and board: $6,780/year

**Website:**
www.cobleskill.edu/ag/

**Type of School:**
Public University

**Description of Program:** The Equine Program is designed to give the student an applied science education in all aspects of the horse industry. The Bachelor of Technology Degree Program includes a fifteen-week internship that provides a valuable experience in the horse industry. The Thoroughbred Management Program is designed for the student who wishes to enter the Thoroughbred racing and breeding industry. The curriculum is centered around a summer at Saratoga, and involves a unique six-week experience in which the student works the backstretch for a successful trainer, works on a commercial breeding farm, assists the National Museum of Racing Hall of Fame with their educational activities, and works at the Fasig-Tipton yearling sales. This summer experience is followed up on-campus in the fall; the students apply the skills they have learned to complete the breaking and early training of yearlings and to prepare yearlings for the Fasig-Tipton Mid-Atlantic Sale.

**Facilities:** Saratoga racetrack, indoor arena, one-mile gallop track, paddocks, heated demo area

**Classroom/Hands-On Equine Classes:** 29/15 credits (Equine Concentration—B.T.), 10/4 (Equine Studies—A.A.S.), 8/4 (Thoroughbred Management)

**Showing:** IHSA, IDA, local and open shows, competitive trail rides

## State University of New York–Morrisville

Equine Studies, State University of New York–Morrisville, Morrisville, NY13408. Phone: (315) 684-6046. Fax: (315) 684-6125. Email: admissions@morrisville.edu.

**Accreditation:** Middle States Commission on Higher Education

**Degrees Offered:** Associate of Applied Science, Bachelor of Technology

**Majors Offered:** Equine Science and Management (A.A.S.), Equine Racing Management (A.A.S.), Equine Science (B.T.) with emphasis in Equine Science and Management, Equine Breeding Management, or Equine Racing Management

**Tuition Costs:** In-state: $14,250/year; out-of-state: $16,900/year

**Description of Program:** The Equine Science and Management Program provides the student with hands-on opportunities to concentrate on breeding, riding, training, nutrition, and management specifically with horses, rather than with a generalized group of livestock. The Equine Program emphasizes "hands-on" participation in breaking, care, training, conditioning, and racing. Students work one-on-one with assigned horses. Upon successful completion of the United States Trotting Association driver/training test and other mandated requirements, students in the racing program are able to race horses on the New York county fair circuit or amateur driving events at a local pari-mutuel track. In addition to the "hands-on" experience, students are exposed to a core of other equine courses. The Equine Science bachelor's degree is designed to further the technical and business knowledge and skills of an individual while developing their management and decision-making ability. Courses ranging from Equine Business Management to Applied Equine Nutrition to Animal Genetics allow the student to advance academically while being actively involved with enterprise management. The focal points of the B.T. in Equine Science are the courses in Advanced Equine Specialization; a work internship or international exchange program is required to complete the degree.

**Facilities:** More than 250 school horses, three indoor arenas (80ft x 264ft and two 100ft x 200ft), two outdoor arenas (100ft x 200ft), half-mile racing track, four horse barns, round pens, hot walkers, trails, paddocks

**Classroom/Hands-On Equine Classes:** Intensive hands-on opportunities

**Showing:** Harness racing and Thoroughbred racing (pari-mutual, fairs), Western and hunt seat, IHSA, open, and breed shows, pleasure and draft driving open and breed shows

**Website:**
www.morrisville.edu

**Type of School:**
Public University

## William H. Miner Agricultural Research Institute

Website:
www.whminer.com

Type of School:
Non-Profit Private Education and
Research Facility

Miner Institute, P.O. Box 90, 1034 Rt. 191, Chazy, NY 12921. Contact: Karen Lassell, Equine Manager.  Phone: (518) 846-7121. Fax: (518) 846-8445.
Email: lassell.whminer.com.
**Degrees Offered:** Internship
**Majors Offered:** Equine Management
**Tuition Costs:** No tuition; students receive stipend of $2,500 minus room and board of $300
**Description of Program:** Summer internship in equine management for college credit. There are approximately two hours of formal lecture or field trip time per week during the thirteen-week internship; the rest of the time is spent working and learning "on the job." Courses are taught in management, basic training, stallion handling, and mare management. The work week is similar to a commercial farm. With three instructors and five students, the program offers an excellent student-to-faculty ratio. Students learn by participating in all aspects of basic training for saddle and harness, as well as breeding farm management. Hunt, dressage, saddle, and driving styles taught.
**Facilities:** Extensive labs, stallion collection lab
**Classroom/Hands-On Equine Classes:** Approximately two hours of lecture or field trip time per week; the rest of the time is hands-on.
**Showing:** Miner attends a few shows during the summer—students have the opportunity to groom and do some showing.

# NORTH CAROLINA

## Martin Community College

Website:
www.martin.cc.nc.us

Type of School:
Community College

Martin Community College, 1161 Kehukee Park Road, Williamston, NC 27892. Phone: (252) 792-1521. Fax: (252) 792-4425.
Email: bwoolard@martin.cc.nc.us and cwennberg@martin.cc.nc.us.
**Degrees Offered:** Diploma, Certificate, Associate of Applied Science
**Majors Offered:** Equine Technology (A.A.S., D, C)
**Tuition Costs:** In-state: $35.50/credit; out-of-state: $197/credit; equine fee: $13.75/credit; activity fee: $19/semester
**Description of Program:** The Equine Technology curriculum is designed to prepare students for positions within the horse industry. The curriculum is management-oriented, preparing graduates for the widest range of available equine jobs; areas of specialization may be pursued during the internship. Farm management, breeding, nutrition, selection/judging, and health are covered in detail; training, teaching, and riding are also included. Students are assigned a horse and practice day-to-day management at the college's equine facility. The equine graduates' wide spectrum of knowledge suits them for jobs with many different types of equine operations: grooms to assistant managers, private to recreational and racing barns, breed to discipline-oriented farms.
**Facilities:** On-campus equestrian center, one indoor arena (100ft x 200ft), one outdoor arena (150ft x 300ft), roundpen, breeding lab
**Showing:** Local and open shows

## NC School of Horseshoeing and Equine Lameness

1165 Overby Rd., Walnut Cove, NC 27052. Phone: (336)994-9497.
Email: moreinfoplease@ncschoolofhorseshoeing.com.
**Accreditation:** Affiliated with the Eastcoast Horseshoer's Association
**Degrees Offered:** Certification
**Majors Offered:** Two-Week, Four-Week, Six-Week, Eight-Week, Nine-Week, Six-Week Evening
**Tuition Costs:** Two-week: $2,000; Four-Week: $3,000; Six-Week: $4,000; Eight-Week: $5,000; Nine-Plus-Week: same as Eight-Week, plus $500/each additional week; includes housing and basic meals
**Description of Program:** This is an apprenticeship program. Students are trained with a hands-on approach, beginning the very first day. All anatomy, lameness, and corrective training takes place through a unique, hands-on approach. The student-to-instructor ratio is low, as no more than five students are accepted at one time. Tuition covers clean, comfortable living quarters, three meals per day, use of all tools, and the instructors' time. Students are trained how to get and keep business, work with local veterinarians, and advertise. Ongoing support after graduation and yearly recertification is offered, with continued contact, support, and training provided free to farriers certified through the East Coast Horseshoer's Association. The school operates a mobile training unit, spending five to six days each week in the field. Programs can be individualized. At least 200 live horseshoeing experiences per student in each six-week course is guaranteed. Prospective students can spend a day with shoeing alongside current students and see for themselves why this shoeing school is Number One!
**Facilities:** Mobile training unit
**Classroom/Hands-On Equine Classes:** 100 percent hands-on

## North Carolina State University

Animal Science Department, North Carolina State University, Box 7621, Raleigh, NC 27695-7621. Contact: Dr. Jeannette Moore. Phone: (919) 515-3028. Fax: (919) 515-8753. Email: Jeannette_Moore@ncsu.edu.
**Degrees Offered:** Bachelor of Science, Doctorate of Veterinary Medicine
**Majors Offered:** Animal Science (B.S.), Pre-Vet track (B.S.), Veterinary Medicine (D.V.M.), Extension Horse Husbandry
**Tuition Costs:** Contact School
**Description of Program:** Opportunities to select equine courses in handling, evaluation, behavioral modification, and management, as part of the Animal Science curriculum.
**Facilities:** Stall barn, breeding area, AI lab, arena
**Showing:** Judging, intercollegiate, local and open shows, rodeos

## St. Andrews Presbyterian College

Sport Studies Department, St. Andrews Presbyterian College, 1700 Dogwood Mile., Laurinburg, NC 28352. Contact: Peggy McElveen, Director of Equestrian Programs or Pebbles Turbeville, Therapeutic Horsemanship Director. Phone: (910) 277-7228 or (910) 276-7771. Fax: (910) 277-7363.
Email: (Peggy) mcelveen@sapc.edu or (Pebbles) turbeville@sapc.edu.
**Degrees Offered:** Certificate, Minor, Bachelor of Art

**Majors Offered:** NARHA (C), ANRC (C), Equine Studies (M), Equine Business Management (B.A.), Therapeutic Riding (B.A.)

**Tuition Costs:** $14,540/year; room and board: $5,500/year; horse board: $350/month; riding fees: $400/semester

**Description of Program:** Hunt seat, jumping, ANRC ratings, dressage styles taught. Five of the six equine studies courses include extensive field work. Many students have the opportunity to participate in equine internships with some of the industry's top professionals, often leading to career opportunities. Even within the instructional program, you can have the opportunity to break and train a two-year-old, bring a green horse through his first show season, campaign a seasoned competitor, train for a National Rider's Rating Exam, compete hunters or jumpers, or trail ride. The Therapeutic Riding major, in keeping with the mission of the college, will offer an integrated educational program that incorporates cross-disciplinary exposure to the knowledge and skills necessary for success in the field, as well as experiential learning components that help students explore and define career options while applying and testing their knowledge base. Students will be prepared to enter the field of therapeutic riding as well-trained and contributing professionals, or to continue on to post-graduate work in a related area.

**Facilities:** Equestrian center is 2 1/2 miles from campus and has 50 school horses, five outdoor arenas (125ft x 275ft, 200ft x 300ft, 80ft x 100ft, 250ft x 120ft, 100ft x 120ft), one covered arena (125ft x 300ft).

**Showing:** IHSA, ANRC, IDA, USA Equestrian, local and schooling shows, dressage

# *OHIO*

## The Andrews School

38588 Mentor Ave., Willoughby, OH 44094. Contact: Roxane Rheinheimer, Equestrian Director. Phone: (440) 942-3600. Fax: (440) 942-3660.
Email: rheinr@andrews-school.org.

**Accreditation:** Independent Schools Association of the Central States

**Degrees Offered:** High School Diploma

**Tuition Costs:** Horse board: $800/month; lessons: $30-$40/half hour or hour

**Description of Program:** All-girls school. The instructional program offers the entire spectrum of hunt seat instruction. From introductory horsemanship to national hunter/jumper competitions, the needs of any rider are met. Lessons are available six days a week (Tuesday-Sunday) and are offered to the general public as well as to Andrews students. For the girl who decides that riding is really her sport, Andrews offers a wide range of horse show opportunities. Participation in a variety of equestrian events, from local schooling shows to OPHA and USA Equestrian "A," "B," and "C"-rated shows is encouraged. Several rated shows are held on campus, in addition to student shows and hunter paces. Some girls like to go on the road to hit the "big" shows and the school is proud to offer one of the most academically supportive programs in the country! The Andrews' faculty understands that a strong student can meet her academic and competitive goals, and the art of balancing both can be the best lesson of all! Andrews is the founding site of the Interscholastic Equestrian Association and was the host site for the 2003 USAE Pony Finals.

**Facilities:** Two indoor arenas, three outdoor arenas, 65 stalls

**Showing:** USA Equestrian A-rated shows and local shows, riding club, drill team, interscholastic team

**Website:**
www.andrews-school.org

**Type of School:**
Middle and Secondary School

# Hocking College

School of Natural Resources & Ecological Sciences, Hocking College, 3301 Hocking Parkway, Nelsonville, OH 45764. Contact: Tina Romine or Lance Booth. Phone: (740) 753-3591 x 2316 (Romine) or (740) 753-3591 x 2540 (Booth). Fax: (740) 753-2021. Email: romine_t@hocking.edu or booth_l@hocking.edu.

**Accreditation:** North Central Association of Colleges and Schools

**Degrees Offered:** Technologists Certificate, Occupational Certificate, Associate of Applied Science, Associate of Technical Study

**Majors Offered:** Backcountry Horse Level I & Level II (O.C.), Equine Health Care and Complementary Therapies (A.A.S.), Equine Health & Complimentary Therapies Level I & II (O.C.), Farrier Science and Business (A.T.S.), Health Care (T.C.), Mounted Police Training Level I (O.C.), Recreation and Wildlife Major in Backcountry Horse (A.A.S.), Shoeing Level I (O.C.), Wilderness Horsemanship (A.T.S.)

**Tuition Costs:** Residents: $84/credit; nonresidents: $168/credit; housing: $1,000/quarter

**Description of Program:** Choose from one of the four associate degrees or meet requirements for certifications. Train in wilderness riding, animal care, and equipment repair. Learn how to run your own business with the equine-specific business classes. Join your classmates and instructors on an advanced packing trip to the western Rockies in Colorado and Wyoming. Combine your horse classes with game management, law enforcement, and interpretive services to diversify your education. If you are interested in expanding your knowledge beyond the associate degree level, Hocking has created an Advanced Technologist Certificate, providing you with nineteen additional hours of specialized training in the equine health care field. Take your turn on "foal watch", and be ready to call your classmates when it's time for the new addition to be born! Be a part of the Campus Mounted Park Patrol. Tailor the program to meet your specific horse career goals by exploring Teaching Riding, Colt Training, Driving Draft Horses, Brood Mare and Foal Care, Reproduction, Nutrition, Conformation, Horse Anatomy and Physiology, Equine Health Care, Complementary Therapies, Equine Massage, Equine Acupressure, Equine Aromatherapy, Leather and Saddle Repair, Shoeing, Corrective Shoeing, Gait Analysis, and Forging.

**Facilities:** Two outdoor arenas, two barns, more than 30 miles of rugged trails

**Classroom/Hands-On Equine Classes:** 2:3/hours per week

**Showing:** Campus Horse Patrol, parades

# Integrated Touch Therapy, Inc.

7041 Zane Trail Road, Circleville, OH 43113-9761. Phone: (800) 251-0007. Fax: (740) 474-2625. Email: wshaw1@bright.net.

**Accreditation:** Approved by the National Certification Board for Therapeutic Massage and Bodywork.

**Degrees Offered:** Certificate

**Majors Offered:** Equine Level I, Equine Level II

**Tuition Costs:** Level I: $899; Level II: $799

**Description of Program:** Equine Massage Level I (Introduction to Massage): Six full days (CEU: 50 hours). This course teaches Swedish and sports massage techniques adapted for the equine. The course is intensive, teaching a full-body relaxation massage choreography, in addition to pre- and post-event sports massage choreographies. Students will learn massage techniques and the theory of application. They will study the muscle anatomy of the horse, learning about muscles and the primary actions produced by these muscles. Discussions include equine wellness, business and ethics, safety, record-keeping, and ideas for how to get started. Equine Level II: Five full days

(CEU: 40 hours). This course covers advanced massage techniques for the equine. Students must have completed Level I or an equivalent equine massage course in order to qualify for Level II. A video of the student performing a horse massage must be sent for review before the class begins. Students are also asked to complete at least 50 massages before attending Level II. The curriculum covers adjunctive topics that affect the performance of the horse, including shoeing, dentistry, and saddle fit. Students will study additional anatomy and physiology topics and discuss case studies. Each student must develop an independent project during the week.

**Facilities:** Heated and air-conditioned classroom, seven-stall barn, limited housing in main house **Classroom/Hands-On Equine Classes:** 50:50

## Lake Erie College

**Website:**
www.lec.edu

**Type of School:**
Private College

Admissions Office, Lake Erie College, 391 W. Washington St., LEC Box 345, Painesville, OH 44077. Contact: Sue Coen, Associate Dean of Equine Studies.
Email: coen@lec.edu.
**Accreditation:** North Central Association of Colleges and Schools
**Degrees Offered:** Bachelor of Science
**Majors Offered:** Equestrian Teacher/Trainer, Equine Facility Management with concentrations in Marketing, General Business, and Equine Stud Farm Management
**Tuition Costs:** $17,400; $5,420/room and board; $800-$1,600/ horse board per semester; $750/first riding class; $450/second riding class (same semester)
**Description of Program:** Two instructed rides per week and recreational riding; riding class size averages six students. Five instructors. Riding styles taught: hunter/jumper, dressage, and combined training. Equine Facility Management: designed for individuals interested in the management of boarding barns, competition stables, training farms, sales facilities, racetracks, horse show complexes, etc. Ideal combination of equine care and business environment. Equestrian Teacher/Trainer: prepares dedicated, talented individuals to become riders, trainers, and riding instructors. Includes preparation to provide quality equestrian facility management. Equine Stud Farm Management Concentration: prepares individuals for positions in the equine breeding industry. Provides opportunities for practical experience at the college's breeding facility. Internships at other breeding farms provide knowledge and expertise in farm management, breeding, foaling, and marketing. Strong foundation for veterinary school. The business concentration focuses on skills required to function well within the business environment. Equine Studies majors may select from several international equestrian experiences. Students may study at an established site in England or arrange an individualized program in Germany, Spain, Ireland, or Australia. LEC intercultural experiences range in duration from two weeks to an academic year, depending upon individual interests and circumstances. Full time students are eligible for a free trip abroad after five semesters enrolled at LEC.
**Facilities:** Equestrian center is six miles from campus and has 65 school horses, two indoor arenas, four outdoor arenas, hunt field, and trails.
**Classroom/Hands-On Equine Classes:** Varies
**Showing:** IHSA, USEF, USDF, Interscholastic Dressage Association shows

## Ohio State University

**Website:**
www.osu.edu

**Type of School:**
Public University

Animal Science, Ohio State University, 2029 Fyffe Rd., Columbus, OH 43210-1095. Contact: Dr. Robert Kline. Phone: (614) 292-2625. Fax: (614) 292-1515.
Email: kline.1@osu.edu.

**Accreditation:** North Central Association of Colleges and Schools
**Degrees Offered:** Bachelor of Science, Doctor of Veterinary Medicine
**Majors Offered:** Animal Science with Equine (B.S.), Veterinary Medicine (D.V.M.)
**Tuition Costs:** In-state: $195/credit; out-of-state: $472/credit; room and board: $8,100/year; horse board: $310/month
**Description of Program:** Three to five instructed rides per week; riding class size averages 30 students. Three instructors. Western and hunt seat riding styles taught. The horse program emphasizes the production and management of horses and an understanding of their behavior. Students have hands-on experience in the introductory course to gain horse-handling ground skills. The reproduction class trains students to collect and evaluate semen, inseminate mares, and participate in the basic training of the foal. The training class requires the student to train a horse that has not been ridden before. The horse courses can be taken as a minor or as an area of emphasis for the B.S. degree in Animal Science.
**Facilities:** The equestrian center is nine miles from campus and has 25 school horses, one indoor arena (75ft x 120ft), and one outdoor arena (150ft x 150ft).
**Classroom/Hands-On Equine Classes:** Varies
**Showing:** Intercollegiate Riding Team, Judging Team

**Website:**
www.ati.ohio-state.edu

**Type of School:**
Community College

## Ohio State University Agricultural Technical Institute

Ohio State University Agricultural Technical Institute, 1328 Dover Rd., Wooster, OH 44691-4000. Contact: Dr. Karen Wimbush, Professor & Technology Coordinator. Email: ati@osu.edu.
**Accreditation:** North Central Association of Colleges and Schools
**Degrees Offered:** Associate of Science, Associate of Applied Science
**Majors Offered:** Equine Science (A.S.), Horse Production/Management (A.A.S.)
**Tuition Costs:** In-state: $120/credit; out-of-state: $251/credit; campus housing: $3,900/year
**Description of Program:** The Ohio State University Agricultural Technical Institute has long been considered a leader in preparing students to enter careers in the horse industry. Ohio State ATI's Equine Facility, dedicated in 2000, is the focal point for an intensively hands-on curriculum that includes classes in feeding and nutrition, animal anatomy and physiology, shoeing, horse facilities management, horse breeding and selection, equine exercise science, riding horse training, and equine reproductive management. The program also includes a ten-week paid industry internship. Students can specialize in Equitation or Breeding, and may earn either an associate of applied science degree in Horse Production and Management, or an associate of science degree in Horse Science, which transfers to the bachelor's degree program in the College of Food, Agricultural, and Environmental Sciences at Ohio State in Columbus. "We foal out 30 mares a year," says Dr. Karen Wimbush, faculty coordinator of the horse program. "Students run our breeding program. There's a lot of hands-on work. That tends to put us in a favorable position with the Standardbred industry. It's nice to have an employee who knows how to artificially inseminate and feels comfortable with it." Three to five instructed rides per week; riding class size averages six students.
**Facilities:** New facility dedicated in 2000 is five miles from campus with a 46-stall barn complex, 100ft x 200ft clear-span indoor arena, outdoor arena, breeding shed and lab, 85 acres of pasture, and 60 school horses.
**Classroom/Hands-On Equine Classes:** 50:50

## Otterbein College

Department of Equine Science, Otterbein College, One Otterbein College, Westerville, OH 43081-2006. Contact: Dr. Lynn Taylor, Associate Prof. & Chairperson. Phone: (614) 823-1843 (Taylor) or (800) 488-8144. Fax: (614) 823-3042.
Email: ltaylor@otterbein.edu.

**Accreditation:** North Central Association of Colleges and Schools

**Degrees Offered:** Certificate, Bachelor of Arts, Bachelor of Science

**Majors Offered:** Equine Pre-Veterinary or Pre-Graduate Studies, Equine Facility Management, Equine Administration, Equine Health Technology, Riding Instructor (C)

**Tuition Costs:** $20,133; $5,952 room and board

**Description of Program:** Three full time faculty and three full time riding instructors. Hunter/jumpers, eventing, dressage, and Western riding styles taught. The Department of Equine Science provides a comprehensive educational experience for students pursuing careers as professionals in the equine industry. A liberal arts foundation prepares students to become productive and effective members of society. The theory and analysis of academic studies are balanced by practical experience. Throughout, ethics and personal responsibility are strongly emphasized. Instruction centers on intensive classroom effort, its practical application, and the opportunity for personal involvement in the various facets of the equine industry. Most equine students complete at least one internship, and many do more than one. On the Foalwatch Team, students monitor the foaling of more than 100 broodmares during winter and spring quarters.

**Facilities:** The equestrian center is five miles from campus, has 25 school horses, one indoor arena (60ft x 120ft), one outdoor arena (80ft x 200ft), pasture, hunt course, paddocks.

**Classroom/Hands-On Equine Classes:** Varies

**Showing:** IHSA, IDA, events, local and open shows

**Website:**
www.otterbein.edu

**Type of School:**
Private Liberal Arts College

## University of Findlay

Equestrian & Pre-Vet Studies, Natural Science Department, University of Findlay, 1000 N. Main St., Findlay, OH 45840. Contact: Craig Harder, Assistant Director of Admissions. Phone: (800) 548-0932 ext. 4738. Fax: (419) 434-4898.
Email: harder@findlay.edu.

**Accreditation:** North Central Association of Colleges and Schools

**Degrees Offered:** Associate of Science, Bachelor of Science

**Majors Offered:** Western Equestrian Studies (A.S., B.S.), English Equestrian Studies (A.S., B.S.), Equine Business Management (B.S.)

**Tuition Costs:** $19,052/year; room and board: $7,000/year; horse board: $240/month; Equestrian Studies surcharge: $3,350/freshman and sophomore years

**Description of Program:** Five instructed rides per week; riding class size averages seven students. Eleven instructors. Horsemanship, showmanship, pleasure, colt breaking, cutting, reining, hunter/jumper, and dressage riding styles taught.

**Facilities:** Two complete equestrian centers are four and eight miles from campus respectively, housing 150 school horses, four indoor arenas, three outdoor arenas, twelve wash stalls, and three hundred stalls.

**Classroom/Hands-On Equine Classes:** 2:1

**Showing:** IHSA (NCAA II), IDA, judging, A Circuit

**Website:**
www.findlay.edu

**Type of School:**
Private Liberal Arts University

## Wilmington College

**Website:**
www.wilmington.edu

**Type of School:**
Small Private College

Admissions, Pyle Center 1325, 251 Ludovic St., Wilmington, OH 45177.
Contact: Monte Anderson. Phone: (937) 382-6661. Fax: (937) 382-7077.
Email: monte_anderson@wilmington.edu.
**Accreditation:** North Central Association of Colleges and Schools.
**Degrees Offered:** Minor, Bachelor of Science
**Majors Offered:** Agriculture with emphasis in Equine Science (B.S.), Equine Science (M)
**Tuition Costs:** $15,746; $6,080 room and board
**Description of Program:** Wilmington College's newest academic offering, an Equine Studies minor, was established in 1999. WC students can bring their horses to college. In contrast with college programs that focus exclusively on horse training, Wilmington's is designed to combine a student's continuing interest in horses with an academic major such as Business, Communications, Agriculture, or Social Science/Pre-Law. The equine coursework involves the technical or scientific basis of equine science, as well as the "hands-on" component of riding and training the horse and rider, in order to prepare students for a career related to equine science.
**Facilities:** Features a 72ft x 328ft barn with 24 horse stalls, paddocks, tack rooms, and other equine amenities. Also, a classroom observation deck is between the barn and a 72ft x 152ft indoor arena. Future expansion possibilities include another barn, a covered outdoor arena, riding trails, and a therapeutic track.
**Classroom/Hands-On Equine Classes:** Varies
**Showing:** Students may participate on the equestrian team and do some showing, but it is not a requirement of the program.

# OKLAHOMA

## Conners State College

**Website:**
www.connors.cc.ok.us

**Type of School:**
Community College

Equine Technology, Conners State College, Rt. 1, Box 1000, Warner, OK 74469-9700.
Contact: Fred Williams. Phone: (918) 463-2931. Fax: (918) 463-6272.
Email fw@conners.cc.ok.us.
**Degrees Offered:** Associate of Science, Associate of Applied Science
**Majors Offered:** Agriculture Equine Technology

## Oklahoma Horseshoeing School

**Website:**
www.horseshoes.net/school

**Type of School:**
Specialty School

Rt. 1, Box 281, Purcell, OK 73080. Phone: (800) 538-1383 or (405) 527-0200.
Fax: (405) 288-1004. Email: okschool@telepath.com.
**Accreditation:** Oklahoma Board of Private Vocational Schools, Veteran's GI Bill, Bureau of Indian Affairs, Workforce Investment Act
**Degrees Offered:** Certificate
**Majors Offered:** Basic Horseshoeing Course, Professional Horseshoeing Course, Advanced Horseshoeing and Blacksmithing Course, Advanced Horseshoeing, Blacksmithing and Horsemanship Course, Horse Owner's Practical Training Course
**Tuition Costs:** $1,200/Basic and Horse Owner; $3,200/Professional; $4,400/Advanced Horseshoeing and Blacksmithing; $5,300/Advanced Horseshoeing, Blacksmithing and Horsemanship

**Description of Program:** The Oklahoma Horseshoeing School was established in 1973 to make available to horsemen and horsewomen a trade in which they can easily earn upwards of $250 per day doing what they love best: working with horses. The director, Jack Roth, D.V.M., is a licensed veterinarian. He is also the Founder and works full-time in the school. Since its inception, the Oklahoma Horseshoeing School has grown to be the largest in the world. The reason for this success is obvious to anyone who has seen the quality of the work performed by the students, which is never compromised. Usable and salable skills are taught. The only entrance requirement is that students must be willing to do the extra work required to produce perfect or near-perfect work on every job. The Oklahoma Horseshoeing School staff consists of two masters, one journeyman, and two assistant instructors at all times.

**Facilities:** The campus includes a clinic, classroom, modern shop with large indoor shoeing area, indoor training pens, exercise track, large round pens, hot walker, and stalls. The shop is open all evening so that you may practice your forgework. Separate men's and women's dormitories, located close to the campus, are provided free of charge. The dormitories include a complete kitchen.

**Classroom/Hands-On Equine Classes:** 15:85

## Oklahoma State Horseshoeing School

Rt. 1, Box 28-B, Ardmore, OK 73401. Phone: (800) 634-2811 or (580) 223-0064. Fax: (580) 223-0729. Email: oshs@brightok.net.
**Majors Offered:** Farrier

**Website:**
www.horseshoes.com/schools/okstate/homepage.htm

**Type of School:**
Specialty School

## Oklahoma State University College of Veterinary Medicine

Admissions, 110 McElroy Hall, Stillwater, OK 74078-2003. Phone: (405) 744-6653. Fax: (405) 744-0356. Email: admissions@cvm.okstate.edu.
**Degrees Offered:** Master of Science, Doctor of Philosophy, Doctor of Veterinary Medicine
**Majors Offered:** Infectious Diseases (M.S., Ph.D.), Pathobiology (M.S., Ph.D.), Physiological Sciences (M.S., Ph.D.), Veterinary Clinical Science (M.S.), Veterinary Medicine (D.V.M.)

**Website:**
www.cvm.okstate.edu

**Type of School:**
Public University

## Oklahoma State University–Okmulgee Technical Branch

Oklahoma State University–Okmulgee Technical Branch, Health and Environmental Technology Department, 1801 E. 4th St., Okmulgee, OK 74447. Contact: Mike Dewitt. Phone: (918) 293-5342. Fax: (918) 293-4653. Email: boots@osu-okmulgee.edu.
**Accreditation:** Central Association of Colleges and Schools
**Degrees Offered:** Associate in Applied Science
**Majors Offered:** Shoe, Boot & Saddlemaking
**Tuition Costs:** Residents: $82/unit; nonresidents: $185/unit
**Description of Program:** Career preparation in shoe repair, bookmaking, and saddlemaking requires experience in such areas as basic and advanced shop practices, pattern design, cutting, shaping, tooling, and sewing leather to the customer's order. While learning to recognize and work with domestic and exotic leathers, students acquire skills required to create and maintain hand-crafted boots and saddles. The popularity of such products and the needs for persons skilled in the repairs of these products create a bright outlook for those pursuing a career in this field. Many graduates elect to

**Website:**
www.osu-okmulgee.edu

**Type of School:**
Public University

establish their own businesses as repair technicians, manufacturers of shoes, boots, or saddles, or in sales. Employment opportunities also exist in many small-business shoe, boot, and saddle repair shops.

**Facilities:** The program laboratories consists of approximately 3,000 square feet and house state-of-the art equipment that provides student learning experiences conducive to industry practices.

## Redland's Community College

**Website:**
www.redlandscc.net

**Type of School:**
Community College

Equine Department, Redland's Community College, 1300 S. Country Club Rd., El Reno, OK 73036. Phone: (405) 262-2552. Fax: (405) 422-1200. Email: studentservices@redlandscc.net.

**Degrees Offered:** Associate of Science, Associate of Applied Science

**Majors Offered:** Agriculture with equine option (A.S.), Equine Science (A.A.S.)

**Tuition Costs:** In-state: $64/credit; out-of-state: $139/credit

**Description of Program:** Equine Management I & II, Anatomy and Physiology, Basic Care & Training, Advanced Care & Training, Horsemanship, Specialized Training, Special Problems, Equine Practicum, Equine Evaluation & Judging

**Facilities:** Equestrian center is four miles from campus and has 35 school horses, one indoor arena (80ft x 160ft), and one outdoor arena (200ft x 300ft).

**Showing:** Local shows, Judging Team

## Sam Howry's Rodeo Academy

**Website:**
www.rodeoacademy.com

**Type of School:**
Specialty School

P.O. Box 1255, Edmond, OK 73083-1255. Phone: (405) 396-2452 or (405) 627-7520. Email: rodeoacedemy@hotmail.com.

**Degrees Offered:** Diploma

**Majors Offered:** Rodeo Announcing

**Tuition Costs:** $750; housing not included

**Description of Program:** Rodeo Academy is a terrific, hands-on, power-packed, weekend workshop that teaches the latest and most effective techniques in the art of professional rodeo announcing. You will learn in one weekend what may take others years to learn by trial-and-error. Whether you are new or presently involved in the rodeo business, this fast-paced, exciting workshop will improve your skills in presentation, communication, and motivation. You will learn practical, effective methods to make each and every one of your rodeo performances outstanding. You will see instant results as you master the proven skills to capture, motivate, and control your audience.

**Facilities:** Hotel Conference Room

# *OREGON*

## Linn-Benton Community College

**Website:**
www.lbcc.cc.or.us

**Type of School:**
Community College

Animal Science, Linn-Benton Community College, 6500 SW Pacific Blvd., Albany, OR 97321. Contact: Jenny Stroobard, Equine Program Director. Phone: (541) 917-4767. Fax: (541) 917-4776. Email: jenny.stroobard@linnbenton.edu.

**Accreditation:** Northwest Association of Colleges and Schools

**Degrees Offered:** Associate of Applied Science, Certificate

**Majors Offered:** Horse Management (A.A.S.)

**Tuition Costs:** $50/credit; $185/month horse board

**Description of Program:** Three instructed rides per week; riding class size averages eighteen students. Six instructors. The curriculum is comprehensive and grounded in developing practical skills that enable the graduates to enter the job market with the types of proficiencies that employers are looking for. In addition to coursework in nutrition, equine marketing, genetics, diseases, and forage crops, students take "hands-on" classes that teach them mastery of such things as administering injections, basic foot trimming, fitting and showing, applying bandages and leg wraps, handling, breeding management, and training. The heart of the curriculum is the horse training classes. In these courses, the student is assigned a green or untrained horse and learns the correct techniques for schooling and training that animal. All training is done in a modern, well-equipped facility, which includes an indoor arena, round pens, box stalls, and access to miles of scenic trails. Breeding management is also a major focus of the program. Students gain skills in stallion handling, teasing mares, semen collection and evaluation, artificial insemination, ultrasound techniques, foaling management, and brood mare management. The program can be joined with the four-year baccalaureate program in Equine Science at nearby Oregon State University.

**Facilities:** Equestrian center is two miles from campus and has ten school horses, an indoor arena, round pens, box stalls, and access to miles of scenic trails. LBCC has little on-campus housing; however, students are eligible to live in the dorms at Oregon State University, which is close by.

**Classroom/Hands-On Equine Classes:** 1:1

**Showing:** Local open and schooling shows

# Oregon State University

**Website:**
www.orst.edu

**Type of School:**
Public University

Animal Sciences, Oregon State University, Withycombe Hall 112, Corvallis, OR 97331-6722. Contact: J. Males, Dept. Head or Angela White, Program Dir. Phone: (541) 737-3431. Fax: (541) 737-4174.

Email: animalsc@ccmail.orst.edu or Angela.White@orst.edu.

**Accreditation:** Certified Horsemanship Association

**Degrees Offered:** Minor, Bachelor of Science, Master of Science, Doctorate

**Majors Offered:** Animal Science (B.S.), Agriculture (B.S.), Equine Science (M), Veterinary Science (M.S.), Comparative Veterinary Medicine (D)

**Tuition Costs:** Residents: $3,987/term; nonresident: $13,935/term; room and board: $5,600

**Description of Program:** Teaching beginning through advanced English and Western riding with a specialty in reining, colt training, and IHSA competition. The Equine Science option is a four-year program offered within the Department of Animal Sciences. The option emphasizes a well-rounded education in equine production, management, training, and marketing, and is unique in the Pacific Northwest. Students have opportunities for extensive hands-on practical experience in many equine career areas. The option also offers a unique equestrian coaching program. An Equine Science minor also exists for students of other majors interested in pursuing equine studies. A diverse recreational riding program with credit classes in both English and Western disciplines complements the core curriculum. Many students have the opportunity for part-time employment at the OSU Horse Center, thereby gaining valuable job-related experience while completing their degree. Internships, available at the Horse Center or through participating farms and stables, offer students the opportunity for extended on-the-job experience with university credit.

**Facilities:** Indoor arena, pasture, turn-outs, trails, 250 acres
**Classroom/Hands-On Equine Classes:** Mostly hands-on
**Showing:** IHSA, reining, Western, eventing, hunter/jumper, dressage, polo, rodeo

## Treasure Valley Community College

650 College Blvd., Ontario, OR 97914. Contact: Roger Findley. Phone: (541) 881-8822. Email: Findley@tvcc.cc.or.us.
**Degrees Offered:** Associate of Applied Science
**Majors Offered:** Ranch Management
**Tuition Costs:** Residents: $1,020/quarter; nonresidents: $1,170/quarter; room and board: $1,351-1,532/term
**Description of Program:** Ranch Management students acquire knowledge and skills in the classroom and in field laboratory settings, and receive practical, hands-on teaching under highly qualified instructors. Upon successful completion of the Ranch Management A.A.S., students will be prepared for a career in some facet of the livestock industry, either working directly with a phase of production, or working indirectly through one of the many support industries. Classes include Artificial Insemination and Beef Pregnancy Checking. Students may also transfer to Oregon State University, Eastern Oregon State College, or the University of Idaho through the "Block Transfer" agreements.
**Showing:** Rodeo Team, Judging Team, Ag Ambassadors

# *PENNSYLVANIA*

## Centered Riding® Inc.

P.O. Box 12377, Philadelphia, PA 19119. Phone/Fax: (215) 438-1286.
**Degrees Offered:** Workshops and Clinics
**Majors Offered:** Centered Riding Instructor
**Tuition Costs:** Varies
**Description of Program:** Centered Riding Instructor's Courses are open to riding instructors who have already become familiar with Centered Riding through an Open Clinic or private work with a Level III or IV instructor. Instructor courses consist of seven teaching days held in two parts. The first part consists of three days, during which the participating instructors are given mounted and unmounted instruction and taught the fundamentals of Centered Riding, including the Four Basics, the Following Seat, and how to do body work on students. The second part of the Instructor Course is four days in length and involves mounted instruction, ground exercises, and practice teaching sessions. Limited space for student riders is available. Centered Riding Instructor Update Clinics are open to Centered Riding Instructors of any level. They are four days in length and are designed to refresh and expand the knowledge of Centered Riding Instructors in their own riding and teaching. Update Clinics provide an opportunity for Centered Riding Instructors to network with each other and share new ideas. The structure is the same as the second half of a Basic Instructor Course, including mounted instruction, ground exercises, and practice teaching sessions.
**Facilities:** Facilities vary depending on workshop location. Housing is usually not included.

## Delaware Valley College

Equine Science, Delaware Valley College, 700 E. Butler Ave., Doylestown, PA 18901.
Phone: (800) 233-5825 or (215) 345-1500. Fax: (215) 230-2968.
Email: admitme@devalcol.edu.
**Degrees Offered:** Bachelor of Science
**Majors Offered:** Equine Studies, Animal Science with emphasis in Equine Science and
Management, Pre-Veterinary Studies

**Website:**
www.devalcol.edu

**Type of School:**
Private College

## George School

Director of Admissions, Box 4000, George School, Newtown, PA 18940. Phone: (215)
579-6547. Fax: (215) 579-6549. Email: admissions@georgeschool.org.
**Accreditation:** Governed by the 29-member George School Committee
**Degrees Offered:** High School Diploma, International Baccalaureate Diploma
**Tuition Costs:** Day: $22,000; Boarding: $30,370
**Description of Program:** The equestrian program at George School is part of the Athletic and Physical Education program. Students may qualify for Varsity (four afterschool practices a week and two shows per term), Junior Varsity (four after-school practices per week and one show per term), or C-Squad (three practices per week during the school day and an on-campus show at the end of the term). There are additional fees for participation in the riding program and for horse boarding. Boarding options include full board, self-care, lesson board, and training board.
**Facilities:** The barn has 21 box stalls with a heated tack room, wash stall and washroom facilities. There is one 100ft x 200ft all-weather surface ring (lighted) and one 100ft x 175ft all-weather surface ring.
**Showing:** Varsity, Junior Varsity, C-Squad Teams

**Website:**
www.georgeschool.org

**Type of School:**
Secondary School

## Grier School

Tyrone, PA 16686-0308. Phone: (814) 684-3000. Fax: (814) 684-2177.
Email: admissions@grier.org.
**Accreditation:** Middle States Association of Colleges and Schools
**Degrees Offered:** High School Diploma
**Tuition Costs:** $25,500; $1,500/riding fee
**Description of Program:** Riding at Grier offers girls the opportunity to develop their skills through a daily instructional program. Hunt seat is taught in all classes. Students may also receive instruction in basic dressage and may compete in dressage events off-campus. The riders are grouped according to their abilities and interests. The size of classes varies but is kept low—about eight riders—so that the students may receive individualized attention from the instructors. Generally, students who participate in the riding program are scheduled to take classes a minimum of three hours a week. It is not uncommon for avid riders to ride six days a week for more than two hours a day. The school's Varsity Riding Team competes in the Tri-State Equitation League throughout the year. Varsity riders may also opt to participate in local weekend shows in the fall and spring semesters. Members of the Varsity Team are selected by their dedication to the sport rather than by their level of ability. During the academic day, Grier's director of riding offers elective classes in Equine Science. Courses offered during the school year are Equine First-Aid, Judging, Stable Management, and Schooling.
**Facilities:** The facilities include a 50-stall stable, indoor and outdoor riding rings, several fields, and miles of forest trails. The 25 horses that the school owns range in abil-

**Website:**
www.grier.org

**Type of School:**
Girls' Private 7-12 Boarding School

ity from well-schooled elementary horses to more challenging advanced horses. Students may also bring their own horses and have them boarded in the school stables from September to June.

**Showing:** Tri-State Equestrian League

**Website:**
www.lindenhall.com

**Type of School:**
Private Girls' 6-12 Boarding School

## Linden Hall

212 East Main Street, Lititz, PA 17543. Phone: (717) 626-8512 or (800) 258-5778. Email: admissions@lindenhall.com.

**Accreditation:** Middle States Association of Colleges and Schools

**Degrees Offered:** High School Diploma

**Tuition:** Contact School

**Description of Program:** Equestrians of all ages and abilities will discover that Linden Hall offers a well-rounded riding program designed to develop a strong foundation of horseback riding skills. The stable and riding facilities are located on the 47-acre campus. Approximately 30 percent of students participate in the riding program. Riders participate in a wide range of equestrian events on and off campus. Riders compete in local and rated horse shows, and the Riding Team is a member of the Tri-State Equitation League, MidAtlantic Association, and Maryland Interschool Association. Students ride two or four days a week in lessons. Additional riding is available in preparation for competitions. Riding a minimum of two days will fulfill the physical education requirement. There is an annual riding trip to County Galway, Ireland.

**Facilities:** The Linden Hall program includes a new 80ft x 200ft indoor riding ring with viewing deck and lounge, an outdoor ring with all-weather footing, a 20-stall, center-aisle stable with heated tack room, many school-owned horses suitable for different levels of riders, and several paddocks for turnout.

**Showing:** Local shows, rated shows, eventing, hunter paces, jumper shows

**Website:**
www.psu.edu

**Type of School:**
Public University

## Pennsylvania State University

Dairy and Animal Science, 324 Henning Building, University Park, PA 16802. Contact: Jana Peters. Phone: (814) 863-4198. Fax: (814) 863-6042. Email: jpeters@psu.edu.

**Accreditation:** Middle States Association of Colleges and Schools

**Degrees Offered:** Bachelor of Science

**Majors Offered:** Animal Sciences with Equine Science minor (B.S.)

**Tuition Costs:** $9,296 resident; $18,918 nonresident

**Description of Program:** Western riding style taught. Penn State has a long history of horse involvement dating from the 1940s. The University has been a leading breeder of AQHA halter and performance horses and once stood the well-known Quarter Horse stallion Skip Sioux. The equine program at Penn State includes teaching, research, and adult and youth extension. Courses: Introductory Horse Production and Management, Advanced Horse Production and Management, Horse Handling and Training, Applied Equine Behavior, Equine Facilitated Therapy, Horse and Man, and multiple courses in selection and judging. Independent Study and Special Topics in Equine Science are also available. Lecture material is widely supplemented with hands-on laboratories and projects. Internships/Job Placement: Internships are available with horse farms, feed and pharmaceutical companies, equine publications, racetracks, veterinary practices, and other equine industry enterprises. Career fairs are held through the college and university; the department also serves as contact or liaison for industry representatives.

**Facilities:** Two horse barns, indoor arena, round pen, breeding herd of Quarter Horses, teaching/research herd of mixed-breed ponies
**Classroom/Hands-On Equine Classes:** 2:1
**Showing:** Intercollegiate Horse Judging Team, IHSA Equestrian Team, Block and Bridle Club

## The Phelps School

P.O. Box 476, 583 Sugartown Road, Malvern, PA 19355-0476. Contact: F. Christopher Chirieleison, Director of Admissions. Phone: (610) 644-1754. Fax: (610) 644-6679. Email: admis@phelpsschool.org.
**Accreditation:** Middle States Association of Colleges and Schools, Licensed by the Commonwealth of Pennsylvania, Pennsylvania Association of Independent Schools (PAIS) member, Pennsylvania Association of Private Academic Schools (PAPAS), National Association of Remedial Teachers, Orton Society, Advancement for Delaware Valley Independent Schools (ADVIS), National Association for College Admission Counseling, CASE, APC, Mid-Atlantic Boarding School Association
**Degrees Offered:** High School Diploma
**Tuition Costs:** Boarding: $25,000; Day: $15,500
**Description of Program:** The equestrian program has been part of the Phelps School since its opening in 1946. Students who participate in the riding program work under the supervision of excellent trainers to improve their riding and jumping skills. Some students also participate in trail rides and competitions.

**Website:**
www.phelpsschool.org

**Type of School:**
All-Boys Secondary School

## Robert O. Mayer Riding Academy

3284 Harts Run Road, Glenshaw, PA 15116. Phone: (412) 767-4902.
Email: dressage@romra.com.
**Accreditation:** Licensed by British Horse Society, German Federation Nationale.
**Degrees Offered:** Certificate, Apprenticeship, Shadow Program, Instructors' Workshops
**Majors Offered:** Dressage (C, A, S.P.), BHS and USDF Riding Instructor (C)
**Tuition Costs:** Application fee: $50; three-month probationary period: $700/month; post-probationary period: $500/month; housing: $220/month
**Description of Program:** Apprenticeship: An excellent program for those who desire to be professionals with careers in the horse industry as trainers, advanced competitors, or riding instructors (including preparation for USDF and BHS certification requirements). The apprenticeship entails a one-on-one teacher/student relationship in which the student has the opportunity to learn under the careful tutelage of the master. Teaching is more intimately conveyed and learning is more profound when the student has the privilege to "sit on the saddle that is still warm from the Master's seat." Apprentices receive a minimum of 50 hours of formal instruction per month and ride at least five educated horses per day. Shadow Program: An intensive course of study in which the student will acquire concentrated education and accelerated development of skills: riding, teaching, training, showing, riding gymnastics, or yoga-related subjects. The program is designed to meet specifically the needs of the individual. Riders at any level are welcome. Instructors' Workshop: Learn the time-proven principles of Classical Dressage, which underlie the entire concept, discipline, correct interpretation, and practice of dressage. Gain valuable insight into teaching and training techniques that will make dressage instruction easier and more efficient.

**Website:**
www.romra.com

**Type of School:**
Specialty School

**Facilities:** Olympic-size outdoor arena, 100ft x 160ft indoor arena, 60-stall boarding stable, on-site housing for seven apprentices, yoga studio, 15 lesson horses (school masters)
**Showing:** Those chosen will be able to participate in showing according to their abilities.

## University of Pennsylvania

**Website:**
www.vet.upenn.edu

**Type of School:**
Public University

School of Veterinary Medicine, University of Pennsylvania, 3800 Spruce Street, Philadelphia, PA 19104. Phone: (215) 898-5434. Fax: (215) 573-8653.
Email: admissions@vet.upenn.edu.
**Degrees Offered:** Veterinary Medicine Doctor
**Majors Offered:** Veterinary Medicine (V.M.D.)

## The Valley Forge Military Academy and College

**Website:**
www.vfmac.edu

**Type of School:**
Private Military Academy
and College

1001 Eagle Road, Wayne, PA 19087. Contact: Ted Torrey, Director of Horsemanship. Phone: (610) 989-1502. Email: ttorrey@vfmac.edu.
**Accreditation:** Middle States Association of Colleges and Schools
**Degrees Offered:** Associate of Arts
**Majors Offered:** No equine majors
**Tuition Costs:** Total tuition and board including horsemanship: $30,500
**Description of Program:** A comprehensive riding program that offers a seven-day-a-week, hands-on and classroom equestrian experience. The program allows for personal riding preferences including, but not limited to, polo, jumping, dressage, combined training, foxhunting, parade/drill, and general riding.
**Facilities:** Stabling and turn out for 40 horses, indoor riding pavilion (300ft x 150ft), outdoor arena (300ft x 150ft), access to foxhunting with Radnor Hunt, full outdoor polo facilities at Brandywine Polo Club
**Classroom/Hands-On Equine Classes:** 30/70 percent
**Showing:** Valley Forge offers a full polo competition schedule, personalized show schedule during season, and foxhunting during season.

## Wilson College

**Website:**
www.wilson.edu

**Type of School:**
Private College

Equestrian Studies Department, Wilson College, 1015 Philadelphia Ave., Chambersburg, PA 17201. Contact: Nicola Walsh, Director of Equestrian Studies.
Phone: (717) 264-4141 x3296. Fax: (717) 264-1578. Email: nwalsh@wilson.edu.
**Accreditation:** Middle States Association of Colleges and Schools, Pennsylvania Department of Education, American Veterinary Medical Association
**Degrees Offered:** Bachelor of Science
**Majors Offered:** Equestrian Management, Equine Facilitated Therapeutics, Pre-Vet, Veterinary Medical Technology
**Tuition Costs:** $16,466; room and board: $6,996; horse board: $365/month; equitation fees: $375/semester
**Description of Program:** Two instructed rides per week; riding class size averages four students. Nine instructors. English-balanced seat, dressage, combined training, hunt equitation, and jumper riding styles taught.
**Facilities:** Equestrian center is on campus and houses 35 school horses, two indoor arenas (100ft x 300ft, 76ft x 204ft), and one outdoor arena (150ft x 300ft).
**Classroom/Hands-On Equine Classes:** All courses have a hands-on component.
**Showing:** IHSA, dressage, hunter

# RHODE ISLAND

## Johnson and Wales University

Website:
www.jwu.edu

Type of School:
Private University

Center for Equine Studies, Johnson and Wales University, 8 Abbott Park Place, Providence, RI 02903. Contact: Stefani Watson, Equine Admission Rep., or Beth Beukema, Center Director. Phone: (508) 252-5700 or (508) 252-9270. Fax: (508) 252-3027. Email: swatson@jwu.edu or bbeukema@jwu.edu.

**Accreditation:** New England Association of Schools and Colleges
**Degrees Offered:** Associate of Science, Bachelor of Science
**Majors Offered:** Equine Studies (A.S.), Equine Business Management (A.S., B.S.), Equine Business Management/Riding (B.S.)
**Tuition Costs:** $19,182; room and board: $7,185-$8,985/year
**Description of Program:** The Johnson & Wales University Equine Studies Department was developed in 1980 from an industry need for professional training in the equine field. Today, the department's associate programs include Equine Studies and Equine Business Management. Both degrees are built on a solid core of business and scientific equine classes. The Equine Studies students take six riding courses as an integral part of their program, whereas the Equine Business Management students elect not to ride for credit. The riding courses emphasize the balanced seat, with concentrations in dressage and eventing. Classes include: Equine Management Practicums, Introduction to Horse Management, Equine Physiology and Genetics, Equine Anatomy and Lameness, Equine Diseases, and Equine Nutrition. Students may continue on for their Bachelor of Science degree in Equine Business Management with or without riding. The bachelor's degree programs offer the following equine academic courses: Equine Reproduction, Horse Show Management and Judging, Horse Farm Management, Equine Co-op/ Internship along with general education studies, and business classes. The students majoring in Equine Business Management /Riding also take the following courses: Foundations of Riding Theory, Methods of Riding Instruction, and Horse Training.
**Facilities:** The University-owned equestrian center is located just fifteen miles from the Providence campus. The University has 31 school horses, many of which have competed at the Federations Equestre Internationale (F.E.I.) level in dressage, on the hunter and jumper circuits, and in combined training. The facility also has three arenas: a 70ftx 170ft heated indoor with leather footing, a 220ft x 80ft outdoor dressage arena, and a 230ft x 90ft outdoor stadium arena, all on 30 acres of beautiful New England farmland adjacent to Massachusetts State Forest.
**Showing:** IHSA Hunt Seat Team, Intercollegiate Dressage Association

# SOUTH CAROLINA

## Clemson University

Website:
www.clemson.edu

Type of School:
Public University

Animal and Veterinary Sciences Department, Clemson University, Clemson, SC 29634-0361. Contact: Pat Evans. Phone: (864) 656-5160. Fax: (864) 646-3131. Email: pevans@clemson.edu.

**Accreditation:** Southern Association of Colleges and Schools
**Degrees Offered:** Bachelor of Science, Master of Science, Doctor of Philosophy
**Majors Offered:** Animal and Veterinary Sciences with emphasis in Equine Business

(B.S.), Animal and Veterinary Sciences Pre-Veterinary (B.S.)

**Tuition Costs:** Residents: $3,467/per semester; nonresidents: $7,266/per semester; includes room and board

**Description of Program:** Stock seat and hunt seat styles taught. The curriculum in Animal and Veterinary Sciences provides students with a broad base of understanding of scientific principles and the application of these principles to scientific, technical, and business phases of equine production and marketing. Completion of general education requirements, basic sciences, applied sciences, and student-selected courses of personal interest, prepares graduates well for successful careers. Students have many opportunities for hands-on experiences involving the breeding, foaling, daily management, and care of sick or injured horses. Students have opportunities to take part in clinics held at the farm or in the local area, and also can be members of the Horse Judging Team that competes each spring and fall.

**Facilities:** The Equine Center is five minutes from campus. The farm maintains approximately 100 head of Quarter Horses and Thoroughbreds. The main farm consists of 60 acres of pastureland, with approximately half of the herd housed there year round. An additional 100 acres of grazing across-town houses the other half of the herd during the year.

**Classroom/Hands-On Equine Classes:** 25:75

**Showing:** IHSA

# SOUTH DAKOTA

## National American University

**Website:**
www.national.edu

**Type of School:**
Private University

321 Kansas City Street, Rapid City, SD 57701. Phone: (605) 394-4827 or (800) 843-8892. Fax: (605) 394-4871. Email: abrumbaugh@rc.national.edu.

**Accreditation:** North Central Association of Colleges and Schools

**Degrees Offered:** Bachelor of Science

**Majors Offered:** Applied Management with emphasis in Equine Management

**Description of Program:** The equine program is designed to help students become aware of the variety of fields in the equine industry, along with horse training. The program will increase their knowledge, ability, and understanding of good horsemanship and training. They will understand that the horse industry requires just as much business sense as any other field, because the program has a basic foundation in business (Applied Management) and Equine Management. Students are already working for breeders, training horses, giving lessons, and preparing horses for sale.

## South Dakota State University

**Website:**
www.sdstate.edu

**Type of School:**
Public University

Animal and Range Sciences Department, South Dakota State University, Box 2170, Brookings, SD 57007-0392. Phone: (605) 688-5165. Fax: (605) 688-6170. Email: SDSU_Admissions@sdstate.edu.

**Accreditation:** North Central Association of Colleges and Schools

**Degrees Offered:** Associate, Bachelor of Science

**Majors Offered:** Animal Science, Range Science, Pre-Veterinary Science

**Tuition Costs:** In-state: $72.10/credit; out-of-state: $229.15/credit; room and board: $4,000/year

**Description of Program:** Instructed rides each week; riding class size averages ten students. One instructor. Stock seat style taught. SDSU is soon to offer a minor in Equine Science, adding classes that specialize in the many topics of horse production, with a special emphasis in Equine Reproduction. Horse Production: lecture and lab; covers all aspects of horse management, including anatomy/physiology, business, reproduction, nutrition, diseases/health, conformation and selection, etc. Horsemanship: Western riding; general equine terms and horse information material included with instructed riding. Yearling/Halter Training and Two-Year-Old Training Classes: Nearly all hands-on instruction; introducing young horses to riding program. Introduction to Horse Management: lecture and lab. This class has no prerequisites, and is open to all students with any level of horse experience or interest. It covers basic principles in caring for horses and provides an introduction to the horse industry. Topics discussed: horse breeds and registry, grooming and safety in handling, care and feeding practices, common lameness and health problems, in addition to other basic management aspects. Laboratory sessions include involvement or instruction with the SDSU horses, activities, and field trips.

**Facilities:** Equestrian center is on campus and houses 50 school horses, one indoor arena (80ft x 130ft), one outdoor arena (140ft x 160ft), and barns.

**Classroom/Hands-On Equine Classes:** Currently, classroom/lecture hours are equaled or exceeded by hands-on learning experiences.

**Showing:** Collegiate rodeo, Horse Club, Little International Ag Exposition, 4-H, FFA, S.D. Horse Fair

# TENNESSEE

## Middle Tennessee State University

Department of Agribusiness & Agriscience, Campus Box 5, Murfreesboro, TN 37132. Contact: Dr. Rhonda M. Hoffman. Phone: (615) 898-2523 or (615) 898-2300. Fax: (615) 898-5169. Email: rhoffman@mtsu.edu or jkelly@mtsu.edu.

**Accreditation:** Tennessee Board of Regents, State University and Community College System of Tennessee

**Degrees Offered:** Minor, Bachelor of Science

**Majors Offered:** Animal Science with Horse Science concentration (B.S.), Animal Science with Pre-Veterinary Medicine concentration (B.S.), Horse Science (M)

**Tuition Costs:** Resident: $2,000/semester; nonresident: $6,000/semester; housing: $1,300-$2,900/semester.

**Description of Program:** Coursework includes equitation, care and training, selection and judging, techniques of teaching, reproduction and breeding, stable management, development of breeds, horse health, nutrition and feeding, horse business management, horse production. Seven full-time faculty and staff in Horse Science are on-site and available to students. Faculty members have specializations including Judging, Veterinary Medicine, Equine Reproductive Physiology, Equine Nutrition, and Horsemanship. Breeds used primarily are Tennessee Walking Horses and Quarter Horses. Tennessee Walking Horse breeding program, including student instruction in artificial insemination and embryo transfer. Riding styles taught include Stock seat, Hunt seat, dressage, and reining. Extracurricular activities include Horse Judging Team (two-time Quarter Horse World Champions, two-time Quarter Horse Congress Champions), Equestrian Team (IHSA National Reserve Champion Western Team, IHSA National Champion High-Point Western Rider), Horseman's Association, and Ten-

**Website:**
www.mtsu.edu

**Type of School:**
Public University

nessee Walking Horse Show Team. Memberships in clubs and teams open to all majors.

**Facilities:** The MTSU Horse Science Center is located seven miles from the main campus. It includes the Tennessee Miller Coliseum arena, 150ft x 300ft, with seating for 4600 and 500 stalls for events. The Horse Science Teaching Facility includes a 100ft x 205ft covered arena, outdoor riding arena, 60 stalls for university horses, high-tech classrooms, breeding laboratory, and opportunities for student work experience.

**Classroom/Hands-On Equine Classes:** 50:50

**Showing:** IHSA Equestrian Team in Hunt Seat and Western. Hosted the National IHSA Championship Show in 2003 and 2004. Bred, showed, and own the World Champion Tennessee Walking Horse Mare and Foal, and the World Champion Tennessee Walking Horse Weanling Colt.

## University of Tennessee–Knoxville

**Website:**
www.utk.edu

**Type of School:**
Public University

Department of Animal Science, 2505 River Dr., Knoxville, TN 37996-4547. Phone: (865) 974-7286. Fax: (865) 974-7297. Email: amathew@utk.edu. Information on University of Tennessee College of Veterinary Medicine programs can be obtained at www.vet.utk.edu.

**Degrees Offered:** Bachelor of Science, Master of Science, Doctor of Philosophy, Doctor of Veterinary Medicine

**Majors Offered:** Animal Science (B.S., M.S., Ph.D.), Veterinary Medicine (D.V.M.)

**Description of Program:** The program in Animal Science can be tailored to fit students' personal needs and career goals while meeting departmental and university requirements. The curriculum has two concentrations. The Production and Business Concentration is designed for students interested in careers in agribusiness and production agriculture. The Science and Technology Concentration is highly flexible and allows students to prepare themselves for careers in veterinary medicine, research, quality control, and non-traditional fields such as laboratory technology. For students interested in veterinary medicine, there are two ways to meet the veterinary college entrance requirements and earn a BS in Agriculture with a major in Animal Science. 1) Complete the requirements for the BS under the Science and Technology Concentration using electives to meet vet school requirements. 2) Participate in the "3-and-1 Program." In this program, all pre-vet requirements and certain courses in animal science are taken during the first three years at UT Knoxville. The BS degree is awarded upon successful completion of the first year in the College of Veterinary Medicine. Extracurricular activities include Equestrian Team, Horse Club, Block & Bridle Club, Pre-Vet Club, Intercollegiate Horse Judging Team, and Collegiate 4-H.

**Showing:** IHSA Zone 5, Region 1, Hunt and Stock Seat Teams

## University of Tennessee–Martin

**Website:**
www.utm.edu

**Type of School:**
Public University

College of Agriculture and Applied Sciences, 250 Brehm Hall, Martin, TN 38238-5008. Contact: James L. Byford, Dean. Phone: (731) 587-7250. Fax: (731) 587-7968. Email: jbyford@utm.edu.

**Accreditation:** Southern Association of Colleges and Schools

**Degrees Offered:** Bachelor of Science

**Majors Offered:** Agriculture with concentration in Animal Science

**Tuition Costs:** In-state: $1,923/semester; out-of-state: $5,748/semester; housing: $955/semester; meals: $945/semester; books and supplies: $400/semester

**Description of Program:** Equine Science is a part of the Animal Science concentration. Four courses in equine science or equitation are offered. Many other animal science courses have portions dealing with horses as well. All have a hands-on component. There is an Equestrian Club, an active IHSA Intercollegiate Equestrian Team, and an active Intercollegiate Rodeo Program.

**Facilities:** The stable on campus provides a place for students to ride, and there are boarding facilities where students can board their horses, either on campus or at the Equine Center and Rodeo Practice Arena about six miles from campus.

**Classroom/Hands-On Equine Classes:** All courses have a hands-on component.

**Showing:** Equestrian Club, IHSA, NIRA, state and regional horse events on campus

## Walters State Community College

Morristown Campus, Walters State Community College, 500 South Davy Crockett Pkwy., Morristown, TN 37813. Phone: (423) 585-2600. Fax: (423) 585-2631. Email: Roger.Brooks@wscc.cc.tn.us.

**Accreditation:** Southern Association of Colleges and Schools

**Degrees Offered:** Associate of Science

**Majors Offered:** Agriculture

**Tuition Costs:** Residents: $64/credit; nonresidents: $193/credit

**Description of Program:** Horse Management and Horsemanship can be electives in Agriculture curriculum.

**Facilities:** Horsemanship classes are taught at stables with 120ft x 240ft arena, round pen, and trails. Housing is not provided, but the school does have a service to help locate housing.

**Classroom/Hands-On Equine Classes:** Horsemanship: 100 percent hands-on; Horse Management: 50:50

**Showing:** Optional

**Website:**
www.wscc.cc.tn.us

**Type of School:**
Community College

# *TEXAS*

## American Association of Horsemanship Safety

P.O. Box 39, Fentress, TX 78622. Phone: (512) 488-2220. Fax: (512) 488-2319. Email: Jzdawson@aol.com.

**Degrees Offered:** Riding Instructor Certification (several types)

**Majors Offered:** Riding Instructor, Assistant Riding Instructor, Riding Instructor–Basic, Assistant Riding Instructor–Basic, Equestrian Safety Supervisor, Assistant Equestrian Safety Supervisor, Trail Guide, Assistant Trail Guide, Head Wrangler, Safety Clinic Participant

**Tuition Costs:** $500-750 (including room and board)/group clinics; $75/certificate and clinic materials

**Description of Program:** AAHS concentrates on producing instructors and support staff who understand equestrian liability issues and who know that the best way to avoid a lawsuit is to avoid the accident. AAHS clinics put a heavy emphasis on teaching all participants how negligence law works and how to apply it to the horse industry environment in which they work. Both the Instructor Basic and the Full Instructor are trained in the Secure Seat[SM] method of teaching, which is the only trademarked, academically validated method of teaching riding. It results in an independent balanced

**Website:**
www.horsemanshipsafety.com

**Type of School:**
Specialty School

seat. Riding Instructor students are able to teach the basics correctly to beginner through advanced riders. Riding Instructor–Basic students are able to teach the basics correctly to beginner and intermediate riders. Trail Guide students are competent in pre-ride instruction, have superior judgment, considerable cross-country riding experience, and an understanding of the hazards of rough-terrain riding in various climates. Trail Guide students must be at least 21 years old. Head Wrangler students have the added qualifications of being able to write a guest ranch program, select horses, and select and train staff in their various duties after they have gone through the two-day AAHS ranch course.

**Facilities:** Facilities vary, as clinics are given around the country at various stables, universities, and summer camps. Clinics are offered year-round at Rocky River Ranch in Wimberley, Texas.

**Classroom/Hands-On Equine Classes:** 50:50

## Central Texas College

Website:
www.ctcd.edu

**Type of School:**
Community College

Science/Agriculture Department, Central Texas College, P.O. Box 1800, Killeen, TX 76540. Contact: Dr. Patrick K. Hidy or Mr. Zhan Aljoe. Phone: (254) 526-1288. Fax: (254) 526-1765. Email: patrick.hidy@ctcd.edu or zhan.aljoe@ctcd.edu.

**Accreditation:** Southern Association of Colleges and Schools

**Degrees Offered:** Certificate, Associate of Applied Science

**Majors Offered:** Equine Management (A.A.S.)

**Tuition Costs:** In-district residents: $30/credit ($90 minimum); out-of-district residents: $35/credit ($105 minimum); room and board: $1,495/semester

**Description of Program:** Instructed rides each week; riding class size averages eight students. The Equine Management program is structured towards those individuals who want to specialize in horse training, riding, production, and management. Small classes for more hands-on experience. Students are permitted to bring their own horses and train with them. The department supports several organizations, such as the active collegiate FFA chapter, which annually competes with other collegiate chapters for state ranking. The Agriculture Department also has scholarships available for those individuals who qualify.

**Facilities:** The equestrian center is one mile from campus. Facilities include an indoor/outdoor riding arena and seven school horses.

**Classroom/Hands-On Equine Classes:** Varies

**Showing:** Local open shows

## Certified Horsemanship Association

Website:
www.cha-ahse.org

**Type of School:**
Specialty School

5318 Old Bullard Rd., Tyler, TX 75703-3612. Contact: Carol Parker. Phone: (800) 399-0138. Fax: (903) 509-2474. Email: Horsesafty@aol.com.

**Degrees Offered:** Certificate

**Majors Offered:** Instructor of Riders with Disabilities, Riding Instructor (English and Western), Trail Guide

**Tuition Costs:** $450-750/five-day clinic; housing included

**Description of Program:** CHA is a non-profit membership organization, operating internationally with a mission to promote safety and excellence in horsemanship. CHA sponsors five-day Certification Clinics all over the U.S., Canada, and Australia, in which instructor candidates are tested and evaluated on their safety awareness, horsemanship knowledge and ability, teaching techniques, group control, and professionalism. Certification may be earned at four levels, from beginner to advanced instruction.

**Facilities:** CHA Certification Clinics are held at approximately 100 different member facilities throughout North America and Australia.

**Classroom/Hands-On Equine Classes:** 90 percent hands-on

## Curragh Equestrian Center

5595 Ben Day Murrin Road, Fort Worth, TX 76126. Phone: (817) 443-3777. Email: curragh@curragh.com.

**Degrees Offered:** BHS Certificates

**Website:**
www.curragh.com

**Type of School:**
Specialty School

## East Texas Horseshoeing School

2761 CR 4670, Atlanta, TX. 75551. Phone: (903) 796-9308. Fax: (903) 796-9308. Email: ethclinics@aol.com.

**Accreditation:** Recommended by James Powell, Director of Community Services and Non Credit programs at Texarkana College

**Majors Offered:** Trimming and Horseshoeing Your Own Horse

**Tuition Costs:** $29.95 video, plus $5 for shipping; $19.95 hoof care notes, plus $2.50 shipping

**Description of Program:** Independent study. Learn to trim and shoe your own horse by video.

**Facilities:** The comfort of your own home—or perhaps even your own backyard.

**Website:**
www.easttexashorseshoeing.com

**Type of School:**
Independent Study

## Josey Ranch Barrel Racing and Roping Clinics

Josey Enterprises, Inc., 8623 SH 43 North, Karnack, TX 75661. Phone: (903) 935-5358. Fax: (903) 935-5366. Email: JoseyRanch@barrelracers.com.

**Degrees Offered:** Certificate of Completion

**Website:**
www.barrelracers.com

**Type of School:**
Specialty School

## North Central Texas College

Agriculture & Equine Science Department, North Central Texas College, 1525 West California St., Gainesville, TX 76240-4669. Contact: Shelly Switzer. Phone: (940) 668-7731 x318. Fax: (940) 668-6049. Email: sswitzer@nctc.edu.

**Accreditation:** Southern Association of Colleges and Schools

**Degrees Offered:** Certificate, Associate of Applied Science

**Majors Offered:** Equine Science (A.A.S.), Breeding Management (C), Horse Management and Training (C)

**Tuition Costs:** County residents: $33/credit; state residents: $54/credit; nonresident: $84/credit; room and board: $1,160-1,350/semester

**Description of Program:** This program offers a very comprehensive series of courses pertaining to all phases of horse management. Aspects of the horse industry as a business, equine breeding, and equine training are all covered in detail. Three levels of training, as well as special topics courses and a detailed breeding course and experience are offered. Each student must complete an internship prior to graduation. This program is designed for the individual who wants to work in the industry at the ranch level, or the individual who wants to continue on for a B.S. degree. Western and English riding styles taught.

**Website:**
www.nctc.edu

**Type of School:**
Community College

**Facilities:** Barn with 20 stalls, covered arena, outdoor arena, college dormitories
**Classroom/Hands-On Equine Classes:** Most courses have a hands-on component.
**Showing:** IHSA, Judging Team

## R.T.S. Professional Team Roping Schools

**Website:**
www.teamroping.com

**Type of School:**
Specialty School

ROPRO Training Systems, 34088 FM 2481, Hico, TX 76457. Phone: (254) 796-1970. Email: RTS@teamroping.com.
**Accreditation:** Official Training System of Teamroping.com
**Majors Offered:** Team Roping
**Tuition Costs:** $50/hour; $300/day; $1250/week
**Description of Program:** A training system that makes team roping much easier to understand and accomplish. The ROPRO Training System staff has produced an approach to training that has achieved tremendous results across the country. By using life-sized training simulators in conjunction with live cattle, proven training techniques can be applied. The practice, scrimmage, and game process used in other professional sports has now been incorporated into team roping training. Students get training in horsemanship and roping. Students are encouraged to bring one or more horses to rope on. Students who attend other ROPRO schools report that they were able to rope extensively; every person is able to rope to the maximum of his or her endurance.
**Facilities:** Stalls or outside pens are available for students' horses and are included in the training costs if students clean up after their horses. Students are invited to bring RVs, which can be hooked up at the ranch.

## Sul Ross State University

**Website:**
www.sulross.edu

**Type of School:**
Public University

Dept. of Animal Sciences, Sul Ross State University, P.O. Box C-11, Alpine, TX 79832. Contact: Dr. Jeff Pendergraft, Ass. Prof. of Equine Science. Phone: (915) 837-8200. Fax: (915) 837-8046. Email: jeffp@sulross.edu.
**Accreditation:** Southern Association of Colleges and Schools
**Degrees Offered:** Certificate, Associate of Science, Bachelor of Science, Master of Science
**Majors Offered:** Farrier (A.S.), Animal Science with Equine Science (B.S., M.S.)
**Tuition Costs:** In-state: $93/credit; out-of-state: $304/credit; room and board: $3,380/year; horse board: $90/month
**Description of Program:** The opportunity to study Equine Science at Sul Ross State University has allowed many students to expand their knowledge about the exciting and constantly evolving equine industry. The SRSU Equine Science program can give you the educational background necessary to gain the skills needed for success in a variety of fields within the equine industry. You will find that the Equine Science program gives you a complete look at the horse and its environment. The objective of the program is to educate you about the diverse uses of horses, as well as equine nutritional needs, reproductive management, training techniques, and business managerial skills. All of the classes are designed to take the student out of the classroom and into the equine facilities. There is a national and international internship program. Over the last five years, the Equine Program has grown by 82 percent. A $6 million renovation and new construction project to allow more hands-on experiences for students should be completed by December 2004.

**Facilities:** The equestrian center is one mile from campus and houses 20 school horses, one covered arena (150ft x 300ft), one outdoor arena (150ft x 300ft). The new Equine Center has 29 stalls, an indoor 50ft round pen, foaling observational lounge, nutritional metabolism room, exercise treadmill room, and reproduction area with lab. An additional 24 stalls are available for student's to board their horses.
**Classroom/Hands-On Equine Classes:** All classes have hands-on experience.
**Showing:** School and open rodeos, IHSA, AQHA, APHA, NRHA, NCHA

## Tarleton State University

Dept. of Animal Sciences, Tarleton Station, Box T-0070, Stephenville, TX 76402. Contact: Dr. David Snyder or Dr. D. Henneke. Phone: (254) 968-9222. Fax: (254) 968-9300. Email: snyder@tarleton.edu.
**Accreditation:** Southern Association of Colleges and Schools
**Degrees Offered:** Bachelor of Science, Master of Science
**Majors Offered:** Animal Science with emphasis in Equine Management (B.S.), Pre-Veterinary Medicine, Agriculture with emphasis is Equine Management (M.S.)
**Tuition Costs:** Residents: $130/unit
**Description of Program:** Limited riding classes. Courses: Introduction to Horse Production, Horse Psychology and Training, Horse Behavior Modification, Farrier Science, Horse Reproduction, Horse Exercise Physiology, Horse Enterprise Management.
**Facilities:** Indoor arena, 30 box stalls, 30 outside runs, pasture, modern breeding facility
**Showing:** Depends on individual

**Website:**
www.tarleton.edu

**Type of School:**
Public University

## Texas A & M University

Animal Science, Texas A & M University, Kleberg Center, Equine Sciences Room 249, College Station, TX 77843-2471. Contact: Dr. Gary Potter, Equine Program Leader. Phone: (409) 845-7731. Fax: (409) 845-6433. Email: g-potter@tamu.edu.
**Accreditation:** Southern Association of Colleges and Schools
**Degrees Offered:** Bachelor of Science, Master of Science, Master of Agriculture, Doctorate of Philosophy, Doctor of Veterinary Medicine
**Majors Offered:** Animal Science with specialty in Equine Science (B.S.), Equine Nutrition (M.S., M.Agr., Ph.D.), Exercise Physiology (M.S., M.Agr., Ph.D.), Equine Reproduction (M.S., M.Agr., Ph.D.), Veterinary Medicine and Surgery (M.S.), Veterinary Medicine (D.V.M.)
**Tuition Costs:** Contact School
**Description of Program:** Research-based Equine Science Program; riding, training, and judging program. Five instructed rides per week; riding class size averages eleven students. Six instructors. Western and hunter seat riding styles taught.
**Facilities:** Equestrian center is one mile from campus. Horse Center on campus includes 40-mare breeding herd and 60 riding horses; modern horse breeding farm, two indoor arenas (100ft x 200ft, 130ft x 260ft), and 150-acre farm.
**Classroom/Hands-On Equine Classes:** Vary
**Showing:** Intercollegiate horse shows, Judging Team, Rodeo Team, Polo Team

**Website:**
www.tamu.edu

**Type of School:**
Public University

## Texas Tech University

**Website:**
www.ttu.edu

**Type of School:**
Public University

Animal & Food Sciences, Box 42141, Lubbock, TX 79409. Phone: (806) 742-2825 or (806) 742-2550. Fax: (806) 742-0898. Email: info.afs@ttu.edu.

**Degrees Offered:** Bachelor of Science, Master of Science, Doctor of Philosophy

**Majors Offered:** Animal Science with equine classes (B.S.. M.S., Ph.D.), Agriculture with Equine Study (M.S., Ph.D.)

**Tuition Costs:** Residents: $2,447/semester; nonresident: $5,987.50/semester

**Description of Program:** Western riding style taught. From informative, hands-on equine classes to an efficient breeding facility, it can all be found at Texas Tech! The mission at the Texas Tech Ranch Horse Center is to provide an excellent education to prepare students for a successful career in a booming equine industry. Along with educating the traditional student, providing information to the non-traditional student through seminars is a focus. During the breeding season, members of the program work hard to provide excellent breeding services and the best mare and foal care possible with a personal touch.

**Facilities:** Research and training unit, 80 acres, a newly donated off-campus equestrian center

**Showing:** Rodeo, intercollegiate judging and showing, local, open and Quarter Horse shows

## West Texas A & M University

**Website:**
www.wtamu.edu

**Type of School:**
Public University

Equine Industry Program, P.O. Box 60998, Canyon, TX 79016. Contact: Dr. John Pipkin, Director. Phone: (806) 651-2550. (806) 651-2938.
Email: jpipkin@mail.wtamu.edu.

**Accreditation:** Southern Association of Colleges and Schools

**Degrees Offered:** Bachelor of Science, Master of Science, Ph.D

**Majors Offered:** Agribusiness with Equine Business (B.S.), Animal Science with equine emphasis (M.S.), Multidisciplinary Ph.D. with equine emphasis

**Tuition Costs:** In-state: $45/credit; horse board: $85/month

**Description of Program:** Two to three instructed rides per week; riding class size averages fifteen students. Four instructors. Hunt and stock seat riding styles taught. West Texas A&M University's Equine Industry Program offers training for undergraduate and graduate students interested in the horse industry and related agribusiness areas. The Equine Industry Program provides students a balance of business and scientific subject matter, integrated with technical and practical skills as they pertain to the horse and related industries. All facets of the industry are addressed, including production, race, recreation, show, and equine-related service industries.

**Facilities:** The equestrian center is 1 1/2 miles from campus and houses 50 school horses, one indoor arena (220ft x 110ft), two outdoor arenas (250ft x 125ft), and a round pen.

**Classroom/Hands-On Equine Classes:** 1:1

**Showing:** Intercollegiate, Varsity Equestrian, NIRA, open, AQHA

# *UTAH*

## Sorenson's Ranch School

Website:
www.sorensonsranch.com

Type of School:
Secondary School for Troubled Youth

P.O. Box 440219, Koosharem, UT 84744-0219. Contact: J.L. Moss, Admission Director. Phone: (435) 638-7318. Fax: (435) 638-7582. Email: srs@scinternet.net.

**Accreditation:** Northwest Association of Schools and Colleges, Joint Commission on Accreditation of Healthcare Organizations (JCAHO), licensed by Utah State Human Services Department as a mental health and substance-abuse treatment center

**Degrees Offered:** High School Diploma

**Tuition Costs:** $1,700 nonrefundable admission fee; $3,900/month; $500/month individualized counseling

**Description of Program:** Sorenson's Ranch School and Residential Treatment Center is located on a ranch with a working farm in southern Utah at a 7,000-foot elevation. The school is situated in an open wilderness area. It is organized and staffed to serve adolescent clients experiencing difficulties with social, family, emotional, behavioral, and substance abuse problems. Sorenson's Ranch uses a holistic approach to adolescent treatment that combines many dimensions, including the use of horseback riding, camp-outs and experiential learning. These and other out-of-doors activities instill in students the values of loyalty, respect, self-worth, goal setting, personal management, respect for property, cleanliness, and trustworthiness.

**Facilities:** Sorenson's Ranch School features a classroom complex, an industrial arts center with three shops, a gym, a media center, a large barn, animal training areas, and corrals. Students sleep in a ranch setting, with an average of four students per room.

**Showing:** Sorenson's Ranch School offers a 4-H program for a variety of animals, including horses. Students are given the opportunity to raise, train, and show animals at fairs and other shows.

## Utah State University

Website:
www.usu.edu

Type of School:
Public Land Grant University

Animal, Dairy and Veterinary Sciences, 4815 Old Main Hill, Logan, UT 84322-4815. Contact: Ms. Tami Spackman. Phone: (435) 797-2150. Fax: (435) 797-2118. Email: tami.spackman@usu.edu.

**Degrees Offered:** Minor, Bachelor of Science, Master of Science, Doctor of Philosophy

**Majors Offered:** Animal Science (B.S.), Bio-Veterinary Science [Pre-Vet] (B.S., M.S., Ph.D.), Horse Production (M), Horse Training (M)

**Tuition Costs:** Residents: $1,307.40/semester; nonresidents: $4,209.87/semester

**Description of Program:** Two instructed rides per week; riding class size averages twelve students. One instructor. The USU Horse Program is designed for the beginning to advanced Western rider. The basic principles of horsemanship are taught, then that foundation is built upon with advanced riders in order to develop their skills so they are prepared to train young horses. The students have the opportunity to compete on an Intercollegiate Equestrian Team in Horsemanship and Equitation Classes, as USU is a member of Zone 8 Region 3 of the IHSA. In addition to horsemanship courses, a horse production course designed for both horse enthusiasts and animal science majors is offered, as well as a senior-level horse management course designed to teach students some of the intricacies of developing and running an equine business. Finally, through USU Extension, students can enroll in a horseshoeing short course.

**Facilities:** The equestrian center is two miles from campus and has 25 school horses, one indoor arena (150ft x 50ft), two outdoor arenas (150ft x 90ft, 90ft x 70ft).

**Classroom/Hands-on Equine Classes:** 1:4 hours on average

**Showing:** NIRA, IHSA, local shows

# VERMONT

## The Putney School

**Website:**
www.putneyschool.org

**Type of School:**
Independent Secondary School

Putney, VT 05346-8675. Contact: Rick Cowan, Director of Admission.
Phone: (802) 387-6219 (Admission Office). Fax: (802) 387-6278.
Email: admission@putneyschool.org.
**Accreditation:** NEASC (New England Association of Schools and Colleges), Vermont Department of Education, TABS (The Association of Boarding Schools) member, NAIS (National Association of Independent Schools), ISANNE (Independent Schools Association of Northern New England), AISNE (Association of Independent Schools in New England)
**Degrees Offered:** High School Diploma
**Tuition Costs:** Boarding: $32,200; Day: $20,100
**Description of Program:** Founded in 1935 by a disciple of John Dewey, the Putney School makes manifest in the daily lives of students one of Dewey's most potent ideas: people learn best what they do. There is a lot of "doing" in the schedule of a Putney student, who is both encouraged to become an independent thinker and required to participate in all areas of school life.

## University of Vermont

**Website:**
www.uvm.edu

**Type of School:**
Public University

Animal Sciences, 102 Terrill Hall, Burlington, VT 05405-0148. Contact: Josie Davis, Equine Studies Coordinator or Kathy Tatro. Phone: (802) 656-0155. Fax: (802) 656-8196. Email: josie.davis1@uvm.edu or ktatro@uvm.edu.
**Degrees Offered:** Bachelor of Science, Master of Science, Doctor of Philosophy
**Majors Offered:** Animal Science with equine concentration (B.S.), Animal Science with pre-professional concentration [pre-vet, pre-med] (B.S.), Animal Science with equine options (M.S., Ph.D.)
**Tuition Costs:** Residents: $8,696; nonresidents: $21,748; room and board: $6,680/year
**Description of Program:** Balance and dressage riding styles taught
**Facilities:** Equestrian center is a quarter mile from campus and has 20 school horses and both indoor and outdoor arenas.
**Showing:** IHSA

# VIRGINIA

## American School of Equine Dentistry

**Website:**
www.amscheqdentistry.com

**Type of School:**
Specialty School

American School of Equine Dentistry, 36691 Sawmill Lane, Purcellville, VA 20132. Contact: Raymond Hyde, DVM. Phone: (540) 668-6505. Fax: (540) 668-7080. Email: rqhydedvm@anent.com.
**Degrees Offered:** Certificate
**Majors Offered:** Equine Dental Technician
**Tuition Costs:** $4,950; housing: $25/day (includes transportation to campus)
**Description of Program:** The Introduction to Equine Dentistry course is a four-week intensive learning experience that prepares a student for entry into a full- or part-time

career as an equine dental technician. This program is designed to provide the student an opportunity to acquire the knowledge needed to pass an Equine Dental Technician Certification written exam and establish a solid foundation for their needed practical skills. Students learn basic dental procedures, including floating, creating bit seats, incisor reduction and realignment, wave and hook correction, wolf teeth removal, canine teeth reduction, and non-surgical extraction techniques. Introductory course also includes the use of power equipment, primarily rotary Dremel burrs. Upon completion of the course, an apprenticeship program with a certified equine dental technician is highly recommended. Placement of the apprentice with a mentor can be arranged by the school, and extended enrollment programs are available for advanced study and more hands-on experience.

**Facilities:** Housing available
**Classroom/Hands-On Equine Classes:** 40:60

## Averett University

Equestrian Studies, Averett University, 420 W. Main St., Danville, VA 24541. Contact: Jane Faulkner. Phone: (434) 791-5727 or (336) 388-9550. Fax: (434) 791-5787. Email: jfaulkne@averett.edu.
**Accreditation:** Southern Association of Colleges and Schools
**Degrees Offered:** Minor, Bachelor of Arts, Bachelor of Science
**Majors Offered:** Equestrian Studies (B.A., B.S.), Equestrian Studies & Business Administration (B.A., B.S.)
**Tuition Costs:** $7,900/semester; room and board: $2,575/semester; Equestrian Studies fee: $50-$800/class; horse board: $325/month
**Description of Program:** Two to three instructed rides per week; riding class size averages four to six students. Three instructors. Balanced seat, eventing, and dressage taught. Teaching, training, management, and equine science classes are also offered as part of the major.
**Facilities:** Equestrian center is nine miles from campus and has a 40-stall barn, 30-35 school horses, extra stall space for students' horses, one indoor arena, two outdoor arenas, round pen, pastures, paddocks, and cross-country jumps.
**Classroom/Hands-On Equine Classes:** 50:50
**Showing:** Combined training, dressage, intercollegiate, schooling shows, TREC

**Website:**
www.averett.edu

**Type of School:**
Private University

## Chatham Hall

800 Chatham Hall Circle, Chatham, VA 24531-3085. Contact: Cricket Stone, Director of Riding. Phone: (434) 432-5500. Fax: (434) 432-1002. Email: cstone@chathamhall.org.
**Degrees Offered:** High School Diploma
**Tuition Costs:** Boarding students: $25,900; Day students: $9,500; horse board: $400-475/month; two school-horse lessons per week: $600/trimester; four school-horse lessons per week: $850/trimester; two student-horse lessons per week: $500/trimester; four student-horse lessons per week: $750/trimester
**Description of Program:** Chatham Hall riders are competitive in the Junior Hunter, Children's Hunter, Children's Jumper, and Equitation classes, winning classes at shows such as House Mountain, Duke Children's Benefit, Reeve Irvine Benefit, Gulf Coast Winter Classics, HITS Ocala, HITS Culpeper, and Atlanta Spring Classic. Chatham Hall also offers a program in which students receive saddle seat instruction on currently competitive show

**Website:**
www.chathamhall.org

**Type of School:**
Private Girl's College-Preparatory Day and Boarding School

horses for physical education credit. This program takes place less than a mile off campus at Longacre Stables. Instructed by Margaret Gardiner, the students compete successfully at all levels, from tournaments to the World Championships at Louisville.

**Facilities:** The Chatham Hall Equestrian Center houses a 125ft x 250ft indoor arena, offices, a conference room, and 12ft x 14ft stalls. A total of 40 box stalls in the new center and the stables accommodate school horses and student horses. The facilities also include a hunter trials course, two all-weather outdoor rings, 362 acres of trails and fields, and indoor hot/cold water wash racks. Longacre Stables, less than a mile off of campus, features a 200ft x 70ft indoor arena, an outdoor ring, 40 box stalls, indoor wash racks, a jogging track, and large turnout fields.

**Showing:** Chatham Hall riders have many opportunities to compete.

## Equissage

**Website:**
www.equissage.com

**Type of School:**
Specialty School

P.O. Box 447, Round Hill, VA 20142. Contact: Mary Schreiber, Founder & President. Phone: (800) 843-0224 or (540) 338-1917. Fax: (540) 338-5569.
Email: info@equissage.com

**Degrees Offered:** Certificate

**Majors Offered:** Equine Sports Massage, Canine Massage Therapy

**Tuition Costs:** $935/Equine Sports Massage; $495/Canine Massage Therapy (home study)

**Description of Program:** Equissage now offers a Distance Education Certificate Program in Canine Massage Therapy, in addition to the original 60-hour, on-site Certificate Program in Equine Sports Massage Therapy. The equine program consists of 40 hours of actual hands-on curriculum with Equissage's fourteen horses, and 20 hours of classroom training. The ratio of students to teachers in the equine program is never more than 5:1. Approximately 65 percent of those enrolled in the equine program intend to start their own practice in equine therapy, with the remaining 35 percent learning the therapy in order to benefit their own horses. Since 1990, Equissage has trained more than 3,500 equine therapists from every state in the union, as well as 21 different foreign countries. Continuing Education Units are awarded through the National Certification Board for Therapeutic Massage and Bodywork.

**Facilities:** State-of-the-art Equissage training facility, 20 acres

**Classroom/Hands-On Equine Classes:** 20:40 hours

## Foxcroft School

**Website:**
www.foxcroft.org

**Type of School:**
Secondary Private Boarding School

P.O. Box 5555, Middleburg, VA 20118-5555. Phone: (540) 687-5555 or (800) 858-2364. Fax: (540) 687-3627. Email: admissions@foxcroft.org.

**Accreditation:** The Virginia Association of Independent Schools

**Degrees Offered:** High School Diploma

**Tuition Costs:** $33,000/boarding; $22,000/day

**Description of Program:** Day and boarding school for grades 9-12. Students are given a classical education in equitation and balance seat. Some are prepared to compete in hunter/jumper shows and combined training events, others to participate in the hunt field. All are prepared to enjoy riding and horses. All levels of riders may enter the program. Beginners learn the basics of riding, including a brief introduction to the preparation and care of the horse and necessary equipment. Intermediate and advanced riders strengthen their skills as they learn to execute more complicated and difficult exercises. Along with regular lessons, intermediate and advanced riders are given the opportunity to ride with well-known professionals in clinics sponsored regularly throughout the year by the school. Students are encouraged to compete at the appropriate levels in horse shows and events held both on and off campus. Advanced riders are invited frequently to participate in local foxhunting meets from early fall through early spring. Foxcroft has a Riding Team and a Riding Club. The Riding Team competes in the Tri-State Equitation League, which consists of seven schools. The Riding Club, comprised of approximately 25-30 members, assists the riding staff in the organization of stable management lectures, clinics, and competitions, which are held on campus.

**Facilities:** Stable with 60 stalls, two tack rooms, two wash stalls (each with cold and hot water and a grooming vacuum), 100ft x 200ft indoor arena with an enclosed viewing gallery, many paddocks, two outdoor sand arenas, outdoor grass arena, beginning novice through training level cross-country courses

**Showing:** Hunter/jumper shows and combined training events

## Hollins University

Hollins University Riding Program, P.O. Box 9611, Roanoke, VA 24020-9611. Contact: Nancy Peterson, Director. Phone: (540) 362-6691. Fax: (540) 362-6446. Email: huadm@hollins.edu.
**Degrees Offered:** Bachelor of Arts
**Majors Offered:** No equine degrees

Website:
www.hollins.edu

Type of School:
Private University

## J. Sargeant Reynolds Community College

Western Campus, (Goochland, VA) C/O P.O. Box 85622, Richmond, VA 23285-5622. Contact: Mary Wilt. Phone: (804) 662-6421. Fax: (804) 556-5741. Email: mwilt@jsr.vccs.edu.
**Degrees Offered:** Career Studies Certificate
**Majors Offered:** Equine Management
**Description of Program:** This program is designed to provide students with the basic skills needed for effective horse care, especially health care, nutrition, stabling, foot care, and business management. The program will meet the needs of both an expanding horse industry in Virginia and students wishing to make a career in this area. Employment opportunities include stable management, training, or small business management in the horse industry.

Website:
www.reynolds.edu

Type of School:
Community College

## Lord Fairfax Community College

Continuing Education, Lord Fairfax Community College, 173 Skirmisher Lane, Middletown, VA 22645. Contact: Nancy Lloyd. Phone: (540) 868-7284. Fax: (540) 868-7020. Email: lfloyn@lfcc.edu.
**Accreditation:** Southern Association of Colleges and Schools
**Degrees Offered:** Certificate
**Majors Offered:** Horse Science (C)
**Tuition Costs:** Resident: $62.71/credit; nonresident: $210.14/credit

Website:
www.lfcc.edu

Type of School:
Community College

## The Madeira School

8328 Georgetown Pike, McLean, VA 22102. Phone: (703) 556-8200.
Email: cphemmer@madeira.org.
**Accreditation:** Virginia Association of Independent Schools
**Degrees Offered:** High School Diploma
**Tuition Costs:** Boarding: $32,800; Day: $22,300
**Description of Program:** All-girls boarding and day secondary school. Offering excellent academics combined with a quality riding program, Madeira is a unique place for the dedicated student who loves to ride. The goal of the Madeira Riding Program is to develop confident and disciplined riders capable of participating in a wide range of equestrian activities. Hunter seat equitation, basic dressage, and principles of cross-country riding are integral parts of the curriculum. Students enroll in the program at the start of each trimester. Riding three times a week in the Madeira Riding Program fulfills the physical education requirement. Instruction in hunter seat equitation is offered for beginning through advanced riders. Extra riding opportunities include hacking outside of class, competitions, clinics, and traditional special events like the Parent's Weekend Horse Show, Founder's Day Gymkhana, and Graduation Gallop.
**Facilities:** A 40-stall barn, Gaines Arena (100ft x 200ft indoor ring), two outdoor sand rings, an abundance of beautiful trails and cross-country jumps, 380-acre campus
**Showing:** Students show both interscholastically and on the circuit.

## Randolph-Macon Woman's College

4762 Hawkins Mill Rd., Lynchburg, VA 24503. Contact: J. T. Tallon, Director of Riding. Email: jttallon@rmwc.edu.
**Accreditation:** Southern Association of Colleges and Schools
**Degrees Offered:** Bachelor
**Majors Offered:** No equine majors
**Tuition Costs:** $550/credit; $2,000/semester horse board; $460-$1,200/riding lesson plan
**Description of Program:** Two instructed rides per week; riding class size averages six students. Three instructors. Instruction is offered for credit in all levels: beginning, intermediate, and advanced. Beginning: emphasis is on the position of the rider and the basic fundamentals of control, with special attention to students with limited riding experience. Intermediate: beginning showing and cross-country riding; learning and improvement of school figures, improving control, jumping gymnastics, and low courses. Advanced: showing, cross-country riding and competition, and individual schooling projects.
**Facilities:** The equestrian center is eight miles from campus, and includes 100 acres in the foothills of the Blue Ridge Mountains, 40 school horses, a jumping amphitheater (360ft x 250ft), a schooling ring (250ft x 150ft), the Claire Noyes Cox indoor arena (at 120ft x 300ft, it is large enough to accommodate two classes simultaneously), all-weather and late afternoon classes, a hunter trial course, outdoor schooling jumps, cross-country jumps throughout the 100-acre tract, a modern 40-stall barn with two wash stalls and a tack room, and stalls available for private boarders (with turn-out paddocks).
**Showing:** IHSA, USAE, SWVHJA

# Sweet Briar College

Physical Education Dept., Riding Program, P.O. Box 6, Sweet Briar, VA 24595. Contact: Shelby French. Phone: (804) 381-6116 or (804) 381-6142. Fax: (804) 381-6457. Email: sfrench@sbc.edu.

**Accreditation:** Southern Association of Colleges and Universities

**Degrees Offered:** Bachelor of Arts, Bachelor of Science, Internships

**Majors Offered:** Liberal Arts with Equine Studies Certificate

**Tuition Costs:** In-state: $12,500; out-of-state: $19,700; room and board: $8,040/year; hunter board: $400/month; full board: $500/month; riding block fees: $150-920/semester

**Description of Program:** Two to five instructed rides per week; riding class size averages five students. Four instructors. Equine classes for physical education credit. At every level, riders have a variety of opportunities, with an emphasis in three major areas: hunter/jumper/equitation, training/schooling young horses, and hunter-oriented cross-country. Concentrations in teaching, schooling, and management are the foundation. You can further enhance your knowledge in pre-veterinary courses, internships, and independent projects. Career-building leadership positions are available as teaching assistants, activity managers, and Riding Council members. The hunter/jumper/equitation program includes schooling the hunter and preparing for competition. You'll develop an awareness of what is expected of the horse in a variety of hunter/jumper and equitation competitions through class work and competitive experiences. Your instructors emphasize developing a quality hunter through a combination of flatwork, gymnastics, and a range of courses. The program also focuses on schooling. You will train on the flat and over fences. Instructional courses provide a systematic approach that applies to a range of horses and specialties. Sweet Briar integrates both young and green horses into the schooling program.

**Facilities:** The riding center is set on 100 acres of rolling hills, just a mile from the main quad of the college, and includes 36 school horses, three spacious outdoor rings with all-season footing, indoor facilities, an enclosed longing ring, more than seven teaching and schooling fields, as well as miles of trails and other fields on the 3,300-acre school campus. Riders can also enjoy a new hunter trials course, fence lines with coops, and a complete inventory of hunter/jumper fences suitable for USA Equestrian competitions.

**Classroom/Hands-On Equine Classes:** 70:30

**Showing:** IHSA, USA Equestrian, ANRC, hunter, riding to hounds, hunter pace and trials

**Website:**
www.sbc.edu

**Type of School:**
Private Women's College

# Virginia Episcopal School

400 VES Road, P.O. Box 408, Lynchburg, VA 24505. Contact: Pam Barile, Director of Admission. Phone: (434) 385-3607. Fax: (434) 385-3603. Email: admissions@ves.org.

**Degrees Offered:** High School Diploma

**Website:**
www.ves.org

**Type of School:**
Secondary School

# Virginia Intermont College

Equine Studies, Virginia Intermont College, Moore St., Bristol, VA 24201. Contact: Eddie Federwisch, Program Director. Phone: (276) 669-6101. Fax: (276) 669-5763. Email: viadmit@vic.edu.

**Degrees Offered:** Minor, Bachelor of Arts, Bachelor of Science

**Majors Offered:** Equestrian Studies (M, B.A., B.S.), Equine-Assisted Growth and Development (M)

**Website:**
www.vic.edu

**Type of School:**
Private College

## Virginia-Maryland Regional College of Veterinary Medicine

Virginia Tech, Duck Pond Drive (0442), Blacksburg, VA 24061. Phone: (540) 231-7666. Email dvmadmit@vt.edu or vmsgrad@vt.edu.

**Degrees Offered:** Master of Science, Doctor of Philosophy, Doctor of Veterinary Medicine

**Majors Offered:** Veterinary Medical Science (M.S., Ph.D.), Veterinary Medicine (D.V.M.)

## Virginia Tech (Virginia Polytechnic Institute and State University)

Animal & Poultry Science Department, Virginia Tech, 2200 Litton Reaves Hall, Blacksburg, VA 24061. Contact: Dr. E. A. Dunnington. Phone: (540) 231-9179.
Fax: (540) 231-3010. Email: dunning@vt.edu.

**Accreditation:** Southern Association of Colleges and Schools.

**Degrees Offered:** Associate, Bachelor of Science, Master of Science, Doctorate, Doctor of Veterinary Medicine

**Majors Offered:** Animal & Poultry Science with equine emphasis (B.S.), Equine Nutrition, Physiology, Management, Veterinary Medical Sciences (M.S., Ph.D.), Veterinary Medicine (D.V.M.)

**Tuition Costs:** In-state: $116/credit; out-of-state: $484/credit; room and board: $4,000/year; equitation classes: $500/semester

**Description of Program:** Two instructed rides per week; riding class size averages nine students. One equitation instructor and two professors. Hunt seat and dressage style taught. The Virginia Tech Equine Program is a science-based program; the emphasis is preparing students for veterinary college, graduate school, or employment in the equine industry. Classes addressing genetics, physiology, anatomy, reproduction, nutrition, behavior, training, and management of horses are offered. The Hokie Harvest Sale, an annual production auction, is organized and conducted by the undergraduate students. Independent studies, special studies, undergraduate research projects, and internships are important parts of this program. Most of the classes include a strong, "hands-on" component.

**Facilities:** The equestrian center is a half-mile from campus and has 40 equitation horses, a livestock teaching arena (125ft x 250ft) with classrooms and housing for large animals, one covered arena (100ft x 130ft), and one outdoor arena (150ft x 250ft). The Breeding Center is a quarter mile from the central campus and has 65 horses including two to three stallions, 25-35 broodmares, and a variety of weanlings, yearlings and two-year-olds.

**Classroom/Hands-On Equine Classes:** 50:50

**Showing:** IHSA, IDA, intramural, and open shows for students

# WASHINGTON

## Experience International

P.O. Box 680, Everson, WA 98247 U.S.A. Contact: Jason Bernstein, Program Manager.
Phone: (360) 966-3876. Fax: (360) 966-4131. Email: ei@expint.org.
**Accreditation:** U.S. State Department Designated J1 Exchange Visitor Training Program
**Degrees Offered:** Apprenticeship/Internship/Quality Work Experience
**Tuition Costs:** Contact School
**Description of Program:** As an internationally-recognized training organization, Experience International provides participants with a high-quality program. Creative, diverse, and challenging placements that fit each individual's needs and career goals are made. Placements can be arranged in agriculture, equine industry, dairy, horticulture, landscaping, winemaking, aquaculture, forestry, environmental education and interpretation, parks and recreation, wildlife, and many related fields. The staff has years of experience, knows what it takes to make it work, and offers the personal support needed to assure the best international experience possible. Two programs are offered: Inbound J1 Exchange Visitor Program to the United States, and Outbound to many countries around the world. Inbound J1 Program: six to 18 months of career-related experience with farms, equine training centers, private companies, and state or federal agencies throughout the Northwest region of the United States. Placements available in Alaska, Oregon, Washington, California, Idaho, and Montana. Outbound Program: three to 18 months of career-related experience in more than 35 countries around the world. See website for full listing of available countries.
**Classroom/Hands-On Equine Classes:** All placements provide quality hands-on work experience.
**Showing:** Varies

**Website:**
www.expint.org

**Type of School:**
Apprenticeship/Internship/
On-the-Job Training

## Mission Farrier School

4404 - 260th Ave. NE., Redmond, WA 98053. Phone: (425) 898-7757.
Email: missionfarrierschool@hotmail.com.
**Degrees Offered:** Certificate
**Majors Offered:** Farrier

**Website:**
www.missionfarrierschool.com

**Type of School:**
Specialty School

## Seattle Knights

340 West Sunset Way A-204, Issaquah, WA 98027. Phone: (425) 557-0311.
Email: Ironwolfe@seattleknights.com
**Degrees Offered:** Accredited by Seattle Knights
**Majors Offered:** Jouster, Lancer, Actor/Combatant
**Tuition Costs:** $300/level
**Description of Program:** The Seattle Knights Academy of Medieval Combat Choreography teaches historical and performance fighting techniques for a variety of weapons as well as for hand-to-hand combat. All classes are conducted by a certified instructor. Classes run between eight and ten weeks. Private lessons are also available. All prospective jousting students must go through ground combat training first. Often, they already have excellent riding skills; if not, they are taught standard dressage and Western riding techniques first. This allows them, while learning jousting, to con-

**Website:**
www.seattleknights.com

**Type of School:**
Specialty School

centrate on the lance work instead of worrying about the horse. Students that excel in their classes are hired to work for the company, and a few go on to work for other people and organizations. The hardest part of the courses is the riding—and the falls. Learning to fall correctly—in order to avoid injury—is frightening at first for most people. But learning to fall at speed is an art, and one that pays well. Special seminars are conducted throughout the year for those who wish to receive a crash course in jousting. However, this course is only for those who are already accomplished riders.

**Facilities:** Facilities consist of two privately-owned outdoor arenas. One is located in Marysville and the other in Hobart. A third, covered arena is being considered for possible use during the winter.

**Showing:** Many students work various Renaissance fairs and other special horse stunt applications, such as film and television.

## U.S. Cavalry School

**Website:**
www.uscavalryschool.org

**Type of School:**
Specialty School

P.O. Box 1171, Twisp, WA 98856. Phone: (509) 997-1015 or (888) 291-4097. Email: horseman@uscavalryschool.org.

**Degrees Offered:** Re-enactor Certification

**Majors Offered:** Cavalry Encampment (RC), Weekend Workshop, School of the Trooper, Cavalry Orientation

## Walla Walla Community College

**Website:**
www.wallawalla.cc

**Type of School:**
Community College

500 Tausick Way, Walla Walla, WA 99362. Phone: (509) 522-2500. Fax: (509) 527-3661. TDD (Hearing Impaired): (509) 527-4412. Email: terri.johnson@wwcc.ctc.edu

**Accreditation:** Northwest Association of Colleges and Schools

**Degrees Offered:** Certificate, Associate of Applied Science

**Majors Offered:** Farrier Science

**Tuition Costs:** $74.15/credit; international students: $245.85/credit

**Description of Program:** The farriery program is designed to provide the student the knowledge and skills to become a qualified farrier, and is offered as a one year certificate program or a two year A.A.S. degree. A farrier must have extensive knowledge of the anatomy and physiology of the horse's feet and legs. The student must be familiar with the farrier's tools so that horseshoes can be made and nailed onto the horse's hooves. With knowledge of the bone structure of the horse's leg and sufficient practice and experience, the farrier will be able to retain true gaits of horses, improve or correct faulty gaits, alleviate disorders of the feet, and furnish relief for injured parts. Farriers must also have the ability to manage their own business and sell their service to the public. High-technology changes are occurring in the farriery industry. Space-age metals and synthetic materials are being used more and more by modern-day farriers. Farriers are becoming more involved in working with veterinarians to treat specific lameness problems. Instructors in the program at Walla Walla Community College are constantly attending workshops and conferences to make certain that these modern innovations are included in the curriculum. This ensures state-of-the-art training at all times.

**Showing:** NIRA

## Washington State University

College of Veterinary Medicine, P.O. Box 647010, Washington State University, Pullman, WA 99164-7010. Phone: (509) 335-9515. Email: webmaster@wsu.edu.

**Degrees Offered:** Master of Science, Doctor of Philosophy, Doctor of Veterinary Medicine

**Majors Offered:** Veterinary Medicine (D.V.M.), Veterinary Science (M.S., Ph.D.)

**Website:**
www.vetmed.wsu

**Type of School:**
Public University

# WEST VIRGINIA

## Bethany Hills College

Office of Admission, Bethany, WV 26032. Contact: Angela Griffen-Jones, Vice President for Enrollment Management and Marketing. Phone: (800) 922-7611 or (304) 829-7611. Fax: (304) 829-7142. Email: admission@bethanywv.edu.

**Accreditation:** The Higher Learning Commision, North Central Association of Colleges and Schools, National Council for Accreditation of Teacher Education, Council for Social Work

**Degrees Offered:** Bachelor of Arts, Bachelor of Science

**Majors Offered:** Equine Studies with tracks in Equine Management (B.A.) and Pre-Veterinary Medicine (B.S.)

**Description of Program:** The Equine Studies major with tracks in Equine Management and Pre-Veterinary Medicine are administered under the Department of Biology. All laboratories and many classroom courses meet at the new Peace Point Equestrian Center. In addition to all-campus requirements for a Bethany College degree, courses in the Equine Management Program include Introduction to Horses, Equine Husbandry, Equine Health and Preventative Medicine, Facility Management, Design and Promotion I and II, Equine Anatomy and Physiology, Training and Schooling, Starting the Young Horse, Stable Management I and II, Show Coordination I and II, Equine Sports Medicine and Lameness, and Equine Reproduction. Management majors are required to take a minimum of four credit horse of mounted/riding courses (Dressage, Hunt Seat, or Stock Seat). Two credit hours toward the mounted requirement can be substituted for the Training and Schooling requirement. Pre-veterinary track majors are required to take courses including Introduction to Horses, Equine Husbandry, Equine Anatomy and Physiology, Equine Nutrition, Equine Genetics. In addition, Pre-Veterinary majors are required to take a minimum of three credit hours of mounted/riding courses. Two credit hours toward the mounted requirement can be substituted with Training and Schooling.

**Facilities:** Two indoor arenas (160ft x 216ft), two outdoor arenas (100ft x 300ft), five barns with 26 stalls per barn, heated wash stalls, student lounge, twelve turnout paddocks, 2,800 total acres

**Website:**
www.bethanywv.edu

**Type of School:**
Private Liberal Arts College

## Meredith Manor International Equestrian Centre

Rt. 1 Box 66, Waverly, WV 26184. Contact: Faith Meredith, Director.
Email: faith@meredithmanor.com.

**Accreditation:** Accrediting Council for Continuing Education and Training (ACCET), licensed by the State College System of West Virginia, approved for Veterans Benefits and by the W.S. Department of Immigration to enroll nonimmigrant alien students

**Degrees Offered:** Certificate

**Majors Offered:** Riding Master I-VI, Teaching Certificate Level I-III, Shoeing Short Course, Equine Massage Therapy.

**Website:**
www.meredithmanor.com

**Type of School:**
Specialty School

**Tuition Costs:** $157 per credit. $795 room and board per year. $120 horse board per month. $120 breeding lab fee. $15 teaching lab fee.

**Description of Program:** Eight to 16 rides per week; average class size is seven students. Eight instructors. The Riding Master I—-VI curriculums include two riding classes, theory, showing, two career areas, and horse and barn care. The Comprehensive Riding Master III and VI curriculums include six riding classes, three theory classes, three showing classes, six career areas, and three classes in horse and barn care. The curriculum for the Shoeing Short Course includes Farrier Craftsmanship I and II, one career area elective, Hoof Care and Maintenance, and Farrier Working Case Study.

**Facilities:** The equestrian center is located on campus. The campus is 64 acres in size, and includes 120 school horses, six indoor arenas (100ft x 230ft, 100ft x 80ft, 60ft x 144ft, 54ft x 144ft, 50ft x 144ft), four outdoor arenas, a 60ft round pen, two jumping fields, a dressage square, and a Western track. The barn complex includes seven barns, a blacksmithing school, feed sheds, bedding storage, classrooms, and laboratories. Students are housed in two dormitories and take their meals together in the cafeteria. Research material, books, periodicals, and audio-visual equipment are available in the school library. The administration building houses the school's administrative offices and reception area. Several residences on campus house several key staff members.

**Classroom/Hands-On Equine Classes:** Vary

**Showing:** Showing is held as a weekly class. The students show throughout each quarter and participate in a big show at the end of each quarter, competing in front of an outside judge.

**Website:**
www.salemiu.edu

**Type of School:**
Private University

# Salem International University

Equine Careers & Industry Management Program, Salem International University, 223 W Main St., P.O. Box 500, Salem, WV 26426. Contact: Dr. Janice L. Holland, Director. Phone: (304) 782-4528. Fax: (304) 782-4916. Email: holland@salemiu.edu. Admissions information: Phone: (800) 283-4562. Fax: (304) 782-5592. Email: admissions@salemiu.edu.

**Accreditation:** North Central Association of Colleges and Schools

**Degrees Offered:** Bachelor of Science, Master of Art

**Majors Offered:** Equine Careers and Industry Management (B.S.), Pre-Vet (B.S.), Education with specialization in Equestrian Education (M.A.)

**Tuition Costs:** $14,100/year; $375/credit; $4,432/year room and board; $250/month horse board

**Description of Program:** Opportunities are available for qualified students to do internships with professionals in the equine industry. In addition, study abroad is available, offering a unique experience in international practices, training, and instruction. Assistance to locate internship sites may be obtained from the director of the Equine Careers and Industry Management Program and must be approved by the coordinator of the Academic Enhancement Center. Field trips are often required as a part of the courses in the Equine Careers and Industry Management curriculum. Transportation for field trips is provided by the university, but students must pay for all other associated expenses. Well-known instructors and trainers in the equine industry periodically offer clinics and workshops. Students are encouraged to participate, but there are additional fees required to do so. The Equine Careers and Industry Management Program at the Barker Equestrian Center is an approved riding establishment of the British Horse Society. The program is an affiliate member of the American Horse Shows Association, Inc. Membership is also held in the American Horse Council and the North American Horsemen's Association. Riding instruction is dependent on the instructor's specialization, but may include several disciplines, including hunt seat (flat and fences), Western horsemanship, reining, dressage, and saddle seat.

**Facilities:** The Barker Equestrian Center is located four miles from the main campus. The center has 59 stalls, with a minimum of 30 school-owned horses available for student use, two arenas (200ft x 150ft, 50ft x 80ft), a solid-wall round pen, access to trails, and outside paddocks.

**Classroom/Hands-On Equine Classes:** 40:60

**Showing:** IHSA, local and open shows

# WISCONSIN

## University of Wisconsin–Madison

School of Veterinary Medicine, 2015 Linden Drive, Madison, WI 53706-1102. Phone: (608) 263-2525. Email: oaa@svm.vetmed.wisc.edu.
**Degrees Offered:** Doctor of Veterinary Medicine
**Majors Offered:** Veterinary Medicine (D.V.M.)

**Website:**
www.vetmed.wisc.edu

**Type of School:**
Public University

## University of Wisconsin–River Falls

Animal and Food Science Department, 410 S. 3rd St., River Falls, WI 54022-5001. Contact: Larry Kasten. Phone: (715)425-3500 or -3704 or -3702. Fax: (715)425-3785. Email: anfdsci@uwrf.edu.
**Degrees Offered:** Bachelor of Science
**Majors Offered:** Animal Science with emphasis in Horse Science

**Website:**
www.uwrf.edu

**Type of School:**
Public University

# WYOMING

## Casper College

Agriculture Department, Casper College, 125 College Dr., Casper, WY 82601. Contact: Samantha Dyer. Phone: (307) 268-2595 or (307) 268-2110. Fax: (307) 268-2530. Email: sdyer@acad.cc.whecn.edu.
**Accreditation:** North Central Association of Colleges and Schools
**Degrees Offered:** Associate of Science, Associate of Applied Science
**Majors Offered:** Agriculture (A.S.), Agriculture Business (A.S., A.A.S.), Animal Science Technician (A.A.S.)
**Tuition Costs:** Resident: $660/semester; nonresident: $1,836/semester; housing: $1,475/semester
**Description of Program:** A few equine classes are offered, but the college is more concerned with preparing students for a four-year degree at a university. Therefore, students take several general education classes to fulfill those requirements. The school has a very competitive rodeo team. The team participates in all the major rodeos in the Central Rocky Mountain Region. Also, the College National Finals Rodeo is currently held in Casper, Wyoming, every June.

**Website:**
www.cc.whecn.edu

**Type of School:**
Community College

**Facilities:** Indoor arena
**Classroom/Hands-On Equine Classes:** Vary
**Showing:** Intercollegiate Rodeo, Livestock Judging

## Central Wyoming College

Equestrian Studies/Rodeo, Central Wyoming College, 2660 Peck Ave., Riverton, WY 82501. Phone: (307) 855-2286 or 855-2231. Fax: (307) 856-6561.
**Degrees Offered:** Associate of Science, Associate of Applied Science, Certificate
**Majors Offered:** Equine Training Technology, Farrier Science, Horse Management (C, A.A.S.), Horse Science (A.S.)

**Website:**
www.cwc.edu

**Type of School:**
Community College

## Global Equine Academy

Box 205, Beulah, WY 82712. Contact Sandy Miller, Director. Phone: (307) 283-2587 Email: globalequine@aol.com.
**Degrees Offered:** Associate Degree, Certification
**Majors Offered:** Equine Marketing, Principles of Training and Ag Sales and Service with emphasis in Equine Management
**Tuition Costs:** Contact School
**Description of Program:** The new era in equine education is great. Get a two-year associate's degree and never leave home. Take online lecture classes from professional college instructors. The classes are very informative and cover anatomy, marketing, business, nutrition, reproduction, and much more. There are two Centered Riding classes offered via lecture online and video.

**Website:**
www.globalequineacademy.com

**Type of School:**
Independent Study

## Laramie County Community College

Laramie County Community College Equine Program, 1400 East College Drive, Cheyenne WY 82007. Phone: (307) 778-1195 or 778-1188. Fax: (307) 778-1189. Email: alindsey@lccc.wy.edu.
**Accreditation:** North Central Association of Colleges and Schools
**Degrees Offered:** Associate of Science, Associate of Applied Science
**Majors Offered:** Equine Training Management (A.A.S.), Equine Science (A.S.), Equine Business Management (A.S.)
**Tuition Costs:** Residents: $822/semester; nonresidents: $2,046/semester; room and board: $3,520/year
**Description of Program:** The Equine Studies program at LCCC offers a balance of classroom instruction and practical laboratory experience covering a wide spectrum of equine interests. The goal of the program is to graduate students who are able to successfully pursue a bachelor's degree or compete for employment in the equine industry. Three majors are available to better assist the student in his/her learning endeavors. Students of the program will learn the basics of training, horsemanship, anatomy and physiology, disease, nutrition, and business of the equine industry. All students will become involved in the equine industry either through the highly competitive judging, show, or rodeo teams, or through involvement in the production of various shows and equine-related activities.
**Facilities:** The equestrian center is on campus and has one indoor arena (126ft x 250ft), one outdoor arena (150ft x 300ft), 52 indoor stalls, and 52 outdoor covered box stalls.

**Website:**
www.lcc.whecn.edu

**Type of School:**
Community College

**Classroom/Hands-On Equine Classes:** 50:50
**Showing:** Horse Show Team (IHSA), Rodeo Team (NIRA), Horse Judging Team, Block and Bridle Club

## Northwest College

**Website:**
www.northwestcollege.edu

**Type of School:**
Community College

231 W. 6th St., Powell, WY 82435. Contact: Brad Hammond, Assistant Director of Enrollment Services. Phone: (800) 560-4692. Fax: (307) 754- 6249.
Email: admissions@northwestcollege.edu.
**Accreditation:** North Central Association of Colleges and Schools
**Degrees Offered:** Associate of Applied Science
**Majors Offered:** Equine Riding and Training, Equine Business Management, Farrier Business Management
**Tuition Costs:** In-state: $1,800/year; out-of-state: $4,304/year; room and board: $3,404/year; horse board: $1,510/year (includes farrier and some veterinary expenses)
**Description of Program:** The Equine Riding and Training option, with competitive entry admission requirements, assists students in learning riding, training, and horse handling skills in both Western and English riding styles, plus related management skills. Students may bring their own horse and board it at the college. Class sizes are limited. Students find employment in training stables, riding academies, summer camps, or other related areas. The Equine Business Management Degree is designed for those who want to be involved in the sales and merchandising aspects of the equine industry. This program has unlimited enrollment. The Farrier Business Management Degree prepares students to own or operate their own farrier business. It combines hands-on farrier courses with an abundance of horses to practice on, along with forge work to create both standard and corrective shoes. A strong group of business courses are provided in this program. All tools are provided in labs, and the instructor is an AFA-certified Journeyman Farrier.
**Facilities:** The Equine Center is a seven-acre complex about one block from the main campus. It features an 80ft x 160ft heated arena with viewing gallery; fully equipped farrier lab and breeding lab; 100ft x 200ft outdoor arena; two round corrals with viewing stands; hot walker; tack room; outdoor hunt course and trail obstacles; indoor/outdoor wash racks; access to country riding from the center; and a 60-stall Porta Stall Barn. Eight turnout paddocks are available. The boarding fee covers college rations, as well as veterinarian services for minor emergencies and routine work.
**Classroom/Hands-On Equine Classes:** Equine Riding and Training: 5/9; Farrier Business Management: 1/4
**Showing:** NIRA

# INTERNATIONAL LISTINGS

## *ARGENTINA*

### El Trebol Polo School

**Website:**
www.haraeltrebol.com

**Type of School:**
Specialty School

Capitan Sarmiento County, Buenos Aires, Argentina. Route No. 8 - kmt. 145. Contact: Mr. Federico Ramos Mejia. Phone: (5411) 46631245. Email: ramomejia@hotmail.com and polomanchaverde@hotmail.com.
**Majors Offered:** Polo School
**Tuition Costs:** $275/day: includes riding fees, stick and ball, room and meals, transportation to and from airport
**Description of Program:** Two instructors supervise the stick and ball in the morning. In the afternoon, the instructors organize the practice and matches (four chukkers).
**Facilities:** One polo field (240m x 150m), twelve school horses
**Showing:** Professional exhibition, the Argentina Open Polo Championship

## *AUSTRALIA*

### Armidale Racing Academy

**Website:**
www.jockeyschool.com

**Type of School:**
Specialty School

P.O. Box 5013, Armidale, NSW 2350, Australia; or C/O Race Course, Barney St., Armidale, NSW 2350 Australia. Contact: Director of Training. Phone: +612 6771 3333. Fax: +612 6771 3330. E-mail: ara@northnet.com.au.
**Degrees Offered:** International Certificates
**Majors Offered:** Certificate II in Racing Stablehand 1, Certificate III in Racing Stablehand 2, Certificate III in Racing Trackwork Rider, Certificate IV Jockey

### Australian Correspondence School

**Website:**
www.acs.edu.au

**Type of School:**
Independent Internationally Accredited School

P.O. Box 2092, Nerang MDC, Qld. 4211 Australia. Phone: (07) 5530 4855. Fax: (07) 5525 1728. Email: admin@acs.edu.au. Victorian Course Counsellor (Australia) 0417 505 573.
**Accreditation:** International Accreditation & Recognition Council, Australian Council of Private Education and Training member, Queensland Nursery Industry Association member
**Courses Offered:** Associate Diploma, Advanced Diploma, Certificate, Advanced Certificate
**Majors Offered:** Agriculture, Applied Management, Animal Husbandry
**Tuition Costs:** (AUD) $374.55/Short Course; $8,314.55/Advanced Diploma Program
**Description of Program:** Formal Courses: Advanced Certificate in Applied Management (Horse Management) is a course designed for managers, supervisors, or people who wish to work up to these positions within their industry. Certificate in Agriculture is designed as a base level qualification for technicians working in Agriculture.

Associate Diploma in Animal Husbandry is a broad-based program that can be adapted to include a number of horse care modules. Advanced Diploma in Agriculture is designed for high level managers in the agricultural industry. Short Courses: Animal Breeding provides a broad understanding of animal breeding and its application in farming; Animal Husbandry I, II, and III provides a solid introduction to the anatomy and physiology of farm animals, animal health, and animal feeding; Horse Care I, II, and III covers terminology, horse psychology, using tack, parts of the body, the digestive system, evaluating the value of a paddock, grooming for different purposes, business applications, management of horses, and health problems.

## Australian College of Natural Animal Medicine

**Website:**
www.acnam.com.au

**Type of School:**
Independent Study, Specialty School

Office: Level 7, 505 St. Kilda Rd., Melbourne VIC 3004 Australia. Mailing address: P.O. Box 54, Beaufort VIC 3373 Australia. Phone: (+61 3) 9868 1680. Fax: (+61 3) 9820 0777. Email: Registrar@acnam.com.au.

**Accreditation:** The Holistic Animal Therapy Association of Australia (HATAA), International Association of Animal Massage & Bodywork (IAAMB) professional member, Australian Complementary Health Association (ACHA), British Complementary Medical Association (BCMA)

**Degrees Offered:** Diploma, Certificate

**Majors Offered:** Veterinary Naturopathy (D), Veterinary Homeopathy (D), Veterinary Botanical Medicine (D), Animal Communication (D), Animal Heath Sciences [for NDs] (D), Natural Animal Therapies (C) with a specialization in Homeopathy, Canine Massage, Equine Massage, Herbal Medicine, Nutrition, Energy Diagnosis, Animal Communication

**Tuition Costs:** (AUD) $700/module; includes books, learning materials, tuition, administration fees, and postage from the college

**Description of Program:** Certificate courses contain three modules; diploma courses—other than Veterinary Naturopathy—contain six modules. The Diploma of Veterinary Naturopathy contains nine modules. All courses are delivered by external study with internships completed at a location in proximity to the student's place of residence. Courses that involve a high degree of hands-on instruction (such as Equine Massage) include video-based instruction. All students must also complete practical hands-on training under the supervision of a qualified practitioner in their area. Regular student online tutorial sessions are also scheduled. Classroom training sessions are held monthly at the Melbourne lecture facility and one- to five-day hands-on clinics are scheduled throughout the year at equine facilities in outer Melbourne. Students who cannot attend these training seminars are able to attend approved training clinics in their own locality, which can be credited toward their practical requirement. In addition to completing both theoretical and practical examinations, students must complete a minimum of 100 hours of supervised practical training to be awarded the Certificate of Natural Animal Therapies (Equine Massage). Veterinary Diploma students must complete internships in all the major ingestive modalities and 550 hours of supervised practical placement training over a three-year study period.

## Charles Sturt University

**Website:**
www.csu.edu.au

**Type of School:**
Public University with Independent Study

School of Agriculture, P.O. Box 588, Wagga Wagga NSW 2678 Australia. Contact: Dr. Karen Affleck, Course Coordinator. Phone: (02) 6933 2147. Fax: (02) 6933 2796. Email: kaffleck@csu.edu.au.

**Degrees Offered:** Bachelor of Applied Science, Bachelor of Applied Science (Honors), Graduate Certificate of Applied Science, Master of Applied Science, Doctor of Philosophy
**Majors Offered:** Equine Studies
**Tuition Costs:** (AUD) $5,366.40/undergraduate; $39/week stable fee
**Description of Program:** Three years of full-time study at the Wagga Wagga Campus, or six years of distance education study complete this course. The Bachelor of Applied Science (Equine Studies), developed in consultation with industry, aims to train you to apply scientific principles and knowledge to the management of breeding and performance enterprises. The course integrates biological sciences, equine sciences and equine husbandry and also develops an understanding of agribusiness and financial management. Practical skills and experience are gained through involvement with the operation of the University's Equine Centre at Wagga Wagga and by eight weeks industry experience in breeding and training establishments. The Equine Center provides the opportunity for students to be involved in all aspects of horse management, husbandry, technology and applied research.
**Facilities:** One indoor arena (80m x 40m), open standard cross-country course, 1200m graded exercise track, 86 stalls, covered yard and handling facilities, high-speed treadmill, 80 ha of horse pastures, sand area for dressage and jumping
**Classroom/Hands-On Equine Classes:** Vary
**Showing:** There is an opportunity for showing during the final year.

**Website:**
www.happyhorses.com.au

**Type of School:**
Independent Study

## A Healthy Horse the Natural Way

P.O. Box 670, Randwick NSW 2031, Australia. Contact: Catherine Bird.
Email: happyhorses@iinet.net.au.
**Degrees Offered:** Certificate
**Majors Offered:** Equine Aromatherapy
**Tuition Costs:** (AUD) $750/course; $150/segment; $30/exam fee
**Description of Program:** Equine Aromatherapy Correspondence Course is designed for massage therapistsor body workers to add to their knowledge. Segment One outlines the history and philosophy of aromatherapy and introduces the student to horses and their responses to essential oils. Segment Two is your *materia medica* of safe essential oils. Segment Three discusses the various ways of choosing your essential oils for use with horses and how to use them. Segment Four discusses massage techniques and understanding your role as an equine aromatherapist. Segment Five discusses subtle energy anatomy in your horse and the spiritual application of essential oils. Segment Six discusses adjunctive therapies that enhance the use of essential oils with horses and requires the submission of the student's case histories. The presenter aims at presenting a weekend clinic in each country where there are enough students. The price is determined at the time of organizing the course and the current exchange rate. Students may also purchase a copy of *Horse Scents: Making Sense with Your Horse Using Aromatherapy* by Catherine Bird, though it is not necessary to do so in order to complete the course, as the notes are extensive.

**Website:**
www.marcusoldham.vic.edu.au

**Type of School:**
Private College

## Marcus Oldham College

Horse Management Studies, Private Bag 116, 145 Pigdons Rd., Geelong Mail Centre, 3221, Victoria, Australia. Contact: Jenny Wotherspoon. Phone: (03) 5243 3533. Fax: (03) 5244 1263. Email: wotherspoon@marcusoldham.vic.edu.au.
**Accreditation:** National Training Authority, Office of Post Secondary Education
**Degrees Offered:** Diploma

**Majors Offered:** Horse Business Management

**Tuition Costs:** (AUD) $26,800; includes room and board, textbooks and two two-week tours, suitable horses, gear and equipment

**Description of Program:** The Diploma of Horse Business Management aims to equip students with the practical, husbandry, and business skills necessary for a successful career in their chosen area. The intensive one-year Diploma of Horse Business Management is structured equally into three broad areas: Practical Skills, Horse Management, and Business Management. The program was developed in close consultation with industry. Students are exposed to a diverse range of prominent leaders specializing in riding, training and management techniques, business philosophies, economic views, marketing strategies, and administrative practices. Exciting study tour and work experience programs are a feature of the course and allow students to visit and work with prominent industry leaders and enterprises in Australia and New Zealand. Dressage, jumping, eventing, and both flat and harness racing are taught.

**Facilities:** Track, breeding facility, cross-country course, indoor arena (23m x 75m), outdoor arenas, outdoor all-weather ménage (60m x 30m), undercover training block, training areas

**Classroom/Hands-On Equine Classes:** 66:33

**Showing:** Varies

## Murdoch University

Australian Applicants - Phone: (61 8) 9360 6538. Fax: (61 8) 9360 6631. Email: admit@central.murdoch.edu.au. International Applicants - Phone: (61 8) 9360 6760. Fax: (61 8) 9310 5090. Email: international@murdoch.edu.au.

**Degrees Offered:** Bachelor of Science, Bachelor of Veterinary Medicine and Surgery

**Majors Offered:** Veterinary Biology (B.Sc.)

**Website:**
www.vetbiomed.murdoch.edu.au

**Type of School:**
Public University

## Queensland Race Training

The Manager, P.O. Box 480, Sandgate QLD 4017 Australia. Phone: (61) (07) 3869-0100. Fax: (61) (07) 3869-0489. Email: info@racetraining.qld.edu.au.

**Accreditation:** Australian National Training Authority, Registered Training Organization, endorsed by Queensland Thoroughbred Racing Board, Harness Racing Board

**Degrees Offered:** Certificate, Diploma

**Majors Offered:** Apprentice Jockeys (C), Farrier (C), Harness Drivers (C), Horse Trainer—Thoroughbred and Harness (D), Stablehands (C), Trackwork Riders (C)

**Tuition Costs:** (AUD) $2,000/month; housing: $160/week

**Description of Program:** Training Program: The training program is specific to the horse racing industries—both Thoroughbred and Standardbred—and is focused on employment outcomes. The training package is nationally accredited and recognized throughout Australia. In many instances, the qualifications are a prerequisite to licensing for the industry. Graduates are presently employed in Japan, Ireland, Dubai, Kentucky, Australia, and New Zealand. Graduates work in the thoroughbred or horse racing industry as: stablehands, track work riders, jockeys, trainers, harness drivers, stud grooms, farriers, and administration.

**Facilities:** The training center includes 62 stables, a farrier workshop, twelve day yards, tack and feed rooms, a mechanical horse, a covered arena, seven classrooms, a fully-equipped computer center, two administration areas, a student common room and staff areas, 1850m grass track, 1700m sand track, four wash bays, and two sand rolls.

**Classroom/Hands-On Equine Classes:** 40:60

**Website:**
www.racetraining.qld.edu.au

**Type of School:**
Specialty School

**Website:**
www.tvtafe.sa.edu.au/tvi

**Type of School:**
Trade/Specialty School

## Torrens Valley Institute of TAFE

Veterinary and Applied Science Centre, Gilles Plains Campus, Blacks Road, Gilles Plains, South Australia 5086. Phone: (08) 8207 1240. Fax: (08) 8207 1199. Or Horse Industries Skills Centre, Cheltenham Racecourse, Torrens Road, Cheltenham South Australia 5014. Phone: (08) 8347 3114. Fax: (08) 8345 4327. Email: Kay.Cameron@tv.tafe.sa.edu.au.

**Accreditation:** Department of Further Education, Employment, Science and Technology

**Degrees Offered:** Certificate, Diploma

**Majors Offered:** Vocational Education: Horse Breeding, Horse Industries, Stablehand, Stablehand/Track Rider, Jockey

**Tuition Costs:** (AUD) $1.55/hour (residents); housing costs vary

**Description of Program:** You can learn basic horsemanship in the Vocational Education Horse Industries course. You will receive expert tuition to perfect your riding technique using the mechanical horse at the Cheltenham Racecourse site. Should you wish to register as a trainee jockey, your professional instruction will include Barrier Training and Race Day Procedures for the Trainee Jockey. There is also a Farriery Certificate, which will equip you for employment in the horse industry. The Agriculture (Horse Breeding) Certificate offers skills in caring for horses, and in particular, the breeding competencies (caring for broodmares, caring for mares at foaling, carrying-out stud stable management duties). Handle Horses Safely and Work Effectively in the Racing Industries are competencies from the Racing Training Package, which is based on industry needs and competency at industry standards. Closely supervised track work is undertaken on the Cheltenham Racetrack. You may wish to complete competencies related to the Harness Racing industry. The three other choices are Breeding, Racing, and Equestrian.

**Facilities:** A complex with stabling for sixteen horses and additional horses on a different site, allows rotation during training; undercover working areas, a mechanical horse, round yard, riding menage, farriery workshop, student amenities, classrooms and office space, and use of the South Australian Jockey Club racetracks and equipment. Horses of various temperaments and racing ability suit the needs of students as they progress throughout the program. Some housing is supplied for international students; local students need to find their own accommodations, though staff will assist in search.

**Classroom/Hands-On Equine Classes:** 30:70

**Website:**
www.unimelb.edu.au

**Type of School:**
Public University, Independent Study

## University of Melbourne

Glenormiston Campus, Institute of Land and Food Resources, The University of Melbourne, PMB 6200, Terang VIC 3264 Australia. Phone: 61 (0)3 5557 8200. Fax: 61 (0)3 5557 8268. Email: glenormiston@landfood.unimelb.edu.au or McMillan Campus, Institute of Land and Food Resources, The University of Melbourne, P.O. Box 353, South Rd, Warragul VIC 3820 Australia. Phone: 61 (0)3 5622 6000. Fax: 61 (0)3 5623 4671. Contact: Institute of Land and Food Resources. Phone: 61 (0)3 8344 0276. Email: enquiries@landfood.unimelb.edu.au.

**Degrees Offered:** Certificate 4, Advanced Diploma, Bachelor of Animal Science, Bachelor of Veterinary Science, Doctor of Philosophy

**Majors Offered:** Equine Dentistry (C), Equine Management (M, Ph.D.), Horse Management (Independent Study), Horse Management (C4, AD), Racing (Standardbred)—Harness Driver/Harness Trainer Level 1 (C4)

**Tuition Costs:** Contact School

**Description of Program:** Equine Management (M, Ph.D.) programs are based on major research projects. The candidate may need to take some formal classes in studies related to the field of expertise or required study. The Institute has research programs and recognized expertise in the fields of behavior and animal welfare, nutrition, pasture and grazing management, agribusiness and marketing, genetics, and reproduction. The Horse Management Program: Certificate IV full-time over one year; Advanced Diploma full time over two years. Both courses are also available by flexible delivery. These programs serve as preparation for a middle or upper management career in the horse industry. The Racing Program is a one-year, full-time course for people seeking a career in the Standardbred racing industry. The course is based on the National Racing Training Package and is designed to provide both theoretical and "hands-on" training in all aspects of managing, handling, feeding, training, driving, and care of the horses, as well as training in the use of all of the latest relevant technical equipment.

**Facilities:** Glenormiston College Horse Stud, indoor arena, outdoor arena, cross-country course, outdoor riding areas, trails, artificial breeding center

**Classroom/Hands-On Equine Classes:** Vary

## The University of Sydney–Orange

Leeds Parade, P.O. Box 883, Orange NSW 2800 Australia. Phone: (02) 6360 5555. Fax: (02) 6360 5590. Email: uso@orange.usyd.edu.au.

**Accreditation:** Commonwealth Department of Education, Science and Training (Australian Federal Government)

**Degrees Offered:** Advanced Diploma, Bachelor

**Majors Offered:** Equine Business Management

**Tuition Costs:** (AUD) Australian students: $5,242/year; international students: $12,450/year; housing: $65-82/week

**Description of Program:** School horses are quality Thoroughbreds and Warmbloods. The course encompasses business management in the context of equine industries and students may focus their learning on breeding and training, equitation, and enterprise and/or organization administration. Studies include Function, Health, and Soundness of Horses; Principles of Horse Nutrition and Grazing Management; Management of a Horse Enterprise; Principles of Business Law, Marketing, and Finance (as related to horse enterprises); Equitation, Horse Preparation, or Breeding. Graduates are expected to have demonstrated recognized management capabilities.

**Facilities:** Covered round yards, large indoor arena, modern stud complex, exercise tracks

**Classroom/Hands-On Equine Classes:** Varies

**Showing:** Shows, eventing, Thoroughbred racing

**Website:**
www.oac.usyd.edu.au

**Type of School:**
Public University

# *AUSTRIA*

## Agricultural School of Lambach

Klosterplatz 1, 4650 Lambach, Austria. Phone: +43-7245-20660. Fax: +43-7245-20660-24. Email: lwbfs-lambach.post@ooe.gv.at.

**Accreditation:** Federal Institute of Physical Training, the Provincial Government of Upper Austria

**Website:**
www.lfs-lambach.eduhi.at

**Type of School:**
Agricultural Technical School

**Degrees Offered:** Certificate
**Majors Offered:** Equine Studies & Horse Management
**Tuition Costs:** (Euros) Government subsidized: 16,4 €/first year; 58,1 €/second and fourth year; 204,5 €/month boarding
**Description of Program:** The Agricultural School of Lambach offers a four-year course in Equine Studies & Horse Management. The students attend this course from age fourteen until age eighteen. The basic aim of this course is the education of young horsekeeping farmers from rural areas and anyone interested in equine studies and management. Equine Studies students get their theoretical education in Lambach.
**Facilities:** The school has a close cooperation with the Austrian Horse Center in Stadl Paura (stables, indoor and outdoor riding schools, a racecourse, and large riding grounds with woods and meadows), and a horse farm in Lambach (owned by Ernst Berger). Most of the practical training takes place at these facilities.

**Website:**
www.pferdewissenschaften.at

**Type of School:**
Veterinary College

# University of Veterinary Sciences and the College of Agriculture

Veterinärplatz 1, 1210 Vienna, Austria. Contact: Markus Sheibenpflug, DVM or Prof. Jorg Aurich, D.V.M., Ph.D., Coordinator of the Equine Science Program. Phone: +43-1-25077-5402. Fax: +43-25077-5490.
Email: markus.scheibenpflug@vu-wien.ac.at.
**Accreditation:** Recognized by European Union members
**Degrees Offered:** Bachelor of Science, Master of Science, Doctor of Veterinary Medicine
**Majors Offered:** Bachelor of Equine Science (Two new Master programs are planned for 2006: Equine Business and Equine Science and Management)
**Tuition Costs:** (Euros) 380 €/semester; living in Vienna, Austria: approx. 900 €/month
**Description of Program:** It is the aim of the Bachelor Program in Equine Science to educate students for leading management positions in the equine industry and to provide them with scientific qualifications. The program is not a vocational course aimed primarily at teaching riding skills. In order to benefit maximally from the program, students should already have good practical skills in equestrian sports and hands-on experience with horses at the time they enter the course. The program starts with basic courses in zoology, chemistry, physics, and equestrian history. Students then obtain a thorough knowledge of equine anatomy and physiology, ethology, nutrition, genetics, reproduction and healthcare as well as the organization of equestrian sports and horse breeding, including selection of breeding stock, business administration/management, legal aspects of the equine industry, and advertising. The courses are taught by faculty members from the Universities of Veterinary Sciences and Agricultural Sciences and by external lecturers from the Equestrian and Breeder's Association and the Vienna Spanish Riding School. Riding courses can be taken as optional modules (dressage, show jumping, eventing, driving, vaulting), however, the number of courses is limited.
**Facilities:** Riding courses are organized in cooperation with the Austrian Military Academy's Equitation Group, the Tullnerback Agricultural School, and the Neustadt/Dosse State Stud in Germany.
**Classroom/Hands-On Equine Classes:** 25 percent hands-on
**Showing:** Students who are interested in showing can compete on their own

# BELGIUM

## The Lord Newcastle Stables

BVBA, Brusselses Teenweg 195, 1560 Hoeilaart, Belgium.  Phone: +32 (0)26 573089.
Fax. +32 (0)26 573089. Email: dsoyer@compuserve.com.
**Accreditation:** British Horse Society
**Degrees Offered:** Certificate
**Majors Offered:** Assistant Instructor, Intermediate Instructor, Instructor
**Tuition Costs:** Contact School
**Description of Program:** The Certificate Courses are primarily designed for those pursuing a career with horses. To this end, students must be able to carry out all aspects of horse care, including grooming, cleaning tack, mucking out, and sweeping yards. Only by learning to do such things well can students become efficient workers and know what standards to demand from others. Thus, students and their parents or guardians must fully appreciate this point before undertaking a Certificate Course. For students who are unsure, it is recommended that they pursue one of the other courses offered by the school. In addition to BHS Certificate Courses, weekly courses are offered throughout the year, designed for riders (of all ability levels) who wish to increase their knowledge and improve their performance. Courses can be tailored to individual requirements, but most students find existing courses that are suitable for them, including general equitation, dressage, combined training, children's courses, side-saddle, in-hand, long-reining, and hacking holidays. (Please inform the school that you saw them listed in this book when contacting.)
**Facilities:** Built in 1912, the facilities include 36 loose boxes (4m x 4m) with heated automatic waterers, 20m x 40m indoor school, 70m x 30m outdoor arena, and clubhouse.
**Classroom/Hands-On Equine Classes:** Vary

**Website:**
www.lordnewcastlestables.com

**Type of School:**
Specialty School

# BERMUDA

## International Group for Qualifications in Training Horse & Rider

Spicelands Riding Centre, P.O. Box HM 1980, Hamilton HM HX, Bermuda.
Contact: Lori Correia. Phone: (441) 238-8212. Fax: (441) 238-6479.
Email: spicelands@northrock.bm.
**Accreditation:** The Bermuda Equestrian Federation
**Degrees Offered:** Certification
**Majors Offered:** Level 1: Preliminary Instructor (must be eighteen years old), Level 2: Instructor (must be 21 years old), Level 3: Advanced Instructor
**Tuition Costs:** Contact School
**Description of Program:** The program runs five days a week. The students have a set number of students they teach every week, and they muck-out five to six stalls a day, learn how to make-up the feeds with supplements, and learn why certain horses are given different supplements. They will groom horses, do laundry, keep the tack room clean, tidy the barn, clean tack, learn how to clip, trim, and braid horses, learn how to school horses, and learn why different techniques are used. Students will learn to prepare for a show: scheduling, tailoring, and organizing tack and participants. They will be able to ride hunt seat, equitation, dressage, and jumping, as well as teach those dis-

**Type of School:**
Specialty School

ciplines. The facility is not considered a formal school for persons learning to be instructors; however, a college in England and a Clinician/Master Instructor of Instructors have helped organize this program. The clinician comes to Bermuda several times each year to work with the students and test them for their Preliminary Instructor and Instructor Certification.

**Facilities:** The equestrian facility has four acres with 50 horses on the property. There are 23 boarders, fifteen trail horses and mules, and twelve school horses and ponies. There is a large main ring and an adjoining collecting ring, which has lights for night riding, as well as a boarders' ring and dressage ring. Adjacent to the property are miles of trails and access to beaches.

**Classroom/Hands-On Equine Classes:** 100 percent hands-on

**Showing:** There are several shows at the facility during the show season (September to May).

# BRAZIL

## Escola de Equitacao do Exercito - Brazillian Army Riding School

**Website:**
www.eseqex.ensino.eb.br

**Type of School:**
Military School
(open to civilian students)

Avenida Duque de Caxias, 2660, Vila Militar, Rio de Janeiro, RJ, Brasil 21615-220. Phone/Fax: 5521 24574152. Email: eseqex@dep.ensino.eb.mil.br or exfmigon@ig.com.br.

**Degrees Offered:** Certificate, Professional, Postgraduate, MBA in Horsemanship, Horse Training and Equine Science

**Majors Offered:** Farrier, Veterinary Assistant, Stages to Develop Proficiency in Show Jumping (SJ), Dressage and Three-Day Event (3DE), Horsemanship/Trainer Assistant, Horsemanship/Trainer Master

**Tuition Costs:** Free to students from any military or government agencies and under agreement of Brazilian Defense Minister. Other students, please contact the school.

**Description of Program:** Eight instructors with three assistants to teach. Students can inquire in Portuguese, English, Spanish or French, but classes are conducted in Portuguese. Horsemanship Master students learn advanced horsemanship skills developed by the International Equestrian Federation (FEI). Students use their personal horse or school horses to help develop theoretical and practice skills in horse training. The students learn dressage, show jumping, three-day event, polo techniques, and young-horse training in theoretical and mounted practical activities. They also learn veterinary first-aid, international and national sports rules, method and psychology of teaching in classroom activities. Horsemanship Assistant students learn intermediate horsemanship skills developed by the Brazilian Equestrian Federation. They also learn veterinary first-aid, international and national sports rules, and stable management in classroom activities. Farrier and Veterinary Assistant students learn horseshoeing and veterinary basic skills with an emphasis on practical activities and teamwork, under supervision of a veterinary doctor. Stages: teaches and develop basics skills in SJ, Dressage, or 3DE disciplines. Sequential stages under I, II and III levels.

**Facilities:** The school has three classrooms (air conditioned, 70 places in total, data show system, PC, etc.), 120 horse boxes, four SJ arenas (two sand and two grass), a polo field, a cross-country area (up to three-star CIC and two-star CCI under FEI classification), veterinary / horseshoe area, three dressage arenas, one indoor multiuse arena (70m x 32m, public access to 2000 persons, W.C, athletes room, press room, etc.), swimming pool for horses, and student center.

# CANADA

## Alberta, Canada

## Fairview College

Website:
www.fairviewc.ab.ca

Type of School:
Public College

Agricultural Sciences - Equine Department, P.O. Box 3000, Fairview AB Canada T0H 1L0. Contact: Wayne Gray, Equine Instructor. Phone: (780) 835-6605. Fax: (780) 835-6697. Email: wgray@fairviewcollege.com.
**Accreditation:** Minister of Advanced Education and Career Development
**Degrees Offered:** Certificate of Achievement, Equine Canada Certification
**Majors Offered:** Equine Studies with majors in Training or Horsemanship (C.A.), Rider Level 1-4 (CEFC)
**Tuition Costs:** (CAD) $43/credit; $450/session room and board; $125/month horse board
**Description of Program:** Five instructors. Five instructed rides per week; riding class size averages seven students. The Horsemanship Major teaches students fundamental horsemanship skills developed by the Equine Canada. Western riding in show or ranch is the focus. Students will use their own personal horse to help them obtain Rider IV. In the Horse Training major, students will use Fairview College horses to learn how a horse is trained and to develop colt breaking and training skills. Students will also improve on their existing riding skills during the colt training portion of the program.
**Facilities:** The equestrian center is on campus and has 16 school horses, heated indoor arena (180ft x 230ft), and a barn.
**Classroom/Hands-On Equine Classes:** 15/34 credits
**Showing:** Stallion exhibition

## Lakeland College

Website:
www.lakelandc.ab.ca

Type of School:
Public College

5707 - 47 Ave. West, Agricultural Sciences, Vermilion, AB, Canada T9X 1K5. Contact: Bill Conrad, Program Head. Phone: (780) 853-8598. Email: admissions@lakelandc.ab.ca.
**Accreditation:** Alberta Learning Department
**Degrees Offered:** Certificate
**Majors Offered:** Ranch and Feedlot Rider
**Tuition Costs:** $4,832 (includes additional costs); housing: $1,122/semester
**Description of Program:** The Ranch and Feedlot Rider Certificate is a unique program combining the recognition and treatment of cattle disease, cattle handling, and horse training. Career possibilities include feedlots, community pastures, and ranches.
**Facilities:** Indoor riding arena, stable
**Classroom/Hands-On Equine Classes:** 50:50
**Showing:** Judging Team, Rodeo Club/Rodeo Club Barn

## Olds College

Website:
www.oldscollege.ab.ca

Type of School:
Public College

4500 - 50 Street, Olds, Alberta, Canada T4H 1R6. Phone: (403) 556-8369 or (403) 556-8344 (extension). Fax: (403) 556-4711. Email: info@admin.oldscollege.ab.ca or extension@admin.oldscollege.ab.ca.
**Accreditation:** Alberta Learning Department

**Degrees Offered:** Certificate, Diploma

**Majors Offered:** Advanced Farrier Science (C), Equine Science (D) with majors in Equine Business Management (EBM), Horsemanship, or Equine Production and Breeding Management (EPBM), Western Rider Development and Coaching Program, Horses on Course

**Tuition Costs:** (CAD) $3,838/Farrier Program plus $2,200/books and equipment; $5,400/Equine Science Program plus $1,500/books and equipment; $3,465-4,580/room and board

**Description of Program:** AFS students will learn the theory, skills, and receive the practical experience and training necessary to become a professional farrier. Students will also learn to recognize and deal with horse hoof and gait problems. The two-year ES program combines theoretical and practical knowledge with hands-on experience to make the student a highly trained paraprofessional capable of working under minimum supervision. Horses are provided by industry breeders and trainers for students use; students can use their own horse if the horse receives the instructor's approval. In the EBM major, the student focuses on equine business and management skills, including computers, accounting, marketing, establishing a business, salesmanship, and tax law. Students should be prepared to run their own successful business or enter the business side of the equine industry. In the Horsemanship major, the students develop their riding skills and learn techniques for the breaking and training of young horses in either the Western or English discipline. In the EPBM major, students learn current reproductive techniques such as hand breeding, artificial insemination, and transported cool semen. Students gain experience managing pregnant mares, foaling, and participating in a commercial breeding operation. The Horses on Course offers several extension horse classes.

**Facilities:** Heated indoor complex with riding arena, classroom, stabling, outdoor riding arena, production complex covering 33 acres, breeding barn complex with artificial insemination laboratory, foaling barn

**Classroom/Hands-On Equine Classes:** EBM: 42/9; Horsemanship: 35/14; PBM: 37/15

**Showing:** Active Rodeo Club, and the students in the Equine Science Program work together to put on a one-day "Equine Extravaganza," which is really a showcase of everything that happens in the program. They also organize a small schooling show.

## Village Farrier School

**Website:**
www.villagefarrier.com

**Type of School:**
Specialty School

51566 Range Road 223, Sherwood Park, AB T8C 1H4 Canada.
Phone/Fax: (780) 922-3672. Email: andy@villagefarrier.com.
**Degrees Offered:** Certificate
**Majors Offered:** Part-Time Farrier Course

# British Columbia, Canada

## BC College of Equine Therapy

**Website:**
www.equinetherapy.ca and
www.saddlefitting.ca

**Type of School:**
Specialty School

7184 L&A Road, Vernon, British Columbia V1B 3S8 Canada.
Phone: (250) 542-5953. Fax: (250) 542-6020. Email: david_collins@telus.net.
**Accreditation:** Registered with the Province of British Columbia, governed by the Private Post-Secondary Education Commission of British Columbia
**Degrees Offered:** Certificate
**Majors Offered:** Equine Therapy Practitioner's Program

**Tuition Costs:** $6,000/entire course; $650/textbooks and course material

**Description of Program:** This college program is a certificate program registered with the Private Post-Secondary Education Commission of BC and is designed for those who wish to acquire the skill and knowledge necessary for a career as an Equine Therapist. The program includes: anatomy, physiology, pathology, equine massage therapy, saddle and tack fitting, applied kinesiology, acupressure techniques, nutritional assessment and balance, structural assessment and balance, business principles, assessing rider imbalances, use of magnetics, lameness analysis, use of herbal remedies, energy balancing techniques, farrier and dental imbalances, treatment of injuries, and principles of movement. The program consists of four components: classroom and hands-on instruction, practicum (case studies and work with horses), course study completed at home, and research projects.

## HJW Equine Therapy

Box 1430 Barriere, B.C. V0E 1E0 Canada. Contact: Helen J. Woods.
Phone: (250) 672-9891. Fax: (250) 672-9831. Email: helenjwoods@Canada.com.
**Degrees Offered:** Certification of Completion
**Majors Offered:** Equine Massage/Chiropractic Therapy
**Tuition Costs:** (CAD) $5,500; room and board: $500/month
**Description of Program:** The course is an extensive two-month course, teaching a complex technique in equine therapy, of chiropractic and massage. When you have passed and are qualified, you will have gained all the skills and learned all that is needed to start your own business and do a very successful job. Students work on all disciplines and all breeds.
**Classroom/Hands-On Equine Classes:** Classroom work is approximately three weeks, with five weeks actually working on horses. Approximately 175 horses are treated per course.

**Website:**
www.helenjwoods.com

**Type of School:**
Specialty School

## Kwantlen University College

12666 - 72nd Ave., Surrey, B.C. V3W 2M8 Canada. Equine Studies: Contact: Ms. Kit Anderson, Program Manager. Phone: (604) 599-3258 or (877) 652-6600.
Email: kit@kwantlen.bc.ca. Farrier Program: Contact: Cindy Eldstrum, Farrier Program Chair. Phone: (604) 599-3349 or (604) 599-3241. CEF Coaching Program: Contact: Christine Hawkins. Phone: (604) 599-3379.
**Accreditation:** Ministry of Education of Victoria, BC
**Degrees Offered:** CEF Certificate, Certificate, Equine Technician's Certificate, Citation
**Majors Offered:** Advanced Farrier Training (C), Equine Studies (T.C.), Equine Studies (Cit.) with emphasis in Equine Health and Nutrition, Equine Reproduction and Breeding, Equine Injury and Lameness, Equine Exercise Physiology, Equine Facilities Management, or Equine Psychology and Behavior. CEF Coaching Program (Level 1)
**Tuition Costs:** (CAD) $6,000/Technician's Certificate; $1,200/farrier tools
**Description of Program:** Equine Studies (EQUA) courses are fifteen weeks in length and are offered evenings and Saturdays. Students are encouraged to enter and exit the program at individual speed and comfort levels. Anyone who meets Kwantlen University College admission requirements is eligible to enroll in EQUA on a first-come, first-served basis. As EQUA is taught almost exclusively by equine veterinarians, students are exposed to the kind of depth and scope that few equine programs have offered to the general public in the past. The Advanced Farrier Training Program prepares stu-

**Website:**
www.kwantlen.bc.ca

**Type of School:**
Public University

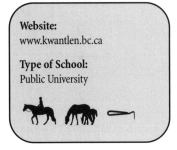

dents to work competently as qualified farriers. The program is nine months in duration and is offered in three-month blocks. Students may complete one or two blocks, leave the program to gain work experience, and return to finish the remainder of the program. Students may enter the program in September, January, or April. Canadian Equestrian Federation Certified Coaching (Level I) prep programs are available through Continuing Education.

**Facilities:** No equine facilities except for the farrier barn. As Langley is the "Horse Capital of BC," students have access to many local training barns, breeding facilities, etcetera, to use for labs and practicums. EQUA courses are offered in the evenings; thus, students are encouraged to work at an equine-related job during the day.

**Classroom/Hands-On Equine Classes:** 1 1/2 :1

**Showing:** Located in the hub of equine "A" rated shows for hunter-jumper disciplines and dressage.

**Website:**
www.qms.bc.ca

**Type of School:**
University Preparatory School

# Queen Margaret's School

Queen Margaret's School, 660 Brownsey Ave., Duncan, B.C. V9L 1C2 Canada.
Contact: Susan Harrison, Director. Phone: (250) 746-4185. Fax: (250) 746-4187.
Email: admissions@qms.bc.ca or sharrison@qms.bc.ca.

**Accreditation:** BC Ministry of Education, NAIS, CAIS, TABS
**Degrees Offered:** High School Diploma, Certificate
**Majors Offered:** E.C. Coaching Certification (C)
**Tuition Costs:** (CAD) $7,000-$10,000/year: day students; $25,000-$30,000/year: boarders.

**Description of Program:** Co-Ed Junior School K-7 and Girls Boarding Grades 6-12. A challenging, structured academic program is offered to girls in Grades 8-12 and to boys and girls in Kindergarten to Grade 7. A safe and nurturing boarding environment is home for 85 girls in Grades 6-12. An English riding program is designed to accommodate riders of all levels, from beginners to serious competitors. Riders are involved in all aspects of horsemanship and stable management. The riding program promotes responsibility, self-esteem, cooperation, and the enjoyment of riding. The Train to Compete Program, for high school credits, provides equine management and animal husbandry theory. Train to Compete is designed for the rider who wishes to bring her own horse or lease one of the school's. It provides applied skills credits for grades 8 to 12, or for those students who wish to pursue their Equine Canada Level 1 Coaching Certification.

**Facilities:** Equestrian center on-campus, 27 country-like acres, indoor and outdoor arena, boarding, turnout, stabling for 40 horses

**Classroom/Hands-On Equine Classes:** Equine Studies: 8/9/10/11

**Showing:** Local B-Circuit hunter/jumper, dressage, Pacific Northwest and California A-Circuit hunter/jumper

## Nova Scotia, Canada

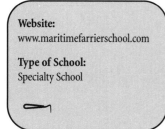

**Website:**
www.maritimefarrierschool.com

**Type of School:**
Specialty School

# Maritime Farrier School

2425 Camden Road, RR# 3, Truro, Nova Scotia B2N 5B2 Canada. Phone: (902) 893-4926. Email: peter@maritimefarrierschool.com.
**Majors Offered:** Farrier

# Ontario, Canada

## Bethany Hills School

727 Bethany Hills Road, Box 10, Bethany, ON L0A 1A0 Canada.
Phone: (705) 277-2866. Fax: (705) 277-1279. Email: info@bethanyhills.on.ca.
**Accreditation:** The Ontario Ministry of Education, Canadian Association of Independent Schools member, CESI, CIS
**Degrees Offered:** High School Diploma
**Tuition Costs:** (CAD) $31,800/International Residential Students; $30,425/Canadian Residential Students; school horse lease: $760/fall, $1,900/winter, $760/spring; student-owned horse fee: $320/fall, $800/winter, $320/spring
**Description of Program:** Offering co-educational programs in grades 1 through 6 and single-sex education for girls at the Iintermediate and Senior Levels. Equestrian sports are offered as a part of the athletic and academic programs. Students are offered equine classes three afternoons per week during sports. Additional opportunities to ride can be provided. The regular weekly programming is complemented with the opportunity to attend workshops offered by guest instructors. Equestrian students are encouraged to volunteer at and organize horse shows and special equine events. Every year, the riders attend events such as the Royal Winter Fair in Toronto. Students are encouraged to understand both the sport and the business of riding. Students at the Bethany Hills School enjoy close proximity to their horses and are encouraged to take full advantage of the country setting.
**Facilities:** The school currently uses stables run by Saddlewood Equestrian Stables, adjacent to the school campus.
**Classroom/Hands-On Equine Classes:** Vary
**Showing:** Students show at both the recreational and competitive level and participate in interschool competitions.

**Website:**
www.bethanyhills.on.ca

**Type of School:**
Private K-12 School

## D'Arcy Lane Institute

627 Maitland Street, London, Ontario N5Y 2V7 Canada. Phone: (519) 673-4420 or (519) 673-3965. Email: info@darcylane.com.
**Degrees Offered:** Diploma
**Majors Offered:** Equine Massage Therapy

**Website:**
www.darcylane.com

**Type of School:**
Specialty School

## Kemptville College/University of Guelph

Continuing Education, Equestrian Program, P.O. Box 2003, Kemptville, ON K0G 1J0 Canada. Phone: (613) 258-8336. Fax: (613) 258-8478.
Email: kcollege@kemptvillec.uoguelph.ca.
**Degrees Offered:** Certificate, Associate Diploma
**Majors Offered:** Agriculture [Equine] (AD), Coaching and Horsemanship (C), Equine Management (C), Riding (C), Standardbred Industry (C)

**Website:**
www.kemptvillec.uoguelph.ca

**Type of School:**
Community College

## Windhurst Riding & Training Centre

1033 Townline Road, R.R.#1, Lowbanks, Ontario N0A 1K0 Canada. Contact: Brenda Robson, Director/Head Coach. Phone: (905) 899-3780.
Email: windhurstwnflt@hotmail.com.

**Type of School:**
Specialty School

**Accreditation:** Recognized as an Educational Institution by Human Resources Development Canada

**Degrees Offered:** Certificate of Achievement, Equine Canada Certification

**Majors Offered:** Equine Studies with major in Western Riding Discipline (C.A.); Rider Levels 1-4 (E.C.F.)

**Tuition Costs:** One & Two Year Coaching Programs: $4,800; stable board: $300/month

**Description of Program:** Ninety-plus-acre equestrian facility located in serene, rural area central to the Niagara and Haldimand/Norfolk regions. E.C. certified coaching. Five riding sessions per week: class size never exceeds eight students. Courses: Stable Management, Coaching/Riding Theory, Anatomy, Conformation & Movement, Nutrition, Emergency First Aid, Equine Sports Physiology, Hoof Care, Tack & Equipment, Training Development. Internships are possible for students who complete the E.C. Instructors Certificate in their first year.

**Facilities:** Indoor arena, heated viewing/classroom area, upscale stable, outdoor sand ring, training round pen, private wooded trails

**Showing:** Show leases available for the show season.

## Prince Edward Island, Canada

### Atlantic Veterinary College

**Website:**
www.upei.ca/~avc/

**Type of School:**
Veterinary College

University of Prince Edward Island, 550 University Avenue, Charlottetown, PEI C1A 4P3 Canada. Phone: (902) 566-0882. Fax: (902) 566-0958. Email: avc@upei.ca.

**Degrees Offered:** Master of Veterinary Science, Doctor of Veterinary Medicine

**Majors Offered:** Veterinary Medicine

## Quebec, Canada

### Institut de Technologie Agroalimentaire

**Website:**
www.italp.qc.ca

**Type of School:**
Technical Institute

401 rue Poire, La Pocatiere, QC G0R 1Z0 Canada. Phone: (418) 856-1110. Email: scitalp@agr.gouv.qc.ca.

**Degrees Offered:** Diploma, CEF Certificate

**Majors Offered:** Equine Techniques, Standardbred Racing, CEF Certification

### Université de Montréal

**Website:**
www.medvet.umontreal.ca

**Type of School:**
Public University

Faculté de médecine vétérinaire, 3200, rue Sicotte, Saint-Hyacinthe (Québec) Canada J2S 2M2. Phone: (514) 345-8521 or (450) 773-8521. Fax: (450) 778-8114. Email: saefmv@medvet.umontreal.ca.

**Degrees Offered:** Doctor of Veterinary Medicine

**Majors Offered:** Veterinary Science

## Saskatchewan, Canada

### Kanadiana International Equestrian Centre, Inc.

**Website:**
www.kanadianalodge.com

**Type of School:**
Specialty School

Box 370, Meadow Lake, Saskatchewan S9X 1YR Canada. Contact: Carole Poche, Program Director. Phone/Fax: (306) 236-1973. Email: kanadiana@sasktel.net. Or Saskatchewan Institute of Applied Science and Technology, 4500 Wascana Parkway

P.O. Box 556, Regina, SK S4P 3A3 Canada. Contact: Grant Zalinko, Program Head. Phone: (306) 798-4003 or in Saskatchewan (800) 667-7730. Fax: (306) 798-9577. E-mail: zalinko@siast.sk.ca.

**Accreditation:** CEF/Equine Canada, Applied Certificate in Equine Studies from SIAST
**Degrees Offered:** CEF Certificate, Applied Certificate
**Majors Offered:** CEF Coach (C), Equine Studies (A.C.), Horsemanship (A.C.)
**Tuition Costs:** (CAD) $5,500: Equine Studies and Horsemanship; $3,100: CEF Coach (included in Equine Studies tuition fee); $2,200: room and board for sixteen weeks; horse board: free if used by school, box stall/$250, tie stall/$200, paddock/$150, pasture/$100
**Description of Program:** The Equine Studies Applied Certificate Program is composed of courses that offer the knowledge and skills necessary for a person to work with horses. This, combined with the practical applications offered by Kanadiana International Equestrian Centre, Inc., helps produce graduates who are ready to work in a variety of areas in the horse industry, including groom, stable manager, assistant trainer, breeding farms, and therapeutic or other riding programs. The sixteen-week intensive program includes English (dressage/jumping) or Western (show/performance), Canadian and German champion trainers and coaches, stable management, feeds and nutrition, horse health and hoof care, breeding and genetics, effective speaking for coaching, farm bookkeeping and entrepreneurship, equitation and showing, judging and cattle work, starting and riding a young horse, CEF Rider Levels and Coaching Preparation, CEF Evaluation, NCCP Coaching Theory, Red Cross First Aid, Kanadiana Riding Master Certificate, and SIAST Applied Certificate. Two German trainers teach jumping and dressage, and the Western trainer is a Canadian champion.
**Facilities:** Working cattle ranch, 600 acres, training stable, 80ft x 200ft heated indoor arena, restaurant and lounge, classroom, breeding program featuring Warmbloods and Quarter Horses
**Classroom/Hands-On Equine Classes:** Vary
**Showing:** Local competitions, Warmblood testing, mock shows, open shows, cutting competition, ropings, sanctioned cattle pennings

## Western College of Veterinary Medicine

University of Saskatchewan, 52 Campus Drive, Saskatoon SK Canada, S7N 5B4. Phone: (306) 966-7447. Fax: (306) 966-8747.
**Degrees Offered:** Master of Veterinary Science, Master of Science, Doctor of Philosophy
**Majors Offered:** Large Animal Clinical Sciences, Veterinary Anatomy, Veterinary Biomedical Sciences, Veterinary Microbiology, Veterinary Pathology

**Website:**
www.usask.ca/wcvm/

**Type of School:**
Veterinary School

# *CHILE*

## Equitation School of the Armored Calvary School–Army of Chile

Casilla 510, Quillota, V Region, Chile. Phone/Fax: (56)(2)6715919.
Email: ayudanteescablin@terra.cl.
**Accreditation:** Féderation Equestre Internationale
**Degrees Offered:** Equitation Master
**Majors Offered:** Horse Military Instructor, Jumping National and International Judge, Eventing National and International Course Designer, Dressage National and Interna-

**Type of School:**
Specialty School

tional Judge, Jumping National and International Course Designer

**Tuition Costs:** Equitation Master: $5,800/year

**Description of Program:** Every year, the Chilean Army offers the Equitation Master Course at the Armored Cavalry School, starting the third week of January until the third week of December. The course includes classes of all equestrian disciplines, giving a full and complete knowledge to all students in specific techniques for the training and teaching of horses and riders. All principles of dressage, show jumping, three-day eventing, driving, polo, basics of veterinary, theory of equitation, and other skills are learned by the students through the course. Classes are held Monday through Saturday from 7:30 a.m. until 8:30 p.m. On Sundays, classes are held for a half-day only. The course includes tours in the country and participation in various international championships as riders. National Judges Courses in all disciplines are also attended by the students, as part of their knowledge and preparation as an Equitation Master. Horses, saddles and equipment are provided on loan by the Army of Chile, and lodging is paid by each student.

**Facilities:** One indoor equestrian stadium, two polo fields, two show jumping courses, two indoor dressage arenas, two outdoor dressage arenas, one cross-country course, one horse swimming pool, a veterinary clinic with operating room, stables for 400 horses, one main saddle storage room, two classrooms, other minor support facilities

**Classroom/Hands-On Equine Classes:** Ride eight to nine horses daily, for one year.

**Showing:** Students participate in all national competitions.

# *ESTONIA*

## Türi School of Technology & Rural Economy

**Website:**
http://tyrikpk.tyri.ee

**Type of School:**
Vocational Institute

Türi TMK, 72101 Särevere, Järvamaa, Estonia. Phone: +372 38 74438 (Department of Studies). Fax: +372 38 74084. E-mail: kool@tyrikpk.tyri.ee.

**Accreditation:** Ministry of Education of Estonia, Ministry of Agriculture of Estonia

**Degrees Offered:** Certificate

**Majors Offered:** Horse Farming

**Tuition Costs:** (Estonian Kroons) Tuition is free; housing: EEK100-175/month

**Description of Program:** This is the only school in Estonia offering training in horse farming as an independent specialty. The program as an independent specialty was started in September of 2001 and is still undergoing alterations in the curriculum. Horse farming is becoming more popular with young people, and the horse farmers from all over the country and the Estonian Horse Farmers Association support the school. The program is 40 weeks in length and is meant for high school graduates. The curriculum modules include Horse Farming (thirteen weeks), Economics (six weeks), Supportive Subjects (six weeks), Apprenticeship/Practical Training on a Horse Farm (twelve weeks), and Writing the Final Thesis (three weeks). The Horse Farming module includes anatomy and physiology of the horse, exterior and work production of the horse, horse breeds and breeding, horse reproduction, horse health care and hygiene, horseback riding and riding as sport, and horse care and feeding. The module of Economics includes basics in entrepreneurship and economics, economic analysis, and bookkeeping. The module of Supportive Subjects includes foreign languages (English or German), IT, environment protection, labor protection, law, communication psychology, and rural tourism.

**Facilities:** Students live in a student hostel.

**Classroom/Hands-On Equine Classes:** 220/300 hours

# FINLAND

## Helsingon Yliopisto

Faculty of Veterinary Medicine, Hämeentie 57(PB 57), 00014 University of Helsinki, Finland. Phone: (09) 1911. Fax: (09) 191 49799.
**Degrees Offered:** Licentiate in Veterinary Medicine, Doctor of Veterinary Medicine

**Website:**
www.vetmed.helsinki.fi/english/

**Type of School:**
Public University

## Päijänne Instituutti

Laurellintie 55, 17320 Asikkala, Finland. Phone: +358 03 828 7123. Fax: +358 03 828 7135. Email: pi@phkk.fi.
**Accreditation:** Finnish Dept. of Education
**Degrees Offered:** Study Program in Horse Care and Management
**Majors Offered:** Groom, Riding Instructor
**Tuition Costs:** None
**Facilities:** Horses—about 20 at two locations Asikkala and Lahti (near trotting track for practice opportunities).

**Website:**
pi.phkk.fi

**Type of School:**
Vocational College

## Raviopisto Kaustinen

Raviradantie 36 B, 69600 Kaustinen, Finland. Phone: +358 06 8612 703.
Fax: +358 06 8612 706. E-mail: info.kaustinen@kpedu.fi.
**Accreditation:** Federation of Municipalities
**Degrees Offered:** Certificate (Level 3 in European Union)
**Majors Offered:** Groom, Horse Trainer
**Tuition Costs:** (Euros) Housing and teaching are free; € 25/year for materials
**Description of Program:** Groom: Students spend half a day in the classroom and half a day in the stables. The school cooperates with professional trainers, and students practice in their stables. Students also have the possibility to work three months abroad. Theory subjects include breeding, feeding, shoeing, and training. The school has its own stable. The horses are trained by students. The school is located at a racetrack. The degree lasts three years.
**Facilities:** There are no equestrian facilities. Students ride one week per year in the riding school. The rest of the time is spent working with trotters.
**Classroom/Hands-On Equine Classes:** 50:50

**Website:**
www.kpedu.fi

**Type of School:**
Vocational School

## Ypäjän Hevosopisto/Equine College Ypäjä

Varsanojantie 63, 32100 Ypäjä, Finland. Phone: +358 02 760 21. Fax: +358 02 7602 200. Email: hevosopisto@ypaja.fi.
**Accreditation:** Ministry of Education
**Degrees Offered:** Professional Degree
**Majors Offered:** Groom, Assistant Rider, Lad Driver, Stable Manager, Farrier, Blacksmith, Saddler, Tourist Leader, Riding Instructor (international levels 1 - 3), Trotting Trainer, Riding Therapist.
**Tuition Costs:** None
**Description of Program:** The education of riding instructors conforms to the European system, and Finland is a member of the International Group for Qualifications

**Website:**
www.hevosopisto.fi

**Type of School:**
Private College

in Training Horse and Rider. The Equine College is the only school in Finland with programs especially for farriers, lad drivers and riders, blacksmiths, saddlers, riding therapists, and riding instructors. As a provider of basic vocational education in trotting, the Equine College is the leading school in Scandinavia and a member of the International Group for Equestrian Qualifications. In addition, the college arranges theoretical studies for those attending apprenticeship education courses. Courses range in length from a couple of months to three years (120 credits). The college can accept only a few international students per year.

**Facilities:** The Equine College functions in an area of nearly 300 hectares. There are stables for 400 horses, several riding arenas, a variety of cross-country training tracks and training roads, and a full-sized trotting track. On the premises, there are four riding halls, three of which are full-sized. Nearly 300 horses live in the college area: Finnhorses, Warmbloods, and Standardbreds. The college has a dormitory for the students, and there are not any housing costs during the schooldays.

**Classroom/Hands-On Equine Classes:** 50:50

**Showing:** Competitions on international, national and local levels in show jumping, dressage, eventing, and carriage driving.

## Yrkesinstitut Sydväst

**Website:**
www.yi.sydvast.fi

**Type of School:**
College

Brusabyvägen, 25700 Kimito, Finland. Phone: +358 02 421 944. Fax: +358 02 423 665.
**Majors Offered:** Horse Management Degree, Animal Husbandry Management Degree, Assistant Instructors Degree, Small Animal/Pet Pre-Nurse/Management Degree, Animal Hotel Management Degree
**Tuition Costs:** Residents: none; international students: please contact school

# *FRANCE*

## Centre de Formation d'Armor

**Website:**
www.centre-formation-armor.fr

**Type of School:**
Specialty School

22450 Pommerit-Jaudy, France. Phone: +33 (0)296 913563. Fax: 02 96 91 34 55.
Email: pommerit-jaudy@cneap.scolanet.org.
**Degrees Offered:** Certificate, Diploma
**Majors Offered:** Grooming (C), Horse Breeding and Horse Riding (D)

## Centre Equestre de la Houssaye

**Website:**
www.eii.fr/club/houssaye/

**Type of School:**
Specialty School

78270 Bonnières-sur-Seine, France. Contact: M & Mme Ismalun. Phone: 01 30 93 37 84 or 06 09 15 32 16. Email: md.ismalun@club-internet.fr.
**Accreditation:** French Equestrian Federation, French Government, Ministry of Youth and Sports
**Degrees Offered:** Premier Degré d'Educateur Sportif (State Diploma of Teacher)
**Majors Offered:** Teacher
**Tuition Costs:** (Euros) €500/month
**Description of Program:** All riders are welcomed—from the beginner to the seasoned competitor. School horses are available for all levels of riders. The center is registered under the auspices of the French Equestrian Federation and specializes in the instruc-

tion of future riding teachers. Six to eight students each year are taught and will receive a diploma issued by the French Government (Brevet d'Etat d'Educateur sportif du 1er degré - Monitorat d'Equitation) at the end of their training. Centre Equestre de la Houssaye offers one- and two-year programs of particular interest to serious equestrians, enabling them to train and compete in France under some of the country's best Grand Prix trainers. Participants will also gain experience in developing young horses, buying and selling, and understanding the international horse market in relation to their country's horse industry. Lower-level riders can also be accommodated. Although English is widely spoken, participants are gladly taught in French. Visits are welcome at any time and assistance in locating horses in France to buy or lease for the jumping season is available.

**Facilities:** Facilities include one indoor riding ring (45m x 25m), three outdoor sand riding rings, cross-country area (four acres) complete with various cross-country jumps, restaurant and club house, 80 stalls divided among three separate stable areas, pony club (fifteen ponies), four cabins, and riding trails through the La Houssaye forest (60 acres). Students are housed in small cabins located in a calm, wooded area, just steps away from the riding activities. The club house and restaurant serve as meeting points. Riders can sit down and relax, watch television, look at videos, have drinks and meals, etc.

**Showing:** Jumpers, hunters

## Cheval Art Action

La Tuilerie, 51140 Muizon, France. Phone: +33 (0)326 029523.
Fax: +33 (0)326 029844.
**Accreditation:** Fédération Française des Ecoles de Cirque (French Circus School Federation) and J&S (Jeunesse et Sport).
**Majors Offered:** Circus, Horse Stunt
**Tuition Costs:** (Euros) € 5,496/first year; € 2,748/year following
**Description of Program:** CAA is a center of professional formation for those interested in careers in equestrian showing, the circus, street-show, live shows, and movies. Students learn how to become artists, with exposure to professional artists, throw shows, and the artist's life. Lessons are given in trick riding, stunt-flying cosaque (circle and straight line), the horse in the show, creation of the show (circus, theater, etc.), and stunt (on horse and on foot). All students have jobs by the time they graduate.
**Facilities:** Possibility of living on site in caravans.

**Website:**
www.cheval-art-action.com

**Type of School:**
Specialty School

## CNEAP

277 rue Saint-Jacques, 75005 Paris, France. Phone: +33 (0)153 737428.
Fax: +33 (0)153 737430. Email: cneap@cneap.scolanet.org.
**Degrees Offered:** CAPE, BTS, BEP
**Majors Offered:** Agricole (CAPE), Agricole Horse Activities (BEP), Agricole Livestock Productions (BTS), Professional VAT Production of the Horse (BEP)

**Website:**
http://cneap.scolanet.org

**Type of School:**
Agriculture School

## Collège Equestre de Conches/Equestrian Village of Conches

Le Fresne, 27190 Conches. Phone: 02.32.30.22.56. Fax: 02.32.30.14.30.
Email: villageequestreconches@wanadoo.fr.
**Degrees Offered:** Certificate
**Majors Offered:** First Class State Sports Instructor [Brevet d'Etat d'Educateur Sportif de 1er degré] (C), The Pony Leader [Brevet d'Animateur Poney] (C)

## École d'Agriculture St. Joseph

25270 Levier, France. Phone: +33 (0)381 895858.
**Accreditation:** French Ministry of Agriculture, French Ministry of Sports
**Degrees Offered:** Official Brevet for teaching equitation, Horse Breeding
**Tuition Costs:** (Euros) €2,000/year
**Facilities:** One closed area and one open area, four teachers in equitation, three teachers in horse breeding

## École Nationale d'Equitation (ENE)

BP 207, 49411 Saumur, France. Phone: +33 (0)241 535055. Fax: +33 (0)241 676308.
Email: nicolas.dugue@cadrenoir.fr.
**Accreditation:** French Ministry of Youth and Sports
**Degrees Offered:** Brevet d'Etat d'Educateur Sportif du 1er degree—B.E.E.S 1st grade
**Majors Offered:** Brevet d'Etat d'Educateur Sportif du 1er degree—B.E.E.S 1st grade
**Tuition Costs:** (Euros) €12,000
**Description of Program:** The course is open to riders of all nationalities. They should have taken part in official competitions in their countries and have acquired a sound technical basis. As most instructors speak English and Spanish, French is not required, but a working knowledge is recommended. French lessons can be organized during the course. The course runs for 44 weeks from the first week of October to the last week of July. Equestrian and pedagogic training: 1630 hours (dressage, show jumping, eventing, vaulting, driving, and endurance). All lessons are taught by the Ecuyers of the Cadre Noir, each an expert in his/her discipline. Horses are provided by the school; students may bring one or more horses capable of being integrated in the course. Included in the course are various visits, dinners, conferences, and competitions. In order to give individual and personal support to each student, only eight positions are open each year. Selection is based on the candidate's file. Two weeks of holidays are programmed during the course. By the end of the course, students will have gained training and competition experience; they will be able not only to teach several riding disciplines, but also to train teams for competitions in their specialty.
**Facilities:** Two-hundred people including 45 instructors, a racetrack, 400 horses stabled in individual boxes, four big barns, five indoor arenas, fifteen Olympic size outdoor riding arenas, about 50km of sand tracks, several hundred cross-country jumps, a modern veterinarian hospital, a well-equipped lecture hall
**Classroom/Hands-On Equine Classes:** Theory/123 hours, pedagogy/113 hours, practice/900 hours
**Showing:** Dressage, show jumping, eventing

## École Nationale Vétérinaire d'Alfort

7, avenue du Général de Gaulle, 94704 Maisons-Alfort, France. Phone: 01 43 96 71 00.
Fax: 01 43 96 71 25. Email: navarre@vet-alfort.fr.
**Majors Offered:** Veterinary Medicine

**Website:**
www.vet-alfort.fr

**Type of School:**
Veterinary School

## École privée Charles Péguy

Route de Nice, 13100 Aix en Provence. Phone: 04.42.27.14.47. Fax: 04.42.27.23.16.
Email: info@val-saint-andre.com.
**Degrees Offered:** High School Diploma

**Website:**
www.val-saint-andre.com

**Type of School:**
Secondary School

## La Chabraque

Sever de Castenet, 12240 Rieupeyroux, France. Phone: +33 (0)565 699197. Fax: +33
(0)565 699687.
**Accreditation:** Minister of Agriculture
**Degrees Offered:** Certificate of Professionnal Aptitude (CAP)
**Majors Offered:** Groom
**Tuition Costs:** Covered by state
**Description of Program:** A professional residential training center that accepts, for a
three-year period, young people who have experienced difficulties at school. During the
first two years, they learn the trade of stablelad. In the second year, the practical work is
longer, and the students are placed with professional riders, who generally form part of
the French Team. When they have obtained the CAP as a groom, they are trained for an
extra year to become an equestrian groom. They are trained by international riders, and
take a heavy-goods vehicle license; they will also know basic equine first aid. They are
then placed with riders who are looking for capable professionals. Some continue their
studies to become children's monitors for ponies, riding instructors, farriers, or equine
dentists. Trainees are placed throughout the world through exchanges with numerous
federations and clubs, both in France and abroad.
**Facilities:** Exchanges with riders of different countries, accommodation with host
families
**Classroom/Hands-On Equine Classes:** First year: two weeks practical time, followed
by two weeks classroom work; second year : one to three months practical, two
hours/day riding time, plus lessons in hippology, horse care, and general matters
**Showing:** Equestrian competitions are available. La Chabraque is the county
headquarters of the Aveyron Equestrian Committee.

**Type of School:**
Specialty School

## La Ferme du Sonvaux

Centre d'Attelage, 55160 Les Eparges, France. Phone: +33 (0)329 873569.
Fax: +33 (0)329 873992.
**Accreditation:** Fédération Française d' Equitation, the Délégation Régionale de la For-
mation Professionnelle, the Ministère de la Jeunesseet des Sports
**Degrees Offered:** Professional Qualifications
**Majors Offered:** Horse-Logging (Forestry), Carriage Driving, Horse-Drawn Tourism,
Harness Making and Saddlery, Horse-Drawn Agricultural Work, Driving for Sport and
Leisure
**Tuition Costs:** (Euros) €45/day; board and lodging: €27.50/day

**Type of School:**
Specialty School

**Description of Program:** Courses vary from five days to one year in length, depending on the individual student's requirements. Other activities offered are fabrication of harness, horse-drawn vehicles, agricultural material, breaking and schooling horses, and help with setting up businesses involving driving horses.

**Facilities:** Stabling for approximately 20 horses, outdoor and indoor schools, classroom, workshops

**Classroom/Hands-On Equine Classes:** 50:50

**Showing:** Demonstrations at the school, parades, fêtes, horse-drawn holidays

## L.A.P. du Tricastin-Baronnies

**Website:**
http://laptb.free.fr

**Type of School:**
Public College

BP 15, 25 Le Courreau, 26130 St. Paul Trois Chauteaux. Phone: +33 (0)475 966227. Fax: 04 75 96 73 64. Email: st-paul-trois-chateaux@cneap.scolanet.org.

**Accreditation:** Ministere de l'Agriculture

**Degrees Offered:** CAPA, BEPA CPA, BAC Professional CGEA

**Majors Offered:** Equine Breeding (BEPA), Breeding of the Horse (BAC), Horse Care (CAPA)

**Tuition Costs:** (Francs) Boarding school for BAC Professional: F 20,400/year; boarding school for CAPA: F 19,650/year; boarding school for BEPA: F 19,800/year; horsemanship fee: F 3,750/year

**Description of Program:** BEPA Equine Breeding: to become a workman specializing in equine breeding. CAPA Horse Care: to become a workman specializing in the care of equines. BAC Breeding of the Horse: to become a specialist in equine breeding.

**Facilities:** Two riding schools

**Classroom/Hands-On Equine Classes:** Vary

## L.A.P. Le Cluzeau

**Website:**
www.cluzeau.asso.fr

**Type of School:**
Public College

CFA Metiers du Cheval, 24240 Sigoules, France. Phone: +33 (0)553 734360. Fax: +33 (0)553 589473. Email: lycee.agricole.le.cluzeau@wanadoo.fr.

**Degrees Offered:** Level IV (Baccalaureate)

**Majors Offered:** Management and Valorization of the Equine Company

**Tuition Costs:** Contact school

**Description of Program:** In partnership with the stud farm Villenueve, the C.F.A. of the Trades of the Horse Villeréal (47) proposed a specialization of local initiative (S.I.L.) in Management and Valorization of the Equine Company. This formation of Level IV (Baccalaureate) is designed for current and future breeders, as well as for stablehands and stable managers who would like to acquire a specific training in equine breeding. Breeders must know how to use a standard to select mares, how to market the offspring and breeding stock, how to manage the company, etc. Considering the diversity of the competencies required in the horse industry, a specialization in the management of equine companies was conceived so that students may acquire the skills necessary for a company management position.

## L'École des Courses Hippiques AFASEC

**Website:**
www.asasec.fr

**Type of School:**
Private Specialty School

AFASEC (Association de Formation et d'Action Sociale des Ecuries de Courses), Allée de Jardy, BP 70419, 60635 Chantilly, France. Phone: 03 44 62 41 60. Fax: 03 44 58 57 37. Contact: Christian Maigret, President, or Didier Budka, Director. Email: dbudka@afasec.fr.

**Accreditation:** Under the supervision of both the Department of Agriculture and the Treasury Department is a grant-maintained school (subsidized by the Racing Institution "France Galop" and the "Société du Cheval Français" ) whose aim is to train racing stable staff and to accompany them during their professional career.

**Degrees Offered:** CAPA (Professional Certificate of Agrarian Aptitude), BEPA (Diploma of Professional Aptitude), Professional Baccalaureate

**Majors Offered:** Stable Lad Galop—Stable Lad Driver (CAPA), Land Management with Option Equine Activities [Specialty Training of Race Horses] (BEPA), Management and Administration of an Agricultural Concern Specialty Horse Breeding (Professional Baccalaureate)

**Tuition Costs:** (Euros) € 2,400/year

**Description of Program:** Stable Lad Galop—Stable Lad Driver is a one-year course. The Land Management with Option Equine Activities (Specialty Training of Race Horses) is a two-year course. The Management and Administration of an Agricultural Concern Specialty Horse Breeding is a two-year course. The aim of the training and education system is based upon the rhythm of three weeks training at the trainers and then three weeks at school. Students and apprentices attend the lessons during three weeks before they can integrate a racing stable under the responsibility of an apprentice or trainee' s tutor (during three weeks). Traditional teaching (Math, French, English) is provided as well as more technical courses like equine science, biology. The practice of trick-riding enables the students to learn how to improve their balance on horses.

**Facilities:** All the schools have their own application center. There are 120 horses for the practical training provided at the Institution.

**Showing:** Specific races called "school races" give the young trainees opportunities to compete on the racecourses in the same conditions as jockeys.

## Lycée Agro-environnemental privé St Joseph

Château St Quentin, 63340 Le Breuil Sur Couze, France. Contact: Laurent Grimault. Phone: 04.73.71.89.60. Fax: 04 73 71 89 69.
Email: le-breuil-sur-couze@cneap.scolanet.org.

**Accreditation:** French Agricultural Minister

**Degrees Offered:** BEPA (Certificate of Professional Agricultural Studies), Baccalauréat Professionnel (Professional Bachelor)

**Majors Offered:** Equine's Ranch and Horse Production

**Tuition Costs:** (Euros) € 30.49

**Classroom/Hands-On Equine Classes:** Vary

**Website:**
www.lyceeagroenvironnemental.com

**Type of School:**
Traditional School

## Lycée d'Enseignement Professionnel Agricole St Hilaire du Harcouet

Rte de Fougères, 50600 Saint Hilaire du Harcouet. Phone: 02.33.91.02.20.
Fax: 02.33.91.02.21. Email: ipa.st-hilaire@educagri.fr.

**Accreditation:** Royal Horse, Ecole Française d' Equitation

**Degrees Offered:** Technical High School Diploma

**Majors Offered:** Horse Breeding, Horse Training

**Facilities:** Riding school

**Type of School:**
State Secondary School

## Lycée General et Technologique Agricole Paysager Equestre

Yssingeaux le Puy, 43200 Yssingeaux, France. Contact: Gilberte Delaille, Vice Principal. Phone: +33 (0)471 657050. Fax: +33 (0)471 655051.
Email: gilberte.delaille@educagri.fr.
**Accreditation:** Ministry of Agriculture
**Degrees Offered:** BEP ARE (Brevet Professionnel Accompagnement de Randonnées Équestres), Bac Professionnel CGEA (Conduite et Gestion d'une Production Agricole)
**Tuition Costs:** (Euros) Tuition: none; boarding and lodging: €1500
**Description of Program:** The BEP prepares students to lead groups on rides and to prepare the trips, including board, lodging, etc. Therefore, the tuition includes communication, tourism, good knowledge of horses, and a good riding level. The BAC specializes in the breeding of horses; this course prepares students to manage a breeding farm or an equestrian center as owner or employee.
**Facilities:** There is an equestrian center about 500 yards from the lycée, where the students are given tuition and may ride during their spare time. The town of Yssingeaux is 30km from the town of St. Etienne, which is a university town.
**Showing:** The students participate in competitions if they wish; there is also a special course to prepare them to compete.

# GERMANY

**Website:**
www.fu-berlin.de

**Type of School:**
University

## Freie Universität Berlin

Dept. of Veterinary Medicine, Oertzenweg 19 b, 14163 Berlin, Germany. Phone: (030) 838-624 24 /-624 26. Fax: (030) 838-624 31. Email: dekanat@vetmed.fu-berlin.de.
**Majors Offered:** Veterinary Medicine

**Website:**
www.uni-leipzig.de

**Type of School:**
University

## Universität Leipzig

Faculty of Veterinary Medicine, An den Tierkliniken 19, 04103 Leipzig, Germany. Phone: (0341) 97-3 80 00. Fax: (0341) 97-3 80 99. Email: dekanat@vmf.uni-leipzig.de.
**Majors Offered:** Veterinary Medicine

# HONG KONG

**Website:**
www.hongkongjockeyclub.com

**Type of School:**
Specialty School

## Beaus River Riding School

Beaus River Country Club, Sheung Shui, New Territories, Hong Kong.
Phone: 2966 1990. Fax: 2679 5521. Email: riding.br@hkjc.org.hk.
**Accreditation:** British Horse Society, Hong Kong Jockey Club
**Degrees Offered:** Certificate
**Majors Offered:** Up To BHS Intermediate Instructor
**Facilities:** Facilities include offices, changing rooms, covered paddock (50m x 30m) lit with floodlights, two outdoor sand arenas (130m x 60m), two smaller sand arenas, and

grass areas with cross-country jumping fences. There is also a hacking trail in the surrounding hills and through local villages.

## Tuen Mun Public Riding School

Website:
www.hongkongjockeyclub.com

Type of School:
Specialty School

Lot 45 Lung Mun Road, Tuen Mun, New Territories, Hong Kong. Phone: 2461 3338. Fax: 2461 8381. Email: riding.tm@hkjc.org.uk.
**Accreditation:** British Horse Society, Hong Kong Jockey Club
**Degrees Offered:** Certificate
**Majors Offered:** Up to BHS Assistant Instructor
**Description of Program:** Courses can be from two weeks to three months. They are tailor-made for individuals. Students get plenty of riding experience and may help to retrain racehorses. The Hong Kong Equestrian Federation, Hong Kong Pony Club, and Riding for the Disabled Association of Hong Kong have offices at the school and make use of the riding venue.
**Facilities:** Facilities in the riding school can accommodate up to 60 horses and ponies and include offices, lecture rooms, changing rooms, horse paddock (95m x 45m), two pony paddocks (65m x 40m and 50m x 25m), and 60 parking spaces.
**Classroom/Hands-On Equine Classes:** 40:60
**Showing:** Students are encouraged to compete in dressage, show jumping and horse trials.

# ICELAND

## Hólar í Hjaltadal

Website:
www.holar.is

Type of School:
Agricultural College

Hólaskóli, Hólum í Hjaltadal, ÍS-551 Sauðárkrókur, Iceland. Contact: Víkingur Gunnarsson, Department Head. Phone: 354-455-6300. Fax: 354-455-6301.
Email: holaskoli@holar.is or vikingur@holar.is.
**Accreditation:** Ministry of Agriculture, collaboration agreement with the Icelandic Horse Trainers Association
**Degrees Offered:** College and University Level
**Majors Offered:** Equine Studies and Basic Riding Instruction, Young Horse Trainer, Trainer and C Riding Teacher,
**Tuition Costs:** 50,000 IKR/year
**Description of Program:** The programs are concerned with practical knowledge and skills in riding, horse breeding, and management, as well as a solid foundation in the main subjects of rural economy: agriculture, animal husbandry, and economics. The programs are meant to further progress in horse breeding, better training methods and management of horses, better riding skills, and enhanced profitability in the industry. The Equine Studies and Basic Riding Instruction program is concerned with a solid foundation in the main subjects of horse breeding, land management, and economics. Main emphasis is on theoretical knowledge and practical skills in horse management, principles of riding/training the Icelandic horse and the basics in riding instruction. The aim is to prepare the student for a vocation in the horse industry, such as horse breeding/farming, horse tourism, riding schools/seminars for beginners, etc. The Young Horse Trainer Program enhances theoretical knowledge and practical skills in starting young horses and in further training of Icelandic horses. The course prepares the student for a professional vocation in the horse industry, such as a young

horse trainer. The Trainer and C Riding Teacher Program prepares students to conduct courses in riding skills and to be able to train and show horses in exhibitions and competitions.

**Facilities:** Stables for 160 horses, veterinary and research facilities, two riding halls (1100m x 1100m and 1500m x 1500m), outdoor riding areas, tracks, fences

**Classroom/Hands-On Equine Classes:** Equine Studies: 60:40; Young Horse Trainer: 20:80; Riding Teacher: 30:70

**Showing:** Competitions are available.

## Landbúnaarháskólinn á Hvanneyri (Hvanneyri Agricultural University)

**Website:**
www.hvanneyri.is

**Type of School:**
Public University

311 Borgarnes, Iceland. Phone: 433-7000. Fax: 433-7001. Email: lbh@hvanneyri.is.

**Accreditation:** The Icelandic Ministry of Agriculture

**Degrees Offered:** Diploma, Bachelor of Science, Master of Science

**Majors Offered:** Agricultural Production (B.Sc., M.S.), Basic Agricultural Education (D), Environmental and Landscape Planning (B.Sc., M.S.)

**Tuition Costs:** None

**Description of Program:** The Agricultural Production program focuses on basic and applied principles relating to all major aspects of agricultural production in Iceland. Crop science, animal nutrition, plant and animal breeding, farm buildings, and animal welfare are among important topics, as well as courses on finance, economy, and farm technology. Basic courses are required in chemistry, biochemistry, plant physiology, zoology, soil science, and more. The goal is to provide students with a firm knowledge on sustainable agricultural production and land use. Specialization in the program is obtained by individually selecting topics within courses and by submitting a B.Sc. thesis, in addition to a selection of optional courses during the third year of study. Students interested in horses can spend one term at Agricultural College Holar, which specializes in Equine Studies. The Agricultural Production Program is intended for students pursuing careers in the Agricultural Extension Service, agricultural production practice and business, research assistantships, or teaching. Further studies for graduates in Agricultural Production include master and doctoral programs within the NOVA University and other universities nationally and internationally.

**Facilities:** Several student residences are located at Hvanneyri, along with a day-care center and elementary school. Stables are provided for those wishing to board their horses. Hvanneyri is fourteen kilometers from the nearest village, Borgarnes, which features shopping and health care centers. The capital city is 80 kilometers away, though the Hvalfjörður tunnel. Hvanneyri has an extensive agricultural library, a well-equipped laboratory, a university farm, and various research facilities, all of which are used for teaching purposes.

**Classroom/Hands-On Equine Classes:** 50:50

# IRELAND, REPUBLIC OF

## Ballingale Farm Riding School

**Website:**
www.nci.ie/yp/fullpage/y3884.htm

**Type of School:**
Specialty School

Taghmon, Co. Wexford, Republic of Ireland. Phone: +353 53 34387. Fax: +353 53 34541. Email: val@ballingale.iol.ie.

**Accreditation:** British Horse Society
**Degrees Offered:** Certificate
**Majors Offered:** BHS Stages 1-4
**Description of Program:** Ballingale Farm prepares students for BHS exams up to Stage IV. These qualifications, recognized internationally, are a particularly good basis for riding, competing, and all equestrian-based employment. The BHS courses are structured as eight-month vocation courses, run in conjunction with a local college (no fees; maintenance grants available).
**Facilities:** Indoor and outdoor schools, cross-country course, full range of show jumps, miles of sandy beaches, local and on-site accommodation

## Brennanstown Riding School Ltd.

Hollybrook, Kilmacanogue, Co. Wicklow, Ireland. Contact: Ms. J. Kennedy.
Phone: 00 353 1 2863778. Fax: 00 353 1 2829590.
Email: info@brennanstownrs.ie.
**Accreditation:** British Horse Society, the Association of Irish Riding Establishments
**Degrees Offered:** BHS Certificate
**Majors Offered:** Training for up to BHS Intermediate Instructor
**Description of Program:** Riding School: instruction for adults and children, cross-country rides, trekking over 1000 acres of scenic Wicklow countryside. Livery Yard: active riding club with regular competitions for livery owners. Training Centre: one-year Career Student/Working Pupil training course for BHS examination.
**Facilities:** Indoor school, three outdoor arenas, cross-country course, access to over 1000 acres of trekking and hacking, mountain, woodland, farmland

**Type of School:**
Specialty School

## Calliaghstown Riding Centre

Calliaghstown, Rathcoole, Dublin, Republic of Ireland. Phone: 00 353 1 4588 322.
Fax: 00 353 1 45 88 171. Email: info@calliaghstownridingcentre.com.
**Accreditation:** British Horse Society
**Degrees Offered:** Certificate
**Majors Offered:** BHS Stages 1-4, BHS Assistant Instructor, BHS Intermediate Instructor
**Tuition Costs:** Vary
**Description of Program:** Riding, stable management, horse knowledge and care
**Facilities:** Limited accommodation
**Classroom/Hands-On Equine Classes:** 1:10

**Website:**
www.calliaghstownridingcentre.com

**Type of School:**
Specialty School

## Curragh House Education Institute

Curragh House, Dublin Road, Kildare, Co. Kildare, Republic of Ireland. Contact: James H. Murphy. Phone: 353-45-522468 or 353-45-522808. Fax: 353-45-521305. Email: racentre@indigo.ie.
**Accreditation:** British Horseracing Training Board/FETAC
**Degrees Offered:** Certificate
**Majors Offered:** Apprentice Jockey, Jump Jockey, Exercise Rider, Qualified Rider, Charity Rider, Permit Holder, Racehorse Trainer, Horse Racing in Ireland Industry Course
**Tuition Costs:** Vary
**Description of Program:** The Curragh House Education Institute (C.H.E.I.) is the

**Website:**
www.racingacademy.ie

**Type of School:**
Specialized Racing School

adult education branch of the Racing Academy and Centre of Education (R.A.C.E). It is based within the R.A.C.E Complex, located on the Dublin Road, just outside Kildare Town. Curragh House Education Institute recognizes the need for ongoing training and education of adults currently working in the horseracing and breeding industries at every level. Racehorse trainers, permit holders, apprentice and amateur jockeys, and secretaries have attended courses and seminars at the R.A.C.E. complex. Apprentice Course includes rules of racing, mock steward's inquiry, communication skills, mock interview, race-riding technique, whip use, safety and fitness, fitness assessment, literacy skills, diet, personal finance, professionalism, trainers association, and jockeys association. Trainers' Course includes rules of racing, administration—Turf Club, sales procedures, maintenance of gallops, racing injuries, horse nutrition, handicapping, trainers association, owners association, business planning, taxation, management issues, legal responsibilities, computer skills, communication skills, human resource management, health and safety, and marketing. Qualified Riders Course includes rules of racing, safety and fitness, race-riding technique, whip use, and pre-race preparation. Permit Holders Course includes rules of racing, administration—Turf Club, sales procedures, maintenance of gallops, racing injuries, veterinary hospital, horse nutrition, handicapping, equine center, breaking procedure, saddling procedure, and turnout for racing.

**Facilities:** The Education Block comprises of an auditorium, which seats 55 people comfortably and has full audio-visual facilities, a video library, anatomical models, and other educational aids. Adjacent to the auditorium is a classroom that has a small library and fourteen desks, and a computer center with fifteen stations and Internet access. There are indoor and outdoor arenas, 34 stables, all-weather gallop, hurdle course, gymnasium, games hall and racehorse simulator room.

**Type of School:**
Specialty School

## Grennan College Equestrian Centre

Newtown, Thomastown, Co. Kilkenny, Ireland. Contact: Mr. Timothy O'Mahony. Phone: 00 353 56 24112.
**Accreditation:** British Horse Society
**Degrees Offered:** Certificate
**Majors Offered:** Up to BHS Assistant Instructor

Website:
www.portlaoiseec.com

**Type of School:**
Specialty School

## Portlaoise Equestrian Centre Ltd.

Timahoe Road, Portlaoise, Co. Laois, Republic of Ireland. Contact: Mr. R. & Mrs. G. Sheehan. Phone/Fax: +353 (0)5026 0880. Email: portlaoiseec@eircom.net.
**Accreditation:** British Horse Society
**Degrees Offered:** Certificate
**Majors Offered:** BHS Stages 1 and 2
**Description of Program:** Portlaoise Equestrian Centre is a purpose-built facility on 40 acres, consisting of stabling for 50 horses, an all-weather outdoor manège, an indoor school, a six-horse walker, and regular SJAI shows (Show Jumping Association of Ireland) and local hunts twice a week during the season.
**Facilities:** Covered school, outdoor manège, cross-country course
**Showing:** SJAI shows, local hunts

## Racing Academy and Centre of Education

Website:
www.racingacademy.ie

Type of School:
Specialty Racing School

Curragh House, Dublin Road, Kildare, Co. Kildare, Republic of Ireland. Contact: James H. Murphy.  Phone: 353-45-522468 or 353-45-522808. Fax: 353-45-521305. Email: racentre@indigo.ie.
**Accreditation:** British Horseracing Training Board-FETAC
**Degrees Offered:** Certificate
**Majors Offered:** Trainee Jockey Course
**Description of Program:** The Racing Academy and Centre of Education (R.A.C.E) opened in September 1973. It began without any experience or facilities, only the desire to improve the social, professional, and human development of young people who work with horses. From these early beginnings, it has developed into a modern and well-equipped educational establishment. The site, which comprises Curragh House and 27 acres of the Irish National Stud, were donated for the project by the Department of Agriculture at the request of the Board of the Stud. It is the officially designated training body of the Irish Turf Club. The Trainee Jockey Course was established in 1977 and is a 42-week residential course comprising three terms. The course is free of charge to E.U. citizens and is sponsored by Fas. Non-E.U. citizens pay a weekly fee. Local trainees go home on weekends.

## University College Dublin

Website:
www.ucd.ie/vetmed/

Type of School:
Public University

Faculty of Veterinary Medicine, University College Dublin, Belfield, Dublin 4, Ireland. Phone: +353 1 716 6100. Fax: +353 1 716 6104. Email: vetmed@ucd.ie.
**Accreditation:** Veterinary Council of Ireland, EAEVE
**Degrees Offered:** Bachelor of Veterinary Medicine, Master of Animal Science, Master of Veterinary Medicine, Doctor of Philosophy, Diploma in Veterinary Nursing.
**Tuition Costs:** (Euros) Veterinary Medicine: 1ˢᵗ-3ʳᵈ year EU students €6,920/year, non-EU students €22,340/year; 4ᵗʰ and 5ᵗʰ year EU students €6,876/year, non-EU students €22,340/year; Master of Animal Science and Master of Veterinary Medicine: 1ˢᵗ and 2ⁿᵈ year EU students €3,270/year, non-EU students €16,540/year; each subsequent year EU students €1,625/year, non-EU students €3,250/year; Veterinary Nursing: EU students €2,400/year, non-EU students €4,800/year; housing: €2,736.56 to €3,039.30 for undergraduate students, €3,825.90 for postgraduate students
**Description of Program:** Basic equine handling and husbandry skills, anatomy and physiology are taught in the first two years of the course, and pathology is taught in the third year. The teaching of Equine Medicine and Surgery is carried out by the Department of Veterinary Surgery and the Department of Large Animal Clinical Studies. Lectures are given in Equine Surgery (including Anaesthesia and Diagnostic Imaging), Equine Medicine (including Equine Cardiology, Neurology, Dermatology, and Ophthalmology), and Equine Reproduction. In addition, during the later years of the course. Students attend tutorials and practical classes in small groups. During the final year of the course, students attend dedicated Large Animal Surgery and Large Animal Medicine Rotations in the University Veterinary Hospital. During these rotations, the students are assigned to clinical cases and are expected to observe and assist in all aspects of patient care, diagnostic and therapeutic procedures (including surgery), under supervision of the clinical staff. The equine caseload presently comprises of mainly surgical cases, with a growing number of medical cases. As well as being a specialized referral center, students also gain some experience of first opinion cases.
**Facilities:** Twenty-five loose box stalls (including adapted mare and foal boxes for foal intensive care and separate isolation facilities), two treatment rooms with stocks, sep-

arate teaching room, two induction/recovery boxes, lunge arena, high-speed treadmill, endoscopy facilities, laparoscopy facilities, two operating theaters, a dedicated Large Animal Diagnostic Imaging Unit

## University of Limerick

**Website:**
www.ul.ie

**Type of School:**
Public University, Independent Study

Department of Life Sciences, Schrodinger Building, University of Limerick, Limerick, Republic of Ireland. Phone: +353 (61) 202880 or +353 (61) 202859. Fax: +353 (61) 331490. Email: admissions@ul.ie. International Equine Institute, University of Limerick, Limerick, Ireland. Phone: +353 (61) 202430. Fax: +353 (61) 202184. Email iei@ul.ie.

**Degrees Offered:** Certificate, Diploma, Bachelor of Science, Master and Doctoral Studies

**Majors Offered:** Equine Science (B.Sc.) with emphasis on Equitation Science or Equine Business Management (D, B.Sc.), Science [Equine Science] (C, D)

**Tuition Costs:** (Euros) EU students: €6190; non-EU students: €15,470

**Description of Program:** B.Sc. in Equine Science is a four-year program that provides students who wish to follow a professional career in the horse industry the opportunity to underpin their career aspirations with specialist knowledge and skills. The course of study has been developed because of the strategic economic importance of equine and related industries and the consequential need to produce highly qualified personnel with the specialized knowledge to exploit the potential of these industries. The overall aim of the program is to equip students with degree level competence in the disciplines of equine science and a choice of professional studies in either the disciplines of equitation science or equine business management. The Certificate in Science (Equine Science) is offered over two years with a similar format to the Degree. The Diploma in Science is a further year of study after the Certificate. Students are required to pass the Certificate in order to progress to the Diploma. Students who obtain the Diploma award may then enter year three of the Degree Program. The Certificate and Diploma Program offered through distance learning are highly flexible in nature, but similar in content to the full-time program.

# ISRAEL

## Koret School of Veterinary Medicine

**Website:**
http://ksvm.agri.huji.ac.il

**Type of School:**
Veterinary School

P.O. Box 12, Rehovot 76100, Israel. Phone: 972-8-9489021 / 31. Fax: 972-8-9467940. Email: ksvm@agri.huji.ac.il.

**Degrees Offered:** Doctor of Veterinary Medicine

# ITALY

## Associazione Sportiva I Due Laghi

**Website:**
www.iduelaghi.it

**Type of School:**
Specialty School

Localita Le Cerque, 00061 Anguillara, Sabazia, Roma, Italy. Contact: Mr. Federicao Nizza. Phone: 00 39 069960 7059. Fax: 0039 069960 7068. Email: info@iduelaghi.it.

**Accreditation:** British Horse Society
**Degrees Offered:** Certificate
**Majors Offered:** BHS Stage 1 and 2

## Eques Coop

Via Donnini, 47-57121 Licorno, Italy. Phone: +39(0)586444074.
Fax: +39(0)586440693. Email: eques@eques.it.
**Degrees Offered:** Certificate
**Majors Offered:** Groom, Farrier, Young Jockey

**Website:**
www.eques.it

**Type of School:**
Specialty School

## Università degla Studi di Milano

Dipartimento di Scienze dell'Informazione, Università degli Studi di Milano, via Comelico 39/41, I-20135 Milano MI, Italia. Phone: +39-02503.16372.
Fax: +39-02503.16373.
**Majors Offered:** Veterinary Medicine

**Website:**
www.dsi.unimi.it

**Type of School:**
University

## Università di Bologna

Faculty of Veterinary Medicine, Via Tolara di Sopra, 50, 40064 - Ozzano dell'Emilia (BO), Italy. Phone: 051-79.28.94 or 051-79.20.03. Fax: 051-65.111.57.
Email: presvet1@vet.unibo.it.
**Majors Offered:** Veterinary Medicine

**Website:**
www.vet.unibo.it

**Type of School:**
University

# JAPAN

## Education Center of Japan Farriers Association

1829-2, Tsuruta, Utsunomiya, Tochigi, Japan 320-0851. Phone: 81 28 648 0007.
Fax: 81 28 648 9944. Email: jfa-ec@farriers.or.jp.
**Accreditation:** Japan Farriers Association
**Degrees Offered:** Certificate
**Majors Offered:** Farrier
**Tuition Costs:** (Yen) 1,400,000 (about $13,000)/year; 400,000 (about $3,700) housing/year
**Description of Program:** Students must be over 18 years old and speak Japanese. Average number of students is sixteen. Entrance examination: Academic Liberal Subject (covering areas such as Japanese language, math, problem solving, logic, and general knowledge) and interview.
**Classroom/Hands-On Equine Classes:** 370 hours/940 hours.
**Facilities:** There is a practice room, which has 20 anvils and coal forges, two lecture rooms, and a library in a two story building. There are sixteen single rooms for individual students and a dining room in the dormitory.

**Type of School:**
Specialty School

## Nihon University College of Bioresource Sciences

**Website:**
www.brs.nihon-u.ac.jp

**Type of School:**
University

Phone: 0466-84-3800. Fax: 0466-84-3805. Email: syomuka@brs.nihon-u.ac.jp.
**Majors Offered:** Veterinary Medicine

# *MALAYSIA*

## Bukit Kiara Resort Berhad

**Website:**
www.berjayaclubs.com

**Type of School:**
Specialty School

Jalan Bukit Kiara, Off Jalan Damansara, 60000 Kuala Lumpur, Malaysia.
Phone: 00603 20941222/20931222. Fax: 00603 20935611/20962825.
Email: kiara@bukit-kiara.com.my.
**Accreditation:** British Horse Society
**Degrees Offered:** Certificate
**Majors Offered:** Beginners Riding Course, Stable Management
**Tuition Costs:** (RM) Three months riding package: registration/RM30 (Individual), first month/RM280 (two lessons per week), second month/RM280 (two lessons per week), third month/RM420 (three lessons per week)
**Description of Program:** Certificate will be given upon completion of the full three months' package. Should the rider/student wish to continue riding after completion of the above package, the rider would have to purchase a membership. The Riding Package is a beginner's riding course, and Basic Stable Management will be included upon the rider's request. On an average, by the end of the third month, the rider would be able to canter. The classes will be conducted in a group of three persons.
**Facilities:** One indoor arena, two grazing paddocks, polo field with track, riding school paddock (sand), grass paddock, three outdoor arenas (sand), housing not supplied
**Showing:** "In-house" dressage and jumping competitions

## Malaysian Equine Council

**Type of School:**
Specialty School

Equestrian Association of Malaysia, No.20, Persiaran Ampang, 55000 Kuala Lumpur, Malaysia. Phone: (60 3) 4251 13 67. Fax: (60 3) 4257 68 48. Email: aem99@tm.net.my.
**Accreditation:** Malaysian Equine Council
**Degrees Offered:** Certificate
**Majors Offered:** Equestrian Coaches, Farriers, Stable Supervisors and Managers

## University Putra Malaysia

**Website:**
www.upm.edu.my

**Type of School:**
University

Dean, Faculty of Veterinary Medicine, University Putra Malaysia, 43400 UPM Serdang, Selangor Darul Ehsan, Malaysia. Phone: 603-9486101 extension 1803.
Fax: 603-9486317. Email: aiini@vet.upm.edu.my.
**Majors Offered:** Equine Studies

# THE NETHERLANDS

## Dutch Equestrian School

Type of School:
Specialty School

Contact: Peter Strijbosch. Email: p.strijbosch.nd@hlcn.nl.
**Accreditation:** The Dutch Government
**Degrees Offered:** Certificate
**Majors Offered:** Instructor/Coaching courses up to International Level III and Stable Management
**Tuition Costs:** (Euros) International Instructor Course: € 3000/year
**Description of Program:** The program includes riding, show jumping, teaching, didactics, horse care, veterinary subjects, lunging, and more. You are linked to a virtual program that helps you through assignments. In the summertime you come to the Netherlands for two- to three-week intense training in riding, jumping, teaching, etc.
**Facilities:** Four indoor riding schools, outdoor arena, 40 school horses, stabling for 220 horses, restaurant, sleeping accommodations, modern classrooms and computer facilities, library
**Classroom/Hands-On Equine Classes:** 30/70
**Showing:** Competition opportunities

## Universiteit Utrecht

Website:
www.vet.uu.nl

Type of School:
University

Faculty bureau of Veterinary Medicine, P.O. Box 80.163, NL-3508TD Utrecht, The Netherlands. Phone: +31 302534851. Fax: +31 302537727. Email: diva@vet.uu.nl.
**Majors Offered:** Veterinary Medicine

# NEW ZEALAND

## Dannevirke High School

Website:
www.dannevirkehigh.school.nz

Type of School:
Secondary School

P.O. Box 23, Dannevirke, New Zealand. Phone: 64-6-374 8302. Fax: 64-6-374 7764. International Students Ph/fax: 64-6-374 5397. Email: info@dannevirkehigh.school.nz or international@dannevirkehigh.school.nz.
**Accreditation:** New Zealand Qualifying Authority
**Degrees Offered:** High School Diploma, National Certificate
**Majors Offered:** Equine—Introductory Skills
**Description of Program:** Students do work experiences at places such as Fayette Park and Tielcey Park and have the chance to observe different facets of the industry at a variety of establishments. Students spend a lot of time during weekends and holidays visiting other equine establishments in the local area: stud farms, riding establishments, and racing stables. Each year, students spend a week at Cambridge Stud, where they live on site, and work with the staff to complete the units that are covered by this part of the course. The school owns a Thoroughbred broodmare, which the students use to help them gain knowledge of the breeding cycle and the raising and handling of foals. They are then able to trace the whole cycle and work with young horses at all stages of their development. The students do all the preliminary work before the horses go to a professional establishment for further education. From there, the students

keep track of their progress, and have the opportunity to do their work experience each holiday at one of these places.

**Facilities:** Hands-on work is completed at a working sheep and beef farm. The facilities are limited to a block that is safely deer-fenced, with a deer shed that students use for handling young horses.

## Eastern Institute of Technology–Hawke's Bay

**Website:**
www.eit.ac.nz

**Type of School:**
Technical Institute

Gloucester Street, Taradale, Napier, Hawke's Bay or Private Bag 1201, Taradale, Napier, Hawke's Bay. Phone: +64 6 974 8000. Fax: +64 6 974 8910. Email: info@eit.ac.nz.

**Accreditation:** Agriculture Industry Training Organisation, Equine Industry Training Organisation, works with Charles Sturt University

**Degrees Offered:** Advanced Diploma, Bachelor of Applied Science (finished at Charles Sturt University AUS)

**Majors Offered:** Applied Science (Equine Studies)

**Tuition Costs:** (NZ) $3,500/34-week program; $100/week accommodation

**Description of Program:** The complete degree program integrates biological sciences, equine sciences, and equine husbandry, and develops an understanding of agribusiness and financial management. Studies will cover the following: Animal Science, Introductory Horse Management, Chemistry, Economics, Pasture Management, Animal Production, Horse Breeding, Biology, Agribusiness, and Statistics. Industry speakers (vets, farriers, nutritionists, owners, breeders, etc.) come on campus to address the class. Bachelor of Applied Science (Equine Studies): EIT Hawke's Bay, Charles Sturt University. By completing the approved Equine Studies papers at EIT Hawke's Bay, successful students are able to enter Year Two or Year Three of what is arguably the best equine degree program in Australia.

**Facilities:** No equine facilities on campus, but extensive use of local equine properties around the region.

**Classroom/Hands-On Equine Classes:** Vary

## Herdword

**Website:**
www.herdword.co.nz

**Type of School:**
Specialty School

P.O. Box 62, Pongaroa, Manawatu 5470 New Zealand. Phone: + 64 6 376 2500. Email: herdword@xtra.co.nz.

**Accreditation:** NZQA

**Tuition Costs:** Contact School

**Description of Program:** Unparalleled eclectic curriculum. Unique psychology and behavior modules are incorporated into practical "hands-on" work. Work involves all areas of equine management, handling, training and breeding. Program includes pasture and environmental management, facility design and development, and analysis of alternative therapy treatments. Rehabilitation work takes place with psychologically damaged, mentally disturbed, emotionally stressed and traumatized horses as well as those with physical conditions. Lessons in dressage and jumping harmonize with the theme principles taught throughout. Peak performance is promoted with each individual horse and student. Opportunities exist for some students to take part in statistical research projects. One-year programs are available for overseas students. Participation visits to two or three additional equine facilities include at least one racehorse trainer. Special packages can be assembled under certain circumstances.

**Facilities:** Facilities include a 320 acre farm, expansive equestrian arena, numerous round training yards, stables, training room, accommodation center, cross-country course, idyllic environment for learning, and a family group of free roaming horses for behavioral study.

**Classroom/Hands-On Equine Classes:** 25 percent/75 percent
**Showing:** Limited opportunities due to remote location

## Insight Learning Academy

Type of School:
Specialty School

570 Tauwhare Road, RD 4, Hamilton, New Zealand. Phone: 07 829 5119.
Email: nzita@xtra.co.nz.
**Accreditation:** New Zealand Qualifications Authority
**Degrees Offered:** National Certificate
**Majors Offered:** Equine Level 2 and 3

## Kyrewood Equestrian Centre Ltd.

Website:
www.kyrewood.co.nz

Type of School:
Specialty School

Oroua Road, R.D. 5, Palmerston North, New Zealand. Phone/Fax: (06) 355 9148.
Email: info@kyrewood.co.nz.
**Accreditation:** N.Z. Qualifications Authority, N.Z. Equine Federation
**Degrees Offered:** National Certificate in Equine
**Majors Offered:** Introductory Skills, Community Coach, Stable Practice, Sport Horse, Thoroughbred Breeding, Race Stable Management
**Tuition Costs:** Fees vary according to the number of teaching weeks and the degree of difficulty of each certificate. Courses are government-subsidized for New Zealand citizens, but overseas students have to pay a higher fee.
**Description of Program:** All certificates except Thoroughbred Breeding have a riding component. Tuition is divided between equitation, horse care, horsemastership, and life skills. Students may bring their own horse, if they wish, to enable them to further its training while they attend the course.
**Facilities:** Kyrewood has an all-weather outdoor arena, a full cross-country course at three different heights, extensive dressage and show jumping facilities, over 50 school horses, stables and saddling stalls, and a horse walker. Accommodation is available on the property, and at the city's university.
**Classroom/Hands-On Equine Classes:** The courses vary in content, but are generally divided into 40 percent riding, 30 percent classroom, and 30 percent hands-on horsemastership.
**Showing:** Kyrewood hosts shows, dressage tournaments, one-day events, and show jumping competitions on the property, and students are welcome to compete if they wish. They also have the opportunity to do some outside competing as well.

## Mark Harris Polo School

Website:
www.polo.co.nz

Type of School:
Specialty School

Physical Address: 44 Topito Road, Tuahiwi, North Canterbury, New Zealand. Mailing Address: 44 Topito Road, R D 1, Kaiapoi, New Zealand. Phone: +64 (3) 313-6387.
Fax: +64 (3) 313-6337. Mobile: +64 274 818 543.
Email: mark@polo.co.nz or rusyl@paradise.net.nz.
**Majors Offered:** Polo
**Tuition Costs:** Contact School
**Description of Program:** The Mark Harris Polo School provides one-on-one training in all aspects of polo. One or two students are accepted at a time, allowing the schedule to be tailored to their individual interests and needs, including sightseeing and

travel arrangements. Most clients stay for a week or so, and attend lessons in riding, schooling, hitting, and so on., in the morning. They may also ride and play stick-and-ball on the beach. Afternoons are usually spent playing chukkas. Some students visit for longer or shorter periods, but a week allows enough time to benefit from the program. Some players come across from the Northern Hemisphere to brush up on their skills prior to the summer season. The school caters to all levels of riding ability, from the novice rider who has not yet been introduce to the game, to riders who want to improve their existing handicap. For spouses or partners not interested in polo, there is plenty to do in the area.

**Facilities:** Playing field, schooling arena for riding instruction, hitting cage (complete with "Tim," the wooden horse).

**Showing:** Tournament polo at Christchurch Polo Club

# Massey University

**Website:**
www.massey.ac.nz

**Type of School:**
Public University

Private Bag 11222, Palmerston North, New Zealand. Phone: +64 6 350 5799 or 0800 MASSEY. Fax: +64 6 350 2263. Email: E.K.Gee@massey.ac.nz.

**Degrees Offered:** Diploma, Bachelor of Applied Science, Bachelor of Veterinary Science, Master of Veterinary Science, Master of Veterinary Studies, Postgraduate Diploma

**Majors Offered:** Equine Studies (B.A.S.), Veterinary Clinical Science (PD), Veterinary Nursing (D), Veterinary Preventative Medicine (PD),Veterinary Public Health (PD), Veterinary Science (B.V.S., M.V.S.), Veterinary Studies (M.V.S.)

**Tuition Costs:** (U.S. Dollars) $5,072; accommodation: (NZ) $175/week

**Description of Program:** A Bachelor of Applied Science (Equine Studies) Degree provides the knowledge base and management skills to meet current and emerging opportunities in the equine industry. It integrates the scientific principles of equine husbandry, agriculture and agronomy with business and management skills. The major is structured to encourage strong links with the equine industry in New Zealand. There is an emphasis on the development of skills for problem solving and analysis of a range of theoretical and practical problems relevant to the equine industry. You will develop skills in written and oral presentation, information technology, innovation, and working with professional colleagues, clients and employers. Students wanting to specialize can continue on into a postgraduate degree.

**Facilities:** The new equine center includes an international size all-weather arena, covered yards (more suitable than stables for New Zealand's temperate climate ), horse grazing, and hacking/riding trails. On-campus accommodation is available for first-year students and a limited number of overseas students.

**Classroom/Hands-On Equine Classes:** Each paper required for the major is based around lectures, study guides, and exams. Some equine papers include a practical component. Students do not ride as part of the qualification.

**Showing:** Competition available in area

# National Equestrian Academy

**Type of School:**
Specialty School

140 East Belt, Rangiora, North Canterbury, New Zealand. Phone: 03 313 5874. Fax: 03 313 7955. Email: bev@northcanterbury.comcol.ca.nz.

**Degrees Offered:** National Certificate

**Majors Offered:** Equine: Stable Practice

# New Zealand Equestrian Federation

**Website:**
www.nzequestrian.org.nz

**Type of School:**
Specialized Certificate Program

The Coaching Director, NZEF, P.O. Box 6146, Wellington. Phone: (04)44998994. Fax: (04)44992899. Email: nzef@nzequestrian.org.nz.

**Accreditation:** New Zealand Equestrian Federation, approved by Equine Industry Training Organization and New Zealand Qualification Authority

**Degrees Offered:** Certificate

**Majors Offered:** Community Coach, Grade One, Grade Two, Grade Three, Grade Four

**Tuition Costs:** (NZ) $15/policy and syllabus manual

**Description of Program:** The coaching certification objectives: To ensure the availability of quality coaching to all members in all parts of the country. To provide a graduated level of achievement for coaches to aspire to. Community Coach: Competent to coach beginner riders of all ages. Grade One: Competent to coach beginner competition riders and horses (up to 1.10 Show Jumping Novice Horse Trials and Dressage). Grade Two: Competent to coach to a Medium standard (Medium Dressage, 1.30 Show Jumping and Intermediate Horse Trials). Grade Three: There is only a specialist discipline strand at this level. Competent to coach to National Championship Standards (Grand Prix Dressage, World Cup Show Jumping and CCI**). Grade Four: National Team and/or Squad Coach Discipline specialist (Nominated by a discipline). There are refresher courses and open coaching days nationwide to help keep coaches at a certain standard.

**Facilities:** Nationwide

# New Zealand Equine Academy

**Type of School:**
Specialty School

New Zealand Equine Academy, Hannon Road, Cambridge, NZ. For information: New Zealand Equine Education Trust, P.O. Box 6665, Te Aro, Wellington, New Zealand. Email: office@nzracing.co.nz.

**Accreditation:** Members: New Zealand Thoroughbred Racing, Harness Racing New Zealand, New Zealand Thoroughbred Breeders' Association, Farriers' Association, and Equine E-Learning Ltd.

**Degrees Offered:** Certificate

**Majors Offered:** Horse Racing (Level 3) with options in Riding or Stable Grooms

**Tuition Costs:** (NZ) $13,500, excluding medical insurance; accommodation: $150/week

**Description of Program:** The Equine Academy is located at Cambridge in the Waikato region, the heartland of the equestrian industry in New Zealand. The facilities are adjacent to the Cambridge Training Track, where 570 horses train each morning. The Academy, established by the NZ Equine Education Trust, is a registered private training establishment offering full-time pre-apprentice jockey training and block courses for other industry sectors. All courses lead towards registered National Qualifications issued by the NZ Qualifications Authority. The Certificate in Horse Racing is a 28-week live-in course with options in riding (for those under 50kg) or stable grooms (for those over 50kg). Modules include stable yard and paddock work, equine health, handling and learning to ride the horse, the racing industry and careers within, personal development and life skills, and preparation for race day or stable management. A typical day includes stable duties before breakfast, classroom learning until lunch, and riding, industry visits, and stable duties in the afternoon. In the final four weeks, students participate in work experience. Students also attend race meetings on alternate weekends.

## New Zealand Equine Training Ltd.

601 Great South Road, RD2, Durdury, Auckland. Contact: Peter Hingston.
Phone: (09)294 7588. Email: nzequineph@xtra.co.nz.
**Degrees Offered:** National Certificate
**Majors Offered:** Equine Introductory Skills Level 2

## New Zealand Riding for the Disabled Association, Inc.

NZRDA Coaching Director, PO Box 48-129, Silverstream, Upper Hutt, Wellington,
New Zealand. Phone: 04 385 1454. Fax: 04 385 4343. Email: nzrda@paradise.net.nz.
**Accreditation:** New Zealand Qualifications Authority
**Degrees Offered:** National Certificate
**Majors Offered:** Equine—RDA Coach
**Tuition Costs:** (NZ) $25/registration; $50/unit (there are five units) for RDA
**Description of Program:** NZRDA offers the following training: Introductory Course,
Volunteer Training Course, NZQA Units 17037-17041, Level III Certificate for
Advanced Practitioners, Therapy Course—Introductory and Advanced—and Special
Workshops. This qualification is designed for those who have a sincere desire to work
with people with disabilities, using horses or ponies; students will receive credit for
horse care, handling, side-walking, and coaching. Those who complete the course may
go on to complete assessment, if they wish; those who complete assessment may, if
they wish, have their Unit Standards accredited and registered with NZQA.

## Palmerston North Girls High School

Fitzherbert Ave., Palmerston North, NZ. Phone: 0-6-357-5690. Fax: 64 6 357 9193.
**Degrees Offered:** High School Diploma, Certificate
**Majors Offered:** NZQA Introductory Certificate in Equine
**Description of Program:** The students who enroll for the equine program have two
lessons on horsemastership theory in school each week, conducted by one of Kyrewood's tutors, and one double period out at Kyrewood one day a week where they
receive riding instruction and practical horsemastership work.
**Facilities:** Equestrian studies are held at Kyrewood Equestrian Centre Ltd. Please
check the listing for Kyrewood for a complete description.

## Queen's High School

195 Surrey St., South Dunedin, Dunedin. Phone: 0 3 455 7212. Fax: 03 455 8644.
**Degrees Offered:** High School Diploma, National Certificate
**Majors Offered:** Equine Introductory Skills, Stable Practice
**Description of Program:** Queen's High School is a secondary-level school for girls
(twelve to eighteen years old). Senior students (fifteen to eighteen years) can take the
Equine Studies option leading to a National Certificate in Equine (Introductory
Skills), Level 2, and a more challenging National Certificate in Stable Practice (Level
4). They spend three hours a week in the classroom doing general research into the
care of horses, and two hours a week at the instructor's Thoroughbred farm doing
practical tasks with the horses. There are fourteen equine units for them to do in the
Introductory Course, including grooming, stable cleaning, maintenance and cleaning
of gear, floating, health care, care of stabled and paddocked horses, preparing for gen-

eral exercise, preparing for a show, knowledge of the industry and related careers, health and safety in the workplace, and the ability to communicate effectively in the workplace. The course can be spread over one to three years depending on knowledge and experience. There is also one basic riding unit: riding safely and leading horses by oneself and from another horse. The last unit is on poisonous plants and how to deal with them. The more advanced Stable Management Course includes most of the above units, plus helping to foal a mare, attending a horse at a race meeting, several units on fencing, and more on paddock care (field-care).

**Facilities:** Queen's is situated in Dunedin City (population about 110,000) and homestays are organized for foreign students.

## St. Peter's School

Private Bag 884, Cambridge, New Zealand. Phone: 0 7 827 9899. Fax: 0 7 827 9812. Email: info@stpeters.school.nz.
**Accreditation:** New Zealand Qualifications Authority
**Degrees Offered:** National Certificates
**Majors Offered:** Y9-13 Equine Studies. National Certificates in Equine: Introductory Skills (Level 2), Stable Practice (Level 3), Sporthorse (Level 4)
**Tuition Costs:** (NZ) Residents: $10,950/tuition, $18,500/boarding; Equestrian Program has additional fees
**Description of Program**: The aim of the Equestrian Program is to provide international and New Zealand students attending St. Peter's with the opportunity to improve their equestrian skills, further their knowledge of horsemastership, and attain unit standards. A special International Riding Program is available for a limited number of students. This program has the major focus on equestrian studies with a core academic program. A booklet outlining this program is available upon request. St. Peter's is one of two New Zealand schools approved to offer a Level 4 qualification, and the only school to offer a program designed specifically for international students. Equine Studies is offered from Y9 onwards. This self-directed study course consists of unit standards, the total course equivalent to approximately two years full-time correspondence study. The number of units completed each year varies from student to student. Modules include self-check questions and practical exercises designed to increase understanding. Unit standards may also be credited towards National Certificates in Equine and the NZ National Certificate of Education (NCEA).
**Facilities:** The 167 hectare farm on which the School is built lies amongst some of the most fertile pastureland in the world. Facilities include classroom, tack room, feed room, wash-down areas, large sand arena, several sets of show jumps, full cross-country training course, six sets of dressage equipment, contoured grass arena for show jumping championships, pens and covered stables, and individual grazing paddocks. All facilities are within a three-minute walk from the academic classroom blocks.
**Showing:** North Island Secondary Schools Dressage and Show Jumping Championships, home of Dressage Waikato (run New Zealand Equestrian Federation Graded dressage tournaments)

**Website:**
www.stpeters.school.nz

**Type of School:**
Private Years 7-13 Day and Boarding School

## Telford Rural Polytechnic

Private Bag 6, Balclutha, New Zealand. Phone: +64 3 418 1550. Fax: +64 3 418 3584. Email: enquiry@telford.ac.nz.
**Degrees Offered:** Certificate, National Certificate
**Majors Offered:** Equine Knowledge (C) via distance learning, Equine Studies (C) with

**Website:**
www.telford.ac.nz

**Type of School:**
Community College

concentrations in Equitation or Stable Management, Sport Horse (NC)

**Tuition Costs:** (NZ) Residents: $450; international: $5,500

**Description of Program:** The Equine Studies Certificate is the ultimate equine experience. The course provides the students with a broad base of knowledge that they will confidently carry with them into the equine industry, nationally and internationally. The course is made up of 34 weeks of full-time study at Telford, Monday to Friday, with weekend work required throughout the year. The program has also been changed to enable students to achieve the National Certificate in Sporthorse, Level 4. The course will become 40 weeks in length if the student chooses to include this. The ever-popular Telford Certificate in Equine Knowledge provides learning opportunities for those interested in horses. It is ideally suited for those who are currently employed in the equine industry; horse owners interested in learning more about horses; and parents of horse-crazy children. The Certificate is a one-year course. There are fourteen theory learning modules to complete, with three small practical assessments (no riding involved). Once the course requirements have been met, the student will receive the Telford Certificate in Equine Knowledge, and the relevant Unit Standards.

**Facilities:** Outdoor arena, covered arena, round yard, pens, stables, cross-country course

**Website:**
www.wintec.ac.nz

**Type of School:**
Community College,
Independent Study

## Waikato Institute of Technology

Dept. of Land Based Technology, Avalon Campus, Waikato Institute of Technology, Private Bag 3036, Hamilton 2020, New Zealand. Contact: Dr. John Simpson, Equine Programs Manager. Phone: +64 7 834 8806. Fax: +64 7 834 8805. Email: ahjxs@wintec.ac.nz.

**Accreditation:** Association of Polytechnics in New Zealand, the New Zealand Equine Industry Training Organisation

**Degrees Offered:** Certificate, Diploma in Technology, Distance Education

**Majors Offered:** Breeding, Sporthorse, Coaching, Stable Practice

**Tuition Costs:** (NZ) $3,500/year; room and board: $8,000/year

**Description of Program:** A leading provider of equine courses in New Zealand since 1989, the Waikato Institute of Technology is located 100 kilometers south of Auckland and in close proximity to many of New Zealand's leading racehorse breeders and trainers, as well as equestrian Olympic medalists. The outstanding facilities at Avalon campus are also home to the New Zealand Monty Roberts Courses. Few other equine institutions can draw on such a diversity of expertise (such as sports therapy, eco-tourism and veterinary nursing), which is in an area world-famous for the quality of its pasture. The Certificate, an amalgam and refining of the old Introductory and Advanced Equine Skills courses, is a 32-week course, eight weeks of which are off-campus with work experience providers. The 24 weeks spent on campus are an even mix of hands-on and classroom-based learning, the intention being to give students a broad theoretical and practical foundation. The Diploma in Technology course, with its Equine Endorsement, is a managerial course that was offered for the first time in 2002. The existing Distance Education course is being developed and adapted into a e-learning mode.

**Facilities:** Indoor arena, outdoor arena, stable block with ten full-size boxes, tack and feed rooms, toilets, workshop, wash-down bays, fifteen stalls

**Classroom/Hands-On Equine Classes:** 50:50

# NORWAY

## Norges veterinærhøgskole

Postboks 8146 Dep, 0033 Oslo, Norway. Phone: 22 96 45 00. Fax: 22 59 73 09.
Email: sekretariatet@veths.no.
**Majors Offered:** Veterinary Medicine

**Website:**
www.veths.no

**Type of School:**
Veterinary School

## Norwegian Equine College

The Norwegian Horse senter, Starum, 2850 Lena, Norway. Phone: +47 61 16 55 00.
Fax: +47 61 16 55 40. Email: nhest@nhest.no.
**Accreditation:** Nor NF, Department of Agriculture
**Degrees Offered:** Riding Instructors Level I-III, corresponding to the International
Group for Qualifications in Training Horse and Rider Levels I-III
**Majors Offered:** Riding Instructors, Grooms, Stable Management, Trotting & Racing
Trainer
**Tuition Costs:** (Euros) € 400-500/five-month course; includes room and board, sta-
bling, and (if necessary) horse rental
**Description of Program:** All teaching is given in Norwegian, so students must speak
at least one Scandinavian language (Danish, Swedish, or Norwegian) in order to take
courses. The NHS is situated in a commanding position overlooking the beautiful lake
of Mjøsa, approximately 100 kilometers north of Oslo, and about 60 kilometers south
of the Olympic town of Lillehammer on the northwest end of the lake. NHS is a foundation made up of sixteen nationwide horse and pony organizations. NHS has two
main departments: Education and Breeding. NHS was founded in 1986 and is under
the supervision of the Department of Agriculture. The education department provides
students with formal training in various aspects of the horse industry. Short courses
are held for private horse owners and horse lovers to improve their equine knowledge.
Courses for professionals include education for riding instructors, grooms, stable
managers, and trotting and racing trainers. The Breeding Department of NHS has an
advisor and staff responsible for organizing the evaluation of breeding stock at shows,
working with breeding plans, and training judges. The Breeding Department also reg-
isters the following breeds: the Dølehorse, the Fjordhorse, the Nordlands/Lyngshorse,
and the Warmblooded Riding Horse.
**Facilities:** Two riding halls (20m x60m and 20m x 40m), outdoor arenas for dressage,
show jumping, eventing, driving, Iceland horse riding, and trotting; student hotel and
dining hall, classroom with overhead projector and widescreen video
**Classroom/Hands-On Equine Classes:** Short courses and seminars are classroom-
only. Most courses are a combination of theory (30 percent) and practice (70 percent).
**Showing:** Dressage, show jumping, eventing, driving

**Website:**
www.nhest.no

**Type of School:**
Specialty School

## Norwegian Top Athelethichs Gymnasium for Elite riders

Skuiveien 40, 1313 Vøyenenga, Norway. Phone: +47 67 15 01 50. Email: ntg@ntg.no.

**Type of School:**
Specialty School

# THE PHILIPPINES

## University of the Philippines Los Baños

**Website:**
www.uplb.edu.ph

**Type of School:**
University

Graduate Schools, College, 4031 Laguna, Philippines. Phone: (63-49) 536-3414. Fax: (63-49) 536-2310. Email: cob@uplb.edu.ph.
**Degrees Offered:** Master of Science, Doctor of Veterinary Medicine
**Majors Offered:** Veterinary Medicine

# PORTUGAL

## Instituto Superior Técnico

**Website:**
www.ist.utl.pt

**Type of School:**
University

Av. Rovisco Pais, 1049-001 Lisboa, Portugal. Phone: +351-218417000. Fax: +351-218499242.
**Majors Offered:** Veterinary Medicine

# SLOVAKIA

## University of Veterinary Medicine in Kosice

**Website:**
www.uvm.sk

**Type of School:**
Public University

Komenského 73, Kosice 04181, Slovakia. Contact: Nicol Beregszásziová. Phone: +421 55 633 21 11-15 or 633 90 14. Fax: +421 55 632 36 66. Email: nicol@uvm.sk.
**Accreditation:** European Union
**Degrees Offered:** Doctor of Philosophy, Doctor of Veterinary Medicine
**Majors Offered:** Biochemistry (Ph.D.), Food Hygiene and Ecology (Ph.D.), Infection and Invasive Diseases (Ph.D.), Internal Diseases of Animals and Pharmacology (Ph.D.), Microbiology (Ph.D.), Veterinary Morphology (Ph.D.), Veterinary Surgery (Ph.D.), Veterinary Reproduction (Ph.D.), Veterinary Physiology (Ph.D.), Veterinary Medicine (D.V.M.)
**Tuition Costs:** (US) $7,700/academic year; $600/entrance fee
**Description of Program:** During the past decade, the University of Veterinary Medicine has established degree courses in Veterinary Medicine taught in English. The university accepts students from the UK/USA and other countries. The degrees are taught in English and qualify recipients for the RCVS entrance exam to practice in the UK and other countries. There are two courses available. The first course is designed for secondary school graduates, lasts five years, and qualifies the recipient for the D.V.M. The second course is designed for successful applicants with a B.Sc. in a life-science-related subject, lasts four years, and qualifies the recipient for the D.V.M. Every applicant for this course is expected to fulfill the terms of entry by passing entrance test in chemistry and biology. These tests are set at the level of the secondary school leaving examination. The university has currently registered undergraduates and postgraduates from the UK, USA, France, Germany, Spain, Israel, and others. Some opportunities are unique to this region (cultural and linguistic) whilst others are unique to the university (horse riding, skiing, etc.). Undergraduate student clubs and university-run courses welcome individuals with time and enthusiasm to devote to social, cultural, and charitable activities.

# SPAIN

## Centro Equestre Epona

Apartado De Correos No 86, Carmona 41410, Sevilla, Spain. Contact: Senor and Senora F. A. Garcia Carvajal. Phone: 00 34 6 08 155359. Fax: 00 34 9 54 148310.
Email: eponasevilla@interbooks.es.
**Accreditation:** British Horse Society
**Degrees Offered:** Certificate
**Majors Offered:** Up to BHS Assistant Instructor

**Website:**
www.btinternet.com/~epona/

**Type of School:**
Specialty School

## Escuela de Arte Ecuestre

Escuela de Arte Ecuestre Costa del Sol, Acuazahara, S.A., N-340 Km. 159 Rio Padron Alto, s/n., Apartado de Correos 266, 29680 - Estepona (Malaga - Spain).
Phone: (+34)952-80-80-77. Fax: (+34)952-80-80-78. Email: arteecue@ctv.es.
**Accreditation:** British Horse Society
**Degrees Offered:** Certificate
**Majors Offered:** BHS Stages 1 and 2
**Tuition Costs:** Vary
**Description of Program:** Students can study for the British Horse Society Examinations. All courses are tailored to suit the individual.
**Facilities:** Covered school, outdoor arena, no housing provided
**Classroom/Hands-On Equine Classes:** Vary
**Showing:** Students have the opportunity to compete.

**Website:**
www.escuela-ecuestre.com

**Type of School:**
Specialty School

## Manas de la Hoz

Escuela de Formacion Ecuestre, 39776 Liendo, Cantabria, Spain. Phone: 00 34 942 643014. Fax: 00 34 9 42 677460. Email: info@manasdelahoz.com.
**Accreditation:** British Horse Society
**Degrees Offered:** Certificate
**Majors Offered:** BHS Stages 1 and 2

**Website:**
www.manasdelahoz.com

**Type of School:**
Specialty School

## Universidad de León

Secretaría General, Pabellón de Gobierno, Avda. de la Facultad n°25, 24071-LEON, Spain. Phone: 987 29 16 19 or 987 29 16 17. Fax: 987 29 16 14.
Email: secgen@unileon.es.
**Majors Offered:** Veterinary Medicine

**Website:**
www.unileon.es

**Type of School:**
University

# SWEDEN

## Swedish University of Agricultural Sciences

**Website:**
www.slu.se or www.slu.se/eng/index.html

**Type of School:**
Public University

Equine Study Program, SLU Box 7046, 750 07 Uppsala, Sweden. Contact: Anna-Lena Holgersson. Phone: 46 (0) 18 672143. Fax: + 46 (0) 18 672199. Email: Anna-Lena.Holgersson@hipp.slu.se.

**Degrees Offered:** University Diploma, Master of Science

**Majors Offered:** Equine Studies (UD), Veterinary Medicine (M.Sc.)

**Tuition Costs:** Contact School

**Description of Program:** The rapidly expanding horse sector in Sweden has created an increasing need for well educated people in the area of horse management in its broadest sense. In 1994, the government gave the Swedish University of Agricultural Sciences the task of developing and heading a specific, two-year, university program in equine studies. This education combines theoretical studies with practical application and also develops the students' riding and driving skills. To make this possible, the program is located at the three main horse establishments in Sweden: Flyinge (stud), Strömsholm (riding pedagogics) and Wången (trotting/racing). In order to participate in the program, candidates need to have completed an upper secondary education (high school) with special attention to biology, riding skills and practical work with horses. The final selection of students takes place after a one-day admission test. The basic year is spent at Flyinge. The main subject is the horse as a biological being from sperm and egg to performance horse. In the second year, the students have to specialize in one of three different areas: Stable Management, Riding Instructor, or Trotting/Racing, all of which are arranged at the three different establishments. The quality of the program is secured by use of internationally recognized trainers and professors.

**Classroom/Hands-On Equine Classes:** 50:50

**Showing:** There are opportunities for competition.

# SWITZERLAND

## Leysin American School

**Website:**
www.las.ch

**Type of School:**
Secondary Boarding School

Families in North and South America: Mr. Paul E. Dyer, U.S. Director of Admissions, P.O. Box 7154, Portsmouth, NH 03802. Phone: (603) 431-7654. Fax: (603) 431-1280. Email: usadmissions@las.ch. Families outside of North and South America: Mr. Timothy Kelley, Director of Admissions, Leysin American School, 1854 Leysin, Switzerland. Phone: +41-24-493-3934. Fax: +41-24-494-1585. Email: admissions@las.ch.

**Accreditation:** European Council of International Schools, the Middle States Association of Colleges and Schools, the Department of Swiss Private Education, Swiss Group of International Schools member, Advanced Placement, College Board, the International Baccalaureate Organization

**Degrees Offered:** High School Diploma

**Tuition Costs:** (US) $29,500

**Description of Program:** Leysin American School offers horseback riding lessons through the Manège de Leysin Riding School. Group lessons are offered as an afternoon activity for beginner, intermediate, and advanced level riders in the fall and spring. Lessons are 1 1/2 hours long and include half an hour of theory and an hour of riding; dressage and jumping according to the students level. A participation certificate will be given out after each session (five weeks) and those students who complete all three sessions within a school year receive a prize. Class divisions are determined by the English-speaking instructor: Beginners: Those with no riding experience. Intermediate: Those who have been through Beginners or who have prior riding experience. Advanced: Those who have prior experience and are able to do jumping and dressage. Advanced riders usually participate in competitions. Private lessons may also be arranged through the activities office. In addition to lessons, there are other activities, such as trail rides, game days, horse carriage, three regular competitions throughout the year and even skijoring—horse surfing!

## University of Bern

Hochschulstrasse 4, CH-3012 Bern, Switzerland. Phone: +41 (0)31 631 39 11.
Fax: +41 (0)31 631 80 08. Email: kanzlei@imd.unibe.ch.
**Majors Offered:** Veterinary Medicine

**Website:**
www.unibe.ch

**Type of School:**
University

## University of Zurich

Faculty of Veterinary Medicine, Tierspital (Deanery), Winterthurstrasse 252, 8057 Zurich, Switzerland. Phone: 01/634 11 11. Fax: 01/634 23 04.
**Degrees Offered:** Doctor of Philosophy, Doctor of Veterinary Medicine
**Majors Offered:** Veterinary Medicine

**Website:**
www.vet.unizh.ch

**Type of School:**
University

# TAIWAN

## National Chung Hsing University

Department of Veterinary Medicine, National Chung Hsing University, 250, Kuo Kuang Road, Taichung, Taiwan 402, Republic of China. Phone: 886-4-2284-0368~9. Fax: 886-4-2286-2073. Email: vmnchu@mail.nchu.edu.tw.
**Degrees Offered:** Bachelor of Science, Master of Science, Doctor of Philosophy
**Majors Offered:** Veterinary Medicine (B.Sc., M.Sc., Ph.D.), Veterinary Microbiology (M.Sc.), Veterinary Pathology (M.Sc.)

**Website:**
www.nchu.edu.tw

**Type of School:**
University

# THAILAND

## Chulalongkorn University

Faculty of Veterinary Medicine, 254 Phyathai Road, Patumwan, Bangkok, Thailand 10330. Phone: +662-215-0871-3. Fax: +662-215-4804. Email: info@chula.ac.th.
**Majors Offered:** Veterinary Science

**Website:**
www.vet.chula.ac.th

**Type of School:**
University

# UNITED ARAB EMIRATES

**Type of School:**
Specialty School

## Dubai Equestrian Centre

P.O. Box 292, Dubai, United Arab Emirates. Contact: Ms. Jennifer Pyke.
Phone: 00 9714 361394.
**Accreditation:** British Horse Society
**Degrees Offered:** Certificate
**Majors Offered:** Up to BHS Assistant Instructor

# UNITED KINGDOM

## England, United Kingdom

### Avon, England

**Type of School:**
Specialty School

## Clevedon Riding Centre

Clevedon Lane, Clevedon, Avon, BS21 7AG England. Contact: R A & J A Sims.
Phone: 01275 858 699.
**Accreditation:** British Horse Society
**Degrees Offered:** Certificate
**Majors Offered:** BHS Stage 1 and 2

**Website:**
www.bris.ac.uk

**Type of School:**
University

## University of Bristol

University of Bristol, Southwell St., Bristol, Avon BS2-8EJ U.K.. Phone: +44 11795
46939. Fax: 44-177-925-4794. Email: admissions@bristol.ac.uk.
**Degrees Offered:** Bachelor of Science (Hons), Bachelor of Veterinary Science
**Majors Offered:** Equine Science (B.Sc.), Veterinary Science (B.V.Sc.)

**Website:**
www.uwe.ac.uk

**Type of School:**
Public University

## University of the West of England–Bristol

Coldharbour Lane, Bristol BS16 1QY England. Phone: 01179 656261.
Email: Admissions@uwe.ac.uk or enquire@hartpury.ac.uk.
**Degrees Offered:** Higher National Certificate, Higher National Diploma, Bachelor of
Arts (Hons), Bachelor of Science (Hons)
**Majors Offered:** Equine Business Management (B.A.), Equine Science (H.N.C.,
H.N.D., B.S.)

**Type of School:**
Specialty School

## Urchinwood Manor Equitation Centre

Congresbury, Avon BS19 5AP. Contact: Capt. P. J. Hall. Phone: +44 01934 833248.
Fax: +44 01934 834683.
**Accreditation:** British Horse Society, Association of British Riding Schools
**Degrees Offered:** Certificate, Diploma, Working Student

**Majors Offered:** ABRS Assistant Groom (C), ABRS Groom (D), BHS Stages 1-4 (C), BHS Assistant Instructor (C), BHS Intermediate Instructor (C), NVQ Levels 1 & 2 (C)

# Berkshire, England

## Berkshire College of Agriculture

Hall Place, Burchetts Green, Nr. Maidenhead, Berkshire, SL6 6QR England.
Phone: 01628 824444. Fax: 01628 824695. Email: enquiries@bca.ac.uk.
**Degrees Offered:** First Diploma, National Certificate, National Diploma, Advanced National Certificate, Higher National Diploma, Bachelor of Arts (Honours)
**Majors Offered:** Horse Care (FD), Horse Management (ND), Equine Business Management (ANC), Equine Studies with Management (HND), Equine Industry Management (B.A.), Equine Sports Performance (HNC, HND, B.A.), Management of Horses (NC)

**Website:**
www.bca.ac.uk

**Type of School:**
Public College

## Blacknest Gate Riding Centre

Blacknest Gate, Mill Lane, Sunninghill, SL5 0PS. Contact: Mrs. J. Newstead.
Phone: 01344 876871.
**Accreditation:** British Horse Society
**Degrees Offered:** Certificate
**Majors Offered:** BHS Stages 1 and 2

**Type of School:**
Specialty School

## Checkendon Equestrian Centre

Lovegrove's Lane, Checkendon, Reading RG8 0NE. Contact: Ms. Tarrant.
Phone: 01491 680225.
**Accreditation:** British Horse Society
**Degrees Offered:** Certificate
**Majors Offered:** BHS Stages 1 and 2

**Type of School:**
Specialty School

## Intelligent Horsemanship from Kelly Marks

Lethornes, Lambourn, Hungerford, Berkshire RG17 8QS England.
Phone: 01488 71300. Fax: 01488 73783. Email: kelly@montyroberts.co.uk.
**Accreditation:** Approved by Monty Roberts
**Degrees Offered:** Monty Roberts' Preliminary Certificate
**Majors Offered:** Horsemanship
**Tuition Costs:** (Pounds) £1,448 for all courses or £75 for one day
**Description of Program:** The "Monty Roberts Preliminary Certificate of Horsemanship" is now in modular form, making it easier and more accessible for the average horseperson to learn these unique methods. Any module can be taken on a freestanding basis, purely for pleasure and education. However, if you would like to work towards gaining the "Monty Roberts Preliminary Certificate of Horsemanship" it is necessary to be a member of the Intelligent Horsemanship Association and successfully complete the program. Stage One: Five-day Foundation Course, plus weekend courses, Handling the Young Foal/Stud Practice, Feeding and Nutrition/The Horse as an Athlete, Horse Psychology Weekend. There will also be a Horse Psychology Project

**Website:**
www.intelligenthorsemanship.co.uk

**Type of School:**
Specialty School

to be completed at home and presented on the final part of the modular program. The Stage Two Five-Day Course is not available to be taken until all other modules are completed.

**Facilities:** A 40-acre stud farm near Witney, Oxfordshire, with an indoor barn for some horse work, as well as heated, indoor facilities for student lectures, etc.

**Classroom/Hands-On Equine Classes:** Horse Psychology is 100 percent classroom-based, Handling the Young Foal/Stud Practice is 75 percent classroom, and Feeding and Nutrition/The Horse as an Athlete is mostly classroom.

# Buckinghamshire, England

## Gillian Watson International Equestrian Training

**Website:**
www.britisheventing.com/training

**Type of School:**
Specialty School

Hyde Farm West, Hyde Lane, Great Missenden, Buckinghamshire HP16 0RF England. Contact: Mrs. Gillian Watson. Phone: 01494 866023. Fax: 01494 863758. Mobile: 07860 533357. Email: gill.watsonfbhs@btinternet.com.

**Accreditation:** British Horse Society; Gillian Watson is a Fellow of the BHS, a British Eventing Accredited Trainer, and an FEI dressage judge.

**Majors Offered:** Eventing

**Tuition Costs:** (Pounds) £40/private lesson, £30/shared lesson

**Description of Program:** Competition training to international level. All standards of horse and rider combinations are welcome, from Pre-Novice to Advanced. As trainer of the British Junior (15 to 18 years) and Young Rider (18 to 21 years) three-day-event teams, Gill specializes in training young people towards all aspects of eventing. Working pupils can train with their horses at the Gill Watson Centre, generally for periods of three months or more, although a shorter stay can be arranged. During this time, the students will receive hands-on training, aiming at practical horsemanship.

**Facilities:** Indoor school, international-size outdoor arena, cross-country schooling fences, show jumping field, horse walker, some off-road riding, small student's room where lectures and other activities take place, stabling for student horses usually available, accommodation for students arranged locally

**Showing:** Students are encouraged to compete in all disciplines during their training.

## Horses and Courses Ltd.

**Website:**
www.horsesandcourses.co.uk

**Type of School:**
Specialty School, Independent Study

Crawley Grange, North Crawley, Buckinghamshire MK16 9HL England. Contact: Beth Maloney, Director of Studies. Phone: 01727 751133. Fax: 08707 065295.

**Accreditation:** BTEC approved

**Degrees Offered:** BTEC National Certificate, BTEC National Diploma, BTEC Advanced Certificate, BTEC Advanced Diploma

**Majors Offered:** Equine Studies

**Tuition Costs:** (Pounds) £55 to £300 per course

**Description of Program:** The Equine Owners Series has been designed for those who are new to home study and want to improve or update their knowledge. Courses are written by experienced professionals, including Beth Maloney author of *Nutrition and the Feeding of Horses* and *The Equine Body*. There are currently ten courses to choose from, and every course is designed to be tailored to your own horse or pony. The Professional Series leads to a BTEC National Certificate and National Diploma in Equine Studies. These courses are divided into Standard Modules, Advanced Modules, and Specialist Modules. Modules can be either studied individually to further your own knowledge or achieve a Certificate of Achievement, or they can be studied in series to build up to a National Certificate or National Diploma Certificate. The Equine National Vocational Qualification Support Packs: This series is designed to support students training in the industry for the N.V.Q level 1, 2, or 3 in Horse Care. National Vocational Qualifications (NVQs) are a qualification offered by many training yards and involves practical training and assessment, along with the production of a "portfolio of evidence." All studies are done from students' homes, and there are no exams to take, as everything is assessed through assignment/case study work.

**Facilities:** Your own backyard and a training center near you.

## Cambridgeshire, England

### The College of West Anglia

Milton Centre, Landbeach Road, Milton, Cambridgeshire CB4 6DB. Phone: (0)1223 860701. Wisbech Centre, Newcommon, Bridge Wisbech, Cambridgeshire PE13 2SJ. Phone: (0)1945 581024. Email: enquiries@col-westanglia.ac.uk.

**Accreditation:** British Horse Society, BTEC

**Degrees Offered:** Certificate, First Diploma, First Certificate, Foundation Course, National Certificate, National Diploma, Higher National Diploma

**Majors Offered:** Up to BHS Intermediate Instructor (C), Horse Care (FD, FC, Fd.C.), Horse Management (NC, ND), Land-Based Industries (HND)

**Website:**
www.col-westanglia.ac.uk

**Type of School:**
College of Further Education Training

### University of Cambridge

Department of Clinical Veterinary Medicine, Madingley Road, Cambridge, CB3 OES, UK Contact: General Admissions: Dr. H.J. Field, or Equine Course: Dr. FMD Henson. Phone: +44 1223 337647. Fax: +44 1223 337610. Email: enquiries@vet.cam.ac.uk or hjf10@cam.ac.uk (Field) or fmdh1@cam.ac.uk (Henson).

**Accreditation:** Royal College of Veterinary Surgeons

**Degrees Offered:** VetMB

**Majors Offered:** Course for veterinary surgeons only

**Tuition Costs:** Contact School

**Description of Program:** Traditional UK program which builds on preclinical courses in anatomy, physiology, genetics, nutrition,and pathology. Lecture courses in Years 4 and 5 are supplemented with introductory clinical rotations; clinical teaching in final year is 100 percent practical rotations in the referral hospital.

**Facilities:** Modern equine referral hospital with four faculty, one resident and one intern, in-patient stabling for twelve horses, day patient center; surgical suites, imaging (scintigraphy, ultrasonography, radiography, thermograpHandhy)

**Classroom/Hands-On Equine Classes:** Equine-specific teaching occurs in Years 4, 5, and 6 of the course. Year 4 Equine Teaching is 20 percent practical; Year 5 Equine Teaching is 30 percent practical; Year 6 Equine Teaching is 100 percent practical (clinical rotations).

**Website:**
www.vet.cam.ac.uk

**Type of School:**
Public University

## Cheshire, England

### Bold Heath Equestrian Centre

Heath House Farm, Bold Heath, Widnes, Cheshire, WA8 3XT England. Contact: Mrs. J. E. Baker. Phone: 0151 424 5151.

**Type of School:**
Specialty School

**Accreditation:** British Horse Society
**Degrees Offered:** Certificate
**Majors Offered:** Up to BHS Intermediate Instructor

## Foxes Riding School

Badgers Rake Lane, Ledsham, South Wirral, Cheshire L66 8PF.
Contact: Mrs. J.E. Davey. Phone: 0151 339 6797. Fax: 0151 339 5926.
**Degrees Offered:** Certificate
**Majors Offered:** BHS Stages 1-4, NVQ Level 3

## Reaseheath College

Reaseheath, Nantwich, Cheshire CW5 6DF England. Phone: 01270 625131. Fax: 01270 625 665. Email: enquiries@reaseheath.ac.uk.
**Accreditation:** British Horse Society
**Degrees Offered:** Edexcel, Certificate, First Diploma, National Award, National Certificate, National Diploma, Higher National Diploma, Bachelor of Science (Hons)
**Majors Offered:** BHS Stage 1, 2, 3, & PTT (C), Equine Management (HND), Equine Studies (ND), Equine Studies, Business Management & Marketing (B.Sc.), Horse Care (FD), Horse Studies (NC), NVQ Stage 2 (C)
**Tuition Costs:** Tuition and housing costs vary
**Description of Program:** The Horse Care Program is designed to give you some practical experience with horses in a safe environment. As part of the course, you will also have a minimum of three weeks planned work experience that will help you to develop a good level of competence when handling horses. The Horse Studies Course comprises both theoretical and practical studies, including practical work experience within the equine industry. Practical yard duties are an essential feature of the course, and will be undertaken on the college equine unit on a rotating basis. In the Equine Studies Course, students will gain an academic qualification and substantial practical skills, enabling them to continue onto higher education or find employment within the equine industry. At least six weeks of work experience is included in the course. The HND in Equine Management Course prepares students for management-level careers in the equine and associated industries once experience is gained, and is a stepping-stone to the B.Sc. (Hons). In the B.Sc. (Hons) Course, the first three semesters are based at Reaseheath College, making full use of the equine facilities. Students then undertake a twelve-month industrial placement. The final three semesters are based at Harper Adams University College for Business Studies and Marketing.
**Facilities:** The superb practical facilities now include tack rooms, a feed room, demonstration areas, a cross-country course, and three lecturing rooms. In addition, there is stabling for over 35 horses, two magnificent 60ft x 30ft arenas, and a veterinary equine clinic for student hands-on experience in a variety of veterinary procedures.
**Classroom/Hands-On Equine Classes:** 50:50
**Showing:** The students can take part in in-house competitions, dressage, and show jumping.

## Ryder Farm Equestrian Centre

Manchester Road, Kearsley, Bolton, Cheshire BL4 8RU England.
Contact: Mr. P. C. Reading. Phone: 0161 7940058.

**Accreditation:** British Horse Society
**Degrees Offered:** Certificate
**Majors Offered:** Up to BHS Assistant Instructor

## Willington Hall Riding Centre

Willington, Nr Tarporley, Cheshire CW6 0NA England.
Contact: Mr. & Mrs. K. Hassett. Phone: 01829 751920.
**Accreditation:** British Horse Society
**Degrees Offered:** Certificate
**Majors Offered:** Up to BHS Assistant Instructor

**Type of School:**
Specialty School

# Cornwall, England

## Association of British Riding Schools

Queen's Chambers, 38/40 Queen Street, Penzance, Cornwall TR18 4BH England.
Phone: 01736 369440. Fax: 01736 351390. Email: office@abrs.org.
**Degrees Offered:** Certificate, Diploma
**Majors Offered:** Preliminary Horse Care & Riding Level 1-2 (C), Grooms (C, D), Initial Teaching Award, Teaching (C), Advanced Teaching (D), Riding School Principal (D)
**Tuition Costs:** Contact ABRS
**Description of Program:** The ABRS Examinations System was created by employers to produce the type of employee the industry requires in teaching and stable management. The ABRS Examiners are carefully selected; they have knowledge, examining and assessing ability, train to all levels of riding and stable management and–above all–are employers in the industry. The number of examiners is kept small so that the same standard is maintained. All ABRS Examinations are of a very practical nature–no written papers are required, but there is a need for an underpinning knowledge and an understanding of the reasons for the various tasks associated with stable routine. There is only an examination fee to pay–no membership fee is required. Jobs available in the horse industry at home and abroad are many and varied, rewarding and interesting. The ABRS qualifications are graded from foundation certificates to diploma standard.
**Facilities:** Vary
**Classroom/Hands-On Equine Classes:** Vary

**Website:**
www.abrs.org

**Type of School:**
Specialty School

## Duchy College

Stoke Climsland, Callington, Cornwall, PL17 8PB. Contact: Admissions. Phone: 01579 372223. Fax: 01579 372200. Email: stoke.enquiries@duchy.cornwall.ac.uk.
**Accreditation:** Associate of Cornwall College
**Degrees Offered:** National Certificate, Advanced Certificate, First Diploma, National Diploma, Foundation Degrees - Fd.Sc., Fd.A
**Majors Offered:** Equine and Business Management (EBM), Equine Sports Performance (Fd.Sc.), Equine Behavior and Training (Fd.Sc.), Horse Studies (ND), Management of Horses (NC, ANC)
**Description of Program:** Progression of Courses: Route 1: (1) First Diploma in Equine Studies (BHS Stages 1 and 2) leads to (2) National Diploma in Horse Studies

**Website:**
www.duchy.ac.uk

**Type of School:**
Further and Higher Education College

(BHS Stages 3 and PTT), which leads to (3) employment or Foundation Degree in Equine Sports Performance or Equine Behavior and Training which leads to (4) B.Sc. (Hons) in Animal Science (Equine) and Applied Equine Studies with the University Plymouth. Route 2: (1) BTEC National Diploma in Business with Equine (EBM) (BHS Stages 1 to 3 and PTT) leads to (2) employment or Foundation Degree in Equine Sports Performance or Equine Behavior and Training which leads to (3) B.Sc. (Hons) in Animal Science (Equine) and Applied Equine Studies with the University of Plymouth. Route 3: (1) NVQ work-based training up to Level 2 or 3 can lead to (2) BTEC National Certificate in the Management of Horses (BHS Stages 1 & 2 and PTT), which leads to (3) employment followed by the Advanced Certificate in Equine Studies (BHS Stage 3 and AI), which leads to (4) employment within the industry.

**Facilities:** Two indoor schools, one international-size outdoor arena, 60 stalls, five-horse covered horse walker, tack rooms, 3,300-meter cross-country course with 40 jumps, including water obstacles

**Showing:** Duchy College Equestrian Centre is one of the largest show centers in the southwest running more than 60 shows per year for outside clients and students. The competitions include the BHTA Horse Trials in July, an international dressage competition in May, and BSJA Showjumping all year.

## TM International School of Horsemanship

**Website:**
www.tminternational.co.uk

**Type of School:**
Specialty School

Sunrising Riding Centre, Henwood, Near Liskeard, Cornwall PL14 5BP England. Phone: 01579 362895. Fax: 01579 363646. Email: enquiries@tminternational.co.uk.
**Accreditation:** British Horse Society. Training center for Duchy College.
**Degrees Offered:** Certificate, Working Pupil
**Majors Offered:** B.H.S. Horse Owner's Certificate Levels 1-4, British National Vocational Qualifications 1-3 in Horse Care, BHS Groom, BHS Assistant Instructor
**Tuition Costs:** (Pounds) No tuition for working pupil; £70 per week room and board
**Description of Program:** Training working pupils to BHSAI (fast track). A B.H.S. approved training center and also a satellite training center for Cornwall's Duchy College. Students are trained for equestrian careers and there is a particularly high pass rate. Tuition in flat work, show jumping, and cross-country jumping, in our all-weather sand school and cross-country course is offered. Lessons are always targeted at individual needs, whether you are looking for a private longe lesson to eradicate a particular fault, or want to brush up on your general skills with a series of lessons. Group lessons seldom include more than six pupils of a similar standard, often only three or four.
**Facilities:** Two outdoor arenas, cross-country course

## Wheal Buller Riding School

**Website:**
www.cornish-riding-holidays.co.uk

**Type of School:**
Working Yard, Specialty School

Buller Hill, Redruth, Cornwall TR16 6ST England. Phone: 01209 211852.
Email: info@cornish-riding-holidays.co.uk.
**Accreditation:** British Horse Society, Association of British Riding Schools, Regional Tourist Board
**Degrees Offered:** Certificate
**Majors Offered:** Horse Care, Stable Management, Riding
**Tuition Costs:** (Pounds) £14/hr; accommodation £495/week for adults, £295 for children
**Description of Program:** Tuition is provided up to and including B.H.S. Stage IV, B.H.S. A.I., ABRS Teaching Certificate, and N.V.Q. III. There is a working yard (cur-

rently 50 horses and ponies) that caters to local riders, residential holiday guests, working students, the yard's own competition horses, and liveries. Courses, lessons, hacks, beach rides, and fully-inclusive riding holidays for adults and unaccompanied children are offered.

**Facilities:** Purpose-built indoor and outdoor arenas, open fields with cross-country jumps, good access to countryside, extensive network of bridleways

# Cumbria, England

## Cumbria School of Saddlery

Redhills, Penrith, Cumbria CA11 0DL England. Phone: 01768 899919.
Email: davidmay@saddlerycourses.com.
**Accreditation:** Society of Master Saddlers, approved City & Guilds Skill Training Centre
**Degrees Offered:** Certificate of Attendance
**Majors Offered:** Handstitching, Intermediate, Saddlery Repairs, Improvers

**Website:**
www.saddlerycourses.com

**Type of School:**
Specialty School

## Lakeland Equestrian Centre

Wynlass Beck, Windermere, Cumbria LA23 1EU England. Phone: 015394 43811.
Fax: 015394 48717. Email: info@lakelandequestrian.co.uk.
**Accreditation:** British Horse Society, Association of British Riding Schools, National Vocational Qualifications
**Degrees Offered:** Certificate, Diploma
**Majors Offered:** ABRS Groom (C, D), BHS PTT & IT, BHS Riding and Road Safety, BHS Stages 1-4, Fire, First Aid at Work, NVQ Breeding, NVQ Driving, NVQ Equitation, NVQ Levels 1-3, Transport

**Website:**
www.lakelandequestrian.co.uk

**Type of School:**
Specialty School

## University of Central Lancashire

Cumbria Campus, Newton Rigg , Penrith, Cumbria CA11 0AH England.
Phone: 01768 863791. Fax: 01772 894990. Email: cumbriainfo@uclan.ac.uk.
**Degrees Offered:** Foundation Degree
**Majors Offered:** Equine Tourism (Fd.Sc.)

**Website:**
www.uclan.ac.uk

**Type of School:**
University

# Derbyshire, England

## Barleyfields Equestrian Centre

Ash Lane, Etwall, Derbyshire DE65 6HT England. Phone/Fax: 01283 734798.
Email: barleyfields@talk21.com.
**Degrees Offered:** Certificate
**Majors Offered:** BHS Stages 1-3, BHS PTT, NVQ Levels 1-3

**Website:**
www.barleyfields.com

**Type of School:**
Specialty School

## Hargate Equestrian

Egginton Rd., Hilton, Derbyshire DE65 5FJ England. Phone: 01283 730 606.
Fax: 01283 732 589. Email: info@hargateequestrian.co.uk.
**Accreditation:** British Horse Society

**Website:**
www.hargateequestrian.co.uk

**Type of School:**
Specialty School

**Degrees Offered:** Certificate
**Majors Offered:** NVQ Level 1-3, BHS Stages 1-4
**Tuition Costs:** Contact School
**Description of Program:** Contact School
**Facilities:** Indoor and outdoor floodlit school, tuition theater, no housing
**Classroom/Hands-On Equine Classes:** NVQ/BHS Students: one hour classroom tuition and the rest practical per day
**Showing:** Unaffiliated and affiliated show jumping, dressage, and trailblazers

**Type of School:**
Specialty School

## Hargate Hill Riding School

Hargate Hill, Glossop, Derbyshire SK13 9JL United Kingdom.
Contact: Mr. and Mrs. Tyldesley. Phone: 01457 865518.
**Accreditation:** British Horse Society
**Degrees Offered:** Certificate
**Majors Offered:** BHS Stages 1 and 2

**Type of School:**
Specialty School

## Ringer Villa Equestrian Centre

Ringer Lane, Clowne, Derbyshire, S43 4BX United Kingdom.
Contact: Mrs. Y. M. Evans. Phone: 01246 810 456.
**Accreditation:** British Horse Society
**Degrees Offered:** Certificate
**Majors Offered:** BHS Stages 1 and 2

# Devon, England

**Website:**
www.bicton.ac.uk

**Type of School:**
Public College

## Bicton College

East Budleigh, Budleigh Salterton, Devon EX9 7BY. England. Phone: 01395 568353. Email: enquiries@bicton.ac.uk.
**Accreditation:** The British Horse Society, City and Guilds, the Government
**Degrees Offered:** Advanced National Certificate, Foundation Degree, National Certificate, National Diploma, National Traineeship
**Majors Offered:** Equine Business Management (ANC), Equine Studies (Fd.Sc.), Management of Horses (NC), Horse Management (ND), Horse Care and Management (NT)
**Tuition Costs:** (Pounds) £738 standard; £1,175 Foundation Degree; £3795 Foundation Degree overseas; £3,500 (estimate) room and board
**Description of Program:** Equine Business Management: The course provides you with comprehensive training in all aspects of equine business management and gives sound practical training in the care and handling of horses. You will be prepared for the British Horse Society Stage Four and Intermediate Instructors Certificate. Equine Studies: The modules include business management, husbandry, veterinary science, and conformation and soundness. Optional modules include equitation, equine behavior, fitness and training, therapy, exercise physiology, competition preparation, and breeding and stud management. Management of Horses: The course provides a sound practical and theoretical training in the care and management of horses, which will prepare you for the British Horse Society Stage Three and Preliminary Instructors Certificate. Horse Management: The course provides you with comprehensive training

in all aspects of management within the horse industry and enables you to take BHS examinations. Horse Care and Management: This course enables you to gain experience in the industry an ideal first step towards taking a full-time course at a later date. Your work is assessed in the workplace; you may come into school for one-week blocks of training during the year.

**Facilities:** Equestrian center is on campus with stabling for 39 horses, indoor school (20m x 40m), outdoor arena (30m x 60m), show jumps, and cross-country fences.

**Classroom/Hands-On Equine Classes:** NC and ND/60:40; F Deg/70:30

**Showing:** Students may show if they have their own horses; if not, they can show within the college when the second-year students organize shows for the first-year students.

## Honeysuckle Farm Equestrian Centre

Type of School:
Specialty School

Haccombe with Combe, Newton Abbot, Devon TQ12 4SA England. Contact: Mr. and Mrs. I. G. Mackay. Phone: +44 (0)1626 355 944. Fax: +44 (0)1626 332 884.
**Accreditation:** British Horse Society
**Degrees Offered:** Certificate
**Majors Offered:** Up to BHS Assistant Instructor

## North Devon Equestrian Centre

Type of School:
Specialty School

Shirwell, Barnstaple, Devon EX31 4HR England.
Contact: Mr. Paul Jennings & Ms Sarah Jeffrey. Phone: 01271 850 864.
**Accreditation:** British Horse Society
**Degrees Offered:** Certificate
**Majors Offered:** BHS Stages 1-3

# Dorset, England

## Bryanston Riding Centre

Type of School:
Specialty School

Bryanston School, Blandford Forum, Dorset DT11 0PX England. Contact: Miss Deborah K Gooden - Head of Riding. Phone: 01258 484565. Fax: 01258 484657.
**Accreditation:** British Horse Society
**Degrees Offered:** Certificate
**Majors Offered:** Up to BHS Intermediate Instructor

## The Fortune Centre of Riding Therapy

Type of School:
Specialty School

Avon Tyrrell, Bransgore, Christchurch, Dorset BH23 8EE England. Contact: Mrs. J. Dixon-Clegg. Phone: 01425 673 297. Fax: 01425 674 320.
**Accreditation:** British Horse Society
**Degrees Offered:** Certificate
**Majors Offered:** BHS Stages 1-2

## Kingston Maurward College

Website:
www.kmc.ac.uk

Type of School:
Community College

Dorchester, Dorset DT2 8PY England. Phone: +44 (0)1305 215 063. Fax: +44 (0)1305 215001. Email: administration@kmc.ac.uk.
**Accreditation:** British Horse Society
**Degrees Offered:** Certificate, First Diploma, National Certificate, National Diploma
**Majors Offered:** Up to BHS Instructor (C), Equine Studies (FD, NC, ND)

## Pound Cottage Riding Centre

Type of School:
Specialty School

Luccombe Farm, Milton Abbas, Blandford, Dorset DT11 0BD England.
Contact: Mrs. J Hardy. Phone: 01258 880057/451240.
**Accreditation:** British Horse Society, Association of British Riding Schools
**Degrees Offered:** Certificate
**Majors Offered:** BHS Stages 1-2 and PTT
**Description of Program:** Instruction for all ages and abilities, safe hacking in forestry and farmland, evening lessons/courses, residential holidays for unaccompanied children, and all types of livery.
**Facilities:** One outdoor arena, one covered arena, cross-country course

## Durham, England

## Low Fold Riding Centre

Type of School:
Specialty School

Low Fold Farm, Sunnybrow, Crook, Co Durham, DL15 0RL England.
Contact: Miss M. Hedley. Phone: 01388 747313. Fax: 01388 747055.
**Accreditation:** British Horse Society
**Degrees Offered:** Certificate
**Majors Offered:** Up to BHS Intermediate Instructor

## Essex, England

## Eastminster School of Riding

Website:
www.eastminster.co.uk

Type of School:
Specialty School

Hooks Hall Farm, The Chase, Upper Rainham Road, Romford, Essex RM7 0SS England. Phone: 01708 447423. Email: david_ackland@hotmail.com.
**Degrees Offered:** Certificate
**Majors Offered:** BHS Stages 1-3

## Rayne Riding Centre

Type of School:
Specialty School

Fairy Hall Lane, Rayne, Braintree, Essex CM8 8SZ England. Contact: Mr. B. R. Pewter. Phone: 01376 322 231.
**Accreditation:** British Horse Society
**Degrees Offered:** Certificate
**Majors Offered:** Up to BHS Assistant Instructor

## Runningwell Equestrian Club

Warren Road, Rettendon Common, Chlemsford, Essex CM3 8DG England.
Contact: Miss R. Nixon. Phone: 01268 711221.
**Accreditation:** British Horse Society
**Degrees Offered:** Certificate
**Majors Offered:** Up to BHS Assistant Instructor

Type of School:
Specialty School

## Writtle College

Chelmsford, Essex CM1 3RR England. Phone: 01245 424200. Fax: 01245 420456.
Email: equine@writtle.ac.uk.
**Accreditation:** British Horse Society
**Degrees Offered:** Certificate, First Diploma, National Diploma, National Certificate, Advanced National Certificate, Higher National Certificate, Foundation Degree, Bachelor of Science (Hons), Master of Science
**Majors Offered:** BHS Stages 2-3 (C), Human and Equine Sports Science (M.Sc.), Equine Science (M.Sc., B.Sc., Fd.Sc.), Equine Studies (FD, ND, NC, ANC, HNC, Fd.Sc., B.Sc.), Equine Studies and Business Management (B.Sc.), Equine Breeding and Stud Management (B.Sc.)
**Facilities:** Equine Training and Development Centre provides stabling for around 70 horses and incorporates a range of stable design features. An indoor arena (50m x 40m), two large outdoor arenas, jumping paddock, and a cross country course provide an excellent teaching resource for practical stable management and equitation teaching and training. The Centre is also equipped with a wieghbridge and horsewalker, used within the teaching of applied Equine Science modules. The Lordship Stud's specialist facilities include modern veterinary examination and AI collection areas, laboratory, manege, indoor school, treadmill, foaling boxes with CCTV, and 20 hectares of permanent pasture. A recent addition includes the arrival of the top class competition stallion Broadstone Landmark and two Fell colts currently doing exceedingly well in the show ring.

Website:
www.writtle.ac.uk

Type of School:
Public University

# Gloucestershire, England

## Cheltenham Ladies College

Bayshill Road Cheltenham GL50 3EP. Contact: Mr. A Siddall. Phone: 01242 520691.
Fax: 01242 227882. Email: riding@cheltladiescollege.org.
**Degrees Offered:** High School Diploma
**Tuition Costs:** (Pounds) Lower and upper boarding: £5,770/term; lower and upper day: £3,840/term
**Description of Program:** Riding is offered at Hartpury College, up to competition standard depending on ability. Polo is also offered.
**Facilities:** Hartpury Equestrian Centre
**Showing:** Students can compete.

Website:
www.cheltladiescollege.org

Type of School:
All Girls Secondary School

## Hartpury College

Hartpury House, Hartpury College, Hartpury, Gloucestershire GL19 3BE England.
Phone: +44 1452 700283. Fax: +44 1452 700629. Email: enquire@hartpury.ac.uk.

**Accreditation:** Approved by British Horse Society to FBHS Level
**Degrees Offered:** First Certificate, First Diploma, National Certificate, National Diploma, Foundation Degree, Bachelor of Science (Hons), Bachelor of Arts (Hons), Master of Science
**Majors Offered:** Horse Care (FC, NC), Horse Management (NC, ND) Stud, Breeding & Stable Management (ND), Equine Science (Fd.Sc., B.Sc., M.Sc.), Equine Business Management (Fd.A., B.A.), Equine Dental Science (B.Sc.), Equine Sports Science (Fd.Sc., B.Sc.)
**Tuition Costs:** (Pounds) Further Education Courses such as National Certificates, National Diplomas: £3,850 per year; Higher Education Courses such as Fd.Sc., Fd.A., B.Sc., B.A.: £6,900 per year; housing £2,000 to £2,500 per year
**Description of Program:** Equine higher education at Hartpury allows students to focus on either the science- or business-related aspects of the equine field. The Fd.Sc./B.Sc. and M.Sc. Equine Science Program provides students with a wide choice of modules, allowing them to tailor their course to suit their interests and career aspirations. The B.A. Equine Business Management Award combines specialist, vocational equine skills and knowledge with business administration skills, allowing graduates to seek employment in a range of specialist equine-related enterprises. Hartpury College offers students the opportunity to study various further education courses prior to entering their degree. These courses vary in content, but give a sound grounding in most aspects of the equine field and prove to be an ideal platform for progressing to the various higher education equine courses available at the college. Students can study British Horse Society qualifications in conjunction with their academic studies. The BHS qualifications are very practical and allow plenty of hands-on work.
**Facilities:** Indoor and outdoor all-weather and grass arenas, 80m x 60m championship arena, sports horse stud standing the world-famous Welton stallions, new stud complex and visitors center at Home Farm, stabling for 208 horses, equine veterinary hospital and operating suite, equine therapy center, water and high-speed treadmills, hunter trial course, horse trials course from novice to advanced and two-star level, two horse walkers, sand playpen, new extensive classrooms and laboratories, IT Centre of Excellence, over 800 new ensuite bedrooms are available, non-ensuite bedrooms and off-campus accommodation is available
**Classroom/Hands-On Equine Classes:** Vary
**Showing:** Dressage, show jumping, horse and hunter trials, combined training

## Huntley School of Equitation

Woodend Farm, Huntley, Gloucestershire GL19 3EY England.
Contact: Mrs. T Freeman. Phone: +44 (0)1452 830440. Fax: +44 (0)1452 830 846.
**Accreditation:** British Horse Society
**Degrees Offered:** Certificate
**Majors Offered:** Up to BHS Instructor
**Description of Program:** Student training and BHS examination center. General improvement of horse knowledge, care, and riding ability.
**Facilities:** Covered school, outdoor arena, cross-country course

## Littledean Riding Centre

Wellington Farm, Littledean, Gloucestershire GL14 2TO England.
Contact: Mrs. G M Chamberlain. Phone/Fax: 01594 823955.

**Accreditation:** British Horse Society
**Degrees Offered:** Certificate
**Majors Offered:** Up to BHS Assistant Instructor
**Description of Program:** Littledean Riding Centre is set in its own 65 acres with two outdoor schools and a cross-country course on the edge of the Royal Forest of Dean. It is not unusual to encounter deer on rides. Fabulous riding on a wide variety of well schooled horses and ponies, faster hacks for experienced riders, and gentle treks for beginners are all available. Ride for one or two hours, or enjoy a five-hour pub ride. Lessons are available from qualified staff. Established 29 years and BHS approved as a riding school and career student training center.
**Facilities:** Outdoor arena, cross-country schooling jumps

## Royal Agricultural College

Cirencester, Gloucestershire GL7 6JS England. Phone: 01285 652531.
Fax: 01285 885730. Email: admissions@royagcol.ac.uk.
**Degrees Offered:** Bachelor of Science (Hons), Master of Science, Masters of Business Administration
**Majors Offered:** Applied Equine Science (M.S.), International Equine and Agricultural Business Management (B.Sc.), Equine Business Management (M.B.A.)

**Website:**
www.royagcol.ac.uk

**Type of School:**
Public University

## Summerhouse Education & Equitation Centre

Hardwicke, Gloucestershire GL2 6RG England. Phone: 01452 720288.
Email: admin@summerhouseec.co.uk.
**Degrees Offered:** Certificate
**Majors Offered:** BHS Stages 1-4, BHS Instructor, NVQ Levels 1-3

**Website:**
www.summerhouseec.co.uk

**Type of School:**
Specialty School

## The Talland School of Equitation

Church Farm, Siddington, Cirencester, Gloucestershire GL7 6EZ England.
Phone: 01285 652318. Fax: 01285 659409. Email: secretary@talland.net.
**Accreditation:** British Horse Society, Association of British Riding Schools
**Degrees Offered:** Certificate
**Majors Offered:** Up to BHS Fellowship, NVQ Level 2—3 in Horse Care
**Tuition Costs:** (Pounds) £27/private lesson; £30/day or £115/week for housing; Career Courses: £2480/four months tuition plus £1880/four months housing; £3360/six months tuition plus £2820/six months housing; £5980/twelve months tuition and housing
**Description of Program:** World-renowned BHS and ABRS approved equestrian center catering to all levels of riders, from beginner to advanced. Tuition in side-saddle, dressage, and jumping with excellent facilities, superb horses, and a Cotswold location. Holiday and Career Courses are a specialty. Unaccompanied children are welcome. As Talland is a professional, working yard, all training is hands-on. However, students do have a daily lecture as well as their riding and stable management tuition.
**Facilities:** Covered school, outdoor arena, cross-country course
**Classroom/Hands-On Equine Classes:** 100 percent hands-on
**Showing:** By arrangement

**Website:**
www.talland.net

**Type of School:**
Specialty School

**Website:**
www.acpat.org

**Type of School:**
Specialty School

## The Association of Chartered Physiotherapists in Animal Therapy Education

Harestock Stud, Kennel Lane, Littleton, Winchester, Hampshire SO22 6PT England. Contact: Amanda Sutton. Phone: 01962 885561. Email: education@acpat.org.

**Type of School:**
Specialty School

## The Naval Riding Centre

HMS Dryad, Southwick, Nr. Fareham, Hampshire, PO17 6EJ. Contact: Cdr. B. W. Holden-Crawford or Mr. G. Passmore. Phone: 023 92379 974.
**Accreditation:** British Horse Society
**Degrees Offered:** Certificate
**Majors Offered:** Up to BHS Instructor

**Type of School:**
Specialty School

## Quob Stables

Church Croft Farm, Durley Brook Road, Durley, Southampton, Hampshire SO32 2AR England. Contact: Mrs. E. Davies. Phone: 02380 694657.
**Accreditation:** British Horse Society
**Degrees Offered:** Certificate
**Majors Offered:** BHS Stages 1-2

**Website:**
www.rycroft-equitation.co.uk

**Type of School:**
Specialty School

## Rycroft School of Equitation

New Mill Lane, Eversley, Hampshire RG27 ORA England. Phone: 01189 732761.
Fax: 01189 730549. Email: rycroft.riding@btopenworld.com.
**Accreditation:** British Horse Society
**Degrees Offered:** Certificate
**Majors Offered:** BHS Stages 1-3, Preliminary Teaching Test
**Tuition Costs:** (Pounds) £680-3,450 for Stages Course; £900-2,500 for Preliminary Teaching Test Course; housing: £80/week
**Description of Program:** Working students receive a wage and training for BHS exams in return for working a five-and-a-half-day week on the yard. This breaks down into four sessions of riding and four sessions of stable management per week, plus practical experience gained with the horses. The chief instructor personally monitors the progress of all the students and will enter them for their exams when she considers them to be ready.
**Facilities:** Indoor and outdoor arena, cross-country course, show-jumping facilities, excellent off-road hacking in the adjacent Bramshill Forest, qualified team of instructors, 45 horses and ponies to suit all abilities, accommodation can be arranged in the village
**Classroom/Hands-On Equine Classes:** Working Students: Four hours of lectures per week/four hours of riding and practical work on the yard. (The training of paying students can be structured towards their individual needs. )
**Showing:** In-house combined training event

## Sparsholt College Hampshire

Website:
www.sparsholt.ac.uk

Type of School:
Public College

Winchester, Sparsholt, Hampshire SO21 2NF England. Phone: +44 (0) 1962 776441. Fax: 01962 776587. Email: enquiries@sparsholt.ac.uk.

**Accreditation:** Learning and Skills Council, approved by Higher Education Funding Council and British Horse Society

**Degrees Offered:** Higher Education: Foundation Degree, Bachelor of Science; Further Education: BTEC First Diploma, BTEC National Diploma

**Majors Offered:** Equine Science and Management (B.Sc.), Equine Studies (Fd.Sc.), Horse Management (ND, FD)

**Tuition Costs:** (Pounds) Higher Education: £1,100/year for residents; £6,995/year for overseas students; Further Education: No tuition for EU residents under nineteen years old; £750/year and £100 exam fees a year for residents over nineteen years old; £3,995/year for overseas students

**Description of Program:** The Bachelor Degree Program has been developed and designed to provide students with a practical and theoretical understanding of the scientific aspects of horse management and the essentials of business practice and administration which are required for effective operation within the industry. The program will provide a broad appreciation of equine science, business management, and current scientific research. After completing their foundation studies, students will be ready for Equine Science or Equine Management. Delivery of the program will be through lectures, practicals, seminars, and tutorials. A program of visiting speakers and off-campus visits will also underpin the course. The Horse Management Course is designed to equip participants with a sound scientific and technical grounding in managing horses across the range of enterprises within the U.K. and Europe. The course will also include a strong business studies element, since all successful candidates are likely to be involved in aspects of financial management. Equitation (riding) skills are taught at a well-equipped external center and the college equitation center and will aim towards BHS (British Horse Society) Stage 3 and Preliminary Teacher's Certificate.

**Facilities:** A "traditional" style yard of ten stables, plus a ten stable "American Barn." Incorporated in the center are a tack room, feed room, office, and demonstration stable. The riding facilities include a floodlit outdoor arena (60m x 30m), and a cross-country course on grass tracks around the college farm is under development. New indoor arena with another 40 stables was completed in 2002.

**Classroom/Hands-On Equine Classes:** Vary

## Wellington Equestrian Education Ltd.

Website:
www.wellington-riding.co.uk

Type of School:
Specialty School

Wellington Riding, Heckfield, Hook, Hampshire RG27 0LJ England. Phone: 01189 326308. Fax: 0118 932 6661. Email: careers@wellington-riding.co.uk.

**Accreditation:** British Horse Society & Association of British Riding Schools

**Degrees Offered:** Certificate, Working Student

**Majors Offered:** Up to BHS Instructor

**Description of Program:** Career training, Intensive BHS Preliminary Instructor course, twelve month Working Student program, tailor-made courses

**Facilities:** Two covered schools, five outdoor arenas, cross-country courses

# Herefordshire, England

## Holme Lacy College

Holme Lacy, Hereford, HR2 6LL United Kingdom. Contact: Mr. P. Savidge. Phone: 01432 870 316. Fax: 01432 870 566. Email: holmelacycollege@compuserve.com.
**Accreditation:** British Horse Society
**Degrees Offered:** Certificate, BHS, NVQ Certificate, First Diploma, National Diploma, National Award
**Majors Offered:** BHS Stages 1 and 2, Horse Care (FD, NVQC), Horse Management (ND, NA)

## Sue Adams Riding School

**Type of School:**
Specialty School

The Ox House, Shobdon, Leominster, Hereford. HR6 9LT. Contact: Ms. S. Adams-Wheeler. Phone: 01568 708 973.
**Accreditation:** British Horse Society
**Degrees Offered:** Certificate
**Majors Offered:** Up to BHS Assistant Instructor

# Hertfordshire, England

## Contessa Riding Centre

**Website:**
www.contessa-riding.co.uk

**Type of School:**
Specialty School

Willow Tree Farm, Colliers End, Nr Ware, Hertfordshire SG11 1EN England. Phone: 01920 821792. Fax: 01920 821496. Email: CONTESSARIDING@aol.com.
**Accreditation:** British Horse Society, Association of British Riding Schools
**Degrees Offered:** Certificate
**Majors Offered:** BHS and ABRS exams
**Description of Program:** Specializes in dressage
**Facilities:** Facilities include a large mirrored indoor school with quality surface, an outside international sized floodlit manège, and small a cross-country course.

## Kent Equine Industry Training Services Ltd.

**Website:**
www.keits.co.uk

**Type of School:**
Specialty School

Unit C Houndswood Gate, Harper Lane, Radlett, Hertfordshire England WD7 7HU. Phone: 01923-854586. Email: keitsco@aol.com.
**Accreditation:** Centre of Vocational Excellence (COVE)—Equine and City and Guilds Approved Centre
**Degrees Offered:** Foundation and Advanced Modern Apprenticeships, direct NVQs (National Vocational Qualifications)
**Majors Offered:** Horse Care and Management
**Tuition Costs:** Tuition is free
**Description of Program:** The Modern Apprenticeship is an industry-based training program for those ages 16 to 24, developed by equine employers and led by the British Horse Society via the National Training Organization, LANTRA. Modern Apprentices have employed status and achieve at least a Level 2 National Vocational Qualification (NVQ) in Horse care and Management. Furthermore, they will gain valuable key skills, including information technology, literacy, and numeracy together with the opportunity to obtain Techinical Certificates in Horse Care. When fully trained from Foundation Level to Advanced Level, modern apprentices should be capable of running a small yard

and taking responsibility for horses and staff. The Modern Apprenticeship is structured around a training agreement between you, an employer, and KEITS, and is supported by government funding. This agreement details the commitment required by everyone to ensure the successful completion of training while in employment. This program offers you the opportunity to establish an attractive career path through a supported modern apprenticeship within the business, ensuring you are an important part of the business.

**Facilities:** Depends on placement (e.g., competition yard, livery yard, stud, riding school, rescue center).

**Classroom/Hands-On Equine Classes:** Training is based in the workplace with the emphasis on building vocational skills. Lectures and classroom based learning are dependent on the placement.

**Showing:** Competing is encouraged by all employers.

## Oaklands College

Smallford Campus, Hatfield Road, St. Albans, Hertfordshire AL4 0JA England.
Phone: 01727 737700. Fax: 01727 737752. Email: help.line@oaklands.ac.uk.
**Accreditation:** British Horse Society (BHS), Edexcel, City and Guilds of London Institute
**Degrees Offered:** First Diploma, National Certificate, Advanced National Certificate, National Diploma.
**Majors Offered:** Equine Studies (FD), Horse Management (ND), Management of Horses (NC)
**Tuition Costs:** (Pounds) EU and UK students: £650/year; non-EU/UK students: £4,150/year; room and board: £2,630/year
**Description of Program:** A range of programs include all relevant subject areas of horse care, training, teaching, riding, applied science, and business management. For specific details of particular programs, please contact the college for an up-to-date brochure. There is an active equestrian group that organizes events, clinics and shows.
**Facilities:** Stabling for 35 horses, indoor school, outdoor arena, horse walker, grazing
**Classroom/Hands-On Equine Classes:** 60:40
**Showing:** Students can assist staff at competitions.

**Website:**
www.oaklands.ac.uk

**Type of School:**
Community College

## South Medburn Farm Ltd.

South Medburn Farm, Watling Street, Elstree, Hertfordshire WD6 3AA England.
Contact: Mrs. M. L. Rose. Phone: 0208 207 4714. Fax: 0208 207 6118.
**Accreditation:** British Horse Society
**Degrees Offered:** Certificate
**Majors Offered:** Up to BHS Intermediate Instructor

**Type of School:**
Specialty School

# Isle of Man, England

## GGH Equitation Centre Ltd.

Ballacallin Beg, Crosby, Marown, Isle of Man IM4 2HD. Contact: Mrs. J. Gilbey.
Phone: 01624 851574/ 851450.
**Accreditation:** British Horse Society
**Degrees Offered:** Certificate
**Majors Offered:** Up to BHS Assistant Instructor

**Type of School:**
Specialty School

## Bedgebury School

**Website:**
www.bedgeburyschool.co.uk

**Type of School:**
Boarding and Day School,
Specialty School

Bedgebury School Riding Centre, Goudhurst, Kent TN17 2SH England. Phone: 01580 211602. Fax: 01580 212296. Email: office@bedgeburyridingcentre.ndo.co.uk.
**Accreditation:** British Horse Society
**Degrees Offered:** BHS Certificate, High School Diploma, National Diploma
**Majors Offered:** BHS Assistant Instructor, Business Studies (Equine Management)
**Tuition Costs:** (Pounds) £5,040 for boarding/upper school; £3,130 for day/upper school
**Description of Program:** Boarding and day school for girls two-and-a-half to eighteen years and boys two-and-a-half to seven years. Bedgebury Riding Centre is part of Bedgebury School. Tuition is required for career students training for exams and competitions. Working trainees (UK only) are accepted on a nonpaying basis; the length of the courses is determined by the students' previous experience. Outstanding riding and horse care instruction is available for BHS examinations, which can be taken at the center. Courses are geared towards BHSAI and are principally aimed at students training for a career in the equestrian industry. On-the-job training and structured work experience are provided in the real environment of a busy working stable with 60 horses, training students for the BHS Groom or Preliminary Teacher Qualification and National Vocational Qualifications. Food, accommodation, in log cabins, and pocket money are provided. Students work in the stable yard as an important part of their practical training. Students are given responsibility for a number of horses; the level of responsibility and number of horses increase as experience is gained. Experienced instructors acts as mentors, taking a personal interest in the students' development and progress.
**Facilities:** Riding center set in the 250 acres of parkland surrounding Bedgebury Independent School for Girls, stabling for 60 horses, two indoor schools and two outdoor schools, full cross-country course, access to several thousand acres of forest riding
**Classroom/Hands-On Equine Classes:** Hands-on, two hours a day
**Showing:** Schoolgirls: Inter-Schools competitions; Working Students: dressage competitions

## Callum Park Riding Centre

**Type of School:**
Specialty School

Lower Halstow, Near Sittingbourne ME9 7ED. Contact: Mr. J & Mrs. L McGee. Phone: 01795 844978/844258. Fax: 01795 844 978. Email: CPRC@Callum-Park.demon.co.uk.
**Accreditation:** British Horse Society
**Degrees Offered:** Certificate
**Majors Offered:** Up to BHS Assistant Instructor
**Description of Program:** Courses tailored for the individual requirements of the client.
**Facilities:** Covered school, outdoor arena, parking for 50 lorries, tack shop, coffee shops, training rooms

## Cobham Manor Riding Centre

**Website:**
www.cobham-manor.co.uk

**Type of School:**
Specialty School

Water Lane, Thurnham, Maidstone, Kent ME14 3LU. Contact: Mr. and Mrs. Brumer. Phone: 01622 738497. Fax: 01622 735600. Email: james@cobham-manor.co.uk.
**Accreditation:** British Horse Society

**Degrees Offered:** Certificate
**Majors Offered:** Up to BHS Assistant Instructor

## Goodnestone Court Equestrian

Goodnestone Court, Graveney, Faversham, Kent, ME13 9BZ. Contact: Mrs. A. L. Hudson. Phone: 01795 535 806.
**Accreditation:** British Horse Society
**Degrees Offered:** Certificate
**Majors Offered:** Up to BHS Intermediate Instructor

**Type of School:**
Specialty School

## Hadlow College

Hadlow, Tonbridge, Kent TN11 0AL England. Freephone: 0500 551434 Fax: 01732 853207. Email: enquiries@hadlow.ac.uk.
**Accreditation:** British Horse Society
**Degrees Offered:** Certificate, First Diploma, National Award, National Diploma, Higher National Diploma
**Majors Offered:** Up to BHS Assistant Instructor (C), Equine Management (HND), Horse Studies (FD, ND), Horse Management/BHS Assistant Instructor (NA)
**Description of Program:** The horse industry is one of the fastest-growing rural sectors, and the care and management of horses is an expanding industry. If you enjoy working with horses, and you are dedicated, there are a vast range of job opportunities for all abilities. The best way to learn is to mix theory with hands-on experience, and Hadlow College provides the perfect solution.
**Facilities:** Facilities include 45 horses, indoor arena with gallery (35m x 60m), outdoor school (40m x 50m), cross-country course, show jumping paddock, jumping lane, college bridle way, horse walker, horse weight bridge, young horses in training, stallions, mares in foal and equine lecture theater.
**Showing:** Affiliated and nonaffiliated dressage and show jumping competitions are held throughout the year, as well as an annual Horse Show and Hunter Trials. Students also have the opportunity to compete at other college shows and events.

**Website:**
www.hadlow.ac.uk

**Type of School:**
Community College

## Imperial College London

Wye Campus, Wye, Ashford, Kent TN25 5AH England. Phone: (+44) (0) 20 7594 2754. Fax: (+44) (0) 20 7594 2669. Email: admissions.wye@imperial.ac.uk.
**Degrees Offered:** Bachelor of Science
**Majors Offered:** Animal Science [Equine], Business Management [Equine]

**Website:**
www.ic.ac.uk or www.wye.ic.ac.uk

**Type of School:**
College

## Limes Farm Equestrian Centre

Pay Street, Hawkinge, Folkestone, Kent CT18 7DZ. Contact: Miss A Berry. Phone: +44 (0)1303 892335. Fax: 01303 894020. Email: info@limesfarmequestriancentre.co.uk.
**Accreditation:** British Horse Society
**Degrees Offered:** Certificate
**Majors Offered:** Up to BHS Intermediate Instructor
**Tuition Costs:** Contact School
**Description of Program:** Career training, NVQ & BHS stage exams
**Facilities:** Covered school, outdoor arena, cross-country course

**Website:**
www.limesfarmequestriancentre.co.uk

**Type of School:**
Specialty School

## Croft End Equestrian Centre

Knotts Lane, Bardsley, Oldham, Lancashire OL8 3JD England. Contact: Mr. and Mrs. S. Kenworthy. Phone: 0161 624 2849.
**Accreditation:** British Horse Society
**Degrees Offered:** Certificate
**Majors Offered:** BHS Stages 1 and 2

## Eccleston Equestrian Centre

Ulnes Walton Lane, Leyland, Preston, Lancashire PR26 8LT England.
Contact: Miss K. A. Green. Phone: 01772 600093. Fax: 01772 600121.
Email: sales@equestrian-northwest.co.uk.
**Accreditation:** British Horse Society
**Degrees Offered:** Certificate
**Majors Offered:** Up to BHS Assistant Instructor
**Description of Program:** Adult lessons and examination preparation
**Facilities:** Covered school, outdoor arena, cross-country course

## Lords House Farm Education Centre

Wilpshire Road, Rishton, Blackburn, Lancashire BB1 4AH England.
Phone: 01254 877400.
**Accreditation:** British Horse Society, Registered Charity #1046173
**Degrees Offered:** NVQ Certificate, BHS Certificate
**Majors Offered:** BHS Horse Care, NVQ Small Animal Care, NVQ Horticulture
**Tuition Costs:** Donation toward cost of riding lessons
**Description of Program:** The Lords House Farm is a totally unique and specialist center specifically designed and built to meet a wide range of needs in the disabled and disadvantaged community. Riding therapy and other activities are offered aimed at the physiotherapy, physical exercise, sensory and social development of the center's beneficiaries. Students with learning difficulties and mainstream students take part in courses leading to BHS, City and Guilds, and other nationally recognized qualifications. These courses are designed to incorporate number power, word power, and social and communication skills by using the center's horses and animals as motivation tools while also developing physical skills in a non-threatening, relaxed environment. Mainstream students work in all subjects to attend up to NVQ Level 2. Over a twelve-month period, the center has over 1000 beneficiaries/visitors or students.
**Facilities:** The center has 25 horses, 26 staff and tutors, and many volunteers.
**Classroom/Hands-On Equine Classes:** Vary
**Showing:** In-house show days

## Myerscough College

Myerscough Hall, Bilsborrow, Preston, Lancashire, PR3 0RY England. Contact: Ms. Susan Pumbley. Phone: 01995 642222. Fax: 01995 642333.
Email: mailbox@myerscough.ac.uk.
**Degrees Offered:** Certificate, First Diploma, National Certificate, National Diploma, Foundation Degree, Bachelor of Science (Hons)

**Majors Offered:** Up to BHS Intermediate Instructor(C), Equine Leisure Management (Fd.Sc.), Equine Science (Fd.Sc.), Equine Science and Management (B.Sc.), Horse Care (FD, NC), Horse Management (ND), NVQ Level 1 Horse Care (C),Veterinary Practice Management (Fd.Sc.)

## Wrea Green Equitation Centre

Bryning Lane, Wrea Green, Lancashire PR4 1TN England. Contact: Miss C.A. Pollitt. Phone: 01772 686576.
**Accreditation:** British Horse Society
**Degrees Offered:** Certificate
**Majors Offered:** Up to BHS Assistant Instructor

Type of School:
Specialty School

# Leicestershire, England

## Brooksby Melton College

Brooksby, Melton Mowbray, Leicestershire LE14 2LJ England. Phone: 01664 850850. Fax: 01664 855355. Email: course.enquiries@brooksbymelton.ac.uk.
**Degrees Offered:** BHS Certificate, NVQ Certificate, First Diploma, National Diploma, Higher National Diploma
**Majors Offered:** Animal Science [including Equine Modules] (HND), BHS Preliminary Teaching (C), BHS Stages 1-4 (C), Foundation Land Based Industries, Horse Care (FD), Horse Management (ND), NVQ Level 1-2 Horse Care (C)

Website:
www.brooksbymelton.ac.uk

Type of School:
Further Education College

## Hinckley Equestrian Centre

Mirfield Farm, Mill Lane, Earl Shilton, Leicestershire, United Kingdom.
Contact: Mr. and Mrs. Clark. Phone: 01455 847464.
**Accreditation:** British Horse Society
**Degrees Offered:** Certificate
**Majors Offered:** BHS Stages 1 and 2

Type of School:
Specialty School

## Swan Lodge Equestrian Centre

Station Road, Upper Broughton, Melton Mowbray, Leics, LE14 3BH United Kingdom.
Contact: Miss D. A. T. Jalland. Phone: 01664 823686. Fax: 01664 822832.
Email: swanlodge@talk21.com
**Accreditation:** British Horse Society
**Degrees Offered:** Certificate
**Majors Offered:** BHS Stages 1 and 2

Type of School:
Specialty School

## Witham Villa Ltd.

Witham Villa Riding Centre, Cosby Road, Broughton Astley, Leicestershire, LE14 6PA United Kingdom. Contact: Mrs. V. Saul. Phone: 01455 282 694.
**Accreditation:** British Horse Society
**Degrees Offered:** Certificate
**Majors Offered:** Up to BHS Assistant Instructor

Type of School:
Specialty School

## Hill House Equestrian Centre

Sand Lane, Osgodby, Market Rasen, Lincs., LN8 3TE. Contact: Ms. L. Tither. Phone: 01673 849 967.
**Accreditation:** British Horse Society
**Degrees Offered:** Certificate
**Majors Offered:** BHS Stages 1 and 2

**Type of School:**
Specialty School

## Lincoln College

Sport and Leisure Studies, Monks Road, Lincoln LN2 5HQ. Contact: Sarah Stainforth, Program Leader. Phone: 01522 876335. Fax 01522 876329. Email: sstainforth@lincolncollege.ac.uk.
**Accreditation:** British Horse Society
**Degrees Offered:** Certificate
**Majors Offered:** Up to BHS Intermediate Instructor (C), NVQ Levels 1-3 (C)
**Tuition Costs:** Contact School
**Description of Program:** Students may study for NVQ Levels 1-3 and British Horse Society examinations up to and including BHS Intermediate Instructor. Students receive a practical training within a commercial equestrian center environment, delivered by college lecturers. Part-time and full-time programs are available. Courses are specifically tailored to meet individual requirements; groups are kept small. Formal riding lessons are offered every day. Students keep a five-day week, with educational term times. Programs last one to three years, depending on the student's ability upon entrance.
**Facilities:** Utilizes a variety of equestrian centers across Lincolnshire, including indoor riding arenas (25m x 20m x 40m), outdoor fibresand arena, outdoor grass arenas, cross-country course, woodland and rural hacking, 46 horses, classroom accommodation, and transport from college to equestrian facility.
**Classroom/Hands-On Equine Classes:** Vary

**Website:**
www.lincolncollege.ac.uk

**Type of School:**
College of Further Education

## Thorpe Grange Equestrian Centre

Newark Road, Lincoln, LN5 9EJ United Kingdom. Contact: Mr. S. Cruickshank. Phone: 01522 680159/500 022.
**Accreditation:** British Horse Society
**Degrees Offered:** Certificate
**Majors Offered:** Up to BHS Assistant Instructor

**Type of School:**
Specialty School

## University of Lincoln

Brayford Pool, Lincoln LN6 7TS. Phone: +44 (0) 1522 882000.
Email: enquiries@lincoln.ac.uk, Risholme Park Equestrian Centre, University of Lincoln, Risholme Hall, Risholme, Lincoln LN2 2LG United Kingdom. Contact: Mrs. Amy Richardson. Phone: 01522 895463. Fax: 01522 545436.
**Degrees Offered:** Certificate, First Diploma, National Diploma, Bachelor of Science (Hons)
**Majors Offered:** Up to BHS Intermediate Instructor (C), Equine Science (B.Sc.), Equine Sports Science (B.Sc.), Horse Care (FD), Horse Management (ND)

**Website:**
www.lincoln.ac.uk

**Type of School:**
University

# Liverpool, England

## University of Liverpool

Website:
www.liv.ac.uk

Type of School:
University

The Admissions Sub-Dean, Faculty of Veterinary Science, The University of Liverpool, Liverpool L69 7ZJ England. Email: vetadmit@liverpool.ac.uk.

**Degrees Offered:** Bachelor of Veterinary Medicine, Bachelor of Science (Hons), Master of Philosophy, Doctor of Philosophy

**Majors Offered:** Bioveterinary Science (B.Sc.), Veterinary Conservation Medicine (B.Sc.), Veterinary Science (B.Sc., B.V.Sc.)

# London, England

## The Royal Veterinary College

Website:
www.rvc.ac.uk

Type of School:
University

University of London, Royal College Street, London NW1 0TU, UK. Phone: +44 (0)20 74685000.

**Degrees Offered:** Bachelor of Veterinary Medicine, Bachelor of Science (Hons), Master of Science, Master of Philosophy, Doctor of Philosophy, Postgraduate Diploma, Doctor of Veterinary Medicine

**Majors Offered:** Bioscience (Ph.M., Ph.D., D.V.M.), Control of Infectious Diseases in Animals (M.Sc., PD), Livestock Health and Production (M.Sc., PD), Veterinary Epidemiology and Public Health (M.Sc., PD), Veterinary Epidemiology (M.Sc.), Veterinary Nursing (B.Sc.), Veterinary Pathology (B.Sc.), Veterinary Physiotherapy (M.Sc., PD), Veterinary Sciences (B.Sc.), Wild Animal Health (M.Sc.), Wild Animal Biology (M.Sc.)

## Trent Park Equestrian Centre

Website:
www.trentpark.com

Type of School:
Specialty School

Bramley Road, London, N14 4XS. Contact: Mrs. S. Martin. Phone: 020 8363 9005. Email: info@trentpark.com.

**Accreditation:** British Horse Society
**Degrees Offered:** Certificate
**Majors Offered:** Up to BHS Intermediate Instructor

## Wimbledon Village Stables

Website:
www.wvstables.com

Type of School:
Specialty Riding School

24 a/b High Street, Wimbledon, London SW19 5DX England. Phone: 020 8946 8579. Fax: 020 8879 0213. Email: admin@wvstables.com.

**Accreditation:** British Horse Society
**Degrees Offered:** BHS Assistant Instructor Certificate
**Majors Offered:** BHS Stages 1-3, BHS Preliminary Teaching Test
**Tuition Costs:** Vary
**Description of Program:** Programs are custom-made to take into account the experience of the student and the examination he/she is aiming for. Riding tuition will include dressage and jumping instruction; teaching instruction is also available.
**Facilities:** Superb London riding school with 25 quality horses and ponies, two schooling arenas, more than 2,000 acres of riding country, lecture room, and video facility.
**Classroom/Hands-On Equine Classes:** As well as lectures and demonstrations, students will be responsible for the care and welfare of one or more horses.
**Showing:** Students will be given the opportunity to compete in certain disciplines.

# Merseyside, England

## Longacres Riding School

**Type of School:** Specialty School

290 Southport Road, Lydiate, Merseyside L31 4EQ England. Contact: Mr. J.E. Kirkham. Phone: 0151 526 0327/527 2439.
**Accreditation:** British Horse Society
**Degrees Offered:** Certificate
**Majors Offered:** Up to BHS Assistant Instructor

# Middlesex, England

## Capel Manor College

**Website:** www.capel.ac.uk

**Type of School:** Further Education College of Agriculture

Bulls Moor Lane, Enfield, Middlesex ENI 4RQ England. Phone: (0)2083 664442. Fax: (0)1992 717544. Email: enquiries@capel.ac.uk.
**Degrees Offered:** Certificate, National Award, National Certificate, National Diploma
**Majors Offered:** BHS Stages 1-4 (C), Horse Care (NA), Horse Management (NA, NC, ND)

## Suzannes Riding School

**Type of School:** Specialty School

Brookshill Drive, Harrow Weald, Middlesex, HA3 6SB. Contact: Mrs. S. Marczak. Phone: 020 8954 3618. Fax: 020 8420 6461.
**Accreditation:** British Horse Society
**Degrees Offered:** Certificate
**Majors Offered:** Up to BHS Assistant Instructor

# Norfolk, England

## Blackborough End Equestrian Centre

**Website:** www.beec.slix.co.uk

**Type of School:** Specialty School

The Stables, East Winch Road, Blackborough End, Kings Lynn, Norfolk PE32 1SF England. Phone: 01553 841212.
**Accreditation:** British Horse Society
**Degrees Offered:** Certificate
**Majors Offered:** BHS Stages 1-3
**Tuition Costs:** Vary
**Description of Program:** Blackborough End Equestrian Centre aims to provide high-quality lessons on horses or ponies for all, from novices to more experienced riders. Group and private lessons are run daily and on weekday evenings until late evening. Class ratio for BHS exams is very high. Unaffiliated competitions are run regularly throughout the year, as are holiday events for youngsters. Full livery is offered with use of all facilities. The well stocked equestrian shop on-site makes the equestrian center a venue to fulfill most needs of the horse and rider.
**Facilities:** Indoor arena (20m x 40m), floodlit outdoor all-weather arena (60m x 30m), 22 boxes, equestrian shop, housing is not supplied
**Classroom/Hands-On Equine Classes:** 50:50

## Easton College

Easton, Norwich, Norfolk NR9 5DX. Phone: +44 (0)1603 742105. Fax: +44 (0)1603 741438. Email: staff@easton-college.ac.uk.
**Degrees Offered:** Certificate, First Diploma, National Diploma, Higher National Diploma
**Majors Offered:** BHS Stage 1 & 2 (C), Equine Studies (HND), Horse Studies (FD), Management of Horses (ND), NVQ Levels 1 & 2 Horse Care (C)

**Website:**
www.easton-college.ac.uk

**Type of School:**
College of Further Higher Education

# Northamptonshire, England

## Brampton Stables

Church Brampton, Northampton, NN6 8AU United Kingdom. Contact: Mr. D. Ward. Phone: 01604 842 051. Fax: 01604 842 051.
**Accreditation:** British Horse Society
**Degrees Offered:** Certificate
**Majors Offered:** Up to BHS Instructor

**Type of School:**
Specialty School

## Moulton College

West Street, Moulton, Northamptonshire NN3 1RR England. Phone: 01604 491131/492653. Fax: 01604 491 127. Email: enquiries@moulton.ac.uk.
**Degrees Offered:** First Diploma, National Certificate, National Diploma, Higher National Diploma, Bachelor of Science (Hons)
**Majors Offered:** Equine Studies (HND, B.Sc.), Horse Care (FD, NC), Horse Management (ND)

**Website:**
www.moulton.ac.uk

**Type of School:**
College of Further Eduation

## University College Northampton

Park Campus, Boughton Green Road, Northampton NN2 7AL, England. Phone: (44) 1604 735500.
**Degrees Offered:** Higher National Diploma, Bachelor of Science (Hons)
**Majors Offered:** Equine and Estate Studies (B.Sc.), Equine Studies with Estate Studies (HND)

**Website:**
www.northampton.ac.uk

**Type of School:**
University

# Northhumberland, England

## Kirkley Hall College

Equine Unit, Kirkley Hall College, Ponteland, Northhumberland NE20 0AQ England. Contact: Mrs. J. McCowie. Phone: 01661 860808.
**Accreditation:** British Horse Society
**Degrees Offered:** Certificate
**Majors Offered:** BHS Assistant Instructor

**Website:**
www.northland.ac.uk

**Type of School:**
College

## Penshaw Hill Equestrian Centre

**Type of School:**
Specialty School

Penshaw Village, Houghton-le-Spring, Tyne & Wear, Northhumberland DH4 7ER England. Contact: Miss J. & Mr. M. Roseberry. Phone: 01915 844828.
**Accreditation:** British Horse Society
**Degrees Offered:** Certificate
**Majors Offered:** Up to BHS Assistant Instructor

# Nottinghamshire, England

## College Farm Equestrian Centre

**Website:**
www.collegefarm.com

**Type of School:**
Specialty School

West Markham, Newark, Nottinghamshire NG22 0PN England. Phone: 01777 870887. Email: enquiries@collegefarm.co.uk.
**Degrees Offered:** Certificate
**Majors Offered:** BHS Escort, BHS Intermediate Stable Manager, BHS Intermediate Teacher, BHS Preliminary Teacher, BHS Riding and Road Safety, BHS Stable Manager, BHS Stages 1-4, NVQ Levels 1-4

## Nottingham Trent University/Brackenhurst

**Website:**
www.ntu.ac.uk

**Type of School:**
Public University

Brackenhurst Equestrian Centre, School of Land-based Studies, The Nottingham Trent University, Brackenhurst, Southwell, Notts. NG25 OQF England. Phone: +44 (0)1636 817000. Fax: 01636 815404. Email: enquiries.lbs@ntu.ac.uk
**Accreditation:** British Horse Society
**Degrees Offered:** University Foundation Degree, National Diploma, National Certificate, Bachelor of Science
**Majors Offered:** Equine Sports Science (B.Sc.), Equestrian Psychology (B.Sc.), Horse Management (ND), Sports Horse Management and Equitation (Fd.Sc.), Management of Horses (NC)
**Tuition Costs:** Contact School
**Description of Program:** Brackenhurst Equestrian Centre has top-flight instructors, facilities, and horses, offering some of the best training in the U.K. B.Sc.: Undergraduates study a range of topics related to equine sports. Within these, they study physiological and psychological principles of sports science. Fd.Sc.: A riding and non-riding option designed for those who wish to study towards BHS Intermediate Instructor Award. Both options revolve around the competition horse. Allows access to the final year of the degree program. NC: Aims to produce reliable, conscientious, and knowledgeable individuals with the ability to care for a stable yard and treat horse ailments with veterinary assistance, exercise and school horses. Students can work towards the BHS stage exams. ND: A highly practical course, which links theoretical horse management to the practical situation. Students can work towards the BHS stage exams. The department offers a unique learning experience. The combination of an idyllic rural setting and friendly dedicated staff results in an atmosphere that generations of students have come to appreciate.
**Facilities:** The equestrian center includes an indoor school (60m 40m) with mirrors, outdoor floodlit school (60m x40m), stabling for 60 horses, covered horse walker, show jumps, and cross-country jumps. The university supplies housing.
**Classroom/Hands-On Equine Classes:** Vary
**Showing:** Students take a Competition Horse module in their second year of the of the Fd.Sc. course.

## Selston Equestrian Centre

Commonside, Selston, Notts., NG16 6FJ United Kingdom. Contact: Mr. Eric Burr.
Phone: 01773 813 817.
**Accreditation:** British Horse Society
**Degrees Offered:** Certificate
**Majors Offered:** Up to BHS Intermediate Instructor

## Wellow Park Stables & Saddlery

Rufford Lane, Wellow, Newark, Notts., NG22 0EQ United Kingdom. Contact: Mrs. M.
M. Willett. Phone: 01623 861 040. Fax: 01623 835 292.
**Accreditation:** British Horse Society
**Degrees Offered:** Certificate
**Majors Offered:** BHS Stages 1 and 2

# Oxfordshire, England

## Abingdon and Witney College

Witney Campus, Holloway Road, Witney, Oxfordshire OX28 6NE England. Phone:
01993 703464. Fax: 01993 703006. Email: inquiry@abingdon-witney.ac.uk.
**Degrees Offered:** BTEC First Diploma, BTEC National Diploma, BTEC Higher
National Certificate, BTEC Higher National Diploma, Bachelor of Science (Hons)
**Majors Offered:** Equine Science International Thoroughbred Management (B.Sc.),
Equine Management (HND), Horse Management (ND), Horse Care (FD)
**Description of Program:** Equine Science International Thoroughbred Management Course modules include The International Thoroughbred Industry, Horse
Husbandry, Introduction to Exercise Science, Equine Science, Health and Preventative Medicine, Training, International Stud Management, Equine Reproductive
Physiology, Genetics, Veterinary Techniques, Equine Injury and Rehabilitation,
Managing Equine Organizations, International Thoroughbred Enterprise Management, Grassland Management, Racecourse and Events Management, Equine Behavior, and Performance Development. Equine Management prepares students primarily for the managerial and administrative roles within the horse industry. By studying a wide range of equine management, science, and business subjects, students
will gain a comprehensive understanding and the practical skills required by
employers in the equine world. The Horse Management Course is designed to equip
students for success in employment within a variety of equine careers, and to develop the knowledge, understanding, and practical skills required in the horse industry at an operational level. Students choosing the Thoroughbred pathways may
complete NVQ Level 2 Racehorse Care (stud or racing options) within the course.
The Horse Care Course provides the ideal first step for those wishing to pursue a
career with horses. Students may choose the Thoroughbred Horse or General Horse
Studies Programs.

## McTimoney College of Chiropractic

Kimber House, 1 Kimber Road, Abingdon, Oxfordshire OX14 0BZ England.
Phone: 01235 523336. Fax: 01235 523576. Email: chiropractic@mctimoney-

college.ac.uk or course-info@mctimoney-college.ac.uk.
**Degrees Offered:** Post-graduate diploma leading to Master of Science
**Majors Offered:** Animal Manipulation Course

## Oakfield Riding School

**Type of School:**
Specialty School

Great Coxwell, Faringdon, Oxon, Oxfordshire SN7 7LU England. Contact: Mr. D C Farrow. Phone: 01367 240126.
**Accreditation:** British Horse Society
**Degrees Offered:** Certificate
**Majors Offered:** BHS Stages 1 and 2

## Oxford Brookes University

**Website:**
www.brookes.ac.uk

**Type of School:**
University

Headington Campus, Gipsy Lane, Oxford OX3 0BP England. Phone: + 44 (0) 1865 741111. Email: query@brookes.ac.uk.
**Accreditation:** In association with Abingdon & Witney College
**Degrees Offered:** Bachelor of Science (Hons)
**Majors Offered:** Equine Science (International Thoroughbred Management)
**Description of Program:** The course has been developed in collaboration with Oxford Brookes University (OBU) to satisfy the ever-changing needs of the Thoroughbred industry. The combination of the excellent facilities and expertise of OBU; the unique Thoroughbred stud enterprise, and extensive industry connections of Abingdon and Witney College provide students with the opportunity to study Equine Science and Thoroughbred Management at degree level. Students are taught at both the OBU campus and at Witney Stud.

## Petersborough, England

## The Farriery Training Service

**Website:**
www.farrier-reg.gov.uk

**Type of School:**
Specialty School

Sefton House, Adam Court, Newark Road, Petersborough PE1 5PP England. Phone: 01733 319770. Fax: 01733 319771. Email: fts@farrier-reg.gov.uk.
**Accreditation:** Farriers Registration Council
**Degrees Offered:** Advanced Modern Apprenticeship
**Majors Offered:** Farriery
**Tuition Costs:** (Pounds) £6,000/entire course; average of £75/week for housing
**Description of Program:** The FTS's role is to administer the Advanced Modern Apprenticeship in Farriery. The AMA includes the following: NVQ Level 3 in Farriery, completion of a course of training approved by the Farriers Registration Council, and Diploma of the Worshipful Company of Farriers Examination. Apprentices are employed by an approved training farrier for the duration of their apprenticeship in Farriery, which is four years and two months. Apprentices undertake a 23-week block release training, which is divided over the entire course at one of the approved assessment locations. During this time, the apprentices undertake practical and theory lessons. For more information, contact one of the assessment locations of the Farriery Training Service. The Farriery Training Service is also a training provider for the Government Funding Agency, the Learning and Skills Council, Herefordshire and Worcestershire, and for the National Training Organisation, Lantra. In addition, it is an approved assessment center for the awarding body of the NVQ, the British Horseracing Training Board.

**Facilities:** Herefordshire College of Technology, Folly Lane, Hereford HR1 1LS. Oatridge Agricultural College, Ecclesmachan, Broxburn, West Lothian EH52 6NH. Warwickshire College, Royal Leamington Spa and Moreton Morrell, Moreton Morrell, Warwick CV35 9BL. Myerscough College, Myerscough, Bilsborrow, Lancashire PR3 0RY
**Classroom/Hands-On Equine Classes:** Contact individual location.

# Shropshire, England

## Berriewood Farm

Condover, Shrewsbury, Shropshire SY5 7NN. Contact: Mrs. S. M. L. Lock and Mrs. P. A. Cowdy. Phone: 01743 718 252. Fax: 01743 718 163.
**Accreditation:** British Horse Society
**Degrees Offered:** Certificate
**Majors Offered:** Up to BHS Intermediate Instructor

**Type of School:**
Specialty School

## Prescott Equestrian Centre

Baschurch, Shrewsbury, Shropshire SY4 2DR. Contact: Mrs. J. C. Haydon. Phone: 01939 260 712.
**Accreditation:** British Horse Society
**Degrees Offered:** Certificate
**Majors Offered:** Up to BHS Assistant Instructor

**Type of School:**
Specialty School

## Walford and North Shropshire College

Admissions, Walford College, Baschurch, Shrewsbury, Shropshire, SY4 2HL England. Phone: 01939 262100. Fax: 01939 261112. Email: webmaster@n-shropshire.ac.uk.
**Degrees Offered:** BTEC First Diploma, BTEC National Diploma, City and Guilds Advanced National Certificate, City and Guilds National Certificate
**Majors Offered:** Horse Studies (FD, ND), Equine Business Management (ANC), Management of Horses (NC)

**Website:**
www.walford-college.ac.uk

**Type of School:**
College

# Somerset, England

## Cannington College

Cannington, Bridgwater, Somerset TA5 2LS England Phone: 01278 652226. Email: enquiries@cannington.ac.uk.
**Degrees Offered:** Certificate, First Diploma, National Award, National Certificate, National Diploma
**Majors Offered:** Association of British Riding Schools Horse Care & Riding Level 2 (C), BHS Stage 2 (C), Horse Care (FD), Horse Management (NC), Horse Management [Equine Business Management] (NA, NC), Horse Management [Equitation] (ND), NVQ in Horse Care Level 1 & 2 (C), NVQ in Horse Care and Management Level 3 (C)

**Website:**
www.cannington.ac.uk

**Type of School:**
Land-Based College

## Lingfield Correspondence

**Website:**
www.horse-care.co.uk

**Type of School:**
Specialty School, Independent Home Study College

Equine Care & Management Home Study Courses, College Office, Leigh Farm Cottage, Exton, Dulverton, Somerset TA22 9LD England. Phone: 01398 371177. Email: info@horse-care.co.uk.

**Accreditation:** Trade Member of the British Horse Society, Member of British Equine Trade Association, Learndirect Scotland, Suffi, Learndirect England

**Degrees Offered:** British Horse Society Horse Owner's Certificates or Lingfield Correspondence Equine Certificates

**Majors Offered:** Level 1, Level 2, Level 3, Level 4

**Tuition Costs:** (Pounds) £126/Levels 1 & 2, £132/Level 3 & 4

**Description of Program:** Lingfield Correspondence offers an informal and friendly approach to learning. The material is written in easy-to-read, every day language. The courses are comprehensive and up-to-date on all aspects of horse care. From basic daily care and psychology to fittening regimes for international events. A personal and friendly course tutor is provided for every student. The Level 1 Course is thought to be the most comprehensive of its kind available in the UK today and is by far the best value for your money. On completion of each course, students have the option to sit the 90-minute theory examinations for the British Horse Society Horse Owner's Certificates 1-4 or to gain a Lingfield Correspondence Equine Care & Management Certificate. Optional exams are arranged in your home—outside invigilators oversee every exam. Overseas students may sit the exams at the offices of the British Council in their own country (www.britishcouncil.org.uk). The college also offers practical, hands-on short courses at three different venues—L & A Riding and Holiday Centre in South Wales, at Hever in Kent, and Bridge House Equestrian Centre, in Slinfold, Sussex.

## Millfield School

**Website:**
www.millfield.co.uk

**Type of School:**
Secondary School

Street, Somerset BA16 0YD England. Phone: 01458 442291. Fax: 01458 447276. Email: postmaster@millfield.somerset.sch.uk or stables@millfield.somerset.sch.uk.

**Degrees Offered:** High School Diploma, BHS Certificates

# Staffordshire, England

## Abbots Bromley Equestrian Centre

**Type of School:**
Specialty School

School of St Mary & St. Anne, Abbots Bromley, Staffordshire WS15 3BW.
Contact: Miss Stephanie Vickers. Phone: 01283 840 203/ 840 841. Fax: 01283 840 988.

**Accreditation:** British Horse Society

**Degrees Offered:** Certificate

**Majors Offered:** Up to BHS Assistant Instructor

## Courses for Horses

**Type of School:**
Specialty School

Lower Stonehouse Farm, Brown Edge, Stoke on Trent, Staffordshire, ST6 8TF.
Contact: Mrs. Mary Stitson. Phone: 01782 503090. Fax: 01782 505404.

**Accreditation:** British Horse Society

**Degrees Offered:** Certificate

**Majors Offered:** Up to BHS Assistant Instructor

## Endon Riding School

Stanley Moss Lane, Stockton Brook, Stoke-On-Trent, Staffs, ST9 9LR.
Contact: Mrs. D. K. Machin. Phone: 01782 502 114. Fax: 01782 504375.
**Accreditation:** British Horse Society
**Degrees Offered:** Certificate
**Majors Offered:** BHS Stages 1 and 2

**Type of School:**
Specialty School

## Ingestre Stables

Ingestre, Staffordshire ST18 0RE England. Phone: 01889 271165. Fax: 01889 271633.
Email: stables@ingestre.com.
**Accreditation:** British Horse Society
**Degrees Offered:** Certificate
**Majors Offered:** Up to BHS Instructor
**Tuition Costs:** (Pounds) £51 to £250 per week; housing: £85/week shared, £110/week single room
**Description of Program:** Established in 1980, the intensive training program is suitable for students who have had previous experience with horses, either at home or in a work situation, but who now wish to gain qualifications to go with their experience. This type of course involves five hours training per day and three hours of skills practice per day. Students who have their own horses at home and who are non- residential may be excused skills practice if they can demonstrate competence in all areas. The regular training program is suitable for students who need to spend time developing skills and fitness in order to become employable, and is generally a long-term course. This type of course involves two hours training per day (eight hours in a four-day period) and six hours of skills practice per day.
**Facilities:** Indoor arena with viewing gallery, small indoor school, outdoor international dressage arena, outdoor training area, cross-country training fences, full set of show jumps, near 26 square miles of open training ground with hills, water, and forestry, as well as plenty of open grassland, accommodation available within the stable yard complex
**Classroom/Hands-On Equine Classes:** Depends on the student's need.
**Showing:** Students compete all over the UK.

**Type of School:**
Specialty School

## Rodbaston College

Rodbaston, Penkridge, Staffordshire ST19 5PH England. Phone: 01785 712209.
Fax: 01785 715701. Email: rodenquiries@rodbaston.ac.uk.
**Accreditation:** British Horse Society, in conjunction with the University of Wolverhampton
**Degrees Offered:** Certificate, First Diploma, National Certificate, National Diploma, Higher National Diploma, Bachelor of Science
**Majors Offered:** BHS Stages (C), Equine Degree (B.Sc.), Equine Studies (HND), Horse Studies (FD, ND), Management of Horses (NC), NVQ Level 1 in Horse Care (C)
**Tuition Costs:** Depends on course.
**Description of Program:** The equine industry is vast and diverse by nature and there are many employment opportunities for people with the necessary qualifications and experience. Courses are available at all levels, and students are able to make use of the excellent equestrian facilities. All of the courses also involve a varying period of work

**Website:**
www.rodbaston.ac.uk

**Type of School:**
Community College

experience, dependent upon the course. This experience, combined with theory, aims to provide students with the necessary qualifications and experience to enter employment in their chosen area. Progression routes are excellent within this department: if they prove capable, students are able to progress right through to degree qualifications.

**Facilities:** Stabling for nearly 50 horses, two outdoor arenas, indoor arena with viewing gallery

**Classroom/Hands-On Equine Classes:** Depends on the course taken.

**Showing:** Students have the opportunity to be involved in the Rodbaston Horse Trials.

# Suffolk, England

## British Horseracing Training Board

Website:
www.bhb.co.uk

Type of School:
Specialty School

Suite 16, Unit 8, Kings Court, Willie Snaith Road, Newmarket, Suffolk CB8 7SG England. Phone: 01638 560743. Fax: 01638 660932. Email: info@bhb.co.uk.

**Degrees Offered:** National Vocational Qualification Certificate

**Majors Offered:** Racehorse Care, Racehorse Care and Management

## British Racing School

Website:
www.brs.org.uk

Type of School:
Specialty School

Snailwell Road, Newmarket, Suffolk CB8 7NU England. Phone: 01638 665103. Fax: 01638 560929. Email: careers@brs.org.uk.

**Accreditation:** British Horseracing Training Board (BHTB), National Vocational Qualification (NVQ)

**Degrees Offered:** Certificate

**Majors Offered:** Professional Jockey, Amateur Jockey, NVQ Racehorse Care and Key Skills (Level 2), NVQ Racehorse Care and Management (Level 3)

**Tuition Costs:** Contact School

**Description of Program:** The Foundation Course includes NVQ Level 2; trainees ride out at least twice every day and are responsible for looking after two horses during their nine-week (fully residential) stay. Seventy-five percent of Level 2 is completed at the school; the other 25 percent is completed at their guaranteed job in a trainer's yard. Advanced Modern Apprenticeships program is based around NVQ Level 3; candidates are also required to complete Key Skills, and are required to compile a portfolio of evidence to prove their competence under the guidance of a mentor. The majority of the training will take place in the workplace, supported by training at the BRS as required. Professional Jockeys Course covers the essential information that they will be required to know before they ride in public. Further development training is available to seven-pound claimers with continuation courses, and apprentices and conditionals will attend the Intermediate Course once they lose their seven-pound claim. Amateur Jockeys: applicants for Amateur Category A and B Licenses must attend mandatory training. Voluntary training is also provided for both flat and National Hunt amateurs as well as point-to-point riders. One-on-one training can be arranged as required.

**Facilities:** Facilities include 52 horses, fully trained and experienced staff, indoor school, two-furlong round all-weather gallop, seven-furlong straight all-weather and grass gallop, stalls and schooling fences, equicisors and horse simulators, radio headsets for instruction while riding, video recording of riding for performance analysis, and hostel with catering and recreational facilities.

## The British Stud Staff Training Scheme

Website:
www.nationalstud.co.uk

Type of School:
Specialty School

The National Stud, Newmarket, Suffolk CB8 0XE Phone: 01638 663464.
Fax: 01638 665173. Email: students@nationalstud.co.uk.
**Accreditation:** The National Stud, the British Horseracing Training Board
**Degrees Offered:** National Stud Diploma, National Vocational Qualifications Level 2 and 3
**Tuition Costs:** No tuition, free boarding and lodging
**Description of Program:** Nine-Week Induction Course for inexperienced sixteen- to nineteen-year-old students. Followed by a period of work placement on a stud to achieve NVQ Level 2, and may move on to NVQ Level 3. National Stud Diploma Course is a five-month residential course from February to July each year, leading to the National Stud Diploma. Students work on a public stud with mares and foals, maiden, barren and foaling mares, attend lectures from industry experts. An excellent introduction to the UK Thoroughbred breeding industry with career opportunities to follow.
**Facilities:** A working stud farm with residential accommodation situated in Newmarket, Suffolk, UK.
**Classroom/Hands-On Equine Classes:** Approximately one to two hours classroom remainder (approximately six hours) work experience

## Newton Hall Equitation Centre

Website:
www.nhec.co.uk

Type of School:
Specialty School

Swilland, Ipswich, Suffolk IP6 9LT England. Phone: 01473 785616. Fax: 01473 785617.
Email: office@nhec.co.uk.
**Degrees Offered:** Certificate
**Majors Offered:** BHS up to Intermediate Instructor, NVQ Levels 1-3

## Open College of Equine Studies

Website:
www.equinestudies.co.uk

Type of School:
Specialty School, Independent Study

Boxted, Bury St. Edmunds, Suffolk IP29 4JT England. Phone: 01787 282123.
Fax: 01787 280278. Email: enquiries@equinestudies.co.uk.
**Accreditation:** Royal Agriculture College, British Horse Society, Edexcel (BTEC)
**Degrees Offered:** BHS Certificate, Certificate, Foundation Degree, National Certificate, Higher National Certificate, Higher National Diploma, Bachelor of Arts, Bachelor of Science
**Majors Offered:** Basic Stable Management (C), BHS Stage 1-4 (BHS C), Equine Behaviour and Welfare (Fd.Sc., B.Sc.), Equine Studies (Fd.Sc., NC, HNC, HND, B.A.), Equine Science (Fd.Sc., B.Sc.), Senior Horsemastership 1 & 2 (C)
**Tuition Costs:** Contact School
**Description of Program:** The Open College of Equine Studies (TOCES) offers an unequaled range of distance learning and residential study weeks covering the care and management of horses. Whether you wish to study for your own pleasure, to complete British Horse Society examinations, or to gain a professional, academic qualification, there is a suitable course for you. In the twelve years since its foundation, TOCES has acquired a reputation for providing the highest standards of training in equine subjects to students all over the world. Course material, written and reviewed by a team of degree-qualified experts, including specialist equine veterinary surgeons, is presented in an easy-to-read, distance learning format. All the information you will need to pass your chosen course is provided. The caliber of course tutors is second-to-none. Many of the

tutors, in addition to their BHS qualifications and wealth of experience, have successfully completed post-graduate degrees in equine subjects. The small, friendly team at TOCES is dedicated to providing you with the best levels of support. Office and tutorial staff are available to assist you at all reasonable times via telephone, fax, or e-mail.

## Pakefield Riding School

**Website:**
www.best.lowestoft.org.uk/Members/PakefieldRS/pakefieldrs.html

**Type of School:**
Specialty School

Carlton Road, Lowestoft, Suffolk NR33 0ND England. Phone: 01502 572257.
**Accreditation:** Approved by British Horse Society, Association of British Riding Schools, Pony Club, Riding for the Disabled Association
**Degrees Offered:** Certificate
**Majors Offered:** BHS Examinations
**Tuition Costs:** (Pounds) £20/hour
**Description of Program:** The school offers four BHSAI-qualified instructors, and its complement of 20 to 30 well-mannered horses and ponies, suitable for all ages. Also available is the BHS' newest equine sport, "Voltige," which is taught by BHS Vaulting Group Coach Arabella Hardy, a qualified disabled persons instructor. The school is the headquarters of the Lowestoft Riding for the Disabled Association Group and also offers driving instruction for both disabled and able-bodied persons.
**Facilities:** Loose box stalls, indoor school, floodlit sanded arena, jumping paddock, car park for patrons, heated club house
**Classroom/Hands-On Equine Classes:** Depends on the program.
**Showing:** Some showing of Lusitano horses.

## Poplar Park Equestrian Training Centre

**Type of School:**
Specialty School

Heath Road, Hollesley, Woodbridge, Suffolk IP12 3NA England.
Contact: Mr. J. Hardwick. Phone: 01394 411 023.
**Accreditation:** British Horse Society
**Degrees Offered:** Certificate
**Majors Offered:** BHS Stage 1 and 2

## Valley Farm Riding & Driving Centre

**Type of School:**
Specialty School

Wickham Market, Woodbridge, Suffolk IP13 0ND England.
Contact: Mrs. S. Ling. Phone: 01728 746 916. Email: sarah@valleyfarmonline.co.uk.
**Accreditation:** British Horse Society
**Degrees Offered:** Certificate
**Majors Offered:** BHS Stages 1 and 2

## Surrey, England

## Ascot Park Polo Club

**Website:**
www.polo.co.uk

**Type of School:**
Specialty School

Windlesham Road, Chobham, Surrey GU24 8SN England. Contact: Nikki Kemp. Phone: 01276 858545. Fax: 01276 858546. Email: info@polo.co.uk.
**Majors Offered:** Polo
**Tuition Costs:** (Pounds) £350 per day; £1,200 four-day course; group discount available; housing not included
**Description of Program:** Weekend classes are the perfect introduction to this great

game. Held on Saturday and Sunday mornings, the two-hour weekend class covers the swing techniques for the four main strokes, the mechanics of hitting, short stick practice, polo riding, stick and ball, and finishes with an opportunity to experience the tactics of team play in a mini-game. Very quiet horses are available and non-riders are welcome. One-day to full-week courses are designed to provide a comprehensive introduction for beginners and an opportunity for the more experienced player to improve their game. Each course is tailored to meet the individual needs of the client, and finishes with a graduation match. The Club provides the ponies, sticks, and helmets. Riding clothes or jeans are recommended. English Country bed-and-breakfast or luxury hotel accommodation can be arranged nearby, and transport can be provided.

**Facilities:** Four playing fields, stick and ball ground with an outside arena area, home to the only mechanical wooden horse in England, livery facilities and stabling available for club members and for visiting players' ponies, more than 50 experienced polo ponies available for hire

**Showing:** Chukkers

## Diamond Centre for Handicapped Riders

Woodmansterne Road, Carshalton, Surrey, England. Phone: 02086 437764. Fax: 02086 438720. Email: riding@diamond.org.uk.
**Accreditation:** British Horse Society and Riding for the Disabled Association
**Degrees Offered:** Certificate
**Majors Offered:** BHS Stages, Riding for the Disabled Group Instructors Exam, Diamond Instructors Badge
**Tuition Costs:** (Pounds) £100/week; housing: £60/week
**Description of Program:** RDA Group Instructors Course is four weeks or more, depending on the student's requirements. There is a practical supervision and four lectures a week. Subjects included are RDA Structure, Taking a Lesson, Stable Management, and Medical Knowledge. Students work alongside Diamond Instructors, taking more responsibility for the instruction as they become more confident and proficient. Working Students can work in exchange for training at the Diamond Centre. Working Students usually spend two to twelve months or at Diamond and work in the stable yard under the direction and supervision of the Stable Manager, Chief Instructor, or another staff member for 20 hours per week. The Working Student helps on rides under the direction and supervision of the staff for ten hours per week. The student takes on more responsibility for instruction as he/she becomes more proficient and confident. The center provides three one-hour lectures, or practical sessions per week, including riding lessons if appropriate. The student is expected to spend a minimum of five hours per week in private study.
**Facilities:** Facilities include 30 working horses, one 20m x 40m indoor school, one 20m x 20m indoor school, one 20m x 40m outdoor school, lecture room, video facilities, and a self-catering student flat for up to five students.
**Classroom/Hands-on Equine Classes:** Virtually 100 percent
**Showing:** Showing is possible if students meet required standards of horsemanship.

**Website:**
www.diamondcentre.org.uk

**Type of School:**
Specialty School

## The Kingston Riding Centre

38 Crescent Road, Kingston-upon-Thames, Surrey, KT2 7RG. Phone: 0181 546 6361.
**Accreditation:** British Horse Society
**Degrees Offered:** Certificate
**Majors Offered:** Up to BHS Assistant Instructor

**Type of School:**
Specialty School

## Merrist Wood College

Worplesdon, Guildford, Surrey, GU3 3PE. Contact: Mr. Robert Pickles.
Phone: 01483 884000.
**Accreditation:** British Horse Society
**Degrees Offered:** Certificate
**Majors Offered:** Up to BHS Instructor

## Orchard Cottage Riding Stables

Babylon Lane, Lower Kingswood, Tadworth, Surrey, KT20 6XA.
Contact: Mrs. C. M. Brugger. Phone: 01737 241 311. Email: riding@ocrs.co.uk.
**Accreditation:** British Horse Society
**Degrees Offered:** Certificate
**Majors Offered:** BHS Stages 1 and 2

## Wildwoods Riding Centre

Ebbisham Lane, Walton on the Hill, Tadworth, Surrey, KT20 5BH. Contact: Mrs. A. C.
Chambers. Phone: 01737 812 146. Fax: 01738 814 872. Email: billtowill@aol.com.
**Accreditation:** British Horse Society
**Degrees Offered:** Certificate
**Majors Offered:** Up to BHS Assistant Instructor

# Sussex, England

## Brinsbury College

Brinsbury College, Pulborough, W. Sussex, RH20 1DL. Phone: +44 (0)1798 873832.
Fax: 01798 875222. Email: principal@brinsbury.ac.uk.
**Degrees Offered:** BHS Certificate, NVQ Certificate, First Diploma, National Diploma,
Higher National Diploma, Bachelor of Science
**Majors Offered:** Equine Level 1 Horse Care (NVQ C), Equine Management (HND),
Equine Science and Management (B.Sc.), Equine Studies Level 1 (BHS/NVQ C), Horse
Care (FD, BHS/NVQ C), Horse Management (ND), Horsemasters Level 2 & 3
(BHS/NVQ C), Intermediate Instructor (BHS C), Stages 1, 2, 3, 4 (BHS C)

## Ditchling Common Stud

Burgess Hill, West Sussex, RH15 0SE England. Contact: Mr. P. G. M. Dudeney.
Phone: 01444 236 678 / 871 900. Fax: 01444 230 389.
**Accreditation:** British Horse Society
**Degrees Offered:** Certificate
**Majors Offered:** Up to BHS Assistant Instructor

## Lavant House Stables

**Website:**
www.lavanthousestables.co.uk

**Type of School:**
Specialty School

Lavant House, Lavant, Chichester, West Sussex PO18 9AH England.
Phone: 01243 530460. Fax: 01243 538129. Email: enquiries@lavanthousestables.co.uk.
**Accreditation:** British Horse Society, Association of British Riding Schools
**Degrees Offered:** Certificate
**Majors Offered:** Up to BHS Assistant Instructor, Specialist Show Jumping and Dressage Training
**Tuition Costs:** (Pounds) Members: £25/45-minute private lesson; nonmembers: £33/45-minute private lesson
**Description of Program:** Students are given individually-tailored programs to suit their other responsibilities. Therefore, students are taught either individually or in very small groups. All instructors are experienced, qualified, and sympathetic. Horses and ponies are well trained and carefully selected to suit the individual. Group lessons have a maximum of six riders and are divided according to age and ability. Adults and children are not mixed in class lessons. A Membership Program–90 percent of clients are members—allows them to enjoy certain benefits.
**Facilities:** Site includes 50 acres, year-round turn-out, 20 stables, two full-size floodlit all-weather arenas, and permanent grass show jumping and dressage arenas. Housing is not supplied.
**Classroom/Hands-On Equine Classes:** Regular practical and theoretical stable management sessions geared toward the British Horse Society syllabus.
**Showing:** Show jumping and dressage competitions are held on-site April to September every year, plus there is one large annual unaffiliated spring show every year, which includes all types of showing and show jumping classes. Students are encouraged to participate in these competitions.

## Plumpton College

**Website:**
www.plumpton.ac.uk

**Type of School:**
Public College

Ditchling Road, Plumpton, Lewes, E. Sussex BN7 3AE England. Phone: +44 (0)1273 890454. Fax: +44 (0)1273 890071. Email: enquiries@plumpton.ac.uk.
**Accreditation:** British Horse Society, BTEC
**Degrees Offered:** BHS Certificate, NVQ Certificate, First Diploma, National Certificate, National Diploma, Higher National Diploma, Bachelor of Science
**Majors Offered:** BHS Preliminary Instructor (C), BHS Stage 1-4 (C), Biological Sciences [Horse Studies] (B.Sc.), Horse Care (FD), Horse Management (NC, ND), Horse Studies (HND), NVQ Level 1-3 (C)
**Tuition Costs:** (Pounds) Further Education: No tuition costs for EU students under age nineteen; £680 for EU students over age nineteen; £4,000 for international students; Higher Education: £1,150 for EU students; £4,350 for international students; Examination Fees: None for students sixteen to eighteen years old; £72-£135 for students nineteen and over; housing: £106-£125/week for students over eighteen years old; £85-£100/week for students under 18
**Description of Program:** FD in Horse Care develops skills and knowledge needed to work in a livery yard or riding school. Routine duties, guided practicals, classroom teaching, riding and work experience will give students a taste of what it is like working full-time with horses. ND/NC/Award in Horse Management is designed for those who wish to become yard managers, competition grooms, or to progress to higher education. Includes routine duties, a supervisory role, stable management, riding, classroom sessions and a period of work experience. NVQ/Outreach in Horse Care are day-release courses designed for those working in the equine industry to develop prac-

tical skills needed to care for horses. Suitable for study at work through a Work-Based Learning Program (Foundation Modern Apprenticeship). HND in Horse Studies provides a high level of practical experience with academic studies and is an excellent qualification for technical, scientific, and management careers. It focuses on the elite equine performer in all disciplines with a thorough understanding of the equine industry. B.Sc. Biological Sciences (Horse Studies) includes elements of modern biological sciences, advanced aspects of equine performance as well as nutrition and industry standards. All students are encouraged to take BHS examinations up to BHSAI/II.

**Facilities:** Two indoor schools  (20m x 40m, 20m x 60m), jump course, cross-country fences, downland hacking, holiday letting, BHS examination center, traditional stabling for sixteen horses, barn stabling for 43 horses, horse walker, demonstration facilities

**Classroom/Hands-On Equine Classes:** FD in Horse Care: 30 percent/70 percent; ND/NC/Award in Horse Management: 50 percent/50 percent; NVQ Horse Care: mostly hands-on; HND in Horse Studies: depends on modules selected; B.Sc. in Biological Sciences (Horse Studies): depends on modules selected; students ride three to five times a week, lunge once a week, guided stable management lesson once a week

**Showing:** Dressage, show jumping

# Wallingford, England

## ACS Distance Education

**Website:**
www.acsedu.co.uk

**Type of School:**
Independent Study

P.O. Box 236, Wallingford, OX10 0WJ, United Kingdom. Phone (UK only): 0800 328 4723. Email: admin@acsedu.co.uk.

**Accreditation:** Recognized by the International Accreditation and Recognition Council

**Degrees Offered:** Associate Diploma, Advanced Diploma, Certificate, Advanced Certificate, Bachelor of Science

**Majors Offered:** Agriculture, Applied Management (Horse Management), Animal Husbandry

**Tuition Costs:** Available at www.acsedu.co.uk/fees.asp

**Description of Program:** Formal Courses: Advanced Certificate in Applied Management (Horse Management) is a course designed for managers, supervisors, or people who wish to work up to these positions within their industry. Certificate in Agriculture is designed as a base level qualification for technicians working in Agriculture. Associate Diploma in Animal Husbandry is a broad-based program that can be adapted to include a number of Horse Care modules. Advanced Diploma in Agriculture is designed for high level managers in the agricultural industry. Bachelor of Science (Agriculture) is a full degree program offered through Warnborough University, with modules developed by ACS Distance Education. Short Courses: Animal Breeding provides a broad understanding of animal breeding and its application if farming. Animal Husbandry I, II, and III provide a solid introduction to the anatomy and physiology of farm animals, animal health, and animal feeding. Horse Care I, II, and III cover terminology, horse psychology, using tack, parts of the body, the digestive system, evaluating the value of a paddock, grooming for different purposes, business applications, management of horses and health problems.

## British Driving Society

BDS Executive Secretary, 27 Dugard Place, Barford, Warwickshire CV35 8DX England. Phone: 01926 624420. Fax: 01926 624633. Email: email@britishdrivingsociety.co.uk.
**Accreditation:** British Driving Society
**Degrees Offered:** Certificate
**Majors Offered:** Preliminary, Intermediate, Advanced, Teaching Element, Grooms Test, Preliminary Grooms Test, BDS Tests for Disabled Drivers
**Tuition Costs:** Vary
**Description of Program:** Whatever your interest, pleasure driving or competing, singles, pairs or multiples, the British Driving Society will help and encourage you. Local area commissioners are on hand to give you guidance. Whether you are a beginner or need to brush up on your technique, the British Driving Society has a panel of qualified instructors throughout the country and runs a Proficiency Test Program, which is respected world-wide as a basis for safe driving. The Society has seven levels of competence set by the Test & Training Committee. This scheme is well established and has recently been completely revised. The tests are completely voluntary, but Preliminary, Intermediate and Advanced Certificates must be taken in sequence, with the Road Driving Assessment being prerequisite to the Intermediate Certificate.
**Facilities:** Vary

**Website:**
www.britishdrivingsociety.co.uk

**Type of School:**
Specialty Society

## British Horse Society

Training & Education, Stoneleigh Deer Park, Kenilworth, Warwickshire CV8 2XZ England. Phone: 01926 707700. Fax: 01926 707800. Email: enquiry@bhs.org.uk.
**Accreditation:** British Horse Society, the Trekking & Riding Society of Scotland, the Association of Irish Riding Establishments, the Welsh Trekking & Riding Association
**Degrees Offered:** Certificate
**Majors Offered:** British Equestrian Tourism: Assistant Ride Leader, Ride Leader, Riding Holiday Centre Manager; Fellowship of the BHS, BHSI: Stable Manager, Equitation and Teaching, Intermediate Teaching Test, Preliminary Teaching Test, Stage 1, Stage 2, Stage 3, Stage 4
**Tuition Costs:** (Pounds) Exam fees: £56 to £750
**Description of Program:** The British Horse Society administers an internationally recognized examination system designed to meet the needs of employers and those who wish to work in the equestrian industry as riding instructors, trainers, or yard managers. While it is not obligatory for candidates to receive their training at BHS Approved Centers, it is certainly advisable to train at a center that understands the requirements of each level and has qualified instructors and suitable horses to ensure training is of the highest caliber. Contact BHS for a list of approved riding and training schools.
**Facilities:** There are a large number of BHS-approved training centers throughout the U.K. and overseas.
**Showing:** TREC

**Website:**
www.bhs.org.uk

**Type of School:**
Registered Educational Charity

## Equi Study

Moreton Hall, Moreton Morrell, Warwickshire CV35 9BL England.
Phone: 01926 651085. Fax: 01926 318300. Email: equistudy@warkscol.ac.uk.
**Accreditation:** British Horse Society, affiliated with Warwickshire College and Harper Adams University
**Degrees Offered:** Certificate of Achievement, Foundation Degree, Higher National Certificate, Higher National Diploma
**Majors Offered:** Advanced Horse Knowledge (CA), Equine Studies (Fd.Sc., HNC, HND), courses to study for BHS Assistant Instructor or BHS Intermediate Instructor certifications, Health and Safety Program (horse handlers and barn workers)
**Tuition Costs:** (Pounds) £30 to £4,500 plus additional postage charges for overseas students
**Description of Program:** You have found the right place if you are looking for the most progressive, yet most established equine distance-learning provider. Courses and qualifications that are recognized and respected by the horse world at large are provided by this program. This respect is built over time, due to the quality of the graduates produced by the learning process. Since Equi Study joined forces with Warwickshire, the premier equine college in the U.K., it has gone from strong to stronger. Equi Study is now part of the delivery routes at Warwickshire College, where students can move between a full-time, part-time, and home-study delivery of their particular course. This partnership allows for the recognized route for gaining further and higher qualifications, which carry weight where it matters. The continued development of on-line learning and assessment means that truly distant learners will be supported in an exciting and innovative way. Further partnerships with the British Horse Society help to ensure the BHS Assistant Instructor and BHS Intermediate Instructor Series that remain part of the most professional and proven training systems. Warwickshire Professional Certificate and Diploma courses enable people to study small units of interest; modules include Equine Anatomy, Equine Behavior, Feeding and Nutrition, and Small Business Management.
**Facilities:** Vary
**Classroom/Hands-On Equine Classes:** Most courses are entirely distance learning; however, higher education programs require some attendance and are classroom/laboratory based. Summer schools are available and are comprised of a mixture of practical riding, stable management, and theory.

## Pittern Hill Stables

Kineton, Warks, Warwickshire CV35 0JF England. Phone: 01926 640370.
Email: info@pitternhillstables.co.uk.
**Accreditation:** British Horse Society, the Side-Saddle Association
**Majors Offered:** Side-Saddle Association Exams
**Tuition Costs:** (Pounds) Lessons: £17/hour group; £30/hour private
**Description of Program:** Students normally ride two hours per day, with additional hands-on instruction in fitting and maintaining side-saddles. Instruction and training towards the Side-Saddle Association Instructors Exams is also provided.
**Facilities:** Lecture room and video facilities, some accommodation on-site
**Showing:** Students are encouraged to take part in shows; horses and transport are provided.

## Warwickshire College

Warwick New Road, Leamington Spa, Warwickshire, CV32 5JE England.
Phone: 08001926318000. Fax: 01926318111. Email: enquires@warkscol.ac.uk.
**Degrees Offered:** NVQ Certificate, Vocational Certificate, First Diploma, National Certificate, Foundation Degree, Higher National Diploma, Bachelor of Science (Hons), Bachelor of Arts (Hons)
**Majors Offered:** Equine and Business Management (B.A.), Equine and Human Sport Science (HND, B.Sc.), Equine Science (HND, B.Sc.), Equine and Human Sports Coaching (HND), Equine Studies (Fd.Sc., HND, B.A.), Horse Studies (NVQ C, VC, FD), Modern Apprenticeships (NVQ C), Pre-Farriery Training (FD), Farriery Registration Council Apprenticeships, Management of Horses (NC)
**Tuition Costs:** (Pounds) £434.50-3,200
**Description of Program:** Part-time, full-time, and distance learning available on selected programs.
**Facilities:** Indoor and outdoor arenas, brand new stable block, BHS Horse Trial Course, 120 horses, two outdoor schools, two indoor schools, BHS Novice Horse Trial Course, cross-country training ground with cantering track, performance development and veterinary units, facilities for polocrosse, driving, and other equine activities

**Website:**
www.warkscol.ac.uk

**Type of School:**
Public University, Independent Study

# West Midlands, England

## Brookfields Riding & Livery Centre

Cannock Road, Shareshill, Wolverhampton, West Midlands WV10 7LZ England. Phone: 01922 414090.
**Accreditation:** British Horse Society, Association of British Riding Schools, South Staffs. Sports Council, licensed by South Staffs. District Council
**Degrees Offered:** Certification
**Majors Offered:** ABRS Exams, BHS Stage 1, BHS Prelim Dressage Tests,
BHS Progressive Tests 1-6
**Facilities:** Two indoor schools, outdoor school

**Type of School:**
Specialty School

## The Walsall College of Arts & Technology

Leather Department, Shelley Campus, Scarborough Road, Walsall, West Midlands WS2 2TY England. Phone: 01922 720889.
**Degrees Offered:** Diploma
**Majors Offered:** Saddlery Studies
**Description of Program:** This course introduces you to saddlery work and includes both traditional rural saddlery and modern production methods. The first year covers all of the basic skills and techniques in saddle- and bridle-making, and leads to City & Guilds Stage 1 and 2 Certificates. During the second year, you will work on a variety of more advanced projects and can opt to specialize in either bridle- or harness-making, or saddlery workshop. Experience is supported by factory exhibitions and factory visits. In addition, you will receive a grounding in business studies, which will be particularly important if you plan to become self-employed.

**Website:**
www.walcat.ac.uk

**Type of School:**
Further Education College

## University of Wolverhampton

Email: enquiries@wlv.ac.uk.
**Accreditation:** Courses run jointly with Rodbaston College
**Degrees Offered:** Higher National Diploma, Bachelor of Science (Hons)
**Majors Offered:** Equine Studies
**Tuition Costs:** Contact School
**Description of Program:** Equine Programs include the following clearly defined study areas: 1) The HND course is aimed at developing and nurturing managers for the equine industry. It is a program that introduces numerous equine avenues that can be explored in greater detail in the final year of the degree. Fundamental aspects of equine issues include behavior and training, practical and academic equitation, equine anatomy and physiology, genetics and equine reproduction, chemical principles with key business and marketing principles for equine enterprises. 2) Detailed aspects of equine science. 3) Current advanced aspects of equine management, physiology and nutrition, together with advances in animal biology and ethical and social issues surrounding genetic modification. 4) IT skills required by the equine industry. 5) Honours Project (B.Sc. only): a current equine topic is selected by the student and studied by investigation of primary literature and research. 6) The principles required to plan, implement, and evaluate research work.
**Facilities:** Rodbaston College's excellent land-based resources include a working farm, animal care unit, veterinary nursing center, equestrian center, floristry center, gardens and hot houses, and a unique fisheries center. A virtual tour of facilities is available at www.rodbaston.com.
**Classroom/Hands-on Equine Classes:** 70/30
**Showing:** Students are encouraged by discounted entry fees to compete in alternate dressage and show-jumping competitions throughout the academic year.

# Wiltshire, England

## The Saddlery Training Centre

14–17 The Malverns, Chery Orchard Lane, Salisbury, Wiltshire SP2 7JG England. Phone: 01722 341144. Fax: 01722 349669. Email: sales@saddlerytraining.co.uk or info@saddlerytraining.co.uk.
**Accreditation:** Partnership with the Society of Master Saddlers
**Degrees Offered:** City & Guilds Certificate
**Majors Offered:** Saddle, Bridle & Harness Making Level 2-3
**Tuition Costs:** (Pounds) £400/week plus materials; £25 housing/night (B & B)
**Description of Program:** Saddle, bridle, and harness making for apprentices, trainees, and others in the trade. Five to six students per course.
**Facilities:** Workshop, tools, and equipment provided.
**Classroom/Hands-on Equine Classes:** All training courses are practically based in the workshop.

## Stonar School

Cottles Park, Atworth, Melksham, Wiltshire SN12 8NT England. Contact: Mrs. Jill Storey, Director of Riding. Phone: 01225 701 765. Fax: 01225 701 767.
Email: ridingoffice@stonar.wilts.sch.uk.
**Accreditation:** British Horse Society

**Degrees Offered:** Certificate
**Majors Offered:** Up to BHS Assistant Instructor, GCSE Riding and A level PE with Riding option
**Tuition Costs:** (Pounds) Starting from £145 per term
**Description of Program:** Independent day and boarding school for girls four to eighteen years old. The British Horse Society has given this unique center its full approval with its indoor school, floodlit outdoor school, and two miles of BE cross-country course. There is stabling for 60 horses, and Stonar can offer a number of different livery options. Girls are able to combine the benefits of an independent education for themselves with excellent livery for their horses.
**Facilities:** Covered school, outdoor arena, cross-country course, stabling for 60 horses
**Showing:** Specialist competition training, dressage, show jumping, eventing

## Wickstead Farm Equestrian Centre

Highworth, Swindon, Wiltshire, SN6 7PP. Contact: Mrs. V. Mace.
Phone: 01793 762 265.
**Accreditation:** British Horse Society
**Degrees Offered:** Certificate
**Majors Offered:** BHS Stages 1 and 2

**Type of School:**
Specialty School

## Wiltshire College, Lackham

Lacock, Chippenham, Wiltshire SN15 2NY. Phone: 01249 466800. Fax: 01249 444474. Email: info@wiltscoll.ac.uk or courses@wiltscoll.ac.uk.
**Degrees Offered:** Certificate, First Diploma, National Diploma, Higher National Diploma
**Majors Offered:** Up to BHS Assistant Instructor (C), Equine Management (HND), Horse Care (FD), Horse Management (ND)

**Website:**
www.wiltscoll.ac.uk

**Type of School:**
College

# Yorkshire, England

## Acre Cliffe Riding School & Equestrian Centre

Ellar Ghyll, Bradford Road, Otley, Yorkshire LS21 3DN England.
Contact: Mrs. A. Everall. Phone: 01943 873912. Fax: 01943 870789.
**Accreditation:** British Horse Society
**Degrees Offered:** Certificate
**Majors Offered:** Up to BHS Assistant Instructor

**Type of School:**
Specialty School

## Askham Bryan College

Central Admissions, Askham Bryan College, Askham Bryan, York, North Yorkshire, YO23 3FR England. Phone: +44 (0) 01904 772211. Fax: +44 (0) 01904 772288.
Email: sf@askham-bryan.ac.uk.
**Degrees Offered:** Certificate, First Diploma, National Diploma
**Majors Offered:** BHS Horse Care NVQ Levels 1-3 (C), Horse Care (FD), Horse Management (ND)

**Website:**
www.askham-bryan.ac.uk

**Type of School:**
Further Higher Education College

## Bishop Burton College

Bishop Burton, Beverley, E. Yorkshire HU17 8QG England. Phone: 01964 553000. Fax: 01964 553101. Email: enquiries@bishopburton.ac.uk.

**Accreditation:** Further Education Funding Council, Beacon College of Excellence, Centre of Vocational Excellence

**Degrees Offered:** ASET, NVQ, BHS Certificate, City & Guilds National Certificate, City & Guilds Advanced National Certificate, BTEC First Diploma, BTEC National Diploma, BTEC National Award Horse Management, Foundation Science Degree, Bachelor of Science, Bachelor of Science (Hons.)

**Majors Offered:** BHS Stages 1-4, NVQ 1-3, Equine Skills Foundation, Horse Care (FD, NC), Horse Management (ANC, NA, ND), Equine Management (Fd.Sc.), Equine Science and Management (B.Sc., B.Sc. [Hons]), Modern Apprenticeship in Horse Care

**Tuition Costs:** Contact School

**Description of Program:** MA program combines the opportunity of working within the equine industry while being paid an allowance or wage with training that leads toward an NVQ in Horse Care. FD in Horse Care Program is aimed at the study of horses and the equine industry. NC in Horse Care Program has been redeveloped to allow students to gain wider practical skills on a work placement during the year. ANC Horse Management Program allows those who have followed the NC in Horse Care Program the opportunity to progress to a more advanced level. NA Horse Management Program allows those who have followed the FD in Horse Care Program the opportunity to progress to a more advanced level. ND Horse Management Program gives a broad-based, yet in-depth study of the industry, preparing students for the wide range of jobs available in this fast-growing area. Fd.Sc. Equine Management Program has options in Therapy and Rehabilitation, and Equitation and Teaching. B.Sc. Equine Science and Management Program aims to allow students with an HND to achieve an ordinary degree in one year of study. B.Sc. (Hons) Equine Science and Management Program provides an in-depth specialist understanding of the equine industry through applied study of the scientific principles and practices of horse management, along with business practice and administration.

**Facilities:** More than 80 horses, large tack rooms, forage barns, outdoor school and two indoor schools, a cross-country schooling paddock and four cross-country courses, equine therapy laboratory and associated laboratory facilities

**Classroom/Hands-On Equine Classes:** Vary

**Showing:** Dressage, show jumping, and carriage driving trials to BHS Pre-Novice, Novice, Intermediate, and Advanced Horse Trials

## Cherry Tree Livery Stables

Gill Lane, Kearby, Nr. Wetherby, West Yorkshire LS22 4BS England.
Contact: Mrs. R. A. Search. Phone: 01132 886460.

**Accreditation:** British Horse Society

**Degrees Offered:** Certificate

**Majors Offered:** Up to BHS Assistant Instructor

## Grove House Stables

Grove Wood Road, Misterton, Doncaster, Yorkshire DN10 4EF England.
Contact: Mr. Andrew Stennett. Phone: 01427 890802. Fax: 01427 891471.
Email: info@grovehousestables.co.uk or andrewstennett@grovehousestables.co.uk.

**Degrees Offered:** Certificate
**Majors Offered:** NVQ Levels 1-3

## Longfield Equestrian Centre

Type of School:
Specialty School

Middle Longfield Farm, Todmorden, West Yorkshire OL14 6JN England.
Contact: Mrs. C. Farnaby. Phone: 01706 812736. Fax: 01706 839 214.
**Accreditation:** British Horse Society
**Degrees Offered:** Certificate.
**Majors Offered:** Up to BHS Assistant Instructor

## Middleton Park Equestrian Centre

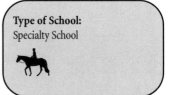

Type of School:
Specialty School

Middleton Grove, Off Dewsbury Road, Leeds, West Yorkshire LS11 5TZ United Kingdom. Contact: Mrs. B. Backhouse. Phone: 0113 277 1962. Fax: 0113 272 3592.
**Accreditation:** British Horse Society
**Degrees Offered:** Certificate
**Majors Offered:** BHS Stages 1 and 2

## Naburn Grange Riding Centre

Type of School:
Specialty School

Naburn, Yorkshire, YO19 4RU England. Contact: Mrs. D. Horn. Phone: 01904 728283.
Email: horses@globalnet.co.uk.
**Accreditation:** British Horse Society
**Degrees Offered:** Certificate
**Majors Offered:** Up to BHS Assistant Instructor

## North Humberside Riding Centre

Type of School:
Specialty School

Easington, Nr. Hull, East Yorkshire, HU12 OUA United Kingdom.
Contact: Mrs. T. Biglin. Phone: 01964 650250.
**Accreditation:** British Horse Society
**Degrees Offered:** Certificate
**Majors Offered:** Up to BHS Assistant Instructor

## Northern Racing College

Website:
www.northernracingcollege.co.uk

Type of School:
Specialty College

The Stables, Rossington Hall, Great North Road, Doncaster, S. Yorkshire DN11 0HN
England. Phone: 01302 861000. Fax: 01302 864151.
Email: info@nrcdonc.demon.co.uk.
**Accreditation:** British Horseracing Training Board (BHTB)
**Degrees Offered:** Certificate
**Majors Offered:** NVQ Levels 1-3 in Horse Care and Race Horse Care and Management
**Tuition Costs:** (Pounds) Free for EU students; £5,000 includes twelve-week residential course
**Description of Program:** A twelve-week fully residential course covering all aspects of horse care leading to the NVQ Level 1 qualification. Students of all levels of experience are welcome. All you will need to bring with you is your passion for horses and a drive

to succeed, and this school will see to it that you receive the best start to your racing career! Job Description: NVQ Level 1 in Horse Care includes mucking out, sweeping, feeding, grooming, exercising and care of horses. Very good career prospects. Entry Requirements: candidates should be motivated, hardworking, and work well with animals, and be able to live away from home. Previous experience with horses is not necessary. Must ideally weigh under [ten stone] if you want to pursue a riding career.

**Facilities:** Fully-equipped stable blocks, outdoor riding schools, all-weather six-and-a-half furlong gallop, grass gallop, indoor riding school, starting stalls, jumping facilities, mechanical racehorse simulator, library and classroom, lecture theater, video teaching facilities, IT Suite, video library, ex-racehorses, residential and training center

**Classroom/Hands-On Equine Classes:** As the qualification is vocational, students spend most of their time working on the yard, with plenty of riding and some classroom work.

**Type of School:**
Specialty College

## Northern Riding Centre

The Stables, Water Lane, Thornhall Road, Dewsbury, W.Yorkshire WF12 9PY United Kingdom. Contact: Mr. Wray. Phone: 01924 466240.
**Accreditation:** British Horse Society
**Degrees Offered:** Certificate
**Majors Offered:** BHS Stages 1 and 2

**Website:**
www.queenethelburgas.edu

**Type of School:**
Private PreK-12 School

## Queen Ethelburga's College/Chapter House Preparatory School

Thorpe Underwood Hall, Ouseburn, York YO26 9SS England. Phone: 08707 423330. Email: remember@compuserve.com.
**Accreditation:** Recognized by the British Council, approved by the British Horse Society
**Degrees Offered:** BHS Certification, NVQ Certification, High School Diploma
**Majors Offered:** BHS Assistant Instructor (BHS C), Horse Care Level 1-3 (NVQ C)
**Tuition Costs:** (Pounds) £6,489/term; room and board included; free livery for pupil's horse if required
**Description of Program:** Queen's Kindergarten is for boys and girls aged three months to three years. Chapter House Preparatory Schools is for boys and girls aged three to eleven years. Queen Etherlburga's College is for boys and girls aged eleven to nineteen years. For those who are interested in riding, Queen Ethelburga's is the school where academic opportunities go hand-in-glove with supreme riding facilities and the highest quality of riding instruction for everyone, from the keen "hobby" rider to those who seek professional qualifications or top competitive riding skills. Pupils can make the fullest use of these riding opportunities, and boarders may bring their own horses to school, in the full confidence that the stabling and livery are among the best in Europe. If you don't own a horse, you can, of course, use the horses provided. Students are able to study Part I, II and III of the BHS Horse Society Assistant Instructor's Certificate. At the same time, you may study for the Equestrian Horse Care NVQ Level I, then go onto Level II and then onto the Horse Care and Management (Level III).
**Facilities:** Top-quality covered stables for more than 185 horses, full set of indoor jumps, 20 floodlit grass day paddocks, parking for 250 horse boxes, plenty of local hacking trails, ten acres of all-weather floodlit outdoor arenas, Olympic-sized indoor arena with full competition twin lighting levels, several tack rooms, three cross-country courses including water jump, two equestrian classrooms with TV/video, outside

hose wash area, all-weather floodlit half-mile jumping track
**Classroom/Hands-On Equine Classes:** Vary
**Showing:** Horse shows, one-day horse trials and events, local competitions and national shows

## Snowdon Farm Riding School

Snowdon Lane, Troway, Marsh Lane, Nr. Sheffield, Yorkshire S21 5RT England.
Phone: 01246 417172. Email: info@snowdonfarmequestrian.co.uk.
**Accreditation:** British Horse Society, Association of British Riding Schools
**Degrees Offered:** Certification
**Majors Offered:** Up to BHS Assistant Instructor
**Tuition Costs:** Vary
**Description of Program:** Full program facilities
**Facilities:** Indoor school, training room, cross-country course, show jumps, viewing area, housing not provided
**Classroom/Hands-On Equine Classes:** Depends on the student.
**Showing:** Eventing, dressage, show jumping

**Website:**
www.snowdonfarmequestrian.co.uk

**Type of School:**
Specialty School

## Wadlands Hall Equestrian Centre

Priesthorpe Road, Farsley, Pudsey, Yorkshire LS28 5RN United Kingdom.
Contact: J. Driver & Partners. Phone: 0113 2363 648. Fax: 0113 290 9233.
**Accreditation:** British Horse Society
**Degrees Offered:** Certificate
**Majors Offered:** BHS Stages 1 and 2

**Type of School:**
Specialty School

## The Yorkshire Riding Centre Ltd.

Markington, Harrogate, N. Yorkshire HG3 3PE England. Phone: 01765 677207.
Email: info@yrc.co.uk.
**Accreditation:** British Horse Society
**Degrees Offered:** Certification.
**Majors Offered:** Stages 1-3, Preliminary Teaching, BHSI Exam
**Tuition Costs:** (Pounds) From £115 per week (including accommodation and all meals)
**Description of Program:** The shortest program lasts three months, where students can achieve Stages I, II, III and PTT Exams. The exact duration of stay depends on the individual's exam goals and previous experience. The center is run by Olympic competitors Jane and Christopher Bartle; training is supervised by Jane and carried out by carefully chosen, mature, and knowledgeable instructors. Horses are carefully chosen, and many have excellent competition records. Above all, this school provides a friendly, relaxed and professional atmosphere.
**Facilities:** Two indoor arenas, one outdoor arena, cross-country course, canter track, full set of show jumps, 60 horses, accommodation for students
**Classroom/Hands-On Equine Classes:** 33:66
**Showing:** Students may compete in on-site shows. If a student has his/her own horse, then there are also opportunities to travel to shows away from the center.

**Website:**
www.yrc.co.uk

**Type of School:**
Specialty School

## Enniskillen College and Greenmount College

**Website:**
www.enniskillencollege.ac.uk or
www.greenmount.ac.uk

**Type of School:**
Land-Based College

Enneskillen College, Levaghy, Enniskillen BT74 4GF Northern Ireland. Phone: 02866 344853. Fax: 02866 344888. Email: enquiries@dardni.gov.uk. Greenmount College, Antrim BT41 4PU Northern Ireland. Phone: 08000 284291. Fax: 02894 426605. Email: enquiries@dardni.gov.uk.

**Degrees Offered:** Certificate, Diploma, First Diploma, National Diploma, Higher National Certificate, Higher National Diploma, Bachelor of Science (Hons)

**Majors Offered:** Equine Studies (HNC, HND, B.Sc.[Hons]), Horse Care (FD), Horse Management (ND), NVQ Level 2 in Racehorse Care (C), Science [Equine Science] via distance learning (C, D)

## Lessans Riding Stables

**Type of School:**
Specialty School

126 Monlough Road, Saintfield, Co. Down, Northern Ireland. Contact: Miss. P. Auret. Phone: 01238 510141.

**Accreditation:** British Horse Society

**Degrees Offered:** Certification

**Majors Offered:** Up to BHS Assistant Instructor

## Necarne Castle

**Type of School:**
Specialty School

The Ulster Lakeland Equestrian Park, Irvinestown, Co. Fermanagh, Northern Ireland. Contact: Mr. Seamus McAlinney. Phone: 01365 621 919. Fax: 01365 628 382.

**Accreditation:** British Horse Society

**Degrees Offered:** Certificate

**Majors Offered:** Up to BHS Assistant Instructor

# Scotland, United Kingdom

## Argyll Trail Riding

**Website:**
www.brenfield.co.uk

**Type of School:**
Specialty School

Brenfield House, Brenfield, Argyll PA30 8ER Scotland. Contact: Ms. T.B. Gray-Stephens. Phone: 01546 603274. Fax: 01546 603225. Email: info@brenfield.co.uk.

**Accreditation:** British Horse Society, Trekking and Riding Society of Scotland, Association of British Riding Schools

**Degrees Offered:** Certificate

**Majors Offered:** BTEC Assistant Ride Leader and Ride Leader

**Description of Program:** Trail riding, by the day or hour, week-long trail riding holidays, endurance riding, swimming with horses, beach gallops, TREC training and competitions

**Facilities:** Outdoor arena, cross-country course, clay pigeon shooting, local hotel accommodation

## Ayrshire Equitation Centre

South Mains, Corton Road, Ayr, KA6 6BY Scotland. Contact: Mr. K. Galbraith.
Phone: 01292 266267. Fax: 01292 610323. Email: ayrequitation@hotmail.com.
**Accreditation:** British Horse Society
**Degrees Offered:** Certificate
**Majors Offered:** Up to BHS Assistant Instructor
**Facilities:** Outdoor arena, indoor school, cross-country course

**Website:**
www.ayrequestrian.co.uk

**Type of School:**
Specialty School

## Easterton Stables

Mugdock, Milngavie, Glasgow, Central Region Scotland G62 8LG United Kingdom.
Contact: Miss R. Brown and Mr. D. Ralston. Phone: 0141 956 1518/2425.
**Accreditation:** British Horse Society
**Degrees Offered:** Certificate
**Majors Offered:** BHS Stages 1 and 2

**Type of School:**
Specialty School

## Gleneagles Equestrian Centre

Auchterarder, Perthshire PH3 1NZ Scotland. Phone: 01764 694351.
Email: resort.sales@gleneagles.com.
**Accreditation:** British Horse Society
**Degrees Offered:** Vocational Qualifications
**Majors Offered:** Up to BHS Instructor
**Tuition Costs:** (Pounds) £220 per week plus VAT for three months of intensive training. Short riding holidays are £275 per week and up, not including accommodation. Career training students receive a training allowance in return for working at the center; accommodation is supplied. Accommodation for the twelve-week intensive course is £1,000 plus VAT. Accommodation for short riding holidays is subject to availability.
**Description of Program:** Career training towards BHSI Level qualifications, fee-paying three-month intensive training for BHS qualifications, short instructional holidays in all disciplines. Career training students receive eight hours of training per week. Fee-paying intensive training students receive 20 hours of training per week. Short instructional holiday students receive up to four hours per day (riding/lecture), depending on chosen course.
**Facilities:** Covered and heated arena (75m x 37m), covered arena (20m x 40m), outdoor arena (60m x 40m), four brand-new cross-country courses from training to novice level
**Classroom/Hands-On Equine Classes:** 25:75 for career training students; 50:50 for fee-paying students
**Showing:** Students get the opportunity to compete.

**Website:**
www.gleneagles.com

**Type of School:**
Specialty School

## Hayfield Equestrian Centre

Hazelhead Park, Aberdeen AB15 8BB Scotland. Phone: +44 (0) 1224 315703.
Email: info@hayfield.com.
**Accreditation:** British Horse Society, Association of British Riding Schools, Trekking and Riding Society of Scotland
**Degrees Offered:** In-house Equiworld Certificate, BHS Certificate, ABRS Certificate, TRSS Certificate

**Website:**
www.hayfield.com

**Type of School:**
Specialty School

**Majors Offered:** All BHS, ABRS, & TRSS Exams
**Tuition Costs:** (Pounds) From £600 to £2,000 per month
**Description of Program:** Hayfield is a friendly training center where pupils train and work with dedicated professional staff on a training program designed to deliver riding instruction, horse training, and stable management to Hayfield clients. Unique to Hayfield, students work almost on a one-to-one basis with qualified staff. Each student has a mentor who will personally set their goals, follow their progress, and is responsible for creating their individual training program.
**Facilities:** Two indoor schools, one outdoor paddock, one outdoor jumping arena, cross-country course, 50 horses and ponies, comfortable accommodations, lounge, clubroom, heated classroom
**Classroom/Hands-on Equine Classes:** Varies according to training level, but all students ride daily and are free to join additional evening classes when appropriate. Lectures set by personal mentor as well as open lectures at the center.
**Showing:** Local competitions available for exam experience.

## Logie Farm Riding Centre

**Website:**
www.angelfire.com/fm/logiefarm/

**Type of School:**
Specialty School

Glenferness, Nairn IV12 5XA Scotland. Phone/Fax: 01309 651226.
**Accreditation:** British Horse Society, Scottish Trekking and Riding Association
**Degrees Offered:** Certificate
**Majors Offered:** BHS Stages 1-3, BHS Preliminary Teaching
**Tuition Costs:** (Pounds) £150 per week
**Description of Program:** BHS Stages
**Facilities:** Include 90-acre farm, extensive cross-country course, outdoor arena, miles of traffic-free riding
**Classroom/Hands-On Equine Classes:** Two to four hours riding daily
**Showing:** Hunter trials, dressage, one-day-events, horse shows

## The North Highland College

**Website:**
www.nhcscotland.com

**Type of School:**
College

Achaurole, Halkirk, Caithness, Scotland KW12 6XQ United Kingdom.
Contact: Mr. James Manro. Phone: 01847 831827. Fax: 01847 893870.
**Accreditation:** British Horse Society
**Degrees Offered:** Certificate
**Majors Offered:** Up to BHS Assistant Instructor

## Portree Riding and Trekking Stables

**Website:**
www.portreeriding.co.uk

**Type of School:**
Specialty School

Garalapin, Portree, Isle of Skye, IV51 9LN Scotland. Contact: Mr. Richard Long. Phone: 01478 613124. Email: info@portreeriding.co.uk.
**Accreditation:** British Horse Society, British Equestrian Tourism
**Degrees Offered:** Certificate
**Majors Offered:** Up to BHS Assistant Instructor, Scottish Vocational Qualifications, BET Assistant Trek Leader, BET Trek Leader, BET Holiday Riding Centre Manager
**Tuition Costs:** (Pounds) £17 to £21 for housing
**Description of Program:** If it is a career you are interested in, take a look at the Training and Skillseeker Programs. Training may be undertaken on a full- or part-time basis (depending on the course selected). This school is the only SVQ (Scottish Vocational Qualifications) Level 3 location in the Highlands that has an indoor school. Students

are taught and trained, from beginner to British Horse Society Assistant Instructor qualification. If you want to be a professional groom, trek leader, rider, or instructor (or just achieve qualification in the equine industry), a formal qualification that is nationally and internationally recognized is the answer.

**Facilities:** Facilities include a huge indoor riding school (the largest north of Perth!), a superb all-weather sand arena, fully qualified instructors on hand at all times, and about 30 well-schooled horses and ponies, to ensure that we can find the right combination for you, whatever your level.

## Oatridge Agricultural College

Ecclesmachan, Broxburn, West Lothian EH52 6NH Scotland. Phone: 01506 854387. Fax: 01506 833373. Email: info@oatridge.ac.uk.
**Degrees Offered:** Certificate, Modern Apprenticeship, Higher National Certificate, Higher National Diploma
**Majors Offered:** BHS Exams, Horse Management (C, HNC, HND), SVQ Levels 2-3 (MA)

**Website:** www.oatridge.ac.uk

**Type of School:** College

## The Royal (Dick) School of Veterinary Studies

The University of Edinburgh, Summerhall, Edinburgh EH9 1QH Scotland, United Kingdom. Phone: +44 (0)131 650 6130. Fax: +44 (0)131 650 6585.
Email: DickVet@ed.ac.uk.
**Degrees Offered:** Bachelor of Veterinary Medicine and Surgery, Master of Science, Doctor of Veterinary Medicine and Surgery
**Majors Offered:** Equine Science (M.Sc.), Veterinary Medicine and Surgery (B.V.M.S., D.V.M.S.)

**Website:** www.vet.ed.ac.uk

**Type of School:** Veterinary School

## University of Aberdeen

Department of Agriculture, University of Aberdeen, Hilton Campus, Block M, Hilton Place, Aberdeen AB24 4FA, Scotland. Phone: +44 (0)1224 274230. Fax: +44 (0)1224 273731. Email: e.watt@abdn.ac.uk.
**Degrees Offered:** Bachelor of Science
**Majors Offered:** Equine Science

**Website:** www.abdn.ac.uk

**Type of School:** University

## University of Glasgow

Faculty of Veterinary Medicine, 464 Bearsden Road, Glasgow G61 1QH Scotland. Contact: Mrs. Joyce Wason. Phone: +44 (0)141 330 5700. Email: j.wason@vet.gla.ac.uk.
**Degrees Offered:** Bachelor of Veterinary Medicine and Surgery

**Website:** www.gla.ac.uk

**Type of School:** University

## Veterinary Field Station

Easter Bush, Roslin, Midlothian EH25 9RG Scotland. Contact: Miss K. Banks. Phone: 0131 650 6284.
**Accreditation:** British Horse Society
**Degrees Offered:** Certificate
**Majors Offered:** Up to BHS Assistant Instructor

**Type of School:** Specialty School

## Coleg Gwent

**Website:**
www.coleggwent.ac.uk

**Type of School:**
Further Education College

Headquarters, The Rhadyr, Usk, Gwent NP15 1XJ Wales. Phone: +44 (0)1495 333333. Fax: +44 (0)1495 333526. Email: info@coleggwent.ac.uk.
**Degrees Offered:** Certificate, First Diploma, National Certificate, Advanced National Certificate, Higher National Certificate, Higher National Diploma
**Majors Offered:** BHS Instructor Training (C), BHS Stages 1-4 (C), Equine Studies (HNC, HND), Horse Care (FD, NC), Management of Horses (ANC), NVQ Levels 1-3 Horse Care (C)

## Coleg Meirion-Dwyfor

**Website:**
www.meirion-dwyfor.ac.uk

**Type of School:**
Community College

Glynllifon Campus, Ffordd Clynnog, Caernarfon, Gwynedd LL54 5DU. Phone: +44 (0)1286 830261. Fax: +44 (0)1286 831597. Email: coleg@meirion-dwyfor.ac.uk.
**Accreditation:** British Horse Society
**Degrees Offered:** Certificate, First Diploma, National Certificate, National Diploma, Higher National Certificate, Higher National Diploma
**Majors Offered:** Up to BHS Assistant Instructor, NVQ Levels 1-3
**Tuition Costs:** (Pounds) No tuition; HND and HNC are approximately £1,000 per year
**Description of Program:** The Higher National Diploma and Higher National Certificate courses are taught in association with Bangor University.
**Facilities:** Indoor school, outdoor school, cross-country course, off-road riding, beautiful country close to the sea and the mountains of Snowdonia
**Classroom/Hands-On Equine Classes:** Vary
**Showing:** Students have the opportunity to compete.

## Coleg Sir Gâr

**Website:**
www.ccta.ac.uk

**Type of School:**
Community College

Pibwrlwyd Campus, Carmarthen, Carmarthenshire, SA31 2NH, Wales UK. Phone: +44 (0)1554 748000.
**Degrees Offered:** Higher National Certificate, Higher National Diploma
**Majors Offered:** Equine Studies, Animal Studies, Agriculture

## The Equestrian Centre

**Type of School:**
Specialty School

Gresford Road, Hope, Wrexham, Clwyd LL12 9SD Wales. Contact: Mr. & Mrs. M.W. Tytherleigh. Phone: 01978 760356/761349. Fax: 01978 762388.
**Accreditation:** British Horse Society
**Degrees Offered:** Certificate
**Majors Offered:** Up to BHS Assistant Instructor

## Institute of Rural Studies, University of Wales, Aberystwyth

**Website:**
www.irs.aber.ac.uk

**Type of School:**
University

The Welsh Institute of Rural Studies, University of Wales, Llanbadarn Fawr, Aberystwyth, Ceredigion, SY23 3AL Wales. Fax: 01970 611264. Email: wirs@aber.ac.uk.

**Degrees Offered:** Foundation Degree, Higher National Diploma, Bachelor of Science (Hons), Master of Science

**Majors Offered:** Equine Science (B.Sc., M.Sc.), Equine Studies (FD, HND, B.Sc.), Equine and Business Studies (HND)

## Isle of Anglesey Stud Farm & Riding Centre

Taly y Foel, Dwyran, Anglesey, North Wales LL61 6LQ Wales. Phone: 01248 430377. Fax: 01248-430977. Email: riding@talyfoel.u-net.com.

**Accreditation:** British Horse Society

**Degrees Offered:** Certificate

**Majors Offered:** BHS Stages 1-3, BHS Riding and Road Safety, NVQ Levels 1-3

**Tuition Costs:** (Pounds) £15 per hack or lesson

**Description of Program:** Regular and holiday riders; students for one-year, part-time courses

**Facilities:** Indoor facilities, cross-country course, riding holidays, beach riding, caravan accommodation or bed and breakfast

**Classroom/Hands-On Equine Classes:** Vary

**Website:**
www.tal-y-foel.co.uk

**Type of School:**
Specialty School

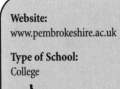

## Liege Manor Farm Equestrian Centre

Liege Manor Farm, Llancarfan Lane, Bonvilston, Vale of Glamorgan CF5 6TQ Wales. Contact: Miss Sarah M. Bassett. Phone: 01446 781648.

**Accreditation:** British Horse Society

**Degrees Offered:** Certificate

**Majors Offered:** Up to BHS Assistant Instructor

**Type of School:**
Specialty School

## Pembrokeshire College

Haverfordwest, Pembrokeshire SA61 1SZ Wales. Phone: +44 (0)1437 765247. Fax: +44 (0)1437 767279. Email: admissions@pembrokeshire.ac.uk.

**Degrees Offered:** NVQ Certificate, Foundation Award, National Award, National Diploma

**Majors Offered:** Horse Care for those with Disabilities (Fd.A.), Horse Studies (NA, ND), NVQ 2 Horse Care (C), NVQ 3 Horse Care and Management (C)

**Website:**
www.pembrokeshire.ac.uk

**Type of School:**
College

## Pencoed College

Bridgend, Mid Glamorgan CF35 5LG Wales. Phone: 01656 302600. Fax: 01656 302601. Email: pencoed.enquiries@bridgend.ac.uk.

**Degrees Offered:** Certificate, First Diploma, National Diploma, Advanced National Certificate, Higher National Certificate, Higher National Diploma

**Majors Offered:** BHS PTT (C), BHS Stages 1-3 (C), Equine (HND), Equine Business Management (ANC), Equine Studies (HNC), Horse Care (FD), Horse Management (ND, HNC), NVQ Level 1 & 2 Horse Care (C)

**Website:**
www.bridgend.ac.uk

**Type of School:**
Land-Based College

## Rheidol Riding & Holiday Centre

**Type of School:**
Specialty School

Felin Rhiw Arthen, Capel Bangor, Aberystwyth SY23 4EL Wales. Contact: Mr. And Mrs. Evans. Phone: 01970 880863.
**Accreditation:** British Horse Society
**Degrees Offered:** Certificate
**Majors Offered:** Up to BHS Assistant Instructor

## Snowdonia Riding Stables

**Website:**
www.snowdonia2000.fsnet.co.uk

**Type of School:**
Specialty School

Waunfawr, Caernarfon, Gwynedd, Snowdonia LL55 4PQ Wales. Contact: Mrs. R. Z. Thomas. Phone/Fax: 01286 650342. Email: riding@snowdonia2000.fsnet.co.uk.
**Accreditation:** British Horse Society
**Degrees Offered:** Certificate
**Majors Offered:** Up to BHS Intermediate Instructor
**Description of Program:** Career training; courses can be conducted in Welsh if required
**Facilities:** Outdoor arena, cross-country jumps

## The University of Wales–Aberystwyth

**Website:**
www.aber.ac.uk

**Type of School:**
Traditional University

Old College, King Street, Aberystwyth, Ceredigion SY23 2AX Wales. Phone: 01970 621614. Fax: 01970 611264. Email: irs-enquiries@aber.ac.uk.
**Accreditation:** University of Wales, British Horse Society
**Degrees Offered:** Higher National Diploma, Bachelor of Science (Hons)
**Majors Offered:** Equine and Human Sports Science (B.Sc. Hons), Equine Science (B.Sc.Hons), Equine Studies (HND, Fd.Sc., B.Sc.Hons)
**Tuition Costs:** (Pounds) International students: £9,276 per annum; EU/UK students: £1,100 per annum; accommodation: £1,313 - £2,350 per annum
**Description of Program:** Details can be found on www.irs.aber.ac.uk, including full details of module content.
**Facilities:** Two equine centers: Lluest Equine Centre is based on Llanbadarn Campus and features an international sized indoor arena with low dust flooring, the Aberystwyth Centre for Equine Research, round pen, horse exerciser and outside manège, plus D.I.Y. livery stabling so you can bring your horse to study with you! Paddocks, rides and a cross-country course (under construction) are available on land adjacent to the Lluest Equine Centre. Frongoch Livery Centre, situated on one of the University's nearby farms, has a small indoor school, outside exercise area, and D.I.Y. livery stabling.
**Classroom/Hands-On Equine Classes:** Vary
**Showing:** The University Riding Club organizes and participates in all types of competitions.

## Welsh College of Horticulture

**Website:**
www.wcoh.ac.uk

**Type of School:**
Land-Based College

Northop, Near Mold, Flintshire CH7 6AA Wales. Phone: 01352 841000.
Email: TAMSIN.HUGHES@wcoh.ac.uk.
**Accreditation:** Edexcel, City and Guilds
**Degrees Offered:** Certificate, BTEC First Diploma, BTEC National Certificate, BTEC National Diploma, BTEC Higher National Certificate, BTEC Higher National Diploma

**Majors Offered:** Animal Science (HND, HNC), Horse Management (FD, ND, NC), NVQ Levels 1-3 (C)

**Tuition Costs:** (Pounds) EU students: £250/term; non-EU students: £1,300/term; HNC students: £375/year; HND students: £1,020/year; room only: £30/week; room and meal: £40/week; room and two meals: £50/week

**Description of Program:** Offers students a rounded experience in a friendly, well-resourced environment, preparing students for real careers in the equine industry. The courses incorporate business and financial management and information technology, providing the students with the skills necessary
for managerial roles in the equine industry. Delivery of the courses is enhanced by access to laboratory facilities, and all courses are supported by the study center. All courses utilize the practical facilities where possible, and students are engaged in yard duties on a rotation basis. Practical skills are further
developed by work experience placements, which are a part of all courses.

**Facilities:** Indoor school (30 x 40m), floodlit outdoor school (60 x 40m), indoor stabling, cross-country course, full set of BSJA show jumps

**Showing:** Students have the opportunity to compete in show jumping and dressage competitions.

# YUGOSLAVIA

## Univerzitet u Beogradu

Veterinarski Fakultet, Bulevar Jugoslovenske Armije 18, Yugoslavia. Phone: +381 11 685936. Fax: +381 11 685939.

**Majors Offered:** Veterinary Medicine

**Website:**
www.bg.ac.yu

**Type of School:**
University

# Scholarships

Perhaps the most common form of financial aid is scholarships. With the emergence of riding as a varsity sport there is now the opportunity to receive athletic scholarships, and many colleges and universities that offer equine programs or have equestrian teams offer scholarships specifically for equestrians. What follows is a list of scholarships that are specifically related to horses.

### American Association of Equine Practitioners Scholarship

Scholarship Committee, 4075 Iron Works Parkway, Lexington, KY 40511. Phone: (859) 233-0147. Email: dgarn@aaep.org. Website: www.aaep.org.
Eight scholarships of $2,500 are offered to fourth-year veterinary students who plan on entering an equine practice.

### American Morgan Horse Institute Educational Scholarships

AMHI Scholarships, P.O. Box 837, Shelburne, VT 05482-0519. Phone: (802) 985-8477. Fax: (802) 985-8430. Email: AMHIOffice@aol.com. Website: www.morganhorse.com or www.fastweb.com (scholarship application).
Application deadline is March 1. Five $3,000 scholarships awarded annually. Selection is based on ability and aptitude for serious study, community service, leadership, financial need, and achievement with Morgan horses.

### American Morgan Horse Institute International Morgan Connection Scholarships

AMHI Scholarships, P.O. Box 837, Shelburne, VT 05482-0519. Phone: (802) 985-8477. Fax: (802) 985-8430. Email: AMHIOffice@aol.com. Website: www.morganhorse.com or www.fastweb.com (scholarship application).
Application deadline is March 1. Three $2,000 educational scholarships awarded annually. One each to a Morgan youth exhibitor in Western Seat (pleasure and equitation), Hunter Seat (pleasure and equitation), and Saddle Seat (pleasure, park, and equitation) divisions.

### American Morgan Horse Institute Graywood Youth Horsemanship Grant

AMHI Scholarships, P.O. Box 837, Shelburne, VT 05482-0519. Phone: (802) 985-8477. Fax: (802) 985-8430. Email: AMHIOffice@aol.com. Website: www.morganhorse.com.
Application deadline is March 1. Provides one to two Morgan youth members per year the opportunity to further their study in the mastery of horse care, and receive tutelage from breed professionals in the categories of breeding, management, training, and/or riding and driving Morgan horses.

### American Morgan Horse Institute van Schaik Dressage Scholarship

AMHI Scholarships, P.O. Box 837, Shelburne, VT 05482-0519. Phone: (802) 985-8477. Fax: (802) 985-8430. Email: AMHIOffice@aol.com. Website: www.morganhorse.com.
Application deadline is November 30. One annual award of $1,000 to a Morgan individual wishing to further his or her skill, knowledge, or proficiency in classically ridden dressage. Selection of candidates emphasizes helping a rider move from the lower levels of dressage to Fourth level and above.

### American Morgan Horse Institute Grand Prix Dressage Award

AMHI Scholarships, P.O. Box 837, Shelburne, VT 05482-0519. Phone: (802) 985-8477. Fax: (802) 985-8430. Email: AMHIOffice@aol.com. Website: www.morganhorse.com.

Application deadline is November 30. $2,500 award available to amateur Morgan riders who compete at the Grand Prix level, receiving five Grand Prix scores with a median of 60% or better while riding a Morgan.

## American Paint Horse Association Youth Development Foundation

American Paint Horse Association, Attn: Rosemary Teate, P.O. Box 961023, Fort Worth, TX 76161. Phone: (817) 834-2742.

Application deadline is March 1. Applicant must be an APHA or AJPHA member in good standing and involved in horse activity using a Paint Horse or contributing actively to a regional club for at least one year prior to, and at the time of, application. Applicants must apply within one year from the date of high school graduation. Approximately 30 scholarships are given out annually at $1,000 each.

## American Quarter Horse Foundation: Arizona Quarter Horse Youth Racing Scholarship

American Quarter Horse Foundation, Attn: Laura Owens, 2601 I-40 East, Amarillo, TX 79104. Phone: (806) 376-5181. Email: lowens@aqha.org. Website: www.aqha.org.

Application deadline is February 1. $500 scholarship will be awarded per year to a crrent member of AQHA or AQHYA who lives in Arizona and intends to pursue a career in American Quarter Horse racing industry.

## American Quarter Horse Foundation: Christopher Junker Memorial Nebraska Scholarship

American Quarter Horse Foundation, Attn: Laura Owens, 2601 I-40 East, Amarillo, TX 79104. Phone: (806) 376-5181. Email: lowens@aqha.org. Website: www.aqha.org.

Application deadline is February 1. $500 scholarship will be awarded per year to a current member of AQHA or AQHYA who lives in Nebraska.

## American Quarter Horse Foundation: Dr. Gerald O'Conner Michigan Scholarship

American Quarter Horse Foundation, Attn: Laura Owens, 2601 I-40 East, Amarillo, TX 79104. Phone: (806) 376-5181. Email: lowens@aqha.org. Website: www.aqha.org.

Application deadline is February 1. $2,000 scholarship will be awarded to a current member of AQHA or AQHYA who live in Michigan. $500 per year will be awarded according to funding guidelines.

## American Quarter Horse Foundation: Education or Nursing Scholarship

American Quarter Horse Foundation, Attn: Laura Owens, 2601 I-40 East, Amarillo, TX 79104. Phone: (806) 376-5181. Email: lowens@aqha.org. Website: www.aqha.org.

Application deadline is February 1. $10,000 scholarship will be awarded to current member of AQHYA or AQHA who is pursuing a degree in education or nursing. $2,500 per year will be awarded according to funding guidelines.

## American Quarter Horse Foundation: Excellence in Equine/Agricultural Involvement Scholarship

American Quarter Horse Foundation, Attn: Laura Owens, 2601 I-40 East, Amarillo, TX 79104. Phone: (806) 376-5181. Email: lowens@aqha.org. Website: www.aqha.org.

Application deadline is February 1. $25,000 will be awarded to a current member of AQHA or AQHYA from a farming or ranching family who exemplifies the qualities developed through a lifetime involvement with horses and agriculture. $6,250 per year will be awarded according to funding guidelines.

## American Quarter Horse Foundation: Farm and Ranch Heritage Scholarships

American Quarter Horse Foundation, Attn: Laura Owens, 2601 I-40 East, Amarillo,

TX 79104. Phone: (806) 376-5181. Email: lowens@aqha.org. Website: www.aqha.org. Application deadline is February 1. $12,500 will be awarded to a current member of AQHYA or AQHA from farm and/or ranch background. $3,125 per year will be awarded according to funding guidelines.

**American Quarter Horse Foundation: Indiana Quarter Horse Youth Scholarship**
American Quarter Horse Foundation, Attn: Laura Owens, 2601 I-40 East, Amarillo, TX 79104. Phone: (806) 376-5181. Email: lowens@aqha.org. Website: www.aqha.org. Application deadline is February 1. $500 scholarship will be awarded per year to a current member of AQHA or AQHYA who live in Indiana.

**American Quarter Horse Foundation: Joan Cain Florida Quarter Horse Youth Scholarship**
American Quarter Horse Foundation, Attn: Laura Owens, 2601 I-40 East, Amarillo, TX 79104. Phone: (806) 376-5181. Email: lowens@aqha.org. Website: www.aqha.org. Application deadline is February 1. $1,000 scholarship to be awarded per year to a current member of AQHA or AQHYA who lives in Florida.

**American Quarter Horse Foundation: Journalism/Communications Scholarship**
American Quarter Horse Foundation, Attn: Laura Owens, 2601 I-40 East, Amarillo, TX 79104. Phone: (806) 376-5181. Email: lowens@aqha.org. Website: www.aqha.org. Application deadline is February 1. $8,000 scholarship will be awarded to a current member of AQHYA or AQHA who is pursuing a degree in journalism, communications, or a related field. $2,000 per year will be awarded according funding guidelines.

**American Quarter Horse Foundation: Nebraska Quarter Horse Youth Scholarship**
American Quarter Horse Foundation, Attn: Laura Owens, 2601 I-40 East, Amarillo, TX 79104. Phone: (806) 376-5181. Email: lowens@aqha.org. Website: www.aqha.org. Application deadline is February 1. $2,000 scholarship will be awarded to a current member of AQHA or AQHYA who lives in Nebraska. $500 per year will be awarded according to funding guidelines.

**American Quarter Horse Foundation: Oklahoma Quarter Horse Youth Scholarship**
American Quarter Horse Foundation, Attn: Laura Owens, 2601 I-40 East, Amarillo, TX 79104. Phone: (806) 376-5181. Email: lowens@aqha.org. Website: www.aqha.org. Application deadline is February 1. $500 scholarship will be awarded per year to a current member of AQHA or AQHYA who lives in Oklahoma.

**American Quarter Horse Foundation: Racing Scholarship**
American Quarter Horse Foundation, Attn: Laura Owens, 2601 I-40 East, Amarillo, TX 79104. Phone: (806) 376-5181. Email: lowens@aqha.org. Website: www.aqha.org. Application deadline is February 1. $8,000 scholarships will be awarded to a current member of AQHA or AQHYA who intends to pursue a career in the American Quarter Horse racing industry. $2,000 per year will be awarded according to funding guidelines.

**American Quarter Horse Foundation: Ray Melton Memorial Virginia Quarter Horse Youth Scholarship**
American Quarter Horse Foundation, Attn: Laura Owens, 2601 I-40 East, Amarillo, TX 79104. Phone: (806) 376-5181. Email: lowens@aqha.org. Website: www.aqha.org. Application deadline is February 1. $500 scholarship will be awarded per year to a current member of AQHYA or AQHA who lives in Virginia.

**American Quarter Horse Foundation: Swayze Woodruff Memorial Mid-South Scholarship**
American Quarter Horse Foundation, Attn: Laura Owens, 2601 I-40 East, Amarillo, TX 79104. Phone: (806) 376-5181. Email: lowens@aqha.org. Website: www.aqha.org. Application deadline is February 1. $8,000 scholarship will be awarded to a current member of AQHA or AQHYA who lives in Alabama, Tennessee, Louisiana, Mississippi or Arkansas. $2,000 per year will be awarded according to funding guidelines.

**American Quarter Horse Foundation: Telephony Scholarship**
American Quarter Horse Foundation, Attn: Laura Owens, 2601 I-40 East, Amarillo, TX 79104. Phone: (806) 376-5181. Email: lowens@aqha.org. Website: www.aqha.org. Application deadline is February 1. $10,000 scholarship will be awarded to a current member of AQHA pursuing a veterinary degree with emphasis in equine medicine. $5,000 per semester will be awarded according to funding guidelines.

**American Quarter Horse Foundation: Working Student Scholarship**
American Quarter Horse Foundation, Attn: Laura Owens, 2601 I-40 East, Amarillo, TX 79104. Phone: (806) 376-5181. Email: lowens@aqha.org. Website: www.aqha.org. Application deadline is February 1. $8,000 scholarship will be awarded to a current member of AQHYA or AQHA who intends to work a minimum of 200 hours per school year. AQHYA Executive Officers or Affiliate Officers may waive the required hours during their term of service. $2,000 per year will be awarded according to funding guidelines.

**American Quarter Horse Foundation: Youth Scholarship**
American Quarter Horse Foundation, Attn: Laura Owens, 2601 I-40 East, Amarillo, TX 79104. Phone: (806) 376-5181. Email: lowens@aqha.org. Website: www.aqha.org. Application deadline is February 1. $8,000 scholarship will be awarded to AQHYA members who have been members for three or more years. $2,000 per year will be awarded according to funding guidelines.

**American Saddlebred Horse Association Foundation**
4093 Iron Works Parkway, Lexington, KY 40511. Phone: (606) 259-2742.
Fax: (606) 259-1628.
Application deadline is April 30. Scholarships are available to applicants who are senior members or special junior members of ASHA. Recipients will be chosen on the basis of academic excellence, financial need, extracurricular activities, involvement with American Saddlebred horses, and personal references. Four scholarships of $5,000 each; one scholarship of $1,000 for an Alabama resident.

**Appaloosa Youth Foundation Educational Scholarships**
ApHC Youth Department, 2720 W. Pullman Road, Moscow, ID 83843. Contact: Keeley Grant, Youth Coordinator. Phone: (208) 882-5578 ext. 264.
Email: kgrant@appaloosa.com. Website: www.appaloosa.com.
Eight scholarships of $1,000 for youth members of the Appaloosa Horse Club, Inc.

**Appaloosa Youth Foundation: Lew & Joann Eklund Educational Scholarship**
ApHC Youth Department, 2720 W. Pullman Road, Moscow, ID 83843.
Contact: Keeley Grant, Youth Coordinator. Phone: (208) 882-5578 ext. 264.
Email: kgrant@appaloosa.com. Website: www.appaloosa.com.
Application deadline is June 10. Scholarship is for junior, senior, or graduate years. Scholarship is awarded to a member or a dependent of a member of the Appaloosa

Horse Club who is studying a field related to the equine industry. Scholarship is a one-time award of $2,000 and is awarded based on merit.

### Arabian Horse Foundation: Don Thompson Memorial Scholarship

Arabian Horse Foundation, Attn: Jean W. Durdin, 10 Farnham Park Dr., Houston, TX 77024-7501. Phone: (713) 952-7081. Fax: (713) 977-9883.

Application deadline is February 1. Scholarship applicants will be selected on the basic of academic ability, financial need, leadership, and equine activities. Preference will be given to students with a 2.8-3.25 GPA and whose financial resources are modest. The final four applications will be sent to a member of the Thompson family for final ranking.

### Arabian Horse Foundation: General Memorial Scholarships

Arabian Horse Foundation, Attn: Jean W. Durdin, 10 Farnham Park Dr., Houston, TX 77024-7501. Phone: (713) 952-7081. Fax: (713) 977-9883.

Application deadline is February 1. Scholarship recipients will be selected on the basic of academic ability, financial need, leadership, and equine activities. The scholarship will be selected on the basis of grade point average and SAT/ACT scores. Requirements will be a B average (85% or better) for high school seniors and 3.5 GPA for college students.

### Arabian Horse Foundation: Foundation Regional Scholarships

Arabian Horse Foundation, Attn: Jean W. Durdin, 10 Farnham Park Dr., Houston, TX 77024-7501. Phone: (713) 952-7081. Fax: (713) 977-9883.

Application deadline is February 1. Scholarship applicants will be selected on the basic of academic ability, financial need, leadership, and equine activities. One winner will be selected from each region; the choice is based on grade point average and SAT/ACT scores. Requirements will be a B average (85% or better) for high school seniors and 3.5 GPA for college students.

### Arabian Horse Foundation: Jon Oostermeyer Memorial Scholarship

Arabian Horse Foundation, Attn: Jean W. Durdin, 10 Farnham Park Dr., Houston, TX 77024-7501. Phone: (713) 952-7081. Fax: (713) 977-9883.

Application deadline is February 1. Scholarship recipients will be selected on the basic of academic ability, financial need, leadership, and equine activities. The scholarship will be selected on the basis of grade point average and SAT/ACT scores. Requirements will be a B average (85% or better) for high school seniors and 3.5 GPA for college students. At least four applications will be sent to Dale Oostermeyer for a final ranking.

### Arabian Horse Foundation: Spirit of a Winner Scholarship

Arabian Horse Foundation, Attn: Jean W. Durdin, 10 Farnham Park Dr., Houston, TX 77024-7501. Phone: (713) 952-7081. Fax: (713) 977-9883.

Application deadline is February 1. Scholarship applicants will be selected on the basic of academic ability, financial need, leadership, and equine activities. Applicant must be either a junior or senior in high school and must show at Youth Nationals. Year of Youth Nationals participation must be on the application to be considered for this award.

### Arabian Horse Trust: The Gladys Brown Edwards Memorial Scholarship

Equine Scholarship, 12000 Zuni Street, Westminster, CO 80234. Phone: (303) 450-4710. Fax: (303) 450-4707.

Application deadline is January 31. Applicant must currently be a sophomore or junior in college, be pursuing an education in a field of media communications, and have an ongoing interest in and commitment to Arabian horses. Award is $1,000.

### Arabian Horse Trust: The William Zekan Memorial Scholarship

Equine Scholarship, 12000 Zuni Street, Westminster, CO 80234. Phone: (303) 450-4710. Fax: (303) 450-4707.

Application deadline is January 31. Applicant must currently be a high school senior, be able to demonstrate a financial need, and have an ongoing interest in and commitment to Arabian horses. Award is $2,500.

### Australian Equestrian Scholarship

Marcus Oldham College, Private Bag 116, Geelong Mail Centre, Victoria 3221. AUSTRALIA. Website: www.marcusoldham.vic.edu.au/scholarships/scholarship.htm. Application deadline is October 1. For students or prospective students of the diploma of Horse Business Management at Marcus Oldham College. If you are over 18 years of age, are an Australian resident, have a passion for horses, and have a strong desire to pursue a career in the horse industry, then you are eligible to apply for this scholarship. Given the nature of the scholarship, it is desirable that applicants can demonstrate above average riding and practical skills/experience in their application. Scholarship is an annual award of AUD$11,500.

### Australian Thoroughbred Scholarship

Marcus Oldham College, Private Bag 116, Geelong Mail Centre, Victoria 3221. AUSTRALIA. Website: www.marcusoldham.vic.edu.au/scholarships/scholarship.htm. Application deadline is October 1. For students or prospective students of the diploma of Horse Business Management at Marcus Oldham College. If you are over 18 years of age, are an Australian resident, have a passion for horses, and have a strong desire to pursue a career in the horse industry, then you are eligible to apply for this scholarship. Given the nature of the scholarship, it is desirable that applicants can demonstrate previous experience in a Thoroughbred/breeding/racing area. Scholarship is an annual award of AUD$11,500.

### Canadian Pony Club: Todd Sandler Memorial Scholarship

Canadian Pony Club National Office, Box 127, Baldur, Manitoba R0K 0B0 Canada. Phone: (888) 286-PONY. Fax: (204) 535-2289. Email: Info@CanadianPonyClub.org. Website: www.canadianponyclub.org.

Application deadline is February 1. The Todd Sandler Memorial Scholarship will be awarded annually to two deserving Pony Club members. One will be chosen from the east and one from the west. The award consists of a two-week residential horsemanship course at The Horse People Inc., located just outside of Wendover, Ontario, (an $1,800.00 value). As well, CPC will cover half of the airfare or gas to get to the site.

### Christian Harness Horseman's Association

1846 Ross Road, Sunbury, OH 43074. Contact: the Youth Foundation. Phone: (317) 848-5132.

Annual scholarships are funded by the Christian Harness Horseman's Association and administered by the Harness Horse Youth Foundation.

### Dude Ranchers Educational Trust

The Dude Ranchers' Association, P.O. Box 471-G, La Porte, CO 80535-0471. Phone: (970) 223-8440. Email: duderanches@compuserve.com. Website: www.duderanch.org (no scholarship information available at website).

The scholarship is open to students who are enrolled in a primary dude ranching state and studying any subject related to dude ranching. They student must also work a guest season at a member dude ranch. There may be multiple awards ranging up to $2,000.

**Florida Standardbred Breeders and Owners Association: The Lester T. Vance Scholarship**
Attn: Jay Sears, Executive Director. 1800 SW Third St., Pompano Beach, FL 33069. Phone: (954) 972-5400.
Application deadline is July 15. Applicant must be a full-time groom, a son or daughter of a full-time groom, or a son or daughter of a member of the FSBOA. Awards $500 annually.

**Governor General's Award of Excellence**
Canadian Pony Club National Office, Box 127, Baldur, Manitoba R0K 0B0 Canada. Phone: (888) 286-PONY. Fax: (204) 535-2289. Email: Info@CanadianPonyClub.org. Website: www.canadianponyclub.org.
Application deadline is January 31. The Governor General's Award of Excellence is a financial scholarship funded by the patron's fund of the Canadian Pony Club. Two awards of $1,000 each, and one award of $500 will be given out to Pony Club members who exemplify the aims and objectives of Pony Club.

**Harness Horse Youth Foundation: Charles Bradley Scholarship**
14950 Greyhound Court, Suite 210, Carmel, IN 46032. Phone: (317) 848-5132. Email: hhyfetaylor@iquest.net. Website: www.hhyf.org/scholarshp.html.
Application deadline is April 30. Scholarship is for a high school senior or undergraduate student who is the child or relative of a racing official who is a member of the North American Judges & Stewards Foundation (NAJSA) and/or licensed USTA officials as presiding, associate, or paddock judge or a marimutual starter. Award can be used for any area of study. Scholarship amount varies.

**Harness Horse Youth Foundation**
**Critchfield-Oviatt Memorial Scholarship**
**Francis McKinzie Memorial Scholarship**
**Margot Taylor Scholarship**
14950 Greyhound Court, Suite 210, Carmel, IN 46032. Phone: (317) 848-5132. Email: hhyfetaylor@iquest.net. Website: www.hhyf.org/scholarshp.html.
Application deadline is April 30. Scholarships are for high school seniors, graduates, or undergraduate college students. One or more scholarships of varying amounts totaling $15,000 go to students who are pursuing or planning on pursuing a horse-related career. Scholarship awards are based on academic record, experience with horses, potential, character, recommendations, and financial need.

**Harness Tracks of America Scholarship Program**
4640 East Sunrise, Suite 200, Tucson, AZ 85718. Contact: Business Manager. Phone: (520) 529-2525. Fax: (520) 529-4753. Email: harness@azstarnet.com. Website: www.harnesstracks.com.
Applications available in late March. Application deadline is June 15. Award notification in early September. Annual scholarships for post-secondary education to students actively involved in the sport of harness racing or to the children of harness racing professionals (living or deceased), including licensed drivers, trainers, caretakers, or management officials. Six scholarships of $7,500 each awarded yearly on the basis of

academic merit, financial need, and active harness racing involvement. Non-U.S. citizens are eligible to apply.

### Horse Expo Committee and The Colorado Horse Council
Colorado Horse Council, Rocky Mountain Horse Expo, 420 E. 58<sup>th</sup> Ave., #145, Denver, CO 80216. Phone: (303) 292-4981. Fax: (303) 293-2412.
Application deadline is January 30. Applicant must be a resident of the state of Colorado, hold at least a 2.5 G.P.A., and be enrolled at Colorado State University in the Equine Science or industry majors. Awards are $1,000 each.

### Indiana Horse Council, Inc.
225 S. East St., Suite #738, Indianapolis, IN 46202-4042. Contact: Grant Coordinator. Phone: (317) 692-7115. Fax: (317) 692-7350.
Application deadline is March 1. Applicant must be a resident of Indiana and be a member, or immediate family of a member, of the Indiana Horse Council. Awards up to six educational grants of at least $500 each annually.

### Indiana Standardbred Association: Distinguished Scholarship Program
ISA, Greenfield, IN 46140. Phone: (800) 565-5725. Contact: Kay Roberts.
Application deadline is May 1. Applicant must be a resident of Indiana and be a member (or have a parent who is a member) of the ISA.

### Intercollegiate Equestrian Foundation
Hollow Rd., Box 741, Stony Brook, NY 11790. Phone: (914) 773-3788. Website: www.IHSAINC.com.
Application deadline is in January. Intercollegiate Horse Shows Association scholarships are offered through standard application process to existing IHSA members (freshmen can apply during the winter of their freshman year, but high school students may not apply). They are awarded primarily on the basis of academic achievement, active participation on the college equestrian team, and financial need, in that order. Scholarships range from $400 to $800, but the standard is $500, and the total number varies from year to year. Certain years, the association will award up to $30,000 in scholarships.

### International Arabian Horse Association
10805 E. Bethany Drive, Aurora, CO 80014-2605. Phone: (303) 696-4500. Fax: (303) 696-4599. Email: iaha@iaha.com. Website: www.iaha.com.
Individual scholarships are awarded to members of the winning teams at the Youth Judging Contest each October at the U.S. National Arabian & Half-Arabian Championship Horse Show. Additionally, some of the IAHA Regions have funds available for scholarship purposes.

### International Buckskin Horse Association
P.O. Box 268, Shelby, IN 46377. Contact: Richard E. Kurzeja, Executive Secretary. Phone: (219) 552-1013.
Application deadline is March 1. Applicant must have participated in IBHA activities for two years prior to applying, be a current member of the IBHA, and be accepted into a college, trade school, or university. Number of scholarships vary, awards are $500-1,500 per scholarship, and recipients may reapply annually for four years.

### International Racehorse Transport: IRT International Equine Scholarship
Marcus Oldham College, Private Bag 116, Geelong Mail Centre Victoria 3221, AUS-

TRALIA. Website: www.marcusoldham.vic.edu.au/scholarships/scholarship.htm. Application deadline is October 1. For students or prospective students of the Diploma of Horse Business Management at Marcus Oldham College. This scholarship is open to students dedicated to pursuing a career in the global horse industry – Thoroughbred or equestrian. Scholarship is an annual award of AUD$10,000. If you are over 18 years of age, can speak fluent English, have a passion for horses and have a strong desire to pursue a career in the horse industry, then you are eligible to apply for this scholarship.

### KTTC Edwin J. Gregson Scholarship

KTTC, EJG Memorial Scholarship Program, 120 South First Ave., Arcadia, CA 91006. Website: www.kttc.org.

Is open to all KTTC members/alumni that have been accepted to attend institutions of higher learning. The scholarship amount is $1,000 per year for four years, and two scholarships are available beginning in 2001. One scholarship must be used to attend the Racetrack Industry Program at the University of Arizona or the Equine Industry Program, College of Business and Public Administration, at the University of Louisville. The other scholarship can be used at any institution of higher learning approved by the scholarship committee.

### The Lois Cochran Finch Youth Excellence Awards

LCF Youth Excellence Awards, 33001 Villanova Street, Dallas, TX 75225.
Fax: (214) 739-9467. Email: kostial@msn.com.

Application request deadline is May 31. Applicants must be 17 years of age or under as of December 31 of the previous year. The focus of this award and scholarship program is "Service to Your Community," which is determined by three short essays regarding how you strive to improve the world around you. Essay topics are: (1) Your involvement with Arabian and Half-Arabian Horses, (2) Your service to your family, friends and community, and (3) Your service to your school, church, or synagogue. Applicants are accepted from the United States and Canada, with scholarships awarded annually to 5-10 selected recipients. Winners are announced in September each year.

### Maine Harness Horsemen's Association

P.O. Box 610, Turner, ME 04252. Contact: Bill Hathaway. Phone: (207) 225-2171.
The applicant or his/her parent must be a member of MHHA and already be accepted into a school. Awards $4,000 annually.

### Maine Standardbred Breeders & Owners Association

Cricket Hill Farm, 257 Hill Road, Lyman, ME 04002.
Contact: Dr. Douglass D. Hutchins. Phone: (207) 499-7244.
Application deadline is April 1. Applicant (or a relative) must be a current member of the MSBOA and be currently involved in the harness racing industry.

### Michigan Harness Horseman's Association

P.O. Box 349, Okemos, MI 48805. Contact: Larry Mallar, General Manager.
Phone: (517) 349-2920.
Application deadline is May 15. Applicants must be an MHHA Active or Life member who has been in good standing for the past three years (or their dependents), or ORC licensed full-time employee (or their dependents), and shall have been accepted or be in current attendance in any accredited program beyond high school. Scholarships awarded are dependent on available funds.

### National FFA Organization: American Association of Equine Practitioners Scholarship

National FFA Organization, Scholarship Office, P.O. Box 68960, Indianapolis, IN 46268-0960. Phone: (317) 802-6060. Website: www.ffa.org.

Application deadline is February 15. One scholarship at $1,000 will be awarded to FFA members pursuing a two or four-year degree in equine science. Applicants must have maintained a 3.5 cumulative GPA. The FFA also offers many other scholarships in animal science and agriculture.

### National Intercollegiate Rodeo Association

2316 Eastgate North, Suite 160, Walla Walla, WA 99362. Phone: (509) 529-4402. Email: nira@bmi.net. Website: www.collegerodeo.com/scholar.html.

There are several scholarships available through the NIRA. National Intercollegiate Rodeo Foundation Scholarship is awarded to eight individuals, each receiving $1,000. RAWHIDE Individual scholarship: (1) man $500, (1) woman $500. Rawhide TEAM Scholarship: $1,000.

### National Intercollegiate Rodeo Association: The Bill Robinson Memorial Scholarship

National Intercollegiate Rodeo Association, 2316 Eastgate North, Suite 160, Walla Walla, WA 99362. Phone: (509) 529-4402. Email: nira@bmi.net. Website: www.collegerodeo.com/scholar.html.

Awarded each year to first-, second-, and third-place steer wrestlers and calf ropers at the CNFR.

### National Intercollegiate Rodeo Association: Ellen Backstrom Memorial Scholarship

National Intercollegiate Rodeo Association, 2316 Eastgate North, Suite 160, Walla Walla, WA 99362. Phone: (509) 529-4402. Email: nira@bmi.net.
Website: www.collegerodeo.com/scholar.html.

Awarded during the CNFR to the cowboy or cowgirl earning the "hard luck" honors during the event.

### National Show Horse Registry

10368 Bluegrass Parkway, Louisville, KY 40299. Phone: (502) 266-5100. Fax: (502) 266-5806. Email: nshowhorse@aol.com. Website: www.nshregistry.org.

Scholarships awarded to the top ten equitation winners at the National Championship Horse Show. In Saddle Seat Equitation, the following is awarded: Champion, $5,000, Reserve, $2,500, and remaining top eight, $1,000.

### New Jersey Equine Advisory Board

NJ Dept. of Agriculture, P.O. 330, Trenton, NJ 08625. Contact: Lynn Mathews. Phone: (609) 984-4389.

Applicant must be a Rutgers University/Cook College senior majoring in Equine Science, demonstrate academic excellence, participate in horse industry activities, and have financial need. One award per year, generally around $1,000.

### New Zealand Equestrian Scholarship

Marcus Oldham College, Private Bag 116, Geelong Mail Centre Victoria 3221, AUSTRALIA. Website: www.marcusoldham.vic.edu.au/scholarships/scholarship.htm.

Application deadline is October 1. For students or prospective students of the Diploma of Horse Business Management at Marcus Oldham College. If you are over 18 years of age, are a New Zealand resident, have a passion for horses, and have a strong desire to pursue a career in the horse industry, then you are eligible to apply for this scholarship. Given the nature of the scholarship, it is desirable that applicants can demonstrate above-average riding and practical skills/experience in their application. Scholarship is an annual award of NZ$11,000.

### New Zealand Thoroughbred Scholarship

Marcus Oldham College, Private Bag 116, Geelong Mail Centre Victoria 3221, AUSTRALIA. Website: www.marcusoldham.vic.edu.au/scholarships/scholarship.htm. Application deadline is October 1. For students or prospective students of the Diploma of Horse Business Management at Marcus Oldham College. If you are over 18 years of age, are a New Zealand resident, have a passion for horses, and have a strong desire to pursue a career in the Thoroughbred industry, then you are eligible to apply for this scholarship. Given the nature of the scholarship, it is desirable that applicants can demonstrate previous experience in a thoroughbred/breeding/racing area. Scholarship is an annual award of NZ$11,000.

### Pony of the Americas Club, Inc.

5240 Elmwood Ave., Indianapolis, IN 46203-5990. Phone: (317) 788-0107. Email: poac@poac.org. Website: www.poac.org.
Two scholarships awarded to members of the Pony of the Americas Club, Inc. Two scholarships of $400 or more are awarded.

### Professional Horseman's Association of America

85 Pawling Lake, Pawling, NY 12564.
Members of PHA or their children. Scholarships are $500 each.

### Race Track Industry Program

University of Arizona College of Agriculture, Scholarship Link, P.O. Box 210069, Tucson, AZ 85721-0069. Phone: (520) 621-5660. Website: ag.arizona.edu/rtip/.
The applicant may apply for scholarship awards linked with the RTIP if he/she has received a university scholarship from a racing industry based organization, accepted into UofA, and is enrolled in the RTIP courses.

### Tennessee Walking Horse Breeders' and Exhibitors' Association

P.O. Box 286, 250 North Ellington Parkway, Lewisburg, TN 37091-1574. Phone: (931) 359-1574 or (800) 359-1574. Fax: (931) 359-7530. Website: www.twhbea.com.
Application deadline is April 1. Provides $20,000 each year to TWHBEA youth members who have been members for 18 months prior to the application date.

### Thoroughbred Racing Associations of North America, Inc.: Fred Russell-Grantland Rice Sportswriting Scholarship

Coordinator of Special Scholarships, Undergraduate Admissions, Vanderbilt University, 2305 West End. Ave., Nashville, TN 37203-1727. Phone: (800) 288-0432.
Application deadline is January 1. Applicant must be a high school senior and interested in becoming a sportswriter. A scholarship of $10,000 per year for four years is awarded annually (to be used at Vanderbilt University.).

### United States Pony Club Scholarships

4041 Iron Works Parkway, Lexington, KY 40511. Phone: (859) 254-7669. Fax: (859) 233-4652. Email: memberservices@ponyclub.org. Website: www.ponyclub.org.
Applicant must be a member of the USPC to apply for the scholarships. Scholarships are awarded through the following universities: Cazenovia College, Centenary College,

University of Findlay, Johnson & Wales University, Lake Erie College, University of Louisville, Midway College, Otterbein College, Salem-Teikyo University, Stephens College, and William Woods University.

## U.S. Tobacco Co. Scholarship Awards Program

National Intercollegiate Rodeo Association, 2316 Eastgate North, Suite 160, Walla Walla, WA 99362. Phone: (509) 529-4402. Email: nira@bmi.net.
Website: www.collegerodeo.com/scholar.html.
Each year, they award more than $200,000 in scholarships.

## Welsh Pony & Cob Foundation

P.O. Box 2977, Winchester, VA 22604. Contact: Lisa Landis. Phone (540) 667-6195.
Application deadline is July 1. Applicants are judged on their academic records and equine involvement. One or two scholarships of $500 are awarded annually.

## Wisconsin State Horse Council

WSHC Scholarship, Attn: Sue Piper, N8849 Hwy. Y, Watertown, WI 53094.
Application deadline is March 1. Applicant must be a Wisconsin resident and a member of the WSHC.

# Intercollegiate Associations

## International Intercollegiate Associations

AIEC Association Internationale des Etudiants Cavaliers/International University Equestrian Federation
Email: info@aiecworld.com.
Website: www.aiecworld.com.

Federation of International Polo
9663 Santa Monica Boulevard PMB 848
Beverly Hills, CA 90210 U.S.A.
Phone: (310) 472-4312. Fax: (310) 472-5220
Email: fippolo@aol.com
Website: www.fippolo.com

## United States Intercollegiate Associations

The International Intercollegiate Equestrian Association, the Intercollegiate/Inter-scholastic Dressage Association (IDA), the Intercollegiate Horse Show Association (IHSA), the Interscholastic Equestrian Association (IEA), the National Intercollegiate Rodeo Association (NIRA), Intercollegiate Polo, and Varsity Horse Teams.

## International Intercollegiate Equestrian Association

The International Intercollegiate Equestrian Association is a nonprofit organization that helps U.S. university students compete internationally at student-sponsored equestrian competitions. In addition, the IIEA acts as the National Responsible for the U.S. in relations with the AIEC (International University Equestrian Federation).

I.I.E.A. Inc.
Julie Chapgier
133 East 17th St.
New York, NY 10003
U.S.A.
Phone: 1-646-334-1300
Email: jvc216@nyu.edu
Website: www.usastudentriding.com

## Intercollegiate Dressage Association

The Intercollegiate Dressage Association (IDA) is a national organization that is divided into regions for the purpose of intercollegiate and interscholastic dressage competition. At each show, individual and team points are earned and count toward regional standings and qualification for the annual National Finals. Riders compete at Intro., Training Level I and II, Training Level III and IV, and First Level. Collegiate and scholastic rider points are totaled in separate categories, and points earned are awarded to individual riders and teams. The IDA is affiliated with the United States Dressage Federation and adheres closely to the U.S.A. Equestrian, Inc. (formerly the AHSA) dressage rules. To learn more about the IDA and how to get involved, visit www.teamdressage.com.

**East Coast Region - New Jersey, New York, Pennsylvania**
Cazenovia College, New Jersey
Centenary College, New Jersey
Delaware Valley College, Pennsylvania
Skidmore College, New York
Wilson College, Pennsylvania

**Midwest Region - Kentucky, Ohio**
Lake Erie College, Ohio
Oberlin College, Ohio
Ohio University Southern, Ohio
Otterbein College, Ohio
University of Findlay, Ohio
University of Kentucky, Kentucky

**Northeast Region - Massachusetts, New Hampshire, Rhode Island, Vermont**
Brown University, Rhode Island
Dartmouth College, New Hampshire
Johnson & Wales University, Rhode Island
Mount Holyoke College, Massachusetts
University of Massachusetts - Amherst, Massachusetts
University of New Hampshire, New Hampshire
University of Vermont, Vermont

**Southeast Region - Georgia, North Carolina, Virginia**
Appalachian State University, North Carolina
Averett University, Virginia
Elon University, North Carolina
Georgia Institute of Technology, Georgia
North Carolina State University, North Carolina
St. Andrews Presbyterian College, North Carolina
Virginia Intermont College, Virginia
Viriginia Tech, Virginia
Wake Forest University, North Carolina

**West Coast Region - California**
Cal Poly State University, San Luis Obispo
California State University-Fresno
University of California-Davis
University of California-Santa Cruz

## Intercollegiate Horse Show Association

The Intercollegiate Horse Show Association was established in 1967 at Fairleigh Dickinson University by Robert Cacchione and John Fritz. The purpose of the IHSA is to promote competition for riders of any skill level regardless of financial status. Students compete individually and as team members at regional and national levels. For all who take part, these IHSA competitions develop sportsmanship, team enthusiasm and horsemanship. Website: www.ihsainc.com.

### Zone 1 - Connecticut, Maine, Massachusetts, New Hampshire, Rhode Island, Vermont

**Region 1 - Connecticut, Rhode Island**
Brown University, Rhode Island
Connecticut College, Connecticut
Johnson & Wales University, Rhode Island
Rhode Island College, Rhode Island
Roger Williams University, Rhode Island
Salve Regina University, Rhode Island
Teikyo Post University, Connecticut
Trinity College, Connecticut
University of Connecticut, Connecticut.
University of Rhode Island, Rhode Island
Wesleyan University, Connecticut

**Region 2 - Maine, Massachusetts, New Hampshire, Vermont**
Bates College, Maine
Bowdoin College, Maine
Colby College, Maine
Colby Sawyer College, New Hampshire
Dartmouth College, New Hampshire
Middlebury College, Vermont
Mt. Ida College, Massachusetts
University of Maine-Orono, Maine
University of New Hampshire, New Hampshire
University of Vermont, Vermont

**Region 3 - Massachusetts, Vermont**
Amherst College, Massachusetts
Becker College, Massachusetts
Clark University, Massachusetts
College of the Holy Cross, Massachusetts
Elms College, Massachusetts
Landmark College, Vermont
Mount Holyoke College, Massachusetts
Smith College, Massachusetts
Springfield College, Massachusetts
University of Massachusetts at Amherst, Massachusetts
Westfield State College, Massachusetts
Williams College, Massachusetts

**Region 4 - Massachusetts**
Boston College
Boston University
Brandeis University
Endicott College
Framingham State College
Harvard University
Stonehill College
Tufts University
University of Massachusetts-Dartmouth

Wellesley College
Wheaton College.

## *Zone 2 - New Jersey, New York, Ontario*

### Region 1 - New Jersey, New York
Centenary College, New Jersey
College of St. Elizabeth, New Jersey
Columbia University - Barnard, New York
Drew University, New Jersey
Manhattanville College, New York
Marist College, New York
New York University, New York
Pace University, New York
Sarah Lawrence College, New York
Stevens Institute of Technology, New Jersey
SUNY New Paltz, New York
The Cooper Union, New York
United States Military Academy, New York
Vassar College, New York

### Region 2 - New York, Ontario
Alfred University, New York
Cazenovia College, New York
Nazareth College, New York
Rochester Institute of Technology, New York
St. Lawrence University, New York
SUNY Geneseo, New York
SUNY Oswego, New York
SUNY Potsdam, New York
Syracuse University, New York
The University of Guelph, Ontario
University of Ottawa, Ontario
University of Rochester, New York

### Region 3 - New York
Binghamton University
Colgate University
Cornell University
Hamilton College
Hartwick College
Ithaca College
Morrisville State College
Rensselaer Polytechnic Institute
Sienna College
Skidmore College
SUNY Cobleskill

## *Zone 3 - Connecticut, Delaware, Maryland, New Jersey, New York, Pennsylvania, West Virginia*

### Region 1 - Connecticut, New York
Dowling College, New York.

Fairfield University, Connecticut
Hofstra University, New York
Long Island University - C.W. Post Campus, New York
Molloy College, New York
Nassau Community College, New York
Sacred Heart University, Connecticut.
St. John's University, New York
St. Joseph's College, New York
Stony Brook University, New York
Yale University, Connecticut

**Region 2 - Delaware, Maryland, New Jersey, Pennsylvania**
Arcadia University, Pennsylvania
Bucks County Community College, Pennsylvania
Delaware Valley College, Pennsylvania
Franklin and Marshall College, Pennsylvania
Gettysburg College, Pennsylvania
Rider University, New Jersey
Temple University - Ambler, Pennsylvania
University of Delaware, Delaware
University of Pennsylvania, Pennsylvania
Washington College, Maryland
West Chester University, Pennsylvania

**Region 3 - New Jersey, Pennsylvania, West Virginia**
Allegheny College, Pennsylvania
California University of Pennsylvania, Pennsylvania
Dickinson College, Pennsylvania
Duquesne University, Pennsylvania
Edinboro University of Pennsylvania, Pennsylvania
Indiana University of Pennsylvania, Pennsylvania
Juniata College, Pennsylvania
Pennsylvania State University, Pennsylvania
Pennsylvania State University - Fayette, Pennsylvania
Saint Vincent College, Pennsylvania
Seton Hall College, New Jersey
Slippery Rock University, Pennsylvania
University of Pittsburgh, Pennsylvania
Washington and Jefferson College, Pennsylvania
Westminster College, Pennsylvania
West Virginia University, West Virginia
Wilson College, Pennsylvania

**Region 4 - New Jersey, Pennsylvania**
Bloomsberg University, Pennsylvania
Bucknell University, Pennsylvania
Cedar Crest College, Pennsylvania
DeSales University, Pennsylvania
East Stroudsberg University, Pennsylvania
Kutztown University, Pennsylvania
Lafayette College, Pennsylvania
Lehigh University, Pennsylvania
Moravian College, Pennsylvania

Princeton University, Pennsylvania
Rutgers University, New Jersey
Susquehanna University, Pennsylvania
University of Scranton, Pennsylvania

## Zone 4 - Maryland, North Carolina, Virginia

### Region 1- Maryland, Virginia
American University, Maryland
Christopher Newport University, Virginia
College of William and Mary, Virginia
Goucher College, Maryland
Hood College, Maryland
John Hopkins University, Maryland
Mary Washington College, Virginia
Mount St. Mary's College, Maryland
Saint Mary's College of Maryland, Marylond
Sweet Briar College, Virginia
University of Maryland, Maryland
University of Richmond, Virginia

### Region 2 - Virginia
Bridgewater College
Hollins University.
James Madison University
Longwood University
Lynchburg College
Mary Baldwin College
Radford University
Randolph-Macon Women's College
University of Virginia
Washington and Lee University

### Region 3 - North Carolina, Virginia
Appalachian State University, North Carolina
Duke University, North Carolina
East Carolina University, North Carolina
Elon University, North Carolina
North Carolina State University, North Carolina
St. Andrews Presbyterian College, North Carolina
University of N.C. Chapel Hill, North Carolina
University of N.C. Greensboro, North Carolina
Virginia Intermont College, Virginia.
Virginia Tech, Blacksburg, Virginia
Wake Forest University, North Carolina
Western Carolina University, North Carolina

## Zone 5 - Alabama, Florida, Georgia, Kentucky, Mississippi, Missouri, South Carolina, Tennessee

### Region 1 - Kentucky, Mississippi, Missouri, Tennessee
Maryville College, Missouri.
Middle Tennessee State University, Tennessee

Mississippi State University, Mississippi
Murray State University, Kentucky
Rhodes College, Memphis, Tennessee
Tennessee Tech University, Tennessee
University of the South, Tennessee.
University of Tennessee, Knoxville, Tennessee
University of Tennessee - Martin, Tennessee
Vanderbilt University, Tennessee
Western Kentucky University, Kentucky

### Region 2 - Alabama, Georgia, South Carolina
Anderson College, South Carolina
Augusta State University, Georgia
Berry College, Georgia
Clemson University, South Carolina
Erskine College, South Carolina
Furman University, South Carolina
Judson College, Alabama
Kennesaw State University, Georgia
Lander University, South Carolina
North Georgia College and State University, Georgia
Presbyterian College, South Carolina
University of South Carolina, South Carolina
Wallace State College, Alabama

### Region 3 - Florida, Georgia, South Carolina
College of Charleston, South Carolina
Emory University, Georgia
Florida State University, Florida
Georgia Institute of Technology, Georgia
Georgia Southern University, Georgia
Georgia State University, Georgia
Savannah College of Art and Design, Georgia
University of Central Florida, Florida
University of Florida, Florida
University of Miami, Florida
Wesleyan College, Georgia

## Zone 6 - Kentucky, Michigan, Ohio, West Virginia

### Region 1 - Ohio, West Virginia
Denison University, Ohio
Hiram College, Ohio
Kent State University, Ohio
Kenyon College, Ohio
Lake Erie College, Ohio
Oberlin College, Ohio
Ohio State University, Ohio
Ohio University, Ohio
Salem International University, West Virginia
University of Akron, Ohio

**Region 2 - Kentucky, Ohio**
Miami University of Ohio, Ohio
Midway College, Kentucky
Morehead State University, Kentucky
Ohio University Southern, Ohio
University of Cincinnati, Ohio.
University of Kentucky, Kentucky
University of Louisville, Kentucky
Wilmington College, Ohio

**Region 3 - Michigan, Ohio**
Albion College, Michigan
Grand Valley State University, Michigan.
Hillsdale College, Michigan
Michigan State University, Michigan
Ohio Wesleyan University, Ohio
Otterbein College, Ohio
University of Findlay, Ohio
University of Michigan, Michigan
Western Michigan University, Michigan

## Zone 7 - Colorado, Kansas, Louisiana, Nebraska, New Mexico, Oklahoma, Texas, Wyoming

**Region 1 - Colorado, Kansas, Nebraska, New Mexico, Wyoming**
Colby Community College, Kansas.
Colorado College, Colorado
Colorado State University, Colorado
Eastern Wyoming College, Wyoming
Laramie County Community College, Wyoming
Nebraska College of Technical Agriculture, Nebraska
New Mexico State University, New Mexico
United States Air Force Academy, Colorado
University of Colorado, Colorado
University of Denver, Colorado
University of Wyoming, Wyoming

**Region 2 - Louisiana, Oklahoma, Texas**
Louisiana State University, Louisiana
North Central Texas College, Texas
Oklahoma State University, Oklahoma
Rice University, Texas
Southern Methodist University, Texas
Southern Nazarene University, Oklahoma
Stephen F. Austin State University, Texas
Sul Ross State University, Texas
Tarleton State University, Texas
Texas A&M University, Texas
Texas A&M University-Corpus Christi, Texas
Texas State University-San Marcus, Texas
Texas Tech University, Texas
Trinity University, Texas

University of Texas - Austin, Texas
West Texas A&M University, Texas

## Zone 8 - California, Idaho, Montana, Nevada, Oregon, Utah, Washington

### Region 1 - California, Nevada
Cal Poly State University - San Luis Obispo, California
California State University - Fresno, California
College of the Sequoias, California
Santa Clara University, California
Sierra Nevada College, Nevada
Stanford University, California
University of California - Davis, California
University of California - Santa Cruz, California
University of Nevada - Reno, Nevada

### Region 2 - California, Arizona
Cal Poly State University - Pomona, California
Mount San Antonio College, California
Pepperdine University, California
University of Arizona, Arizona
University of California - Los Angeles, California
University of California - San Diego, San Diego, CA 92093
University of Redlands, California
University of San Diego, California
University of Southern California, California

### Region 3 - Idaho, Montana, Utah
Albertson College of Idaho, Idaho
College of Southern Idaho, Idaho
Idaho State University, Idaho
Montana State University, Montana
Montana Tech of the University of Montana, Montana
University of Montana, Montana
University of Montana - Western, Montana
Utah State University, Utah

### Region 4 - Oregon, Washington
Linn Benton Community College, Oregon
Oregon State University, Oregon
Seattle University, Washington
University of Oregon, Oregon
University of Washington, Washington
Washington State University, Washington
Western Washington University, Washington

## Zone 9 - Illinois, Indiana, Iowa, Kansas, Minnesota, Missouri, Nebraska, North Dakota, South Dakota, Wisconsin

### Region 1 - Illinois, Indiana
Ball State University, Indiana
Butler University, Indiana

Earlham College, Indiana
Indiana University, Indiana
Indiana University - Purdue University Indianapolis, Indiana
Parkland College, Illinois
Purdue University, Indiana
Saint Mary-of-the-Woods College, Indiana
Taylor University, Indiana
University of Illinois, Illinois
University of Indianapolis, Indiana
University of Notre Dame/Saint Mary's College, Indiana

**Region 2 - Illinois, Iowa, Kansas, Missouri**
Black Hawk College, Illinois
Iowa State University, Iowa
Kansas State University, Kansas
Northern Illinois University, Illinois
Northwest Missouri State University, Missouri
Northwestern University, Illinois
Southern Illinois University at Carbondale, Illinois
Southwest Missouri State University, Missouri
Truman State University, Missouri
Washington University in St. Louis, Missouri

**Region 3 - Iowa, Minnesota, Nebraska, North Dakota, South Dakota, Wisconsin**
Carleton College, Minnesota
Ellsworth Community College, Iowa
Gustavus Adolphus College, Minnesota.
North Dakota State University, North Dakota
South Dakota State University, South Dakota
Southeast Community College, Nebraska
St. Cloud State University, Minnesota
University of Minnesota - Crookston, Minnesota
University of Minnesota - Twin Cities, Minnesota
University of Nebraska, Nebraska
University of Wisconsin - Madison, Wisconsin
University of Wisconsin - River Falls, Wisconsin

# Interscholastic Equestrian Association

The Interscholastic Equestrian Association (IEA) is a national organization dedicated to introducing students in private and public primary and secondary schools to equestrian sports and to developing understanding and appreciation of equestrian sports through organized student competitions and educational opportunities. Membership is available to schools, student riders, coaches and interested parties. The organization sanctions shows at hosting schools that are run very much along the lines of the Intercollegiate Horse Show Association (IHSA) with the hosting school providing horses, tack and facilities. Finals competitions are held each year to award championships to teams and individuals. IEA adheres closely to the hunter equitation rules established by the IHSA and the USAE (USA Equestrian, Inc.).

IEA
P.O. Box 354
Willoughby, OH 44096-0354
Phone: (440) 463-4452
RheinR@andrews-school.org

Here is a list of high schools with teams competing in the IEA:

Academy of the Sacred Heart, Grand Coteau, Louisiana.
Andrews School, Willoughby, Ohio
Chatham Hall, Chatham, Virginia
Cherokee High School, Canton, Georgia
Culver Academies, Culver, Indiana
Dana Hall School, Wellesley, Massachusetts.
Garrison Forest School,  Owings Mills, Maryland
Kell High School, Marietta, Georgia
The Madeira School, McLean, Virginia.
Milton High School, Alpharetta, Georgia
Miss Porter's School, Farmington, Connecticut
St. Francis High School, Alpharetta, Georgia
St. Magaret's Episcopal, San Juan Capistrano, California
Stoneleigh-Burnham School, Greenfield, Massachusetts

## National Intercollegiate Rodeo Association

The National Intercollegiate Rodeo Association (NIRA) is the governing body of U.S. college rodeo. One of the primary goals of the NIRA is to establish and maintain standards for conducting intercollegiate rodeo competition. It seeks to promote intercollegiate rodeo on a national scale by bringing national recognition as an organized and standard collegiate sport and to promote interest, understanding and appreciation and vigilance over western life and culture.

National Intercollegiate Rodeo Association
2316 Eastgate North, Suite 160
Walla Walla, WA 99362
Phone: (509) 529-4402.
Email: info@collegerodeo.com
Website: www.collegerodeo.com

Here is a list of schools that have teams that compete under the National Intercollegiate Rodeo Association.

**Big Sky Regional - Montana, Wyoming**
Dawson Community College, Montana
Miles Community College, Montana
Montana State University Rodeo, Montana
Northern Montana College, Montana
Northwest College, Wyoming
University of Montana, Montana
University of Montana-Western, Montana

**Canadian Regional - Alberta**
Lakeland College

Lethbridge Community College
Olds College
University of Lethbridge

**Central Plains Regional - Kansas, Missouri, Oklahoma**
Bacone College, Oklahoma
Colby Community College, Kansas
Connors State College, Oklahoma
Dodge City Community College, Kansas
Eastern Oklahoma State College, Oklahoma
Fort Hays State University, Kansas
Fort Scott Community College, Kansas
Garden City Community College, Kansas
Kansas State University, Kansas
Northeastern OK A&M College, Oklahoma
Northwest MO State University, Missouri
Northwestern OK State University, Oklahoma
Oklahoma State University, Oklahoma
Panhandle State University, Oklahoma
Pratt Community College, Kansas
Rogers State University, Oklahoma
Southeastern OK State University, Oklahoma
Southwestern OK State University, Oklahoma
Western Oklahoma State College, Oklahoma

**Central Rocky Mountain Regional - Colorado, Nebraska, Wyoming**
Casper College, Wyoming
Central Wyoming College, Wyoming
Chadron State College, Nebraska
Colorado State University, Colorado
Colorado State University-Pueblo, Colorado
Eastern Wyoming College, Wyoming
Lamar Community College, Colorado
Laramie County Community College, Wyoming
Mesa State College, Colorado
Northeastern Junior College, Colorado
Sheridan College, Wyoming
University of Wyoming, Wyoming

**Grand Canyon Regional - Arizona, New Mexico**
Central Arizona College, Arizona
Cochise Community College, Arizona
Crownpoint Institute of Technology, New Mexico
Dine College, Arizona
New Mexico State University, New Mexico
Northland Pioneer College, Arizona
University Of Arizona, Arizona

**Great Plains Regional - Iowa, Minnesota, Nebraska, North Dakota, South Dakota, Wisconsin**
Dickinson State University, North Dakota
Iowa State University, Iowa
Mitchell Technical Institute, South Dakota

National American University, South Dakota
Nebraska College of Tech., Nebraska
North Dakota State University, North Dakota
Northeast Community College, Nebraska
Sitanka/Huron University, South Dakota.
South Dakota State University, South Dakota
University Of Nebraska-Lincoln, Nebraska
University Of Wisconsin-River Falls, Wisconsin
Western Dakota Tech Institute, South Dakota

**Northwest Regional - Idaho, Oregon, Washington**
Blue Mountain Community College, Oregon
Central Oregon Community College, Oregon
Central Washington University, Washington
Columbia Basin College, Washington
Eastern Oregon University, Oregon
Treasure Valley Community College, Oregon
University Of Idaho, Idaho
Walla Walla Community College, Washington
Washington State University, Washington

**Ozark Regional - Alabama, Arkansas, Kentucky, Michigan, Missouri, Mississippi, Tennessee**
Arkansas State University, Arkansas
East Central Community College, Mississippi
Faulkner State Community College, Alabama
Michigan State University, Michigan
Mississippi State University, Mississippi
Missouri Valley College, Missouri
Murray State University, Kentucky
Northwest MS Community College, Mississippi
Southern Arkansas University, Arkansas
Southern Illinois University-Carbondale, Illinois
Southwest MO State University, Missouri
Troy State University, Alabama
University of Arkansas-Monticello, Arkansas
University of Tennesse-Martin, Tennessee
University of West Alabama, Alabama

**Rocky Mountain Regional - Idaho, Utah**
Boise State University, Idaho
College Of Southern Idaho, Idaho
Dixie State College of Utah, Utah
Idaho State University, Idaho
Salt Lake Community College, Utah.
Southern Utah University, Utah
Utah State University, Utah
Utah State University -Uintah Basin, Utah
Utah Valley State College, Utah
Weber State University, Utah

**Southern Regional - Louisiana, Texas**
Coastal Bend College, Texas

Hill College, Texas
McNeese State University, Louisiana.
Northeast Texas Community College, Texas
Northwestern State University, Louisiana
Sam Houston State University, Texas
Stephen F. Austin State University, Texas
Southwest Texas Junior College, Texas
Texas A&M University, Texas
Texas A&M University-Kingsville, Texas
Trinity Valley Community College, Texas
Tyler Junior College, Texas
Wharton County Junior College, Texas

**Southwest Regional - New Mexico, Texas**
Angelo State University, Texas
Clarendon College, Texas
Eastern New Mexico University, New Mexico
Frank Phillips College, Texas
Howard County Junior College, Texas
Meslands Community College, New Mexico
New Mexico Junior College, New Mexico
Odessa College, Texas
South Plains College, Texas
Sul Ross State University, Texas
Tarleton State University, Texas
Texas Tech University-Lubbock, Texas
Vernon College, Texas
Weatherford College, Texas
Western Texas College, Texas
West Texas A&M University, Texas

**West Coast Regional - California, Nevada**
California State University-Fresno, California
Cal Poly State University-San Luis Obispo, California
Cal State Poly University- Pomona, California
Lassen College, California
University of Nevada-Las Vegas, Nevada
Western Nevada Community College, Nevada
West Hills College, California

# Intercollegiate/Interscholastic Polo

United States Polo Association
Suite 505
771 Corporate Drive
Lexington, KY 40503
Phone: (859) 219-1000 or (800) 232-USPA
Fax: (859) 219-0520.
E-mail: uspa@uspolo.org. Website: www.uspolo.org

List of schools that have intercollegiate polo teams:

**Eastern - Connecticut, Indiana, Masachusetts, Michigan, New York, Virginia**
Cornell University, New York
Michigan State University, Michigan
Ohio State University, Ohio
Purdue University, Indiana
Skidmore College, New York
University of Connecticut, Connecticut
University of Massachusetts, Massachusetts
University of Michigan, Michigan
University of Virginia, Virginia
Vassar College, New York
Yale University, New York

**Central - Colorado, New Mexico, Oklahoma, Texas**
Colorado State University, Colorado
New Mexico State University, New Mexico
Oklahoma State University, Oklahoma
Texas A&M University, Texas
Texas Tech University, Texas
University of Oklahoma, Oklahoma
University of Texas, Texas

**Western - California, Idaho, Oregon, Washington**
Boise State University, Idaho.
California Poly State University, San Luis Obispo, California
Eastern Oregon University, Oregon
Oregon State University, Oregon
Stanford University, California
University of California at Davis, California
University of California at San Diego, California
University of California at Santa Barbara, California
University of San Diego, California
University of Southern California, California
Washington State University, Washington
Westmont College, California

List of schools that have interscholastic polo teams:

**Eastern - Connecticut, Florida, Kentucky, Maryland, New York, Ohio, Ontario, Pennsylvania, Rhode Island, Virginia**
Baltimore Polo Club, Maryland
Charlottesville Junior Polo Club, Virginia
Cornell Polo Club, New York
Cowtown Polo Club, Pennsylvania
Dillon Country Day Polo Club, Florida
Garrison Forest School Polo, Maryland
Hardscuffle Polo Club, Kentucky
Ligonier Polo Club, Ohio
Natania Polo Club, Virginia
Pot of Gold Stables Polo Club, Ontario, Canada

Potomac Polo Club, Virginia
Shallowbrook Polo Club, Connecticut
Toronto Polo Club, Ontario, Canada
University of Connecticut Polo Club, Connecticut
Valley Forge Military Academy, Pennsylvania
Westchester Polo Club, Rhode Island

**Central - Illinois, Indiana, Kansas, Texas**
Culver Academies Polo Club, Indiana
Fairfield Polo Club, Kansas
Ft. Worth Polo Club, Texas
Las Colinas Polo Club, Texas
Midland Polo Club, Texas
Peoria Polo Club, Illinois
Texas Tech Junior Polo Club, Texas

**Western - California, Hawaii, Washington**
California Polo Club, California
Central Coast Polo Club, California
Eldorado Polo Club, California
Hawaii Polo Club, Hawaii
Maui Polo Club, Hawaii
Modesto Polo Club, California
Napa Valley Poly Club, California
Poway Polo Club, California
Tacoma Polo Club, Washington
Thacher School Polo Club, California

## Varsity Horse Teams

Below is a list of colleges and universities that offer Varsity Horse Teams. Contact the individual schools to find out about their programs.

**Division I**
Auburn University, Alabama
Brown University, Rhode Island
California State University, Fresno, California
College of Charleston, South Carolina
Cornell University, New York
Dartmouth College, New Hampshire
Kansas State University, Kansas
New Mexico State University, New Mexico
Oklahoma State University, Oklahoma
Sacred Heart University, Connecticut
Southern Methodist University, Texas.
Texas A&M University, Texas
University of Georgia, Georgia
University of South Carolina, South Carolina

**Division II**
Molloy College, New York
Pace University, New York

Stonehill College, Massachusetts
University of Findlay, Ohio
University of Minnesota, Crookston, Minnesota
West Texas A&M University, Texas

## International

### Algerian Intercollegiate Association

Tewfik Bougandoura
Phone: 213-61-50 44 76 or 213-21-63 03 23. Fax: 213-21-63 08 74
Email: tewfikb@hotmail.com

### Austrian Intercollegiate Association

Austrian Student-Riding-Federation
Christian Moritsch
Landscha 7
A-8435 Wagna
Austria
Phone: 43-664-3869510
Email: christian.moritsch@arcaustria.at
Website: www.arcaustria.at

### Belgium Intercollegiate Association

Bjorn WARIN Kaaistraat 43
B-1790 Affligem
Belgium
Phone: 32-477-237105
Email: bjornwarin@hotmail.com

### Canadian Intercollegiate Association

Since its foundation in 1976, the Canadian Universities Riding Clubs Association (CURCA) has been providing Canada's college and university students with a unique opportunity to gain international equestrian experience and meet other student riders from around the world, all while attending post-secondary school. Canadian students riders not only represent Canada on the International Student Riding Association (AIEC) circuit but also are diplomats and skilled individuals.

C.U.R.C.A.
Anna Kate Shoveller, Canadian National Responsible to AIEC
Phone: (780)433-3748. Fax: (780)492-4265
Email: shovellercurca@hotmail.com
Website: www.geocities.com/curca_2001/index.html

### Denmark's Intercollegiate Association

Cecilie Anthony
Lottesvej 15, st. 6
DK-8220 Brabrand
Denmark
Phone: 45-86-255256
Email: cecilieanthony@hotmail.com

## France's Intercollegiate Association

Marie-Xavière Loyer
Email: mariexloyer@aol.com

## Germany's Intercollegiate Association

Stephan Munk
Hauffstr. 10
D-72649 Wolfschlugen
Germany
Phone: 49-7022-52634. Fax: 49-7022-51737
Email: Munk.Stephan@t-online.de
Website: www.deutscher-akademischer-reiterverband.de

## Great Britain's Intercollegiate Association

Polly McGuigan
Email: pollymcguigan@hotmail.com

## Ireland's Intercollegiate Association

Sarah Campbell
24 Glenavy Road
Lisburn, Co.Antrim
Northern Ireland
BT28 3UT
Email: sarahjc1@aol.com

Ashlin Noonan
61 Donard Rd
Drimnagh
Dublin 12
Ireland
Phone: 353-87-2297799. Fax: 353-1-4121939
Email: Ashlin.noonan@kpmg.ie

## Italian Intercollegiate Association

Nicola Pittoni
Piazzale Cadorna 3/1
I-33100 Udine
Italy
Phone: 39-0432-505760 or 39-349-4585694. Fax: 39-0432-505760
Email: nicpit@tin.it
Website: www.geun.it

## Japanese Intercollegiate Association

Japan Equestrian Federation
Minoru Osada
1-2 Kanda-surugadai, Chiyoda-ku
Tokyo 101-0062
Japan
Phone: 81-3-3291-9971. Fax: 81-3-3291-9974
Email: jef@japan-sports.or.jp

## Luxemburg's Intercollegiate Association

Joëlle Kinnen
Doblbachstrasse 14
D-85665 MOOSACH
Germany
Phone: 004971716441498
Email: joelle.kinnen@t-online.de
Website: www.hippoline.lu/lsr

## Netherlands' Intercollegiate Association

Erik Hamoen
Oostzeedijk 32A
3063 BC Rotterdam
Netherlands
Phone: 31-6-21831281
Email: hamoen83@hotmail.com
Website: www.paardensport.nl/sns

## Norway's Intercollegiate Association

Annicken Jegersberg
N. Aas Gard, Jelöy
N-1514 Moss
Norway
Email: Jegers99@hotmail.com

## Poland's Intercollegiate Association

Kaja Koczurowska
ul. Sklodowskiej Curie 5/2
81-703 Sopot
Poland
Phone: 48-58-5551295. Cell: 48-602-390230. Fax: 48-58-5519605
Email: kajusia@2com.pl

## Romanian Intercollegiate Association

The ASCR (Romanian Studentriders Association) is a very young association, organized in 1996 by Alex and Mihnea Virgolici. We are looking forward to getting the new generation into ASCR. Since 1996, our main purpose has been to improve the image of our country among student riders. Romanian student riders are very friendly and open, so any student rider that comes to Romania is welcome to contact us.

Romanian Studentriders Association
Mihnea (Mick) Virgolici
Bd. M. Kogalniceanu 51, app.3
Bucuresti
Romania
Phone: 40-94-500457. Fax: 40-12-322936
Email: mihneav@yahoo.com

## Spain's Intercollegiate Association

Carolina Aróstegui
Castillo de Játiva nº 21
Villafranca del Castillo
Madrid 28692
Spain
Phone: 34-91-8150084
Email: carol1717@hotmail.com

## Switzerland's Intercollegiate Association

Rahel Alder
Hafnerstrasse 17
CH-8005 Zürich
Switzerland
Phone: 41-79-623 27 60
Email: rahelalder@hotmail.com

## Swedish Intercollegiate Association

Swedish Student Riders
Anna Godsk
Vildandsvägen 2 W:201
S-23427 Lund
Sweden
Phone: 46-46-335585 or 46-70-4856334
Email: a_godsk@hotmail.com
Website: www.etek.chalmers.se/~mia/SAR/

# Equestrian Federations

Fédération Equestre Internationale / International Equestrian Federation
Avenue Mon Repos 24, PO Box 157
1000 Lausanne 5, Switzerland
Phone: 41 21 310 47 47. Fax: 41 21 310 47 60
Email: info@horsesport.org
Website: www.horsesport.org

## Algeria
Federation Equestre Algerienne
B.P. Nr. 183/ Hussein-Dey 148 Av. de L'A.L.N. Caroubier
Alger
Algeria
Phone: (213 21) 49 74 00. Fax: (213 21) 49 81 06
Email: sq@fea.org.dz
Website: www.fea.org.dz

## American Samoa
American Samoa Equestrian Federation
1278 Glenneyre #244
Laguna Beach, 92651 CA
U.S.A.
Phone: (949) 716-7742. Fax: (949) 494-8667
Email: shwjmpca@aol.com

## Andorra
Federacio Andorrana D'Hipica
B.P. 43 - Correu Francès Baixada del Moli n°32 - Entresol
Andorra La Vella
Andorra
Phone: (376) 86 11 16. Fax: (376) 86 11 16
Email: fah@andorra.ad

## Antigua
Antigua Horse Society
English Harbour Post office
Antigua West Indies
Antigua
Phone: (1 268) 463 20 51. Fax: (1 268) 460 15 24
Email: norma@candw.ag

## Argentina
Federacion Ecuestre Argentina
Gorostiaga 2287 C.C. 59 - Sucursal 26B
1426 Buenos Aires
Argentina
Phone: (54 11) 47 72 04 28. Fax: (54 11) 47 75 44 23
Email: fea@fibertel.com.au
Website: www.fedecuarg.com.ar

**Armenia**
Equestrian Federation of Armenia
7, Grigor Lousavorich Street
375015 Yerevan
Armenia
Phone: (374 1) 51 00 10. Fax: (374 1) 54 44 04

**Australia**
Equestrian Federation of Australia
P.O. Box 673
Sydney Markets, NSW 2129
Australia
Phone: +61 2 8762 7777. Fax: +61 2 9763 2466
Email: info@efanational.com
Website: www.efanational.com

**Azerbaijan**
Equestrian Federation of Azerbaijan
36 A Z. Buniyadov St.
370069 Baku
Azerbaijan
Phone: (994 12) 61 04 19. Fax: (994 12) 67 03 35
Email: equestrian_federation@baku.az

**Austria**
Bundesfachverband Fuer Reiten Und Fahren in Oesterreich
Geiselbergstrasse 26-32/512
1110 Wien
Austria
Phone: (43 1) 749 92 61. Fax: (43 1) 749 92 61 91
Email: office@fena.at
Website: www.fena.at

**Bahamas**
Bahamas National Equestrian Federation
P.O. Box N-7123
Nassau
Bahamas
Phone: (001 242) 323 1317. Fax: (001 242) 323 1318
Email: slobosky@bahamas.net.bs

**Bahrain**
Bahrain Royal Equestrian & Endurance Federation
P.O. Box 25200
Awali
Kingdom of Bahrain
Phone: (973) 754 300. Fax: (973) 754 424
Email: breef@batelco.com.bh
Website: www.find4sure.net

## Barbados

Barbados Equestrian Association
"Bucklebury House" Cottage Terrace
St. George, West Indies
Barbados
Phone: (1 246) 228 91 44. Fax: (1 246) 228 62 47
Email: bea@sunbeach.net

## Belgium

Federation Royale Belge Des Sports Equestres
Avenue Houba de Strooper 156
1020 Bruxelles
Belgium
Phone: (32 2) 478 50 56. Fax: (32 2) 478 11 26
Email: info@equibel.be
Website: www.equibel.be

## Belarus

Equestrian Federation of Belarus
Pos. Ratomka
223035 Minskij Raion
Belarus
Phone: (375 17) 502 42 90. Fax: (375 17) 502 42 90.
Email: blrfdh@bas-net.by
Website: www.horses.org.by

## Bermuda

Bermuda Equestrian Federation
P.O. Box DV 583 37 Front Street, Hamilton HM11
Devonshire DV BX
Bermuda
Phone: (1 441) 234 0485. Fax: (1 441) 234 3010
Email: jacherry@northrock.bm
Website: www.bef.bm

## Bolivia

Federacion Boliviana de Deportes Ecuestres
Av. Ballivian N° 555 P.O.Box 3-12296
La Paz
Bolivia
Phone: (591 2) 278 45 57. Fax: (591 2) 278 45 57
Email: fede@hotmail.com

## Botswana

The Horse Society of Botswana
Suite 232 Postnet Broadhurst, Private Bag BR 351
Broadhurst Gaborone
Botswana
Phone: (267) 316 16 55. Fax: (267) 316 16 55
Email: hsb@it.bw
Website: www.hsb.co.bw

## Brazil

Confederacao Brasileira de Hipismo
Rua 7 de Setembro, 81 - 3 Andar Centro
CEP 20050-005 Rio de Janeiro RJ
Brazil
Phone: (55 21) 2539492. Fax: (55 21) 2539492.
Email: cbh@cbh-hipismo.com.br
Website: www.cbh-hipismo.com.br

## Brunei

Brunei Equine Association
c/o TEMC Sdn Bhd, Royal Stable Block H, Jerudong Park, Jerudong
BG3122 Negara Brunei Darussalam
Brunei
Phone: (673 2) 612 347. Fax:  (673 2) 611 432
Email: bea_brunei@hotmail.com

## Bulgaria

Bulgarian Equestrian Federation
Bd. Vassil Levski 75
1040 Sofia
Bulgaria
Phone: (359 2) 930 06 03. Fax: (359 2) 986 53 99
Email: horse@sportbg.com
Website: www.sportbg.com

## Canada

Equine Canada
2460 Lancaster Road Suite 200
Ottawa, K1B 4S5 Ontario
Canada
Phone: (613) 248-3433. Fax: (613) 248-3484
Email: info@equinecanada.ca
Website: www.equinecanada.ca

## Chile

Federacion Ecuestre de Chile
Avda. Vicuna Mackenna No.40 of 5 Providencia
Santiago de Chile
Chile
Phone: (56 2) 635 18 96. Fax: (56 2) 222 90 17
Email: fedecuestre@entelchile.net
Website: www.fecuestre.cl

## China, People's Republic of

Equestrian Association of the People's Republic of China
Laoshan, Shijingshan District
100043 Beijing
People's Republic of China
Phone: (86 10) 68862550. Fax: (86 10) 68862596
Email: swb422@163.com

**Chinese Taipei**
Chinese Taipei Equestrian Association
Room 808 No. 20, Chu-Lun St.
Taipei, Taiwan (R.O.C.)
Chinese Taipei
Phone: (886 2) 2775 72 78. Fax: (886 2) 2778 37 40
Email: ctea@ctea.org.tw
Website: www.ctea.org.tw

**Colombia**
Federacion Ecuestre de Colombia
Carrera 13 No. 77A-59 P.O.Box 16987
Bogota
Colombia
Phone: (57 1) 256 29 92. Fax: (57 1) 618 12 76
Email: fedecuestre@hotmail.com

**Congo Democratic Rep.**
Federation Congolaise des Sports Equestres (F.C.S.E.)
C/O Jean-Michel Turlot, Building Mercure Avenue Kalemie 37, P.O. Box 12709
Kinshasa 1
Congo Democratic Republic
Phone: (243 ) 88 445 78. Fax: (243 ) 880 46 85
Email: jmturlot@hotmail.com

**Costa Rica**
Federacion Ecuestre de Costa Rica
Oficina Ricardo Rojas Diaz S.A. 125 mts Norte del Gran Hotel Costa Rica Edificio
Vazquez Dent 2 Piso Calle 3 Avenida 3 y 5
San Jose
Costa Rica
Phone: (506 ) 222 55 55. Fax: (506 ) 221 57 03
Email: ofrrojas@racsa.co.cr

**Croatia**
Croatian Equestrian Federation
Radoslava Cimermana 5
10020 Zagreb
Croatia
Phone: (385 1) 6520790. Fax: (385 1) 6520790
Email: cef@zg.hinet.hr

**Cuba**
Federacion Ecuestre Cubana
Calle 13 no. 601 Zona postal 4, Vedado Plaza
Ciudad de la Habana
Cuba
Phone: (53 7) 203 14 33. Fax: (53 7) 203 15 93
Email: equs@inder.co.cu

**Cyprus**
Cyprus Equestrian Federation
20 Ionos str. PO Box 14043

2153 Nicosia
Cyprus
Phone: (357 99) 67 33 33. Fax: (357 22) 33 88 66
Email: notorious.equ@cytanet.com.cy

## Czech Republic
Czech Equestrian Federation
Atleticka' 100/2 P.O. Box 40
160 17 Praha 6
Czech Republic
Phone: (420 2) 2051 11 05. Fax: (420 2) 333 543 99
Email: info@cjf.cz
Website: www.cjf.cz

## Denmark
Dansk Ride Forbund
Idraettens Hus Brondby Stadion 20
2605 Brondby
Denmark
Phone: (45 43) 26 28 28. Fax: (45 43) 26 28 12
Email: pev@rideforbund.dk
Website: www.rideforbund.dk

## Dominican Republic
Federacion Ecuestre Dominicana Inc.
Calle Aberto Larancuent #20 Naco
Santo Domingo
Dominican Republic
Phone: (1 809) 567 34 00. Fax: (1 809) 567 48 01
Email: fedrd@tricom.net
Website: www.ecuestrerd.com

## Ecuador
Federacion Ecuatoriana de Deportes Ecuestres
Av.Atahualpa #1116 y Juan Gonzales Piso 6 Oficina B, P. O. Box 17-17-1323
Quito
Ecuador
Phone: (593 2) 43 17 76. Fax: (593 2) 43 17 78
Email: fede@pi.pro.ec

## Egypt
Egyptian Equestrian Federation Sports Fed. Building
El-Estad El Bahary Street Nasr City, Federations Building
Cairo
Egypt
Phone: (20 2) 402 92 65. Fax: (20 2) 261 65 75

## El Salvador
Federacion Salvadorena de Ecuestres
Alameda Juan Pablo II Instituto Nacional de los Deportes de El Salvador, Indes
Apartado Postal 01-586
San Salvador
El Salvador

Phone: (50 3) 257 05 85. Fax: (50 3) 257 05 84
Email: fesades@telesal.net

**Estonia**
Equestrian Federation of Estonia
Pirita tee 12
10127 Tallinn
Estonia
Phone: (372) 603 1 5 25. Fax: (372) 603 15 26
Email: erl@sport.ee
Website: www.ratsaliit.ee

**Ethiopia**
Ethiopian Equestrian Federation
c/o Ethiopian Olympic Committee P.O. Box 3241
Addis Abeba
Ethiopia
Phone: (251 1) 51 65 26. Fax: (251 1) 51 33 45

**Finland**
The Equestrian Federation of Finland
Radiokatu 20 00093 SLU
00240 Helsinki
Finland
Phone: (358 9) 22945240. Fax: (358 9) 149 68 64
Email: ratsastus@ratsastus.fi
Website: www.ratsastus.fi

**France**
Fédération Française d'Equitation
81, Avenue Edouard Vaillant
92517 - Boulogne Billancourt Cedex
France
Phone: (33 1) 58 17 58 17. Fax: (33 1) 58 17 58 60
Email: dtnadj@ffe.com
Website: www.ffe.com

**Georgia**
National Equestrian Federation of Georgia
10, Antonovskov
380077 Tbilisi
Georgia
Phone: (995 32) 38 33 24. Fax: (995 32) 38 33 24
Email: Itogeorg@access.sanet.ge

**Germany**
Deutsche Reiterliche Vereinigung (FN) e.V.
Petra Schaffer
Mitgliederservice
Postfach, 48229 Warendorf
Phone:  02581 / 6362-222. Fax: 6362-333
Email: fn@fn-dokr.de
Website: www.pferd-aktuell.de

**Great Britain (United Kingdom)**
British Equestrian Federation
National Agriculture Centre
Stoneleigh Park
Kenilworth
Warwickshire CV8 2RH
Great Britain
Phone: (44 24) 76 69 88 71. Fax: (44 24) 76 69 64 84
Email: info@bef.co.uk
Website: www.bef.co.uk

**Greece**
Hellenic Equestrian Federation
37, Dimitriou Ralli str.,
15124 Maroussi, Athens
Greece
Phone: (30 210) 614 19 86. Fax: (30 210) 614 18 59
Email: eoi@ath.forthnet.gr
Website: www.equestrian.org.gr

**Grenada**
Grenada International Sports Foundation
P.O. Box 897
St. George's West Indies
Grenada
Phone: (43 676) 575 00 31. Fax: (1 508) 374 79 64
Email: office@grensports.com
Website: www.grensports.com

**Guatemala**
Asociacion Nacional de Ecuestres de Guatemala
6 a Calle 8-00, Zona 13
Guatemala City
Guatemala
Phone: (502 ) 471 08 25. Fax: (502 ) 471 08 23
Email: aneg@internetdetelgua.com.gt

**Honduras**
Federacion Ecuestre de Honduras
Km.1 Salida a Valle de Angeles
Tegucigalpa
Honduras
Phone: (504 ) 236 64 34. Fax: (504 ) 236 64 34
Email: feh@disnet.hn

**Haiti**
Federation Equestre Haitienne
P.O. Box 15788
Petion-Ville
Haiti
Phone: (509) 404-0498. Fax: (509) 250-1083/249-4126
Email: fehaiti@hotmail.com

**Hong Kong**
Hong Kong Equestrian Federation
Lot 45, Lung Mun Road
Tuen Mun NT
Hong Kong
Phone: (852 ) 2464 2800. (852 ) 2460 9499
Email: hkef@netvigator.com
Website: www.equestrian-hk.com

**Hungary**
Hungarian Equestrian Federation
Kerepesi u. 7
1087 Budapest
Hungary
Phone: (36 1) 323 26 40. Fax: (36 1) 323 26 41
Email: hunhorse@axelero.hu
Website: www.lovasszovetseg.hu

**Iceland**
The National Association of Riding Clubs in Iceland
Landssamband hestamannafélaga Ipróttamiostoeiin Laugardal
104 Reykjavik
Iceland
Phone: (354) 514 40 30. Fax: (354) 514 40 31
Email: lh@isisport.is
Website: www.lhhestar.is

**India**
Equestrian Federation of India
Room No 164, Gate 29, Ground Floor Jawaharlal Nehru Stadium, Lodhi Road
110 003 New Dehli
India
Phone: (91 11) 436 71 07. Fax: (91 11) 436 70 25
Email: india.efi@indiatimes.com

**Indonesia**
Pordasi-Equestrian Commission of Indonesia (ECI)
c/o Mrs I. Thalib Jl. Madrasah no. 10-12, Cilandak Timur, Ps. Minggu
12560 Jakarta
Indonesia
Phone: (62 21) 781 16 28. Fax: (62 21) 7883 1988
Email: justreelax@hotmail.com

**Iran**
Equestrian Federation of the Islamic Republic of Iran
P.O. Box 19395/4755 Soul Ave. Engelab sport Complex
1589 Tehran
Iran
Phone: (98 21) 201 35 24.  Fax: (98 21) 204 41 14
Email: irief@neda.net

## Ireland

Equestrian Federation of Ireland
Ashton House Castleknock
Dublin, 15
Ireland
Phone: (353 1) 868 82 22. Fax: (353 1) 868 38 05/882 37 82
Email: efi@horsesport.ie
Website: www.horsesport.ie

## Israel

Israel Equestrian Federation
Wingate Institute for Sport
42902 Nethanya
Israel
Phone: (972 9) 885 09 38. Fax: (972 9) 885 09 39
Email: office@ief.org.il
Website: www.ief.org.il

## Italy

Italian Equestrian Federation
Viale Tiziano 74 -76
00196 Rome
Italy
Phone: (39 06) 36 85 81 05. Fax: (39 06) 323 37 72
Email: fise@fise.it
Website: www.fise.it

## Jamaica

The Equestrian Federation of Jamaica
Constant Spring Road P.O.Box 1796
Kingston 8
Jamaica
Phone: (876) 861-4213. Fax: (876) 903-0224
Email: efj@cwjamaica.com
Website: www.jamaicanhorse.com

## Japan

Japan University Equestrian Federation
c/o Japan Equestrian Federation
2-6-16 Shinkawa, Chuo-ku
Tokyo 104-0033
Japan
Phone: (81 3) 32 97 56 11. Fax: (81 3) 32 97 5617
Email: info@juef.jp
Contact Person: Mr. Mitsunori Nagatomo

## Jordan

Royal Jordanian Equestrian Federation
P.O. Box 5271 Zahran
11183 Amman
Jordan
Phone: (962 6) 565 08 21. Fax: (962 6) 565 08 23
Email: rjef@arabia.com

**Kazakhstan**
Equestrian Federation of the Republic of Kazakhstan
33/1 Osennayay Street
480037 Almaty
Kazakhstan
Phone: (7 3272) 35 16 09. Fax: (7 3272) 63 12 07
Email: equestr@academset.kz

**Kenya**
Horse Association of Kenya
P.O. Box 24555
00502 Karen
Kenya
Phone: (254 20) 891911. Fax: (254 20) 891911
Email: hak@swiftkenya.com

**Korea**
Korean Equestrian Federation
Room 603, Olympic Center 88 Oryun-Dong, Songpa-Ku
138-749 Seoul
Korea
Phone: (82 2) 422 75 63/4. Fax: (82 2) 420 42 64
Email: kef7563@yahoo.co.kr

**Kuwait**
Kuwait Equestrian Federation
c/o Hunting & Equestrian Club
P.O. Box 22436, Safat
13085 Kuwait
Kuwait
Phone: (965) 471 72 71. Fax: (965) 473 92 51
Email: frousaya@hotmail.com

**Kyrgyzstan**
Horse Racing Federation of the Republic of Kyrgyzstan
204 a Bakinskaya Str.
720015 Bishkek
Kyrgyzstan
Phone: (996 312) 67 20 37. Fax: (996 312) 67 20 37
Email: kg_equestrian_federation@netmail.kg
Website: www.equifed.elcat.kg

**Latvia**
Latvian Equestrian Federation
Kleistu 75
1067 Riga
Latvia
Phone: (371 2) 42 71 35. Fax: (371 2) 42 71 35 / 42 67 27
Email: lef@ljf.lv
Website: www.ljf.lv

**Lebanon**

Federation Equestre Libanaise Sin el Fil - Horch Tabet
P.O. Box 55 162 Sinn El Dekwane Mar. Daher Group
Dekouaneh Mar Roukoz
Lebanon
Phone: (961 1) 68 48 39. Fax: (961 1) 68 38 71
Email: lebolymp@cyberia.net.lb
Website: www.lebolympic.org

**Lesotho**

Lesotho Equestrian Federation
P.O. Box 138
Maseru, 100
Lesotho
Phone: (266) 321 292. Fax: (266) 310 494
Email: mjmakoele@nul.ls

**Libya**

Libyan Arab Equestrian Federation
Maidan Abi-Sitta P.O. Box 879
Tripoli
Libya
Phone: (218 21) 334 43 91. Fax: (218 21) 333 91 50

**Liechtenstein**

Liechtensteiner Pferdesport - Verband
P.O. Box 310 Sportfeldstr. 632
FL-9493 Mauren
Liechtenstein
Phone: (423 ) 373 35 47. Fax: (423 ) 373 34 23
Email: fnlie@lpsv.li

**Lithuania**

Lithuanian Equestrian Association.
Kedru 6
2009 Vilnius
Lithuania
Phone: (370 2) 260415. Fax: (370 2) 263957
Email: romasz@takas.lt

**Luxemburg**

Federation Luxembourgeoise des Sports Equestres
14, Avenue de la Gare
1610 Luxembourg
Luxemburg
Phone: (352 ) 48 49 99. Fax: (352 ) 48 50 39
Email: flse@hippoline.lu
Website: www.flse.lu

**Malawi**

Malawi's Equestrian Federation
Msamba Estate, Thondwe P.O. Box 54

Zomba
Malawi
Phone: (265 1) 535 248. Fax: (265 1) 514 249
Email: mzkayes@malawi.net

**Malaysia**
Equestrian Association of Malaysia
No.20, Persiaran Ampang
55000 Kuala Lumpur
Malaysia
Phone: (60 3) 4251 13 67. Fax: (60 3) 4257 68 48
Email: eam99@tm.net.my

**Malta**
National Equestrian Federation of Malta
Sammut Buildings, Insolja Str.
Burmarrad
Malta
Phone: (356 3) 576280. Fax: (356 3) 576862
Email: mef@kemmunet.net.mt

**Mauritius**
Mauritian Equestrian Sports Federation
Les Ecuries du Domaine les Pailles
Pailles
Mauritius
Phone: (230) 286 42 40. Fax: (230) 286 42 26

**Mexico**
Federacion Ecuestre Mexicana
Cda de Agustin Ahumada no. 31 Lomas de Chapultepec Box 41-951
Mexico D.F. , 11000 Lomas de Chapultepec
Mexico
Phone: (52 5) 540 58 20. Fax: (52 5) 520 37 39
Email: info@fem.org.mx
Website: www.fem.org.mx

**Moldova**
Federatia Ecvestra a Republicii Moldova
Hincheshti 38 B
MD 2009 Chisinau
Moldova
Phone: (373 2) 73 39 38. Fax: (373 2) 73 30 09
Email: agros@agros.net.md

**Monaco**
Federation Equestre de la Principaute de Monaco
Villa Gardénia 3, Avenue Saint Michel
MC 98000 Monte-Carlo
Monaco
Phone: (377) 93 50 80 54. Fax: (377) 93 50 80 56
Email: jumpmc@monaco.net
Website: www.federation-equestre.mc

**Mongolia**
Mongolian National Horse Racing Association
Olympic House, Chinggis Avenue Baga Toiruu - 55, Box - 29
Ulaanbaater, 210648
Mongolia
Phone: (976 11) 991 830 79. Fax: (976 11) 313 811
Email: mongolhorsedava@yahoo.com

**Morocco**
Federation Royale Marocaine des Sports Equestres
Dar-es-Salam 742 Agdal Rabat
Rabat
Morocco
Phone: (212 37) 75 44 24. Fax: (212 37) 75 47 38
Email: frmse@menara.co.ma

**Myanmar**
Myanmar Equestrian Federation
Pyidaung Su Road North Dagon Township
Yangon
Myanmar
Phone: (230 ) 212 08 18. Fax: (230 ) 208 88 50

**Namibia**
Namibian Equestrian Federation
P.O. Box 5445 Ausspannplatz
Windhoek
Namibia
Phone: (264 61) 246 637. Fax: (264 61) 246 637
Email: equest@mweb.com.na

**Netherlands**
Royal Dutch Equestrian Federation
De Beek 125 P.O. Box 3040
3852 Pl Ca Ermelo
Netherlands
Phone: (31 577) 40 82 00. Fax: (31 577) 40 17 25
Email: info@knhs.nl
Website: www.paardensport.nl

**Netherlands Antilles**
Stichting Nederlandse Antilliaanse Hippische Sportbond
P.O. Box 3641
Willenstad Curaçao
Netherlands Antilles
Phone: (599 9) 560 60 40. Fax: (599 9) 864 73 14

**New Zealand**
New Zealand Equestrian Federation
PO Box 6146 Level 4,Credit Consultants House 3 - 9 Church Street
Wellington
New Zealand

Phone: (64 4) 499 89 94. Fax: (64 4) 499 28 99
Email: nzef@nzequestrian.org.nz
Website: www.nzequestrian.org.nz

**Nicaragua**
Federacion Ecuestre de Nicaragua
Reparto Bolonia Casa #27 Contiguo Consulado Canada
Managua
Nicaragua
Phone: (505) 266-8661. Fax: (505) 266-8661
Email: esanchez75@yahoo.com

**Norway**
Norges Rytterforbund Norwegian Equestrian Federation
Serviceboks 1 U.S., Sognsveien 75
0840 Oslo
Norway
Phone: (47 21) 02 96 50. Fax: (47 21) 02 96 51
Email: nryf@rytter.no
Website: www.rytter.no

**Oman**
Oman Equestrian and Camel Federation
P.O. Box 1485 CPO Postal Code III
Seeb
Sultanate of Oman
Phone: (968) 695 688. Fax: (968) 698 776
Email: omaneque@omnatel.net.om

**Pakistan**
Equestrian Federation of Pakistan
Care of the President's Body Guard Near Qasim Market
P.O. Box 837
Rawalpindi
Pakistan
Phone: (92 51) 927 02 56. Fax: (92 51) 552 83 54
Email: ppa@isb.comsets.net.pk

**Palestine**
Equestrian Federation of Palestine
P.O. Box 122
Jericho
Palestine
Phone: (970 2) 232 50 07. Fax: (970 2) 232 50 07
Email: jerichoridingclub@yahoo.com

**Panama, Republic of**
Organizacion Ecuestre de Panama
P.O. Box 0832-2374 WTC
Panama 5
Rep. of Panama
Phone: (507) 269 38 21. Fax: (507) 264 48 75
Email: dacris@sinfo.net

**Paraguay**

Federacion de Deportes Ecuestres del Paraguay (F.E.D.E.P.A.)
P.O. Box 2130, Iturbe no. 823 Esq. F.R. Moreno
Asuncion
Paraguay
Phone: (595 21) 49 55 49. Fax: (595 21) 44 56 43
Email: fenix@quanta.com.py

**Peru**

Federacion Peruana de Deportes Ecuestres
Estadio Nacional Puerta 14 2ºPiso
Lima 1
Peru
Phone: (51 1) 425 11 93. Fax: (51 1) 425 11 93
Email: fpde@terra.com.pe
Website: www.fpdecuestres.com

**Philippines**

Philippine Equestrian Federation
119 dela Rosa cor. Alvarado Sts., Legaspi Village
Makati City
Philippines
Phone: (63 2) 818 88 82. Fax: (63 2) 817 93 09
Email: philippine_equestrian_federation@hotmail.com

**Poland**

Federation Equestre Polonaise
Rue Ceglowska 68/70
01-809 Warszawa
Poland
Phone: (48 22) 834 73 21. Fax: (48 22) 834 52 28
Email: pzj@pzj.pl
Website: www.pzj.pl

**Portugal**

Federacao Equestre Portuguesa
Avenida Manuel da Maia No.26 4eme Droite
1000-201 Lisbon
Portugal
Phone: (351 21) 847 87 74. Fax: (351 21) 847 45 82.
Email: secgeral@fep.pt
Website: www.fep.pt

**Puerto Rico**

Federacion Ecuestre de Puerto Rico
Apartado 8
00902 San Juan P.R.
Puerto Rico
Phone: (1 787) 283 26 10. Fax: (1 787) 283 23 10
Email: dcgonza@attglobal.net

## Qatar

Qatar Equestrian Federation
P.O. Box 24464
Doha
Qatar
Phone: (974 4) 810 368. Fax: (974 4) 813471
Email: info@q-ef.com
Website: www.q-ef.com

## Romania

Federation Equestre Roumaine
Rue Vasile Conta 16 Sect. 2
70139 Bucarest
Romania
Phone: (40 1) 331 00 49. Fax: (40 1) 250 25 69
Email: ecvestra@logicnet.ro

## Russia

Federation of Equestrian Sports of Russia
Luzhnetskaya Naberezhnaya 8
119992 Moscow
Russia
Phone: (70 95) 234 32 28. Fax: (70 95) 234 32 27
Email: efr@mail.sitek.ru

## San Marino

Federazione Ippica Sammarinese
Sede C.O.N.S., Via Rancaglia 30
47899 Serravalle
San Marino
Phone: (378 549) 88 56 00. Fax: (378 549) 88 56 52

## Saudi Arabia

Saudi Arabian Equestrian Federation
P.O. Box 60602 Al Maathar Olympic Complex
11555 Riyadh 11555
Saudi Arabia
Phone: (966 1) 482 38 37. Fax: (966 1) 482 37 95

## Senegal

Federation Senegalaise des Sports Equestres
Stade Leopold Sedar Sengor B.P. 8559
Dakar-Yoff
Senegal
Phone: (221) 638 29 89 or (221) 638 63 18. Fax: (1 928) 447 08 36
Email: fsse@enselle.net
Website: www.enselle.net

## Singapore

Equestrian Federation of Singapore
51 Fairways Drive
286965 Singapore

Phone: (65) 6466 5123. Fax: (65) 6466 1178
Email: admin@efs.org.sg
Website: www.efs.org.sg

## Slovakia
Slovak Equestrian Federation
Junacka 6
83280 Bratislava
Slovakia
Phone: (421 2) 49249138. Fax: (421 2) 49249584
Email: svkeqfed@hotmail.com
Website: www.jazdectvo.sk

## Slovenia
Equestrian Federation of Slovenia
Celovska 25
1000 Ljubljana
Slovenia
Phone: (386 1) 43 47 265. Fax: (386 1) 43 47 265
Email: KZS@konj-zveza.si
Website: www.konj-zveza.si

## South Africa
South African National Equestrian Federation
1st floor, Crowthorne Shopping Centre
Cor Arthur and Main Rds, Crowthorne
P.O. Box 30875
1684 Kyalami
Republic of South Africa
Phone: (27 11) 468 32 36. Fax: (27 11) 468 32 38
Email: sanef@iafrica.com
Website: www.sanef.co.za

## Spain
Real Federacion Hipica Espanola
c/ Menorca, No 3. 4'
28009 Madrid
Spain
Phone: (34 91) 436 42 00. Fax: (34 91) 575 07 70
Email: rfhe@rfhe.com
Website: www.rfhe.com

## Sudan
Sudan Equestrian Federation
P.O.Box 417
Khartoum
Sudan
Phone: (249 11) 477990. Fax: (249 11) 46 36 46

## Swaziland
Swaziland National Equestrian Federation
P.O. Box 182

Matsapha
Swaziland
Phone: (268) 550 24 08. Fax: (268) 550 24 08
Email: snef@africaonline.co.sz

## Sweden
Svenska Ridsportforbundet
Ridsportens Hus, Strömsholm
73040 Kolbäck
Sweden
Phone: (46 220) 45 600. Fax: (46 220) 45 670
Email: kansliet@ridsport.se
Website: www.ridsport.se

## Switzerland
Federation Suisse des Sports Equestres
Papiermühlestrasse 40 H Case Postale 726
3000 Bern 22
Switzerland
Phone: (41 31) 335 43 43. Fax: (41 31) 335 43 57/58
Email: vst@svps-fsse.ch
Website: www.svps-fsse.ch

## Syria
Federation Arabe Syrienne des Sports Equestres
Avenue Baramkeh B.P. 967 - 421
Damas
Syria
Phone: (963 11) 666 46 30. Fax: (963 11) 666 46 30
Email: ociee@scs-net.org
Website: www.horses-sy.com

## Thailand
Thailand Equestrian Federation
206/665 Paholyotin Road Samsen-nai, Payathai
10400 Bangkok
Thailand
Phone: (66 2) 615 03 51. Fax: (66 2) 615 03 52

## Trinidad and Tobago
The Trinidad and Tobago Equestrian Association
P.O. Box 3409 Maraval
Port of Spain
Trinidad & Tobago
Phone: (1868) 622 65 80. Fax: (1868) 622 67 13
Email: baxters@wow.net

## Tunisia
Federation Tunisienne des Sports Equestres et Tir
La Soukra
2036 Tunis
Tunisia
Phone: (216 1) 76 56 19. Fax: (216 1) 76 51 74

**Turkey**
Turkish Equestrian Federation/Turkiye Binicilik Federasyionu
Ciftlik Caddesi Saim Onhon Kapali Maneji
06510 Bestepe/Ankara
Turkey
Phone: (90 312) 215 37 42. Fax: (90 312) 215 72 65
Email: info@binicilik.org.tr
Website: www.binicilik.org.tr

**Turkmenistan**
Turkmen Equestrian Federation
Bulvar Kosmonavtov 2-1
Ashgabat
Turkmenistan
Phone: (99 312) 361 147. Fax: (99 312) 438 634
Email: annaklychev@mail.ru

**Ukraine**
The Equestrian Federation of Ukraine
62 Vel. Vasilkivska str.
03150 Kiev
Ukraine
Phone: (38 044) 201 64 66. Fax: (38 044) 201 63 34
Email: info@efu.org.ua
Website: www.efu.org.ua

**United Arab Emirates**
United Arab Emirates Equestrian & Racing Federation
P.O. Box 3234 Khalidya Street
Abu Dhabi
United Arab Emirates
Phone: (971 2) 66 61 800. Fax: (971 2) 66 55 700 / 66 54 555
Email: uaefed@emirates.net.ae
Website: www.equafed.ae

**United States of America**
United States Equestrian Federation, Inc.
4047 Iron Works Parkway
Lexington, KY 40511-8483
U.S.A.
Phone: (859) 258-2472. Fax: (859) 253-1968
Email: aice@equestrian.org
Website: www.usef.org

**Uruguay**
Federacion Uruguaya de Deportes Ecuestres
Canelones 980/82
11100 Montevideo
Uruguay
Phone: (598 2) 902 08 77. Fax: (598 2) 902 51 07
Email: cud@adinet.com.uy

**Uzbekistan**
Uzbekistan Equestrian Sport Federation
25, Navoi Street
700011 Tashkent
Uzbekistan
Phone: (998 712) 139 13 80. Fax: (998 712) 139 13 80/139 43 00

**Venezuela**
Federacion Venezolana de Deportes Ecuestres
Centro Empresarial La Lagunita Avenida Sur, Piso 1, Of. 114/116
1060-A Caracas La Lagunita
Venezuela
Phone: (58 212) 961 60 80. Fax: (58 212) 963 20 55
Email: fedecuestre@cantv.net

**Virgin Islands**
Virgin Islands Equestrian Association
Post Box 24160 Gallows Bay, Christiansted,
00824 St.Croix
Virgin Islands
Phone: (1 340) 773 51 67. Fax: (1 340) 773 51 67
Email: isv_equestrian@yahoo.com

**Zambia**
Zambia Horse Society
P.O. Box 20133
Kitwe
Zambia
Phone: (260 1) 29 12 27. Fax: (260 1) 22 51 23
Email: kentjaeg@zamnet.zm

**Zimbabwe**
The Horse Society of Zimbabwe
P.O. Box U.A. 340 Union Avenue 2 Bryce Road New Ardbennie
Harare
Zimbabwe
Phone: (263 4) 620705-6. Fax: (263 4) 620 709 or 780 967
Email: chrisl@cmb.co.zw

# Bibliography

The majority of the information in this book came from the schools and associations themselves, other sources referenced include:

British Horse Society. "Where to Train."
    URL: http://www.bhs.org.uk/Where-to-Train (20 Jan. 2004).
Federation Equestre Internationale (FEI). "Reference."
    URL: http://www.horsesport.org/fei/reference/reference_01/ref_01_01.html
    (12 Nov. 2003).
Kreitler, Bonnie. *50 Careers With Horses! From Accountant to Wrangler*.
    Breakthrough Publications, 1995.
Horse Country. "Horse Country's Vet Schools."
    URL: http://www.horse-country.com/vet/schools.html (14 Jan. 2004).
Intercollegiate Dressage Association. "IDA Member Colleges."
    URL: http://www.teamdressage.com/teams.asp (23 Nov. 2003).
International University Equestrian Federation(AIEC). "Contacts-countries."
    URL: http://www.aiecworld.com/nresps.htm (14 Nov. 2003).
Reynolds, Sue. *The Complete Guide to Horse Careers*.
    Colorado: New Horizon's Equine Educational Center, Inc., 1998.
U.S. Equestrian. "Intercollegiate."
    URL: http://www.usef.org/content/intercollegiate/ (24 Jan. 2004).

# Index of Schools

University of the Philippines Los Baños, 206
University of the West of England–Bristol, 210
University of Vermont, 150
University of Veterinary Medicine in Kosice, 206
University of Veterinary Sciences and the College
  of Agriculture, 170
University of Wales–Aberystwyth, The, 264
University of Wisconsin–Madison, 161
University of Wisconsin–River Falls, 161
University of Wolverhampton, 252
University of Zurich, 209
University Putra Malaysia, 196
Univerzitet u Beograd, 265
Urchinwood Manor Equitation Centre, 210
Utah State University, 149

**V**

Valley Farm Riding & Driving Centre, 244
Valley Forge Military Academy and College,
  The, 138
Verde Valley School, 46
Veterinary Field Station, 261
Village Farrier School, 174
Virginia Episcopal School, 155
Virginia Intermont College, 155
Virginia-Maryland Regional College of Veterinary
  Medicine, 156
Virginia Tech, 156

**W**

Wadlands Hall Equestrian Centre, 257
Waikato Institute of Technology, 204
Walford and North Shropshire College, 239
Walla Walla Community College, 158
Walsall College of Arts & Technology, The, 251
Walters State Community College, 143
Warwickshire College, 251
Washington State University, 158
Wellington Equestrian Education Ltd., 225
Wellow Park Stables & Saddlery, 237
Welsh College of Horticulture, 264
Wesleyan College, 77
West Texas A & M University, 148
Western College of Veterinary Medicine, 179
Western Kentucky University, 93
Western School of Horseshoeing, 46
Wheal Buller Riding School, 216
Wickstead Farm Equestrian Centre, 253
Wildwoods Riding Centre, 246
William H. Miner Agricultural Research Institute,
  123
William Woods University, 108
Willington Hall Riding Centre, 215
Wilmington College, 130
Wilson College, 138
Wiltshire College, Lackham, 253
Wimbledon Village Stables, 233
Windhurst Riding & Training Centre, 177
Witham Villa Ltd., 231
Wolverine Farrier School, 103
Woodcock Hill Riding Academy, Inc., 71
Workshops for Riding Instructors, 43

Wrea Green Equitation Centre, 231
Writtle College, 221

**Y**

Yorkshire Riding Centre Ltd., The, 257
Ypäjän Hevosopisto/Equine College Ypäjä, 181
Yrkesinstitut Sydväst, 182

# School Tracking Form

| Name of School | Page # | Possibility | Contacted School | Received Packet |
|---|---|:---:|:---:|:---:|
| _____ | _____ | ❏ | ❏ | ❏ |
| _____ | _____ | ❏ | ❏ | ❏ |
| _____ | _____ | ❏ | ❏ | ❏ |
| _____ | _____ | ❏ | ❏ | ❏ |
| _____ | _____ | ❏ | ❏ | ❏ |
| _____ | _____ | ❏ | ❏ | ❏ |
| _____ | _____ | ❏ | ❏ | ❏ |
| _____ | _____ | ❏ | ❏ | ❏ |
| _____ | _____ | ❏ | ❏ | ❏ |
| _____ | _____ | ❏ | ❏ | ❏ |
| _____ | _____ | ❏ | ❏ | ❏ |
| _____ | _____ | ❏ | ❏ | ❏ |
| _____ | _____ | ❏ | ❏ | ❏ |
| _____ | _____ | ❏ | ❏ | ❏ |
| _____ | _____ | ❏ | ❏ | ❏ |
| _____ | _____ | ❏ | ❏ | ❏ |
| _____ | _____ | ❏ | ❏ | ❏ |
| _____ | _____ | ❏ | ❏ | ❏ |
| _____ | _____ | ❏ | ❏ | ❏ |
| _____ | _____ | ❏ | ❏ | ❏ |
| _____ | _____ | ❏ | ❏ | ❏ |
| _____ | _____ | ❏ | ❏ | ❏ |
| _____ | _____ | ❏ | ❏ | ❏ |
| _____ | _____ | ❏ | ❏ | ❏ |
| _____ | _____ | ❏ | ❏ | ❏ |
| _____ | _____ | ❏ | ❏ | ❏ |
| _____ | _____ | ❏ | ❏ | ❏ |
| _____ | _____ | ❏ | ❏ | ❏ |
| _____ | _____ | ❏ | ❏ | ❏ |
| _____ | _____ | ❏ | ❏ | ❏ |
| _____ | _____ | ❏ | ❏ | ❏ |

| Name of School | Page # | Possibility | Contacted School | Received Packet |
|---|---|---|---|---|
| _____ | _____ | ❑ | ❑ | ❑ |
| _____ | _____ | ❑ | ❑ | ❑ |
| _____ | _____ | ❑ | ❑ | ❑ |
| _____ | _____ | ❑ | ❑ | ❑ |
| _____ | _____ | ❑ | ❑ | ❑ |
| _____ | _____ | ❑ | ❑ | ❑ |
| _____ | _____ | ❑ | ❑ | ❑ |
| _____ | _____ | ❑ | ❑ | ❑ |
| _____ | _____ | ❑ | ❑ | ❑ |
| _____ | _____ | ❑ | ❑ | ❑ |
| _____ | _____ | ❑ | ❑ | ❑ |
| _____ | _____ | ❑ | ❑ | ❑ |
| _____ | _____ | ❑ | ❑ | ❑ |
| _____ | _____ | ❑ | ❑ | ❑ |
| _____ | _____ | ❑ | ❑ | ❑ |
| _____ | _____ | ❑ | ❑ | ❑ |
| _____ | _____ | ❑ | ❑ | ❑ |
| _____ | _____ | ❑ | ❑ | ❑ |
| _____ | _____ | ❑ | ❑ | ❑ |
| _____ | _____ | ❑ | ❑ | ❑ |
| _____ | _____ | ❑ | ❑ | ❑ |
| _____ | _____ | ❑ | ❑ | ❑ |
| _____ | _____ | ❑ | ❑ | ❑ |
| _____ | _____ | ❑ | ❑ | ❑ |
| _____ | _____ | ❑ | ❑ | ❑ |
| _____ | _____ | ❑ | ❑ | ❑ |
| _____ | _____ | ❑ | ❑ | ❑ |
| _____ | _____ | ❑ | ❑ | ❑ |
| _____ | _____ | ❑ | ❑ | ❑ |
| _____ | _____ | ❑ | ❑ | ❑ |
| _____ | _____ | ❑ | ❑ | ❑ |
| _____ | _____ | ❑ | ❑ | ❑ |

# Want to Be in This Guide?

Don't see your school included in this guide? Just fill out the form below and mail it off to (Horse Schools, P.O. Box 18848, S. Lake Tahoe, CA 96151 U.S.A.), send it via email (horseschools@thoroughweb.com), or go to **www.horseschools.net** and fill out the electronic form there. Check the listings in the book that are similar to your own school to give yourself an idea on how to fill out the form.

Name of School: _____

Contact Info.
Address: _____
_____
Phone/Fax: _____
Email: _____
Website: _____

Accreditation: _____

Degrees Offered: _____
_____

Majors Offered: _____
_____

Tuition Costs: _____

Type of School: _____

Description of Program: _____
_____
_____
_____
_____
_____
_____
_____
_____
_____
_____

Facilities: _____

Classroom/Hands-On Equine Classes: _____

Showing: _____